Theory into

C000144057

Theory into Practice

A READER IN MODERN LITERARY CRITICISM

EDITED AND INTRODUCED

BY K. M. NEWTON

MACMILLAN

First published 1992 by
THE MACMILLAN PRESS LTD
Houndmills, Basingstoke, Hampshire RG21 2XS
and London
Companies and representatives
throughout the world

ISBN 0–333–56767–6 hardcover
ISBN 0–333–56768–4 paperback

A catalogue record for this book is available
from the British Library

Phototypeset by Intype, London
Printed in Hong Kong

CONTENTS

ACKNOWLEDGEMENTS

The author and publishers wish to thank the following for permission to use copyright material:

Basil Blackwell Ltd for Edward W. Said, 'Jane Austen and Empire' in *Raymond Williams: Critical Perspectives*, ed. Terry Eagleton (Polity Press, 1989); and Catherine Belsey on some short poems of Milton from *John Milton: Language Gender, Power* (1988); Cornell University Press for Barbara Johnson, 'Is Female to Male as Ground is to Figure?' in *Feminism and Psychoanalysis*, eds Richard Feldstein and Judith Roof, copyright © 1985 by Cornell University; Columbia University Press for Cleanth Brooks, 'Literary Criticism: Marvell's "Horatian Ode"' in *The English Institute Essays* (1946); Stephen Greenblatt for 'The Cultivation of Anxiety: *King Lear* and His Heirs', *Raritan*, 2, 1968; Harvard University Press for Shoshana Felman, 'The Case of Poe: Applications/Implications of Psychoanalysis', in *Jacques Lacan and the Adventure of Thought: Psychoanalysis in Contemporary Culture* (1987); copyright © 1987 by the President and Fellows of Harvard College; the Johns Hopkins University Press for Wolfgang Iser, 'The Role of the Reader in Fielding's *Joseph Andrews*' in *The Implied Reader* (1974); and J. Hillis Miller, 'Thomas Hardy, Jacques Derrida, and the 'Dislocation of Souls' in *Taking Chances: Derrida, Psychoanalysis, and Literature* eds William Herrigan and Joseph H. Smith (1984) and in *Tropes, Parables, Performatives: Selected Essays on Twentieth Century Literature* by J. Hillis Miller (Harvester Wheatsheaf, 1991); Oxford University Press, Inc., for Henry Louis Gates, Jr., 'Binary Oppositions' in *Figures in Black: Words, Signs, and the 'Racial' Self* copyright © 1987 by Henry Louis Gates, Jr.; Random Century Group and the Estate of F. R. Leavis for F. R. Leavis, '*Antony and Cleopatra* and *All for Love*' in *The Living Principle* (1975, Chatto and Windus); Routledge for Elaine Showalter, 'Representing Ophelia' in *Shakespeare and the Question of Theory*, eds P. Parker and G. Hartman (Methuen, 1985); and material from David Lodge, *Working with Structuralism* (1981); Alan Sinfield for '*Macbeth*: History, Ideology, Intellectuals', *Critical Quarterly*, 28, 1986; Stanford University Press for Stanley Fish, 'Transmuting the Lump: *Paradise Lost* 1942–1982' in *Literature and History* ed. Gary Saul Morson (1986); University of Chicago Press for Gayatri Chakrovorty Spivak, ' "Draupadi" by Mahasweta Devi', *Critical Inquiry*, 8,

1981; University of Michigan, Department of Slavic Languages and Literatures, for Victor Shklovsky, 'The Mystery Novel: *Little Dorrit*' in *Readings in Russian Poetics*, eds. Ladislaw Matejka and Krystyna Pomorska (1978); University of Texas Press for M. M. Bakhtin, 'Heteroglossia in the Novel' in *The Dialogic Imagination*, ed. Michael Holquist, copyright © 1981 by the University of Texas Press; Verso for Terry Eagleton, 'Ideology and Literary Form: Joseph Conrad' in *Criticism and Ideology: A Study in Marxist Literary Theory* (New Left Books, 1976).

Every effort has been made to trace all the copyright-holders, but if any have been inadvertently overlooked the publishers will be pleased to make the necessary amendment at the first opportunity.

INTRODUCTION

In the last few years students of literature who wish to be better acquainted with the shift towards theory in recent literary criticism have been well catered for by the publication of numerous Readers which have made readily available texts by the major modern literary theorists.[1] In addition several general introductions to critical theory have been published.[2] But anyone who takes part in a theory course with students will know that one is constantly being asked to direct them to where they can find theory being applied to practice. One reason for this may be that the power of empiricism in the English-speaking world creates a distrust of theory divorced from the question of its application. But a more basic reason is that much literary theory operates at such a high level of abstraction that students find it difficult to grasp. This book is a response to that situation.

There would also be little point in producing theory Readers and introductions to theory if there was no intention of encouraging students to apply theory themselves when they interpret texts. Yet such volumes are unlikely on their own to have a significant influence on critical practice. If the practice of criticism at a general level is to be significantly changed by developments in modern theory, students must be convinced both that the theory does work in critical engagement with texts and that they can apply it. Theory collections therefore need to be supplemented by examples of theory operating in relation to the interpretation of texts, especially as it is often not clear from theoretical discourse alone what form of critical practice it would entail.

This volume aims to provide such supplementation by reprinting readings of texts by critics who write from a particular theoretical perspective. Moreover, in selecting the material for the volume I have endeavoured not only to cover the range of modern theoretical approaches but also to choose essays which will be as accessible as possible to a general literary readership. The intention of the volume is thus both to give students of literary criticism and theory a better understanding of the implications of particular theories and also to aid them in the application of theory by learning from the practice of others. I hope it may also prove useful to those who teach literary theory.

But this raises the question of how students will select a theoreti-

1

cal approach to apply to critical interpretation since modern literary criticism consists of opposed and competing approaches. Though one has to accept, whether or not one approves of the situation, the existence of pluralism in present-day literary study, the practice of criticism necessarily involves favouring certain approaches and rejecting others. In other words, literary critical practice entails choice and commitment. Students who read through the various Readers in literary theory may feel like inexperienced shoppers in a supermarket who are confronted by numerous brands of the same type of product, none of which they have tried. It is surely necessary therefore that students, at the very least, should be acquainted with how the various theories work in practice before making their choice.

One possible way of acquainting students with the practical dimension of theory is to construct examples of readings of texts which employ the various theories that are dominant at the present time. Though this may have the benefit of illustrating clearly and simply how a particular theory may be applied, its drawback is that it will not necessarily help the student make a choice. Such exemplary essays are unlikely to be of great critical interest in themselves since they have been created not so much out of belief in or commitment to a particular theoretical approach but rather to provide demonstrations of how various theories would work in practice. Students would therefore not be seeing theory applied to practice at its most powerful and persuasive. One can only make an informed choice, I think, if one studies the work of the best practitioners of a particular theoretical perspective, those who are committed to it and who implicitly believe that it has greater explanatory power than alternative approaches. Thus in this Reader I have selected essays applying theory to practice across the literary critical spectrum by critics who are generally regarded as major exponents of the theoretical perspective they favour.

Since I have tried to find examples which will be accessible to a general literary readership, inevitably most of the essays chosen are on texts which will be fairly familiar to such a readership, that is texts which are generally regarded as being 'canonic'. However, the 'canon' itself is an issue in modern critical theory. For example, feminist and black critics question a canon that includes very few texts by women or non-whites. A volume such as this must therefore take account of such questioning of the canon. However, I have endeavoured to try to reconcile this with accessibility by, for instance, reprinting an essay by Henry Louis Gates which discusses the first chapter of the autobiography of the black writer, Frederick

Douglass, and one by Gayatri Chakravorty Spivak which applies deconstruction to a short story by a modern Indian woman writer, Mahasweta Devi, but which provides a translation of the story within the essay.

I mentioned above that this collection sets out to supplement the literary theory Readers which have attempted to introduce theory to a general literary readership. Those acquainted with the writings of Jacques Derrida, who has had a crucial influence on modern literary theory, will be aware that the concept of 'supplement' is one that he has subjected to a deconstructive analysis. Such concepts impose structures on our thinking which always require to be questioned and scrutinised even if in the final analysis we cannot do without them. Derrida has provided cogent deconstructions of binary oppositions which show that what was conventionally or traditionally regarded as supplementary or marginal can be placed in a central or dominant position, while what was formerly thought of as central in turn becomes marginal or secondary. Most famously he has argued that writing, often regarded as merely supplementary to speech in relation to language, should in fact be central in our thinking about the nature of language since writing is a better model than speech for understanding how language functions.

The division between theory and practice is similarly one that we should be suspicious of since it implies that theory precedes and therefore occupies a superior position to practice. But if one examines practice, it soon becomes clear that no absolute separation from theory is possible. Theory and practice continually interact and are mutually dependent on each other. Clearly there are distinctions to be made but one should beware of erecting such distinctions into a fundamental division in which one form of discourse is intrinsically prior to the other. Practice is almost never merely the simple application of theory; applying theory to practice inevitably introduces difference which must have a knock-on effect on theory, thus changing the theory and developing it. This is particularly the case in literary theory where many of the major figures are both theorists and practitioners of criticism and one sees a continual interaction between the two forms of discourse. Such critics as J. Hillis Miller and Stephen Greenblatt whose criticism is clearly dependent on certain theoretical concepts but whose major work has been in the area of critical practice rather than theory in the narrow sense cannot be seen as merely passively applying theory; their literary critical practice has an independent theoretical force which has had an impact on 'pure' theory. Though this volume therefore is primarily intended to show how theory is applied to practice, many of the essays make a contribution to theory in their own right and demonstrate that the division between theory and practice is finally artificial.

I said above that pluralism reigns in current criticism. This does not mean that different critical perspectives are not in competition with each other. What perhaps marks the present critical situation off from the past is that it does not seem likely, in the short term at least, that one particular critical approach will achieve a position of dominance similar to that attained by the New Criticism in America in the late 1940s and 1950s. Anglo-American New Criticism was a version of formalism that succeeded in displacing historical and scholarly criticism from their previously dominant position, though they continued to have considerable support.

The formalism-historicism conflict is still a major feature of modern criticism, though in the past twenty years or so both formalism, with its emphasis on the text itself, and historical criticism, which sees context as crucial, have undergone radical changes. The impact of structuralist and post-structuralist thinking has had a fundamental effect on formalism, particularly post-structuralism which challenged traditional formalism through its concentration on instabilities and impasses within the text, while historical criticism has been radically affected by such thinkers as Althusser and Foucault. But whereas in the past formalists and historicists tended to pursue their aims without paying much attention to each other, in recent criticism there has been continual interaction. Many new historicists have clearly been influenced by a post-structuralist like Derrida even if he, notoriously, has declared that 'there is nothing beyond the text', while a deconstructionist like Hillis Miller, though afraid that the ascendancy of contextualist criticism will make literature 'no more than a minor by-product of history, not something that in any way makes history' has nevertheless stated: 'Nothing is more urgently needed these days in humanistic study than the incorporation of the rhetorical study of literature into the study of the historical, social, and ideological dimensions of literature.'[3] Thus contemporary historicists do not ignore the force of the text and contemporary formalists recognise the force of ideology and politics. In fact the division between formalists and historicists, or textualists and contextualists as they might be better described today, like that between theory and practice, is one that in the present situation of literary criticism should not be viewed too rigidly even if a complete reconciliation between the two seems a Utopian aim.

Though the formalism-historicism opposition may constitute the major conflict within contemporary literary criticism other forces have also had a powerful influence, notably reader- and gender-based approaches. Both have made an independent contribution and have also had an impact on the formalism-historicism conflict, which in turn has shaped their development. Perhaps contemporary literary criticism is best seen as a continuing debate in which certain critical tendencies – such as formalism, historicism, reader- and gender-based criticism – interact with each other and are changed in the process. This makes current criticism a rapidly developing field which it is difficult to keep up with. For example, the last twenty years have been notable for quite dramatic changes in the critical perspectives of many of the most significant critics. This may be disorienting and troubling to those who value stability and consistency, but undeniably it has created one of the liveliest periods ever in the history of criticism. I hope this volume, as well as giving examples of theory being applied to practice, also gives some indication of the vitality and excitement of modern criticism.

Though this volume is on one level a follow-up to my literary theory Reader it is different in that it includes fewer selections, the great majority being complete articles or chapters from books. In the theory Reader I endeavoured to present a theoretical position in a concentrated form through editing the material, in the hope and expectation that readers would both gain insight into the range of twentieth-century theory and also read the complete versions of those pieces which they found particularly interesting or appealing. Also, even in edited form it was possible to experience the power of theoretical arguments. With readings of particular texts, however, I think it is less easy to convey the power of the reading if the text is edited to the same degree. One needs the detail and the elaboration more so than one does with most theoretical texts.

Since I have space only for fifteen pieces, in contrast to the fifty pieces in the theory Reader, I have concentrated on the contemporary critical scene. It is here that readers are more likely to have difficulty and have the greater need to read accessible applications of theory to specific texts. However, much contemporary criticism is a reaction to the previous dominant approaches. I have therefore included examples of the latter in order that the reader has some knowledge of what many contemporary critics are reacting against. Obviously the most influential critical approach in America up until the 1960s was the New Criticism and for this reason I have included an essay by one of the major New Critics, Cleanth Brooks. In Britain the most powerful critical influence before the advent of theory-based criticism was undoubtedly F. R. Leavis and I have also included an essay by him.

It is difficult to predict how contemporary criticism is going to develop. One cannot even rule out the possibility that the New Criticism in some kind of modified form may make a comeback. One of its major advantages was that it was made accessible to students at virtually all levels through the publication of textbooks such as Brooks's and Warren's *Understanding Poetry* and *Understanding Fiction*. Both the New Criticism and Leavisite criticism also appeared to encourage a kind of equality between teacher and student before the text, even if this equality was something of an illusion. Teachers inevitably possessed greater implicit knowledge than their students which placed them in a position of dominance. A danger of the present situation, however, is that many students may feel that contemporary criticism is so difficult that they have little or nothing to contribute and they may therefore be inclined to accept passively the authority of the teacher. It would be ironic if a consequence of the ascendancy of theory-based criticism was to reproduce the situation that obtained before the emergence of New Critical close analysis and practical criticism, when scholars dominated criticism and tended to make their students feel that they could never compete with the kind of learning that such scholars possessed. One of the aims of this volume is to counteract such a situation by making available accessible examples of contemporary theory-based criticism in order both to illustrate how it operates in practice and to encourage students to apply theoretical concepts in their own criticism. Though much contemporary literary criticism is difficult, it is unhealthy in my view to accept passively the elitist assumption that it is the preserve of experts. Clearly developments in modern criticism present a challenge to teaching and I hope this book will help both teachers and students to rise to that challenge.

Notes

1. See, for example, *Issues in Contemporary Critical Theory: A Casebook*, ed. Peter Barry (Basingstoke and London, 1987); *Modern Criticism and Theory: A Reader*, ed. David Lodge (Harlow, Essex, 1988); *Twentieth-Century Literary Theory: A Reader*, ed. K. M. Newton (Basingstoke and London, 1988); *Modern Literary Theory: A Reader*, eds Philip Rice and Patricia Waugh (London, 1989); *Debating Texts: A Reader in Twentieth-Century Literary Theory and Method*, ed. Rick Rylance (Milton Keynes, 1987). For a long review of most of the theory Readers available see James R. Bennett, *Textual Practice*, 4 (1990), pp. 113–22.

2. See, for example, *Contemporary Literary Theory*, eds G. Douglas Atkins and Laura Morrow (Basingstoke and London, 1989); Terry Eagleton, *Literary Theory: An Introduction* (Oxford, 1983); *Modern Literary Theory: A Comparative Introduction*, eds Ann Jefferson and David Robey (London, 1986); K. M. Newton, *Interpreting the Text: A Critical Introduction to the Theory and Practice of Literary Interpretation* (Hemel Hempstead, 1990); Raman Selden, *A Reader's Guide to Contemporary Literary Theory* (Brighton, 1985);

3. J. Hillis Miller, *The Ethics of Reading* (New York, 1987), pp. 8, 7.

1 THE NEW CRITICISM AND LEAVISITE CRITICISM

Much contemporary criticism is a reaction in one way or another to the New Criticism, which was the dominant critical mode in America between the 1940s and the 1960s. It had its origins in Britain through the work of T. S. Eliot, I. A. Richards, and William Empson, but it never had as great an impact in Britain as it had in America, though many British critics were strongly influenced by it. Traditional scholarly and historical criticism retained greater power and influence in Britain than in America and, more important, the influence of F. R. Leavis and his supporters, centred on the journal *Scrutiny*, provided a kind of equivalent to it in the British context. The New Criticism and Leavisite criticism, however, had many points of contact. Both had been strongly influenced by Eliot's critical preferences, adhered to an organicist aesthetics which claimed that in the greatest works form and content were unified, viewed modern social developments with their emphasis on the technological and the utilitarian in negative terms and looked back nostalgically to more spiritually unified societies which supposedly existed in the past. A major difference, however, was that the New Critics favoured interpretation more than Leavis, who was much less concerned with questions of meaning.

Cleanth Brooks mainly devoted himself to applying New Critical methods but he also wrote some influential theoretical essays. He saw himself as a formalist, and though he recognised the importance of historical considerations and the dimension of reader-response, these were very much secondary in his mind to the literary work as an objective structure. Unity, form, structure, however, were not to be seen in mechanical terms in relation to literature, since in major literary works they must be able to accommodate contradictory or apparently logically opposed elements. In one of his most important theoretical essays, 'The Heresy of Paraphrase', Brooks claims that the unity that informs structure in literature is 'an achieved harmony' and must be able to embrace ambiguity, paradox, or irony. The structure of the literary work, therefore, always contains tensions: 'The essential structure of a poem (as distinguished from the rational or logical structure of the "statement" which we abstract from it) resembles that of architecture or painting: it is a pattern of resolved stresses.' This unity, he declares, is not achieved through logic but through 'a dramatic process'[1] which resolves in a dialectical way the conflicts intrinsic to the drama which the work embodies.

Irony is the term he most often uses for the existence of incongruities or contradictions within literary texts and he claims that irony in this sense pervades all authentic literary works. Part of Brooks's critical project is to demonstrate that this is the case. On the surface the kind of irony he values was most obviously to be found in metaphysical poetry and in the work of certain modernists, such as T. S. Eliot, but Brooks endeavoured to demonstrate that it applied across the range of literature. Though Marvell is usually grouped among the metaphysical poets and thus is the kind of poet one would expect a critic like Brooks to focus on, the poem he chooses to discuss in this essay – the Horatian ode – is one that clearly presents difficulties for a critical method that places the emphasis on poetic structure and regards historical and authorial considerations as secondary, since these considerations have been primary in much discussion of the poem. The interest of Brooks's reading lies in whether he is able to demonstrate that the poem can be persuasively discussed in New Critical terms.

It is often said that the New Critics were anti-historical and viewed the literary text as a 'verbal icon', dissociating the text from any context and concentrating solely on the words on the page. Brooks's essay clearly shows that the New Critics did not reject or ignore historical considerations. He recognises that the critic must pay attention to the linguistic context and know what words meant at a particular period, and clearly some knowledge of the historical situation is essential in a poem concerned with historical figures such as Cromwell and Charles I. But Brooks argues that even in a poem that seems so caught up in history in a very specific sense, in the final analysis the poem is dramatic, in his terms, and creates a poetic unity that incorporates ambiguity and irony.

Leavis resembles Brooks in that the emphasis in his criticism is on practical engagement with literary texts, but unlike Brooks Leavis had objections to any theoretical elaboration of his critical position. As against the abstraction demanded by a discipline like philosophy Leavis claimed that 'Words in poetry invite us, not to "think about" and judge but to "feel into" or "become" – to realize a complex experience that is given in the words', and that the critic's 'first concern is to enter into possession of the given poem . . . in its concrete fulness, and his constant concern is never to lose his completeness of possession, but rather to increase it'.[2]

Leavis clearly has strong connections with the Arnoldian critical tradition which believed that literature could form the spiritual basis for a society in which religion in the formal sense had ceased to be a major force. He refused to make any separation between formal or aesthetic values and moral values, and his more ambitious claims that English as a discipline should form the spiritual centre of the university was much attacked and ridiculed. But it has been argued convincingly that to see Leavis only as a critic in the Arnoldian tradition is greatly to narrow his significance; that he should also be seen as having strong connections with literary modernism and its belief that the literary text is irreducible and beyond paraphrase; and also that the emphasis he places on 'life' in his discussion of literature has similarities with the work of a philosopher like Heidegger and his concern with 'Being', that both are in an anti-Cartesian tradition that seeks to break down dualistic thinking.[3] Whereas language as used in ordinary situations constantly reinforces dualism through such concepts as form and content, meaning and expression, signifier and signified, for Leavis the language of literature is enactive in such a way that such dualisms do not apply.

Though Leavis is associated with close reading and practical criticism, his criticism has little in common with New Critical close analysis and even less with Empsonian interrogation of the text. Indeed Leavis considered Empson's criticism as a warning to the critic. Empson's relentless analysis of texts ignored the kind of questions that Leavis was interested in, such as the integrity of the text, the fusion between feeling and intellect, the question of value. Leavis's constant emphasis is on the wholeness of literary works, the way in which they achieve 'concrete realisation' and 'sensuous particularity'. As in the essay reprinted here, which focusses on Shakespeare's *Antony and Cleopatra* and Dryden's play on the same subject, *All for Love*, he often employs comparison in order to demonstrate why a particular literary text is a major artistic achievement.

Notes

1. Cleanth Brooks, *The Well Wrought Urn: Studies in the Structure of Poetry* (London, 1949), pp. 186, 189.

2. F. R. Leavis, 'Literary Criticism and Philosophy', in *Twentieth-Century Literary Theory: A Reader*, ed. K. M. Newton (London, 1988), p. 67.

3. See Michael Bell, *F. R. Leavis* (London, 1988).

Further Reading

Cleanth Brooks, *Modern Poetry and the Tradition* (London, 1948).
Cleanth Brooks and Robert Penn Warren, *Understanding Poetry* (New York, 1976).
F. R. Leavis, *The Common Pursuit* (London, 1962).

Cleanth Brooks: Literary Criticism: Marvell's 'Horatian Ode'

The easiest error into which we may fall in defining the relationship between historical and critical studies is illustrated by the preface of Maurice's Kelley's interesting book on Milton, *This Great Argument*. For Kelley, the problem of exegesis is almost amusingly simple: we will read Milton's *Christian Doctrine* to find out what Milton's ideas are, and then we shall be able to understand his *Paradise Lost*, explaining the tangled and difficult poetic document by means of the explicit prose statement. But Kelley's argument rests not only upon the assumption that the Milton who wrote the *Christian Doctrine* was precisely and at all points the same man who composed *Paradise Lost* – a matter which, for all practical purposes, may well be true; it rests upon the further and much more dangerous assumption that Milton was able to *say* in *Paradise Lost* exactly what he intended to say; and that what he supposed he had put into that poem is actually to be found there. In short, Mr Kelley tends to make the assumption about poetry which most of us constantly make; namely, that a poem is essentially a decorated and beautified piece of prose.

But I propose to deal here with a more modest example than Milton's epic. I propose to illustrate from Marvell's 'Horatian Ode'. If we follow the orthodox procedure, the obvious way to understand the 'Ode' is to ascertain by historical evidence – by letters and documents of all kinds – what Marvell really thought of Cromwell, or, since Marvell apparently thought different things of Cromwell at different times, to ascertain the date of the 'Ode', and then neatly fit it into the particular stage of Marvell's developing opinion of Cromwell. But this is at best a relatively coarse method which can hope to give no more than a rough approximation of the poem; and

Reprinted from *Explication as Criticism: Selected Papers from the English Institute 1941–1952*, ed. W. K. Wimsatt, Jr (New York and London, 1963), pp. 99–128.

there lurk in it some positive perils. For to ascertain what Marvell the man thought of Cromwell, and even to ascertain what Marvell as poet consciously intended to say in his poem, will not prove that the poem actually says this, or all this, or merely this. This last remark, in my opinion, does not imply too metaphysical a notion of the structure of a poem. There is surely a sense in which any one must agree that a poem has a life of its own, and a sense in which it provides in itself the only criterion by which what it says can be judged. It is a commonplace that the poet sometimes writes better than he knows, and, alas, on occasion, writes worse than he knows. The history of English literature will furnish plenty of examples of both cases.

As a matter of fact, Marvell's 'Ode' is not a shockingly special case. Indeed, I have chosen it for my example, not because it is special – not because I hope to reveal triumphantly that what it really says is something quite opposed to what we have supposed it to be saying – but because it seems to me a good instance of the normal state of affairs. Yet, even so, the 'Ode' will provide us with problems enough. To the scholar who relies upon the conventional approach, the problems become rather distressingly complicated.

Let us review the situation briefly. Hard upon his composition of the 'Ode' in 1650, Marvell had published in 1649 a poem 'To his Noble Friend, Mr Richard Lovelace', and a poem 'Upon the Death of the Lord Hastings'. Both Margoliouth and Legouis find these poems rather pro-Royalist in sentiment and certainly it is difficult to read them otherwise. If we add to these poems the 'Elegy upon the Death of My Lord Francis Villiers', a Cavalier who was killed fighting for the King in 1649, the Royalist bias becomes perfectly explicit. As Margoliouth puts it: 'If [the elegy on Villiers] is Marvell's, it is his one unequivocal royalist utterance; it throws into strong relief the transitional character of *An Horatian Ode* where royalist principles and admiration for Cromwell the Great Man exist side by side. . . .'

A transition in views there must have been, but the transition certainly cannot be graphed as a steadily rising curve when we take into account Marvell's next poem, 'Tom May's Death'. May died in November, 1650. Thus we have the 'Horatian Ode', which was almost certainly written in the summer of 1650, preceding by only a few months a poem in which Marvell seems to slur at the Commander of the Parliamentary armies – either Essex or Fairfax – as 'Spartacus', and to reprehend May himself as a renegade poet who has prostituted the mystery of the true poets. The curve of Marvell's political development shows still another surprising quirk when we recall that only a few months after his attack on May, Marvell was to be living under Spartacus Fairfax's roof, acting as tutor to his little daughter Mary.

Let me interrupt this summary to say that I am not forcing the evidence so as to crowd the historian into the narrowest and most uncomfortable corner possible. On the contrary, whatever forcing of the evidence has been done has been done by the editors and the historians. If we limit ourselves to historical evidence, it is possible to suppose that 'Tom May's Death' was actually written on the Hill at Billborrow; and Margoliouth chooses early 1651 as the probable date for Marvell's arrival at Appleton House only because, as he says, ' "Tom May's Death" is not the sort of poem Marvell would have written under Fairfax's roof'.

There is no need, in view of our purposes, to extend the review of Marvell's political development through the late 1650's with their Cromwellian poems or through the Restoration period with its vexed problems concerning which of the anti-court satires are truly, and which are falsely, ascribed to Marvell. The problem of Marvell's attitude through the years 1649–51 will provide sufficient scope for this examination of some of the relations and interrelations of the historical approach and the critical approach. For there is still another complication, which has received less attention than it deserves. It is the curious fact that the 'Horatian Ode' in which Marvell seems to affirm the ancient rights of the monarchy –

> Though Justice against Fate complain,
> And plead the antient Rights in vain –

is full of echoes of the poetry of Tom May, the poet whom Marvell was, a few months later, to denounce for having failed poetry in the hour of crisis:

> When the Sword glitters ore the Judges head,
> And fear the Coward Churchmen silenced,
> Then is the Poets time, 'tis then he drawes,
> And single fights forsaken Vertues cause.
> He, when the wheel of Empire, whirleth back,
> And though the World's disjointed Axel crack,
> Sings still of *antient Rights* and better Times,
> Seeks wretched good, arraigns successful Crimes.

The echoes of May's poetry, of course, may well have been unconscious: to me it is significant that they are from May's translation of Lucan's poem on the Roman civil wars. (The relevant passage from Margoliouth's notes will be found on pp. 129–30.)* I must say that I find the parallels quite convincing and that I am a little

---

* These page numbers are from *Explication as Criticism*, ed. Winsatt.

surprised at Margoliouth's restraint in not pushing his commentary
further. For one is tempted to suppose that in the year or so that
followed the execution of Charles, Marvell was obsessed with the
problem of the poet's function in such a crisis; that the poet May
was frequently in his mind through a double connection – through
the parallels between the English and the Roman civil war, Lucan's
poem on which May had translated, and through May's conduct
as a partisan of the Commonwealth; and that the 'Horatian Ode'
and 'Tom May's Death', though so different in tone, are closely
related and come out of the same general state of mind. But to
hazard all this is to guess at the circumstances of Marvell's composition of these poems. It can be only a guess, and, in any case, it
takes us into a consideration of what must finally be a distinct
problem: how the poem came to be; whereas our elected problem
is rather: what the poem is. I am, by the way, in entire sympathy
with the essay 'The International Fallacy', by W. K. Wimsatt and
M. C. Beardsley, recently published in *The Sewanee Review*. We had
best not try to telescope the separate problems of 'the psychology
of composition' and that of 'objective evaluation'. I have no intention of trying to collapse them here.

Well, what is 'said' in the 'Horatian Ode'? What is the speaker's
attitude toward Cromwell and toward Charles? M. Legouis sees in
the 'Ode' a complete impartiality, an impartiality which is the
product of Marvell's nonparticipation in the wars. Legouis can even
speak of the poem as *'ce monument d'indifférence en matière de régime
politique'*. But the 'Ode', though it may be a monument of impartiality, is not a monument of indifference. To read it in this fashion
is to miss what seems to me to be a passionate interest in the issues,
an interest which is manifested everywhere in the poem. It is true
that we have no evidence that Marvell ever served in the civil war,
but we had better not leap to conclusions of his indifference from
that. My own guess is that some young Cavaliers who shed their
blood for the King thought and felt less deeply about the issues
than does the speaker of this poem. The tone is not that of a 'plague
o' both your houses' nor is it that of 'the conflict provided glory
enough to be shared by both sides'.

Mr Margoliouth comes much closer to the point. He sums up as
follows:

The ode is the utterance of a constitutional monarchist, whose sympathies
have been with the King, but who yet believes more in men than in parties
or principles, and whose hopes are fixed now on Cromwell, seeing in him
both the civic ideal of a ruler without personal ambition, and the man of
destiny moved by and yet himself driving a power which is above justice.

This statement is plausible, and for its purposes, perhaps just. But does it take us very far – even on the level of understanding Marvell the man? What sort of constitutional monarchist is it who 'believes more in men than in . . . principles'? Or who can accept a 'power which is above justice'? I do not say that such a monarchist cannot exist. My point is that Margoliouth's statement raises more problems than it solves. Furthermore, in what sense are the speaker's hopes 'fixed . . . on Cromwell'? And how confident is he that Cromwell is 'without personal ambition'? I have quoted earlier Margoliouth's characterisation of the 'Ode' as a poem 'where royalist principles and admiration for Cromwell the Great Man exist side by side'. I think that they do exist side by side, but if so, how are they related? Do they exist in separate layers, or are they somehow unified? Unified, in some sense, they must be if the 'Ode' is a poem and not a heap of fragments.

I hope that my last statement indicates the kind of question which we finally have to face and answer. It is a problem of poetic organisation. As such, it addresses itself properly to the critic. The historical scholars have not answered it, for it is a question which cannot be answered in terms of historical evidence. (This is not to say, of course, that the same man may not be both historical scholar and critic.) Moreover, I have already taken some pains to indicate how heavily the critic, on his part, may need to lean upon the historian. To put the matter into its simplest terms: the critic obviously must know what the words of the poem mean, something which immediately puts him in debt to the linguist; and since many of the words in this poem are proper nouns, in debt to the historian as well. I am not concerned to exalt the critic at the expense of specialists in other disciplines: on the contrary, I am only concerned to show that he has a significant function, and to indicate what the nature of that function is.

But I am not so presumptuous as to promise a solution to the problem. Instead, the reader will have to be content with suggestions – as to what the 'Ode' is not saying, as to what the 'Ode' may be saying – in short, with explorations of further problems. Many critical problems, of course, I shall have to pass over and some important ones I shall only touch upon. To illustrate: there is the general Roman cast given to the 'Ode'. Marvell has taken care to make no specifically Christian references in the poem. Charles is Caesar; Cromwell is a Hannibal; on the scaffold, Charles refuses to call with 'vulgar spight', not on God, but on 'the Gods', and so on. Or to point to another problem, metaphors drawn from hunting pervade the poem. Charles chases himself to Carisbrooke; Cromwell is like the falcon; Cromwell will soon put his dogs in 'near / The *Caledonian* Deer'. Or, to take up the general organisation of the poem: Marvell seems to have used the celebrated stanzas on Charles's execution to divide the poem into two rather distinct parts: first, Cromwell's rise to power; and second, Cromwell's wielding of the supreme power. This scheme of division, by the way, I intend to make use of in the discussion that follows. But I shall try, in general, to limit it to the specific problem of the speaker's attitude toward Cromwell, subordinating other critical problems to this one, which is, I maintain, essentially a critical problem too.

From historical evidence alone we would suppose that the attitude toward Cromwell in this poem would have to be a complex one. And this complexity is reflected in the ambiguity of the compliments paid to him. The ambiguity reveals itself as early as the second word of the poem. It is the 'forward' youth whose attention the speaker directs to the example of Cromwell. 'Forward' may mean no more than 'high-spirited', 'ardent', 'properly ambitious'; but the *New English Dictionary* sanctions the possibility that there lurks in the word the sense of 'presumptuous', 'pushing'. The forward youth can no longer now

> in the Shadows sing
> His Numbers languishing.

In the light of Cromwell's career, he must forsake the shadows and his 'Muses dear' and become the man of action.

The speaker, one observes, does not identify Cromwell himself as the 'forward youth', or say directly that Cromwell's career has been motivated by a striving for fame. But the implications of the first two stanzas do carry over to him. There is, for example, the important word 'so' to relate Cromwell to these stanzas:

> So restless *Cromwel* could not cease. . . .

And 'restless' is as ambiguous in its meaning as 'forward', and in its darker connotations even more damning. For, though 'restless' can mean 'scorning indolence', 'willing to forego ease', it can also suggest the man with a maggot in the brain. 'To cease', used intransitively, is 'to take rest, to be or remain at rest', and the *New English Dictionary* gives instances as late as 1701. Cromwell's 'courage high' will not allow him to rest 'in the inglorious Arts of Peace'. And this thirst for glory, merely hinted at here by negatives, is developed further in the ninth stanza:

> Could by industrious Valour climbe
> To ruine the great Work of Time.

'Climb' certainly connotes a kind of aggressiveness. In saying this we need not be afraid that we are reading into the word some smack of such modern phrases as 'social climber'. Marvell's translation of the second chorus of Seneca's *Thyestes* sufficiently attests that the word could have such associations for him:

> Climb at *Court* for me that will
> Tottering favors Pinacle;
> All I seek is to lye still.

Cromwell, on the other hand, does not seek to lie still – has sought something quite other than this. His valour is called – strange collocation – an 'industrious valour', and his courage is too high to brook a rival:

> For 'tis all one to Courage high
> The Emulous or Enemy;
> > And with such to inclose,
> > Is more then to oppose.

The implied metaphor is that of some explosive which does more violence to that which encloses it, the powder to its magazine, for instance, than to some wall which merely opposes it – against which the charge is fired.

But the speaker has been careful to indicate that Cromwell's motivation has to be conceived of as more complex than any mere thirst for glory. He has even pointed this up. The forward youth is referred to as one who 'would appear' – that is, as one who wills to leave the shadows of obscurity. But restless Cromwell 'could not cease' – for Cromwell it is not a question of will at all, but of a deeper compulsion. Restless Cromwell could not cease, if he would.

Indeed, the lines that follow extend the suggestion that Cromwell is like an elemental force – with as little will as the lightning bolt, and with as little conscience:

> And, like the three-fork'd Lightning, first
> Breaking the Clouds where it was nurst,
> > Did thorough his own Side
> > His fiery way divide.

We are told that the last two lines refer to Cromwell's struggle after Marston Moor with the leaders of the Parliamentary party. Doubtless they do, and the point is important for our knowledge of the poem. But what is more important is that we be fully alive to the force of the metaphor. The clouds have bred the lightning bolt, but the bolt tears its way through the clouds, and goes on to blast the head of Caesar himself. As Margoliouth puts it: 'The lightning is conceived as tearing through the side of his own body the cloud'. In terms of the metaphor, then, Cromwell has not spared his own body: there is no reason therefore to be surprised that he has not spared the body of Charles.

I do not believe that I overemphasized the speaker's implication that Cromwell is a natural force. A few lines later the point is reinforced with another naturalistic figure, an analogy taken from physics:

> Nature that hateth emptiness,
> Allows of penetration less:
>   And therefore must make room
>   Where greater Spirits come . . .

The question of right, the imagery insists, is beside the point. If nature will not tolerate a power vacuum, no more will it allow two bodies to occupy the same space. (It is amusing, by the way, that Marvell has boldly introduced into his analogy borrowed from physics the nonphysical term 'Spirits'; yet I do not think that the clash destroys the figure. Since twenty thousand angels can dance on the point of a needle, two spirits, even though one of them is a greater spirit, ought to be able to occupy the same room. But two spirits, as Marvell conceives of spirits here, will jostle one another, and one must give way. True, the greater spirit is immaterial, but he is no pale abstraction – he is all air and fire, the 'force of angry Heavens flame'. The metaphor ought to give less trouble to the reader of our day than it conceivably gave to readers bred up on Newtonian physics.)

What are the implications for Charles? Does the poet mean to imply that Charles has angered heaven – that he has merited his destruction? There is no suggestion that Cromwell is a thunderbolt hurled by an angry Jehovah – or even by an angry Jove. The general emphasis on Cromwell as an elemental force is thoroughly relevant here to counter this possible misreading. Certainly, in the lines that follow there is nothing to suggest that Charles has angered heaven, or that the Justice which complains against his fate is anything less than justice.

I began this examination of the imagery with the question, 'What is the speaker's attitude toward Cromwell?' We have seen that the speaker more than once hints at his thirst for glory:

> So restless *Cromwel* could not cease . . .
> Could by industrious Valour climbe . . .

But we have also seen that the imagery tends to view Cromwell as a natural phenomenon, the bolt bred in the cloud. Is there a contradiction? I think not. Cromwell's is no vulgar ambition. If his valour is an 'industrious Valour', it contains plain valour too of a kind perfectly capable of being recognised by any Cavalier:

> What Field of all the Civil Wars,
> Where his were not the deepest Scars?

If the driving force has been a desire for glory, it is a glory of that kind which allows a man to become dedicated and, in a sense, even selfless in his pursuit of it. Moreover, the desire for such glory can become so much a compulsive force that the man does not appear to act by an exercise of his personal will but seems to become the very will of something else. There is in the poem, it seems to me, at least one specific suggestion of this sort:

> But through adventurous War
> Urged his active Star. . . .

Cromwell is the marked man, the man of destiny, but he is not merely the man governed by his star. Active though it be, he cannot remain passive, even in relation to it: he is not merely urged by it, but himself urges it on.

Yet, if thus far Cromwell has been treated as naked force, something almost too awesome to be considered as a man, the poet does not forget that after all he is a man too – that 'the force of angry Heavens flame' is embodied in a human being:

> And, if we would speak true,
> Much to the Man is due.

The stanzas that follow proceed to define and praise that manliness – the strength, the industrious valour, the cunning. (You will notice that I reject the interpretation which would paraphrase 'Much to the Man is due' as 'After all, Cromwell has accomplished much that is good'. Such an interpretation could sort well enough with Legouis's picture of Marvell as the cold and detached honest broker between the factions: unfortunately it will not survive a close scrutiny of the grammar and the general context in which the passage is placed.)

One notices that among the virtues composing Cromwell's manliness, the speaker mentions his possession of the 'wiser art':

> Where, twining subtile fears with hope,
> He wove a Net of such a scope,
>   That *Charles* himselfe might chase
>   To *Caresbrooks* narrow case.

On this point Cromwell has been cleared by all the modern historians (except perhaps Mr Hilaire Belloc). Charles's flight to Carisbrooke Castle, as it turned out, aided Cromwell, but Cromwell could have hardly known that it would; and there is no evidence that he cunningly induced the King to flee to Carisbrooke. Royalist pamphleteers, of course, believed that Cromwell did, and used the item in their general bill of damnation against Cromwell. How does the speaker use it here – to damn or to praise? We tend to answer, 'To praise'. But then it behooves us to notice what is being praised. The things praised are Cromwell's talents as such – the tremendous disciplined powers which Cromwell brought to bear against the King.

For the end served by those powers, the speaker has no praise at all. Rather he has gone out of his way to insist that Cromwell was deaf to the complaint of Justice and its pleading of the 'antient Rights'. The power achieved by Cromwell is a 'forced Pow'r' – a usurped power. On this point the speaker is unequivocal. I must question therefore Margoliouth's statement that Marvell sees in Cromwell 'the man of destiny moved by . . . a power that is above justice'. Above justice, yes, in the sense that power is power and justice is not power. The one does not insure the presence of the other. Charles has no way to vindicate his 'helpless Right', but it is no less Right because it is helpless. But the speaker, though he is not a cynic, is a realist. A kingdom cannot be held by mere pleading of the 'antient Rights':

> But those do hold or break
> As Men are strong or weak.

In short, the more closely we look at the 'Ode', the more clearly apparent it becomes that the speaker has chosen to emphasize Cromwell's virtues as a man, and likewise, those of Charles as a man. The poem does not debate which of the two was right, for that issue is not even in question. In his treatment of Charles, then, the speaker no more than Charles himself attempts to vindicate his 'helpless Right'. Instead, he emphasises his dignity, his fortitude, and what has finally to be called his consummate good taste. The portraits of the two men beautifully supplement each other. Cromwell is – to use Aristotle's distinction – the man of character, the man of action, who 'does both act and know'. Charles, on the other hand, is the man of passion, the man who is acted upon, the man who knows how to suffer. The contrast is pointed up in half a dozen different ways.

Cromwell, acted upon by his star, is not passive but actually urges his star. Charles in 'acting' – in chasing away to Carisbrooke – actually is passive – performs the part assigned to him by Cromwell. True, we can read 'chase' as an intransitive verb (the *New English Dictionary* sanctions this use for the period): 'that Charles himself might hurry to Carisbrooke'. But the primary meaning asserts itself in the context: 'that Charles might chase himself to Carisbrooke's narrow case'. For this hunter, now preparing to lay his dogs in 'near / The *Caledonian Deer*', the royal quarry has dutifully chased itself.

Even in the celebrated stanzas on the execution, there is ironic realism as well as admiration. In this fullest presentation of Charles as king, he is the player king, the king acting in a play. He is the 'Royal Actor' who knows his assigned part and performs it with dignity. He truly adorned the 'Tragick Scaffold'

> While round the armed Bands
> Did clap their bloody hands.

The generally received account is that the soldiers clapped their hands so as to make it impossible for Charles's speech to be heard. But in the context this reference to hand-clapping supports the stage metaphor. What is being applauded? Cromwell's resolution in bringing the King to a deserved death? Or Charles's resolution on the scaffold as he suffered that death? Marvell was too good a poet to resolve the ambiguity. It is enough that he makes the armed bands applaud.

It has not been pointed out, I believe, that Robert Wild, in his poem on 'The Death of Mr. Christopher Love', has echoed a pair of Marvell's finest lines. Love was beheaded by Cromwell on 22 August 1651. In Wild's poem, Marvell's lines

> But with his keener Eye
> The Axes edge did try

become: 'His keener words did their sharp Ax exceed'. The point is of no especial importance except that it indicates, since Wild's poem was evidently written shortly after Love's execution, that in 1651 the 'Horatian Ode' was being handed about among the Royalists. For Wild was that strange combination, an English Presbyterian Royalist.

I have pointed out earlier that the second half of the poem begins here with the reference to

> that memorable Hour
> Which first assur'd the forced Pow'r.

Cromwell is now the *de facto* head of the state, and the speaker, as a realist, recognizes that fact. Cromwell is seen henceforth, not primarily in his character as the destroyer of the monarchy, but as the agent of the new state that has been erected upon the dead body of the King. The thunderbolt simile, of the first part of the poem, gives way here to the falcon simile in this second part of the poem. The latter figure revises and qualifies the former: it repeats the suggestion of ruthless energy and power, but Cromwell falls from the sky now, not as the thunderbolt, but as the hunting hawk. The trained falcon is not a wanton destroyer, nor an irresponsible one. It knows its master: it is perfectly disciplined:

> She, having kill'd, no more does search,
> But on the next green Bow to pearch . . .

The speaker's admiration for Cromwell the man culminates, it seems to me, here. Cromwell might make the Fame his own; he *need* not present kingdoms to the state. He might assume the crown rather than crowning each year. Yet he forbears:

> Nor yet grown stiffer with Command,
> But still in the *Republick's* hand . . .

Does the emphasis on 'still' mean that the speaker is surprised that Cromwell has continued to pay homage to the republic? Does he imply that Cromwell may not always do so? Perhaps not: the emphasis is upon the fact that he need not obey and yet does. Yet the compliment derives its full force from the fact that the homage is not forced, but voluntary and even somewhat unexpected. And a recognition of this point implies the recognition of the possibility that Cromwell will not always so defer to the commonwealth.

And now what of the republic which Cromwell so ruthlessly and efficiently serves? What is the speaker's attitude toward it? To begin with, the speaker recognises that its foundations rest upon the bleeding head of Charles. The speaker is aware, it is true, of the Roman analogy, and the English state is allowed the benefit of that analogy. But it is well to notice that the speaker does not commit himself to the opinion that the bleeding head is a happy augury:

> And yet in that the *State*
> Forsaw it's happy Fate.

The Roman state was able to take it as a favourable omen, and was justified by the event. With regard to the speaker himself, it seems to me more to the point to notice what prophecy he is willing to commit himself to. He does not prophesy peace. He is willing to predict that England, under Cromwell's leadership, will be powerful in war, and will strike fear into the surrounding states:

> What may not then our *Isle* presume
> While Victory his Crest does plume!
> What may not others fear
> If thus he crown each year!

Specifically, he predicts a smashing victory over the Scots.

But what of the compliments to Cromwell on his ruthlessly effective campaign against the Irish? Does not the speaker succumb, for once, to a bitter and biased patriotism, and does this not constitute a blemish upon the poem?

> And now the *Irish* are asham'd
> To see themselves in one Year tam'd:
> So much one Man can do,
> That does both act and know.
> They can affirm his Praises best,
> And have, though overcome, confest
> How good he is, how just. . . .

Margoliouth glosses the word 'confessed' as follows: 'Irish testimony in favor of Cromwell at this moment is highly improbable. Possibly there is a reference to the voluntary submission of part of Munster with its English colony.' But surely Margoliouth indulges in understatement. The most intense partisan of Cromwell would have had some difficulty in taking the lines without some inflection of grim irony. The final appeal in this matter, however, is not to what Marvell the Englishman must have thought, or even to what Marvell the author must have intended, but rather to the full context of the poem itself. In that context, the lines in question can be read ironically, and the earlier stanzas sanction that reading. Cromwell's energy, activity, bravery, resolution – even what may be called his efficiency – are the qualities that have come in for praise, not his gentleness or his mercy. The Irish, indeed, are best able to affirm such praise as has been accorded to Cromwell; and they know from experience 'how good he is, how just', for they have been blasted by the force of angry Heaven's flame, even as Charles has been. But I do not mean to turn the passage into sarcasm. The third quality which the speaker couples with goodness and justice is fitness 'for highest Trust', and the goodness and justice of Cromwell culminate in this fitness. But the recommendation to trust has reference not to the Irish, but to the English state. The Irish are quite proper authorities on Cromwell's trustworthiness in this regard, for they have come to know him as the completely dedicated instrument of that state whose devotion to the purpose in hand is unrelenting and unswerving.

To say all this is not to suggest that Marvell shed any unnecessary tears over the plight of the Irish, or even to imply that he was not happy, as one assumes most Englishmen were, to have the Irish rebellion crushed promptly and efficiently. It is to say that the passage fits into the poem – a poem which reveals itself to be no panegyric on Cromwell but an unflinching analysis of the Cromwellian character.

The wild Irish have been tamed, and now the Pict will no longer be able to shelter under his particoloured mind. It is the hour of decision, and the particoloured minds affords no protection against the man who 'does both act and know'. In Cromwell's mind there are no conflicts, no teasing mixture of judgments. Cromwell's is not only an 'industrious valour', but a 'sad valour'. Margoliouth glosses 'sad' as 'steadfast', and no doubt he is right. But sad can mean 'sober' also, and I suspect that in this context, with its implied references to Scottish plaids, it means also drab of hue. It is also possible that the poet here glances at one of Virgil's transferred epithets, *maestum timorem*, sad fear, the fear that made the Trojans sad. Cromwell's valour is *sad* in that the Scots will have occasion to rue it.

Thus far the speaker has been content to view Cromwell from a distance, as it were, against the background of recent history. He has referred to him consistently in the third person. But in the last two stanzas, he addresses Cromwell directly. He salutes him as 'the Wars and Fortunes Son'. It is a great compliment: Cromwell is the son of the wars in that he is the master of battle, and he seems fortune's own son in the success that has constantly waited upon him. But we do not wrench the lines if we take them to say also that Cromwell is the creature of the wars and the product of fortune. The imagery of the early stanzas which treats Cromwell as a natural phenomenon certainly lends support to this reading. Cromwell can claim no sanction for his power in 'antient Rights'. His power has come out of the wars and the troubled times. I call attention to the fact that we do not have to choose between readings: the readings do not mutually exclude each other: they support each other, and this double interpretation has the whole poem behind it.

Cromwell is urged to march 'indefatigably on'. The advice is good advice; but it is good advice because any other course of action is positively unthinkable. Indeed, to call it advice at all is perhaps to distort it: though addressed to Cromwell, it partakes of quiet commentary as much as of exhortation. After all, it is restless

Cromwell who is being addressed. If he could not cease 'in the inglorious Arts of Peace' when his 'highest plot' was 'to plant Bergamot', one cannot conceive of his ceasing now in the hour of danger.

> And for the last effect
> Still keep thy Sword erect.

Once more the advice (or commentary) is seriously intended, but it carries with it as much of warning as it does of approval. Those who take up the sword shall perish by the sword: those who have achieved their power on contravention of ancient rights by the sword can only expect to maintain their power by the sword.

What kind of sword is it that is able to 'fright the spirits of the shady night'? Margoliouth writes: 'The cross hilt of the sword would avert the spirits . . .'. But the speaker makes it quite plain that it is not merely the spirits of the shady night that Cromwell will have to fight as he marches indefatigably on. It will not be enough to hold the sword aloft as a ritual sword, an emblematic sword. The naked steel will still have to be used against bodies less diaphanous than spirits. If there is any doubt as to this last point, Marvell's concluding lines put it as powerfully and explicitly as it can be put:

> The same *Arts* that did *gain*
> A *Pow'r* must it *maintain*.

But, I can imagine someone asking, What is the final attitude toward Cromwell? Is it ultimately one of approval or disapproval? Does admiration overbalance condemnation? Or, is the 'Ode', after all, merely a varied Scottish plaid, the reflection of Marvell's own particoloured mind – a mind which had not been finally 'made up' with regard to Cromwell? I think that enough has been said to make it plain that there is no easy, pat answer to such questions. There is a unified total attitude, it seems to me; but it is so complex that we may oversimplify and distort its complexity by the way in which we put the question. The request for some kind of summing up is a natural one, and I have no wish to try to evade it. For a really full answer, of course, one must refer the questioner to the poem itself; but one can at least try to suggest some aspects of the total attitude.

I would begin by reemphasising the dramatic character of the poem. It is not a statement – an essay on 'Why I cannot support Cromwell' or on 'Why I am now ready to support Cromwell'. It is a poem essentially dramatic in its presentation, which means that it is diagnostic rather than remedial, and eventuates, not in a course of action, but in contemplation. Perhaps the best way therefore in which to approach it is to conceive of it as, say, one conceives of a Shakespearean tragedy. Cromwell is the usurper who demands and commands admiration. What, for example, is our attitude towards Macbeth? We assume his guilt, but there are qualities which emerge from his guilt which properly excite admiration. I do not mean that the qualities palliate his guilt or that they compensate for his guilt. They actually come into being through his guilt, but they force us to exalt him even as we condemn him. I have chosen an extreme example. I certainly do not mean to imply that in writing the 'Ode' Marvell had Shakespeare's tragedy in mind. What I am trying to point to is this: that the kind of honesty and insight and whole-mindedness which we associate with tragedy is to be found to some degree in all great poetry and is to be found in this poem.

R. P. Warren once remarked to me that Marvell has constantly behind him in his poetry the achievement of Elizabethan drama with its treatment of the human will as seen in the perspective of history. He had in mind some of the lyrics, but the remark certainly applies fully to the 'Ode'. The poet is thoroughly conscious of the drama, and consciously makes use of dramatic perspective. Charles, as we have seen, becomes the 'Royal Actor', playing his part on the 'Tragick Scaffold'. But the tragedy of Charles is merely glanced at. The poem is Cromwell's – Cromwell's tragedy, the first three acts of it, as it were, which is not a tragedy of failure but of success.

Cromwell is the truly kingly man who is *not* king – whose very virtues conduce to kingly power and almost force kingly power upon him. It is not any fumbling on the poet's part which causes him to call Cromwell 'a Caesar' before the poem ends, even though he has earlier appropriated that name to Charles. *Both* men are Caesar, Charles the wearer of the purple, and Cromwell, the invincible general, the inveterate campaigner, the man 'that does both act and know'. Cromwell is the Caesar who must refuse the crown – whose glory it is that he is willing to refuse the crown – but who cannot enjoy the reward and the security that a crown affords. The tension between the speaker's admiration for the kingliness which has won Cromwell the power and his awareness that the power can be maintained only by a continual exertion of these talents for kingship – this tension is never relaxed. Cromwell is not of royal blood – he boasts a higher and a baser pedigree: he is the 'Wars and Fortunes Son'. He cannot rest because he is restless Cromwell. He must march indefatigably on, for he cannot afford to become fatigued. These implications enrich and qualify an insight into Cromwell which is as heavily freighted with admiration as it is with a great condemnation. But the admiration and the condemnation do not cancel each other. They define each other; and because there is responsible definition, they reinforce each other.

Was this, then, the attitude of Andrew Marvell, born 1621, sometime student at Cambridge, returned traveller and prospective tutor, toward Oliver Cromwell in the summer of 1650? The honest answer must be: I do not know. I have tried to read the poem, the 'Horatian Ode', not Andrew Marvell's mind. That seems sensible to me in view of the fact that we have the poem, whereas the attitude held by Marvell at any particular time must be a matter of inference – even though I grant that the poem may be put in as part of the evidence from which we draw inferences. True, we do know that Marvell was capable of composing the 'Ode' and I must concede that the fact may tell us a great deal about Marvell's attitude towards Cromwell. I think it probably does. I am not sure, for reasons given earlier in this paper, that it tells us everything: there is the problem of the role of the unconscious in the process of composition, there is the possibility of the poet's having written better than he knew, there is even the matter of the happy accident. I do not mean to overemphasise these matters. I do think, however, that it is wise to maintain the distinction between what total attitude is manifested in the poem and the attitude of the author as citizen.

Yet, though I wish to maintain this distinction, I do not mean to hide behind it. The total attitude realised in the 'Ode' does not seem to me monstrously inhuman in its complexity. It could be held by human beings, in my opinion. Something very like it apparently was. Listen, for example, to the Earl of Clarendon's judgement on Cromwell:

He was one of those men, quos vitupare ne inimici quidem possunt, nisi ut simul laudent [whom not even their enemies can inveigh against without at the same time praising them], for he could never have done halfe that mischieve, without great partes of courage and industry and judgement, and he must have had a wonderful understandinge in the nature and humours of men, and as greate a dexterity in the applyinge them, who from a private and obscure birth (though of a good family), without interest of estate, allyance or frenshippes, could rayse himselfe to such a height, and compounde and kneade such opposite and contradictory humours and interests, into a consistence, that contributed to his designes and to ther owne distruction, whilst himselfe grew insensibly powerfull enough, to cutt off those by whom he had climed, in the instant, that they projected to demolish ther owne buildinge. . . .
He was not a man of bloode, and totally declined Machiavells methode . . . it was more then once proposed, that ther might be a generall massacre of all the royall party, as the only expedient to secure the govern-

ment, but Crumwell would never consent to it, it may be out of to much contempt of his enimyes; In a worde, as he had all the wickednesses against which damnation is denounced and for which Hell fyre is praepared, so he had some virtues, which have caused the memory of some men in all ages to be celebrated, and he will be looked upon by posterity, as a brave, badd man.

The resemblance between Clarendon's judgment and that reflected in the 'Ode' is at some points so remarkable that one wonders whether Clarendon had not seen and been impressed by some now lost manuscript of the 'Ode': 'Who from a private and obscure birth' – 'Who, from his private Gardens, where/He liv'd reserved and austere' – 'could rayse himself to such a height . . . by whome he had climed' – 'Could by industrious Valour climbe', and so on and so forth. But I do not want to press the suggestion of influence of Marvell on Clarendon. Indeed, it makes for my general point to discount the possibility. For what I am anxious to empha-sise is that the attitude of the 'Ode' is not inhuman in its Olympian detachment, that something like it could be held by a human being, and by a human being of pronounced Royalist sympathies.

I have argued that the critic needs the help of the historian – all the help that he can get – but I have insisted that the poem has to be read as a poem – that what it 'says' is a question for the critic to answer, and that no amount of historical evidence as such can finally determine what the poem says. But if we do read the poem successfully, the critic may on occasion be able to make a return on his debt to the historian. If we have read the 'Ode' successfully – *if*, I say, for I am far from confident – it may be easier for us to understand how the man capable of writing the 'Ode' was also able to write 'Tom May's Death' and 'On Appleton House' and indeed, years later, after the Restoration, the statement: 'Men ought to have trusted God; they ought and might have trusted the King'.

F. R. Leavis: *'Antony and Cleopatra'* and *'All for Love'*

All for Love is beyond doubt a proud and lovely masterpiece; it is the fine flower of Dryden's genius. It was at one time, indeed for a very long time, fashionable to decry it in comparison with *Antony and Cleopatra*, but Dryden

Reprinted from F. R. Leavis, *The Living Principle: 'English' as a Discipline of Thought* (London, 1975), pp. 144–54.

was not trying to do at all the same kind of thing as Shakespeare. Free opinion will be forced to admit that though Shakespeare's play contains finer poetry than Dryden could ever write – as he would have been the first to admit – Dryden's has a more tragic effect.

I take this from the Introduction to the 'World's Classics' volume of *Restoration Tragedies*, and I take it as representative. The critical position would not be generally found surprising either in the academic world or in the world of literary fashions (the critic, Professor Bonamy Dobrée, had standing in both). So, though to myself Dryden and Shakespeare seem to be doing things so different in kind as to make a serious and sustained comparison obviously impossible, the quotation serves to countenance me in offering to enforce this view critically by way of illustrative exercise – a suggestion of critical method.

The superiority in poetry that makes it seem to me absurd to compare the two plays in tragic effect (not to speak of attributing the other superiority to Dryden) is conclusively manifest in the first twenty lines of *Antony and Cleopatra*. It is an immediately felt superiority in the life of the verse – superiority in concreteness, variety and sensitiveness – that leaves us with 'eloquence' instead of 'life' as the right word for Dryden's verse. This superiority asserts itself everywhere; it is a matter of the general texture of the play, and could in spoken discussion be exemplified point by point in the least eloquent and exalted places. Nevertheless, the exigencies of written criticism dictate the choice of some sustained passage, where demonstration can be effected with force and economy. There is an obvious choice, and it will, in fact, serve peculiarly well:

> *Enobarbus.* I will tell you.
> The barge she sat in, like a burnish'd throne,
> Burn'd on the water; the poop was beaten gold;
> Purple the sails, and so perfumed that
> The winds were love-sick with them; the oars were silver,
> Which to the tune of flutes kept stroke, and made
> The water which they beat to follow faster,
> As amorous of their strokes. For her own person,
> It beggar'd all description: she did lie
> In her pavilion – cloth of gold, of tissue –
> O'er-picturing that Venus where we see
> The fancy outwork nature: on each side her,
> Stood pretty dimpled boys, like smiling Cupids,
> With divers-colour'd fans, whose wind did seem
> To glow with delicate cheeks which they did cool,
> And what they undid did.
> *Agrippa.* O, rare for Antony!

> *Enobarbus.* Her gentlewomen, like the Nereides,
> So many mermaids, tended her i' the eyes,
> And made their bends adornings; at the helm
> A seeming mermaid steers: the silken tackle
> Swell with the touches of those flower-soft hands,
> That yarely frame the office. From the barge
> A strange invisible perfume hits the sense
> Of the adjacent wharfs. The city cast
> Her people out upon her; and Antony,
> Enthroned i' the market-place, did sit alone,
> Whistling to the air; which, but for vacancy,
> Had gone to gaze on Cleopatra too
> And made a gap in nature.*

How does that look in comparison with Dryden's rendering of it?†

> *Antony.* To clear her self,
> For sending him no Aid, she came from Egypt.
> Her Silver Gally down the Silver Cydnos row'd,
> The tackling Silk, the Streamers wav'd with Gold,
> The gentle Winds were lodg'd in Purple Sails:
> Her Nymphs, like Nereids, round her Couch, were plac'd;
> Where she, another Sea-born Venus, lay.
> *Dollabella.* No more: I would not hear it.
> *Antony.* O, you must!
> She lay, and leant her Cheek upon her Hand,
> And cast a Look so languishingly sweet,
> As if, secure of all Beholders Hearts,
> Neglecting she could take 'em: Boys, like Cupids,
> Stood fanning, with their painted Wings, the Winds
> That plaid about her Face: But if she smil'd,
> A darting Glory seem'd to blaze abroad:
> That Mens desiring Eyes were never weary'd
> But hung upon the Object: to soft Flutes
> The Silver Oars kept Time; and while they plaid,
> The Hearing gave new Pleasure to the Sight;
> And both to Thought: 'twas Heav'n or somewhat more;
> For she so charm'd all Hearts, that gazing Crowds
> Stood panting on the shore, and wanted Breath
> To give their welcome Voice.

It should be plain that a formal comparison is hardly possibly; Dryden's version offers in itself little lodgment for detailed commentary, and must serve mainly as a foil to the Shakespearean passage. The juxtaposition invites us to point to this, that and the other in

---

* *Antony and Cleopatra*, Act II, sc. ii.
† *All for Love*, Act iii; page 58 in *Five Restoration Tragedies* (World's Classics).

Shakespeare and note that Dryden offers nothing corresponding. Our general observation is that Shakespeare's verse seems to enact its meaning, to do and to give rather than to talk about, where Dryden's is merely descriptive eloquence. The characteristic Shakespearean life asserts itself in Enobarbus's opening lines.

> The barge she sat in, like a burnish'd throne,
> Burn'd on the water . . .

– The assonantal sequence, 'barge' – 'burnish'd' – 'burn'd,' is alien in spirit to Dryden's handling of the medium (it reminds us of Hopkins who, though he has a technical deliberateness of his own, is, in his use of English, essentially Shakespearean). The effect is to give the metaphor 'burn'd' a vigour of sensuous realisation that it wouldn't otherwise have had; the force of 'burn' is reflected back through 'burnish'd' (felt now as 'burning' too) upon 'barge,' so that the barge takes fire, as it were, before our eyes: we are much more than merely told that the barge 'burn'd'. Further, the assonantal repetition, following immediately upon the quiet

> I will tell you,

has the effect of the ejaculatory superlative – the tone explicit in

> It beggar'd all description

Even if, by the way, this 'beggar'd' is not, here, an original metaphorical creation (though the *New English Dictionary* gives this as the earliest instance of the phrase), we feel it as such; as we take it in its context surrounding life seems to inform it, so that there is an effect of re-creation, in spite of our familiarity with the phrase as a cliché.

But there has, before this, been something else to notice. Shakespeare's superiority over Dryden is not merely an affair of metaphors; it is equally observable – if not as amenable to written commentary – in tone and movement. These too exhibit Shakespeare's marvellous power of realisation, of making language create and enact instead of merely saying and relating. There is in them a life corresponding to – bound up with – the metaphorical life. We become aware of it as sensitive variation. As already noted, the narrator's introductory

> I will tell you

sets off by contrast the restrained-intense of the assonantal passage, in which the thing described seems present and not merely told of.

In

> the poop was beaten gold

there is relaxation; we slip back into telling, the 'was' getting its full value. But with the succeeding inversion (in which the verb is omitted) –

> Purple the sails

– we have again the tone of immediacy, and in the next clause the superlative intensity is explicit. After this,

> the oars were silver

comes as a relapse into mere telling, into narration at a distance. What it introduces is an effect of movement that may be said to be implicitly of the order of metaphor; while there is nothing obviously mimetic in the rhythm, the water following faster seems to be more than told about, it seems to be done:

> the oars were silver,
> Which to the tune of flutes kept stroke, and made
> The water which they beat to follow faster,
> As amorous of their strokes.

– The relapse into comment in this last line (with the closing pun) sets off the amorous eagerness of the water, which is conveyed observably by the even hurry of

> and made
> The water which they beat to follow faster . . .

The fluid movement of this (overflowing the line-division) is again felt to be enhanced by the preceding succession of stressed and consonantally packed monosyllables:

> Which to the tune of flútes képt stróke . . .

These three rigid-seeming stresses suggest both the oars and the strokes which the hurrying water follows (it is, perhaps, well to say again that there is nothing directly and simply mimetic – *e.g.*, no approach to the rhythm of rowing; the suggestive process is a subtler matter).

This kind of action in the verse (if 'kind' does not misrepresent, for there is indefinite variety) cannot be done justice to in written analysis. In the mature Shakespeare it is pervasive, but it can be fixed on for convincing comment only where the working is comparatively simple and obvious. At the most obvious we have:

> With divers-colour'd fans, whose wind did seem
> To glow the delicate cheeks which they did cool,
> And what they undid did.

– The 'undid did', with its repetition that is at the same time reversal, plainly enacts the sense. But even this effect owes its full force to the movement of the preceding three or four lines, which is not so easily annotated. Here, then, is what as much as the metaphorical life makes the difference between Shakespeare's poetry and Dryden's eloquence.*

One aspect of the difference is that Dryden's text would give little lodgment to the commentator who finds so much to explain or puzzle over in Shakespeare's. Not that there would appear to be any notable crux in the passage under examination. The Arden editor of my old edition, however, does find a difficult one here:

> Her gentlewomen, like the Nereides,
> So many mermaids, tended her i' the eyes,
> And made their bends adornings . . .

– Against this last line ('this much vexed passage') there is a note directing the reader to an appendix. Perhaps it is a long untroubled familiarity with the passage that makes me, after reading the half-dozen large pages of the appendix, unable to see that any vexing was necessary. At any rate, the obvious meaning still seems to me obviously the intended one: the stylised deference – movements, gestures, obeisances – of the attendant gentlewomen as they wait upon Cleopatra plays up to the *décor* in a kind of ballet ('adornings', the verbal form, is clearly the right word for movement and action).

The lines that follow exemplify well Shakespeare's characteristic sensuous strength:

* Cf.
>   What you do
> Still betters what is done. When you speak, sweet,
> I'ld have you do it ever: when you sing,
> I'ld have you buy and sell so, so give alms,
> Pray so; and, for the ordering your affairs,
> To sing them too: when you do dance, I wish you
> A wave o' the sea, that you might ever do
> Nothing but that; move still, still so,
> And own no other function: each your doing,
> So singular in each particular,
> Crowns what you are doing in the present deeds,
> That all your acts are queens.
>   *The Winter's Tale*, Act IV, sc. iv, l.135

> at the helm
> A seeming mermaid steers: the silken tackle
> Swell with the touches of those flower-soft hands,
> That yarely frame the office. From the barge
> A strange invisible perfume hits the sense
> Of the adjacent wharfs

– The tactual imagery of the second clause derives its strength partly from contrast: the hard and energetic associations of 'tackle' (they are not overtly felt as such, but are transformed, as it were, into their opposite) give the adjective 'silken' a strength of sensuous evocation that it would not otherwise have had. 'Tackle' here, no doubt, is inclusive, and it is the sails that swell; so that to feel, as I have done (and do still), that the verb makes the reader's hand grasp and compress the silken rope was perhaps a mere private vagary. Yet the 'touches' insist that 'tackle' (to which they are drawn by alliteration) also includes here what it ordinarily denotes – hands take hold of cordage, and it seems impossible to dissociate 'swell' from the tactual effect. The hands are made more 'flower-soft' by the contrasting 'yarely,' with its suggestion of brisk seaman-like efficiency ('ay, ay!').

In the next sentence the explicit 'strange' is curiously enforced by 'invisible': we shouldn't expect visibility in a perfume, and the unexpected adjective (intimating, no doubt, that there was no smoke or vapour to see) adds to the suggestion of a mysterious spell. The contrast between 'perfume' and the associations of 'wharfs' itself 'hits the sense,' and 'hits,' taken simultaneously with the soft suggestions of 'perfumes,' has already an oddly immediate force. The whole phrase –

> A strange invisible perfume *hits the sense*
> *Of the adjacent wharfs*

– conveys the multitudinous impersonality of the packed masses of onlookers:

> The city cast
> Her people out upon her . . .

What follows –

> and Antony,
> Enthron'd i' the market-place, did sit alone,
> Whistling to the air; which, but for vacancy,
> Had gone to gaze on Cleopatra too
> And made a gap in nature

– comes as an invitation to make the shift from considering verse as verse to the plane on which we discuss 'characters.'

Dryden's Antony couldn't have sat in the market-place whistling to the air; his dignity wouldn't have permitted it. Or rather, to ask whether he could or not is to introduce a criterion of reality in the presence of which he doesn't exist. His Cleopatra couldn't have hopped in the public street, or anywhere. His tragic *personae* exist only in a world of stage-postures; decorum gone, everything is gone. Shakespeare's have a life corresponding to the life of the verse; the life in them is, in fact, the life of the verse. Correspondingly, his poem as drama – in situation, larger rhythm, cumulative effect – has an actuality, a richness and a depth in comparison with which it becomes absurd to discuss Dryden's play as tragedy. It is, of course, understood that in a sustained reading Shakespeare's poetry conveys an organisation such as cannot be examined in an extracted passage. But the passage analysed exhibits representatively the difference from Dryden.

About Dryden's rendering there is nothing to say except that it has none of the poetic – and that is, we have seen, the dramatic – life of the original. It is accomplished verse, and verse that lends itself to stage-delivery, but it is hardly poetry. It is not poetry, in the sense that it is not the product of a realising imagination working from within a deeply and minutely felt theme. Dryden is a highly skilled craftsman, working at his job from the outside. The superior structure with which his play is credited as a theatre-piece is a matter of workmanship of the same external order as is represented by his verse. He aims at symmetry, a neat and obvious design, a balanced arrangement of heroic confrontations and 'big scenes'. The satisfaction he offers his audience is that of an operatic exaltation and release from actuality, a ballet-like completeness of pattern, and an elegantly stylised decorum.

It may, of course, be urged on his behalf that he does not offer a poetic concentration comparable with Shakespeare's, but exhibits his strength only to the more inclusive view, in more spacious relations, so that it is peculiarly unfair to represent him, as above, in a short passage. To this it must be replied that his quality is still the quality of his verse, his virtue still a matter of taste, judgment and workmanship. The point may be fairly coercively made by an observation regarding what, in Dryden's verse, takes the place of the life of metaphor and imagery in Shakespeare's. What we find, when we can put a finger on anything, is almost invariably either a formal simile, or a metaphor that is a simile with the 'like' or the 'as' left out. The choice is so wide and the showing so uniform that illustration must be random:

> He could resolve his mind, as Fire does Wax,
> From that hard rugged Image, melt him down,
> And mould him in what softer form he pleas'd.
> And yet the Soul, shut up in her dark Room,
> Viewing so clear abroad, at home sees nothing;
> But, like a Mole in Earth, busie and blind,
> Works all her folly up and casts it outward
> To the World's open view.

>   the least kind word, or glance,
> You give this Youth, will kindle him with Love.
> Then, like a burning Vessel set adrift,
> You'll send him down amain before the wind,
> To fire the Heart of jealous Antony.

> With fiery Eyes, and with contracted Brows,
> He Coyn'd his Face in the severest stamp;
> And fury shook his Fabrick like an Earthquake;
> He heav'd for vent, and burst like bellowing Aetna,
> In sounds scarce humane . . .

> I find your Breast fenc'd round from humane reach,
> Transparent as a Rock of solid Chrystal;
> Seen through, but never pierc'd.
> But I am made a shallow-forded Stream,
> Seen to the Bottom: all my clearness scorn'd,
> And all my Faults expos'd!

The structure, it will be seen, is always that of simple, illustrative, point-by-point correspondence. One analogy may give way to another, and so again, but the shift is always clean and obvious, there is never any complexity, confusion or ambiguity. When there is development, it is simple, lucid and rational.

This habit of expression manifests plainly the external approach, the predominance of taste and judgment. It is an approach equally apparent in the treatment of emotion in what are meant to be the especially moving places – as, for instance, in the scene in which Octavia and the childen are loosed upon Antony:

> *Antony.*   Oh, Dollabella, which way shall I turn?
> I find a secret yielding in my Soul;
> But Cleopatra, who would die with me,
> Must she be left? Pity pleads for Octavia
> But does it not plead more for Cleopatra?

> [Here the Children go to him, etc.
> *Ventidius.*   Was ever sight so moving! Emperor!
> *Dollabella.*   Friend.
> *Octavia.*   Husband!
> *Both Children.*   Father!
> *Antony.*   I an vanquished: take me,
>   Octavia; take me, Children; share me all.
>   (Embracing them).

– The emotion doesn't emerge from a given situation realised in its concrete particularity; it is stated, not presented or enacted. The explicitness is of the kind that betrays absence of realisation.

It would be unprofitable to carry the show of formal comparison any further: the terms, it is plain, are too disparate. And it should be plain too that we needn't take the disparateness as an excuse for the implication that judgments of comparative value are out of place. They are only out of place in the sense that they should hardly need making explicitly. But they do need making when it is urged that, though Shakespeare's play contains fine poetry, Dryden's has a more tragic effect. It doesn't, of course, follow that, because it becomes impossible to talk seriously about tragic effect or of 'characters' in connection with Dryden's play when Shakespeare's is placed by it, *Antony and Cleopatra* is among Shakespeare's greatest tragedies. In fact, there seem good grounds for some such conclusion as A. C. Bradley came to.* Nevertheless, *Antony and Cleopatra* is a very great dramatic poem, and if the comparison with *All for Love* is proposed it can be seriously taken up only as an approach to Shakespeare – a way of setting off the character of the Shakespearean genius.

It might, for instance, be an introduction to the study of Shakespeare's imagery. Commentators on Shakespeare's text too commonly betray a notion of metaphor that would make Dryden's practice the standard, and one might start with the Arden editor's note on

> the bellows and the fan
> to cool a gipsy's lust:

'Johnson suggests *to kindle and to cool*, misled by the usual use of bellows; for which, as a cooling implement . . .' etc. It would be fair to comment here that even when Shakespeare's metaphors are most like Dryden's he cannot be counted on to exhibit the same tidiness,

---

* See *Oxford Lectures on Poetry*.

and that there is no need to establish the use of bellows as a cooling implement. It seems probable that, though Johnson's emendation is unnecessary, he takes the meaning rightly, and that the effect here is much that of 'what they undid did'. If that is so, Shakespeare's metaphor is, characteristically, less simple, as well as less tidy, than one of Dryden's.

We might then pass to one we have already considered – one that, though it is not more difficult, we recognise immediately as not of Dryden's kind:

> Her tongue will not obey her heart, nor can
> Her heart inform her tongue – the swan's down-feather,
> That stands upon the swell at the full of tide,
> And neither way inclines.

'It is not clear whether Octavia's heart is the swan's down-feather, swayed neither way on the full tide of emotion . . . or whether it is merely the *inaction* of heart and tongue . . . which is compared to that of the feather.' Dryden would not have left it not clear. And Dryden could not have evoked the appropriate dramatic feeling with that vividness and particularity. When we try to say in what ways the passage is incomparably superior to anything Dryden could have produced, we have to think of metaphor as something more immediate, complex and organic than neat illustrative correspondence. And as we pass from example to example in *Antony and Cleopatra* it becomes less and less easy to suppose that a neat line can be drawn round the study.

2 FORMALISM, DIALOGISM, STRUCTURALISM

Though Russian Formalism has a strong claim to be the earliest analytic and theoretical approach to literature to emerge in the twentieth century, having its origins shortly before the Russian Revolution, it was little known in the English-speaking world until the emergence of structuralism in France aroused interest in earlier critical schools which had influenced structuralist critics. But whereas structuralism as a method came to prominence first – especially through the work of Claude Lévi-Strauss – in the field of social anthropology and then was applied to other areas, Russian Formalism was almost entirely concerned with literature. Indeed, one of its primary concerns was to make literary criticism a separate and coherent discipline. As one of its exponents, Boris Eikhenbaum, remarks in his essay, 'The Theory of the Formal Method', published as long ago as 1926, Russian Formalism's method was 'derived from efforts to secure autonomy and concreteness for the discipline of literary studies'. It endeavoured to establish the study of literature on a scientific basis and rejected the impressionistic or intuitive approaches of previous critics because they lacked rigour or method. Indeed, Eikhenbaum stresses Formalism's connections with positivism when he writes of the need to break with 'subjective-aesthetic principles' in favour of 'an objective-scientific attitude toward facts' which is 'the source of the new spirit of scientific positivism that characterizes the Formalists'.[1]

Victor Shklovsky was one of the earliest of the Formalists to make an impact, particularly through his claim that there was a fundamental opposition between 'poetic' and 'practical' language, which he elaborated in his widely reprinted article, 'Art as Technique'. He argued that in contrast to language used for ordinary, practical purposes, literary language undermined the tendency of perception to become governed by habit and routine through its ability to 'defamiliarise' our perception. One of the prime means of achieving this was through 'the principle of the palpableness of form'[2] by which certain artistic devices were highlighted in such a way that they could not be perceived merely as the passive means of mediating a literary work's content. Art was thus justified as a means of resisting the tendency of perception to become automatised.

As Russian Formalism developed, greater emphasis was laid on how the work of art is perceived against the background of other works of art than on the opposition between poetic and practical language. Literary devices, for example, could not be adequately understood if they were seen as being fundamentally different from linguistic usage in non-literary situations, since they could not be defined intrinsically but only differentially by perceiving them within the context of the use of devices in other literary works. For example, a literary device could be created by the use of some linguistic feature common in ordinary 'practical' forms of discourse but unusual in literary contexts. An especially influential concept was that of the 'dominant': the idea that in order for art to retain its vitality, new devices had to be highlighted since all devices eventually become over-familiar. As Shklovsky put it: *'New form comes about not in order to express new content but in order to replace an old form that has already lost its artistic viability'.*[3]

Shklovsky was particularly interested in the novel as a form, and here his work was especially influential on structuralist critics, who tended to concentrate on fiction. Formalism's interest in the novel is understandable, for on the surface the novel is a literary mode in which literary devices are absent and formal concepts avoided, since the narrative normally appears to be produced by merely mirroring social reality. Shklovsky attempts to demonstrate that this is an illusion, as his essay on the mystery novel (in which he concentrates primarily on Dickens's *Little Dorrit*) illustrates. His major concern was with plot, and the division he established between *'fabula'* or story and *'sjuzet'* or how story is shaped into narrative form has been central to theory of narrative in later criticism.

Mikhail Bakhtin's 'dialogism' has many connections with Formalism in that both are preoccupied with how literature works rather than with what it means, but a basic difference is that while the work of the Formalists applied scientific positivism to literary study Bakhtin's intellectual influences, such as German philosophy, Marx, Russian mysticism, were anti-positivist. Fundamental to his thought is the idea that language is not a unified system but incorporates a struggle that Bakhtin sees as being intrinsic to the world itself. Like the Russian Formalists, he attended to the formal aspect of literary works, but he believed that form could not be dissociated from social reality in which ideologies were in conflict and in which language cannot be separated from social struggle. Literary texts could not be legitimately seen as autonomous linguistic phenomena but were social products. Thus he valued the novel most among literary genres because it was potentially the most dialogic; that is, it could incorporate in its form the diversity of voices that made up society. He particularly admired the works of Dostoevsky. In his book on the novelist, he argued that Dostoevsky was distinctive because the various voices in his novels, including the narrator's, were on the same level with no one voice dominating the rest, but he later came to believe that Dostoevsky's work exemplified a tendency intrinsic to the novel as a form.

Bakhtin uses a number of different terms to express how literary form breaks with unitary concepts: 'polyphony', 'carnivalisation', 'heteroglossia'. The latter is perhaps the most fundamental to his thought and is defined as follows by Michael Holquist:

Heteroglossia is Bakhtin's way of referring, in any utterance of any kind, to the peculiar interaction between the two fundamentals of all communication. On the one hand, a mode of transcription must, in order to do its work of separating out texts, be a more or less fixed system. But these repeatable features, on the other hand, are in the power of the particular context in which the utterance is made; this context can refract, add to, or, in some cases, even subtract from the amount and kind of meaning the utterance may be said to have when it is conceived only as a systematic manifestation independent of context.[4]

Thus any living utterance, spoken or written, incorporates multiplicity rather than unity. Here Bakhtin's thought anticipates poststructuralism, despite the fact that Bakhtin gives priority to the spoken rather than the written (in contrast to Jacques Derrida whom I shall discuss later) whereas the major influence on structuralism was the linguistics of Saussure, which focussed on language as a synchronic system. Bakhtin, in contrast to Saussure, believes that any systematisation of language is undermined by the fact that dialogue is intrinsic to any language use.

For him, the novel is the most important literary form because the novel is driven by an impulse to break with the constraints and systematic ordering associated with other literary modes. He does not view the novel as a form which had its origins in the modern era, but in his later writing reserves the term for any text that is predominantly dialogic and which breaks with systematic forms of ordering. It is interesting that like Shklovsky he wrote on Dickens, and indeed on *Little Dorrit* in particular, and it is instructive and useful to compare and contrast their different approaches.

Whereas both Russian Formalists and Bakhtin concentrated primarily on literature, structuralists saw literature as just one of many semiotic (or semiological, the term preferred by Saussure) systems.

For Saussure language was subsumed by semiology, but structural-ists viewed language as the basis of all semiotic systems. Thus Saussurean linguistics, which concentrated on '*langue*', that is the language system as it exists at a particular point in time, was adapted to study activities which, by analogy with linguistics, could also be viewed as '*langues*'. Literature therefore was viewed as a system and the role of the critic was like that of a linguist studying language synchronically: the critic's role was to show the structure of the system, the set of relations that enabled it to function.

Whereas there was no doubt that critics such as Shklovsky and Bakhtin placed great value on literature and that their criticism attempted to enhance that value, French structuralism, particularly the work of Roland Barthes, was motivated by a more demystifying spirit, revealing for example how the structures that governed liter-ary texts were related to the power structures of society. Both Russian Formalism and the early New Criticism had focussed on the literary text itself, rejecting earlier criticism's concern with the author and the reader, but structuralism took this much further and gave it a more philosophical dimension. Structuralism was philosophically opposed to the subject and as part of this opposition reduced the roles of the author and reader to mere epiphenomena of writing and reading as activities, thus denying that they existed as independent forces. This might seem to have little in common with the humanist impulse of Bakhtin's work, with its emphasis on language as dialogue and communication, but the structuralist concept of intertextuality, in which texts are related to each other without any human dimension such as intersubjectity being men-tioned, obviously owes a good deal to the Bakhtinian concept of heteroglossia.

Structuralism had relatively little influence on criticism in the English-speaking world: in America in particular, few critics showed any interest in it. Its anti-humanism and the fact that it tended to concentrate on forms and genres rather than the close reading of texts made it difficult to accommodate. However, David Lodge is one critic who believes it can be reconciled with Anglo-American formalism. In contrast to the early New Critics his major interest has been in the novel as a form, and structuralist criticism had tended to focus mainly on fiction. In the essay reproduced here, as well as providing a useful overview of structuralist approaches to fiction, he shows how structuralism can be applied to a single text, Hemingway's short story, 'Cat in the Rain'.

Notes

1. Boris Eikhenbaum, 'The Theory of the Formal Method', in *Readings in Russian Poetics: Formalist and Structuralist Views*, eds Ladislav Matejka and Krystyna Pomorska (Michigan, 1978), p. 7.
2. Quoted in Eikhenbaum, p. 13.
3. Quoted in Eikhenbaum, p. 17.
4. M. M. Bakhtin, *The Dialogic Imagination: Four Essays*, trans. Caryl Emerson and Michael Holquist; ed. Michael Holquist (Austin and London, 1981), pp. xix–xx.

Further Reading

M. M. Bakhtin, *Problems in Dostoevsky's Poetics*, trans. R. W. Rotsel (Michigan, 1973).
Seymour Chatman, *Story and Discourse: Narrative Structure in Fiction and Film* (Ithaca and London, 1978).
Victor Erlich, ed., *Twentieth-Century Russian Literary Criticism* (New Haven, Conn., 1975).
Gérard Genette, *Narrative Discourse*, trans. Jane E. Lewin (Oxford, 1980).
Robert Scholes, *Semiotics and Interpretation* (New Haven, Conn., 1982).

Victor Shklovsky: The Mystery Novel: Dickens's *Little Dorrit*

Anne Radcliffe, one of the originators of the mystery novel, organised her tales on such a pattern: the heroine finds herself in a castle; she sees a decomposing corpse behind a curtain; spirits wander through the castle; someone invisible interjects his remarks into the conversations of drunken robbers, and so on. The solutions to these mysteries are revealed only at the end of the volume. The corpse is made of wax; it was placed there as a penance by one of the proprietor's ancestors, a count, under the Pope's instructions. The mysterious voice belongs to a prisoner who wanders through the castle through secret passages. As you see, the solutions to these

Excerpts from 'Roman tajn', *O teorii prozy* (Moscow, 1925), pp. 117–138. Translated by Guy Carter. Reprinted from *Readings in Russian Poetics*, eds Ladislav Matejka and Krystyna Pomorska (Michigan, 1978), pp. 220–6.

mysteries (as a contemporary remarked) are at best only partially satisfactory.

In the second part, the scenario begins again. A new castle. New mysterious voices are heard. These prove subsequently to belong to smugglers. Music resounds all around the castle: this turns out to be a nun playing, and so forth. . . .

It is noteworthy, however, that these mysteries at first present false solutions (as is also the case with Dickens); we usually suspect something far more terrifying than what we actually find. In the second part, for example, the author quite pointedly suggests the idea of incest in a manner reminiscent of obscene ditties with risqué rhymes, a device that is also canonical for Russian folk riddles, such as: 'It hangs dangling. Everybody grabs for it.' The solution: 'A towel.'[1]

In solving these riddles a pause takes place which stands for the 'false', obscene solution. Here is an example of how a similar riddle is worked into the plot. The tale cited below was recorded as narrated by an old peasant woman. It is interesting because it displays the device of the false or misleading solution. The play of riddles furnishes the tale's content:

A young tailor used to live at my place, and he gave me a riddle to figure out: 'Two years pass in a crow's life; what comes next?' I answer him, 'The third year'. The tailor thinks it's funny that I guessed his riddle. I give him another riddle: 'If daddy didn't keep busy, mother's. . . . would have overgrown long ago'. The young tailor thinks that it has a bad meaning. He can't solve it. I give him the answer: 'Bushes grow quickly on the furrows, on the furrows of Mother Earth'.

Thus we see that the false or misleading solution is a very common element of either a tale or a mystery novel. The manipulation of false and true solutions is what constitutes the method of organising the mystery. The dénouement consists in shifting from one to the other. The interrelation of the parts is the same as that found in plots based on puns.

The mystery type is characterised by its kinship with the device of inversion, that is, the rearrangement of the parts. The most common type of mystery in the novel is the narration of an earlier event after the depiction of the present one. The mystery of the 'watch' in Dickens's *Little Dorrit* and the 'double' are examples of such riddles.

On the other hand, the mystery of the 'house', Dorrit's secret love for Clennam, and Clennam's love for Pet are built up without a plot inversion. In this case, the mystery is achieved by means of the exposition; the metaphorical and factual series form a parallel. In mysteries based on a rearrangement of cause and effect, the parallel is formed from a false solution.

In Dickens's last novel, *Our Mutual Friend*, the organisation of the mystery is most interesting. The first mystery is the secret of John Rokesmith: the author seems to conceal the fact that Rokesmith is none other than John Harmon. Boffin's secret is the second mystery. We see how wealth destroys the Golden Dustman, and we do not know that Boffin is playing a hoax on us. Dickens himself says that he did not even consider hiding Rokesmith's true identity from the reader. In this case John Harmon's secret is a false plot line. It does not allow us to solve or even notice Boffin's secret. The novelistic technique is therefore quite complex.

The direct heir to the mystery novel is the detective novel in which the detective is a professional solver of mysteries. First, a mystery is presented, the crime, then a misleading solution appears, and the police investigation follows. Only later is the truth about the murder established. In such a work inversion is obligatory, and it sometimes takes the form of a complex omission of separate details. That is how the mystery in *The Brothers Karamazov* is achieved (but without a detective). For a more detailed analysis of the mystery technique, I have chosen Dickens's *Little Dorrit*.

This novel is built around several simultaneous actions. The link between these parallel actions is achieved: (1) through the participation of characters of one line in the action of another, and (2) through locale. The heroes move next door to each other. Thus Arthur Clennam lives in the Bleeding Hearts yard. The 'patriarch' also lives here, as does Baptist, the Italian. The *fabula*[2] of the work consists of: (1) Dorrit and Clennam's love; (2) the history of the rise to wealth and the subsequent ruin of the Dorrit family: (3) Rigaud's attempted blackmail and his threat to expose Mrs Clennam.

However, the novel can be related in the above form only after we have finished reading it. While reading we have before us a collection of mysteries. The interrelationships of the characters are also presented as interwoven mysteries. We can distinguish the following mysteries running throughout the novel:

1. The mystery of the watch. } These are basic mysteries.
2. The mystery of dreams. } They frame the plot, but are unresolved.
3. Mr Pancks' mystery (the inheritance). This is a partial mystery, one which does not run the length of the novel. It creates an imbalance between Dorrit and Clennam through the device of plot inversion.

4. Mr Merdle's secret (likewise an auxiliary mystery) which plays the same role as Pancks's above.
5. The mysterious noises in the house. They prepare the solution to the first two mysteries.
6. The mystery of Dorrit and Clennam's love. These belong to the central plot, but technically they represent a developed negative parallelism.[3]

The device of using several simultaneous actions whose inter-relationship is not immediately specified by the author serves as plot impediment, a special continuation of the mystery technique.

Little Dorrit begins with such a device. In this novel two plot lines are given in the very beginning: Rigaud's line and Clennam's. The beginning of each line is worked up into a chapter. In the first chapter, 'Sun and Shadow', Monsieur Rigaud and the Italian, John Baptist, appear. They are both in prison – Rigaud on a murder charge, and Baptist for smuggling. Rigaud is taken away to court. As he leaves, a boisterous crowd gathers round the prison and threatens to tear him to pieces. Neither Rigaud nor his cellmate Baptist is a major character in the novel.

Beginning a novel in such a fashion, with a secondary character, is quite common for Dickens. *Nicholas Nickleby, Oliver Twist, Our Mutual Friend*, and *Martin Chuzzlewit* all begin in this way. This device may be related to the technique of the riddle. The second group of characters appears in the second chapter, 'Fellow-travellers'. This chapter is linked to the first by the sentence: 'No more of yesterday's howling, over yonder, today, sir; is there?'

Little Dorrit is a multilevelled novel. In order to unite these levels, it is necessary to contrive the assemblage of all the characters at the beginning of the novel. Dickens chooses a quarantine for this task. In this context the quarantine corresponds to the tavern or monastery found in collections of tales (e.g., *The Heptameron* of Marguerite d'Angoulême or the tavern in the *Canterbury Tales*). The Meagles, husband and wife, their daughter Pet, their servant Tattycoram (whose story is told in that chapter), Mr Clennam, and Miss Wade are all in quarantine at the beginning of *Little Dorrit*. The same situation exists in *Our Mutual Friend*. In the first chapter, 'On the Look-Out', Gaffer is introduced together with his daughter on the boat, which is towing a corpse. This chapter is permeated with mystery: we do not know exactly what the people in the boat are looking for, and the corpse is presented through negation.

Lizzie's father, composing himself into the easy attitude of one who had asserted the high moralities and taken an unassailable position, slowly lighted a pipe, and smoked, and took a survey of what he had in tow. What he had in tow, lunged itself at him sometimes in an awful manner when the boat was checked, and sometimes seemed to try to wrench itself away, though for the most part it followed submissively. A neophyte might have fancied that the ripples over it were dreadfully like faint changes of expression on a sightless face but Gaffer was no neophyte and had no fancies.

It is interesting to compare this description with the 'angling for fish' in *A Tale of Two Cities*.

The second chapter, 'A Man from Somewhere', describes Veneering's house. The lawyer Mortimer is introduced along with the whole of higher society, which will later function as a 'chorus', as does Anna Pavlovna's salon in *War and Peace*. At the end of the second chapter we learn, by way of connection with the first, that a certain heir to an enormous estate has drowned; and we link his fate to that of the corpse trailing the boat.

In the third chapter, 'Another Man', a new character, Julius Handford, is introduced; in the fourth chapter, the Wilfer family; and in the fifth, the Boffins, and so forth.

The given plot lines are maintained to the end of the novel, and they tend not so much to intersect as to converge from time to time. The plot lines intersect even less frequently in *A Tale of Two Cities*. In this novel, the transitions from one plot line to another seemingly unrelated to it are perceived as a sort of mystery. Moreover, the identification of the characters from various plot lines is postponed until we are well into the heart of the novel.

In recent times we have seen a revival of the mystery novel with a new interest in complicated and entangled plots. An original example of the mystery technique is offered by Andrej Belyj. He gives us a transformed version of the riddle technique which is quite interesting. In his *Kotik Letaev*, for example, two levels are presented, 'heaven' and 'order'. Order is 'real life which has already formed'; 'heaven' is the swelling of life in flux, before its formation. 'Heaven' is formed either through a series of metaphors or through puns. In this arrangement 'heaven' first appears, then 'order' – in other words, an inversion takes place. The puns usually take the form of a riddle.[4]

Belyj also supplies us with the mystery technique in its pure form. *Saint Petersburg* may serve as an example. Belyj's followers, in particular, Boris Pil'njak, have developed the device of parallelism to a high degree. This parallelism is one in which the connection between the parallel levels is obscured and moved to the background. Such novels create an impression of great complexity when they are, in fact, quite elementary. The connecting link between the parts is presented either through the most rudimentary device, such as the kinship of the characters, or else through the episodic participation of a character of one line in another line. See, for example, 'A Petersburg Tale', 'Rjazan' Apple', or 'The Snowstorm'. It is interesting to observe in this connection Pil'njak's method of making separate stories take form as a novel.

In the mystery novel both the riddle and the solution are important. Such a novel offers the possibility of impeding the action, throwing it into strange perspective, and thus exciting the reader's interest. The main thing is not to give the reader an opportunity of recognising the object. Once an object is recognisable, it no longer frightens us. For this reason, in Maturin's novel *Melmoth the Wanderer*, the author repeatedly conceals from us the proposals Melmoth makes to assorted people in terrible predicaments, prisoners of the Inquisition, people dying of hunger and selling their blood, inmates of a madhouse, people wandering lost in underground passageways, etc. Whenever the action reaches Melmoth's proposal, the manuscript breaks off – the novel consists of separate parts which have only a confused relationship to one another. The traditional duty to solve the mystery weighs heavily on many novelists, who nevertheless tend to avoid fantastic solutions. If fantasy is introduced at all, then it occurs at the end of the novel within the confines of the dénouement. The fantastic element is offered as a sort of final judgment, as a cause of the action, but rarely in the course of the action itself. And if fantasy is introduced, then it appears in a special form, as a premonition, for example, or a prediction, so that the novel will develop according to predetermined conditions.

The element of fantasy appears in Lewis's novel *The Monk*, in which the cast of characters includes a devil with a companion spirit and a phantom nun. In the last act the devil carries the monk away and reveals the whole intrigue to him. Such revelations, of course, do not occur in the novel accidentally. Dickens with his many involved plot constructions constantly had to resort to this type of device. This explains the 'mystery of the watch' in *Little Dorrit*, in which it again becomes necessary to gather all the people together in one room – a device common to many novels and parodied over and over in V. Kaverin's novel *A Chronicle of the City of Leipzig*. In Dickens people are literally dragged together by the scruff of their necks. In *Little Dorrit* Pancks and Baptist dragged Rigaud to Clennam's mother in such a way.

'And now,' said Mr Pancks . . . 'I've only one other word to say before I go . . . If Mr Clennam was here, he would say, "Affery, tell your dream!" '

The dénoument is achieved in the following way: Affery tells her dreams. Dreams function here as a new type of ironic motivation and deformation of the old device of eavesdropping. In Dickens, eavesdropping is usually performed by office clerks (as in *Nicholas Nickleby*) and sometimes by the main characters. There is a renovation of this device in Dostoevsky's *A Raw Youth*, in which the eavesdropping occurs as if by accident

The main reason for the artificiality of the dénoument in *Little Dorrit* is the fact that it takes place without the presence of outsiders and that people tell one another things that they themselves already know quite well.[5]

How does one explain the success of the mystery novel from Radcliffe to Dickens?

I see the matter in this light. The adventure novel had outlived its day. It was revived by satire. Elements of the adventure novel in Swift's *Gulliver's Travels* played a purely subordinate role. A time of crisis had arrived. In *Tom Jones*, Fielding parodied the old novel form in his depiction of the main character's amorality. Instead of the traditional lover's fidelity, sustained through various trying adventures, we are presented with Jones's carefree adventures.

Sterne wrote an even more radical parody and parodied the very structure of the novel, mustering all of its devices for review. Simultaneously, the younger genres began to rise and strive for canonisation. Richardson canonised the genre of the epistolary novel. According to legend, he intended to write a collection of edifying letters, but instead wrote an epistolary novel. At the same time the Gothic tales appeared (the Pinkertons of that day), as did Anne Radcliffe and Charles Maturin with their mystery novels.

The old novel form attempted to increase the effectiveness of its devices with the introduction of parallel plot intrigues. The technique of the mystery novel offered a convenient means of connecting several parallel intrigues. Dickens's complicated plot constructions were a result.

The mystery novel permits the author to incorporate into a work large passages of local-colour description which, while serving the goal of retarding the plot, themselves undergo pressure from the plot and are perceived as belonging to the work of art. The descriptions of the debtor's prison, the Ministry of Circumlocution, and the Bleeding Hearts Yard are incorporated into *Little Dorrit* in such a way. Thus we see how the mystery novel came to be used by the social novel.

Notes

1. Shklovsky's example of the Russian song has been omitted here.
2. The Russian Formalists distinguished between *fabula* and *sjužet* in discussing plot construction. *Fabula* refers to the raw material of a story, the story stuff, the basic causal-temporal relationships. *Sjužet* refers to the presentation and manipulation of this basic story stuff – what we would call plot. Shklovsky's discussion here is an excellent example of these two concepts. The fabula consists of the three main relationships: Clennam-Dorrit, the Dorrit family, and Mrs. Clennam-Rigaud – but not in any particular order, nor even clarity. In fact, because of their ordering by *sjužet*, they appear cloudy and mysterious until the very end of the novel.
3. Pages 119–129 of the Russian text have been omitted.
4. Pages 131–132 of the Russian text have been omitted.
5. Pages 133–137 of the Russian text have been omitted.

M. M. Bakhtin: Heteroglossia in the Novel

The compositional forms for appropriating and organising heteroglossia in the novel, worked out during the long course of the genre's historical development, are extremely heterogeneous in their variety of generic types. Each such compositional form is connected with particular stylistic possibilities, and demands particular forms for the artistic treatment of the heteroglot 'languages' introduced into it. We will pause here only on the most basic forms that are typical for the majority of novel types.

The so-called comic novel makes available a form for appropriating and organising heteroglossia that is both externally very vivid and at the same time historically profound: its classic representatives in England were Fielding, Smollett, Sterne, Dickens, Thackeray and others, and in Germany Hippel and Jean Paul.

In the English comic novel we find a comic-parodic re-processing

Reprinted from M. M. Bakhtin, *The Dialogic Imagination: Four Essays*, trans. Caryl Emerson and Michael Holquist, ed. Michael Holquist (Austin and London, 1981), pp. 301–9.

of almost all the levels of literary language, both conversational and written, that were current at the time. Almost every novel we mentioned above as being a classic representative of this generic type is an encyclopedia of all strata and forms of literary language: depending on the subject being represented, the storyline parodically reproduces first the forms of parliamentary eloquence, then the eloquence of the court, or particular forms of parliamentary protocol, or court protocol, or forms used by reporters in newspaper articles, or the dry business language of the City, or the dealings of speculators, or the pedantic speech of scholars, or the high epic style, or Biblical style, or the style of the hypocritical moral sermon or finally the way one or another concrete and socially determined personality, the subject of the story, happens to speak.

This usually parodic stylisation of generic, professional and other strata of language is sometimes interrupted by the direct authorial word (usually as an expression of pathos, of Sentimental or idyllic sensibility), which directly embodies (without any refracting) semantic and axiological intentions of the author. But the primary source of language usage in the comic novel is a highly specific treatment of 'common language'. This 'common language' – usually the average norm of spoken and written language for a given social group – is taken by the author precisely as the *common view*, as the verbal approach to people and things normal for a given sphere of society, as the *going point of view* and the going *value*. To one degree or another, the author distances himself from this common language, he steps back and objectifies it, forcing his own intentions to refract and diffuse themselves through the medium of this common view that has become embodied in language (a view that is always superficial and frequently hypocritical).

The relationship of the author to a language conceived as the common view is not static – it is always found in a state of movement and oscillation that is more or less alive (this sometimes is a rhythmic oscillation): the author exaggerates, now strongly, now weakly, one or another aspect of the 'common language', sometimes abruptly exposing its inadequacy to its object and sometimes, on the contrary, becoming one with it, maintaining an almost imperceptible distance, sometimes even directly forcing it to reverberate with his own 'truth', which occurs when the author completely merges his own voice with the common view. As a consequence of such a merger, the aspects of common language, which in the given situation had been parodically exaggerated or had been treated as mere things, undergo change. The comic style demands of the author a lively to-and-fro movement in his relation to language, it demands a continual shifting of the distance between author and language, so that first some, then other aspects of language are thrown into relief. If such were not the case, the style would be monotonous or would require a greater individualisation of the narrator – would, in any case, require a quite different means for introducing and organising heteroglossia.

Against this same backdrop of the 'common language', of the impersonal, going opinion, one can also isolate in the comic novel those parodic stylisations of generic, professional and other languages we have mentioned, as well as compact masses of direct authorial discourse – pathos-filled, moral-didactic, sentimental-elegiac or idyllic. In the comic novel the direct authorial word is thus realised in direct, unqualified stylisations of poetic genres (idyllic, elegiac, etc.) or stylisations of rhetorical genres (the pathetic, the moral-didactic). Shifts from common language to parodying of generic and other languages and shifts to the direct authorial word may be gradual, or may be on the contrary quite abrupt. Thus does the system of language work in the comic novel.

We will pause for analysis on several examples from Dickens, from his novel *Little Dorrit*.

(1) The conference was held at four or five o'clock in the afternoon, when all the region of Harley Street, Cavendish Square, was resonant of carriage-wheels and double-knocks. It had reached this point when Mr Merdle came home *from his daily occupation of causing the British name to be more and more respected in all parts of the civilized globe capable of appreciation of wholewide commercial enterprise and gigantic combinations of skill and capital.* For, though nobody knew with the least precision what Mr Merdle's business was, except that it was to coin money, these were the terms in which everybody defined it on all ceremonious occasions, and which it was the last new polite reading of the parable of the camel and the needle's eye to accept without inquiry. [book 1, ch. 33]

The italicised portion represents a parodic stylisation of the language of ceremonial speeches (in parliaments and at banquets). The shift into this style is prepared for by the sentence's construction, which from the very beginning is kept within bounds by a somewhat ceremonious epic tone. Further on – and already in the language of the author (and consequently in a different style) – the parodic meaning of the ceremoniousness of Merdle's labours becomes apparent: such a characterisation turns out to be 'another's speech', to be taken only in quotation marks ('these were the terms in which everybody defined it on all ceremonious occasions').

Thus the speech of another is introduced into the author's discourse (the story) in *concealed form*, that is, without any of the *formal* markers usually accompanying such speech, whether direct or indirect. But this is not just another's speech in the same 'language' – it is another's utterance in a language that is itself 'other' to the author as well, in the archaicised language of oratorical genres associated with hypocritical official celebrations.

(2) In a day or two it was announced to all the town, that Edmund Sparkler, Esquire, son-in-law of the eminent Mr Merdle of worldwide renown, was made one of the Lords of the Circumlocution Office; and proclamation was issued, to all true believers, that this admirable *appointment was to be hailed as a graceful and gracious mark of homage, rendered by the graceful and gracious Decimus, to that commercial interest which must ever in a great commercial country – and all the rest of it, with blast of trumpet.* So, bolstered by this mark of Government homage, the *wonderful* Bank and all the other *wonderful* undertakings went on and went up; and gapers came to Harley Street, Cavendish Square, only to look at the house where the golden wonder lived. [book 2, ch. 12]

Here, in the italicised portion, another's speech in another's (official-ceremonial) language is openly introduced as indirect discourse. But it is surrounded by the hidden, diffused speech of another (in the same official-ceremonial language) that clears the way for the introduction of a form more easily perceived *as* another's speech and that can reverberate more fully as such. The clearing of the way comes with the word 'Esquire', characteristic of official speech, added to Sparkler's name; the final confirmation that this is another's speech comes with the epithet 'wonderful'. This epithet does not of course belong to the author but to that same 'general opinion' that had created the commotion around Merdle's inflated enterprises.

(3) It was a dinner to provoke an appetite, though he had not had one. The rarest dishes, sumptuously cooked and sumptuously served; the choicest fruits, the most exquisite wines; marvels of workmanship in gold and silver, china and glass; innumerable things delicious to the senses of taste, smell, and sight, were insinuated into its composition. *O, what a wonderful man this Merdle, what a great man, what a master man, how blessedly and enviably endowed* – in one word, what a rich man! [book 2, ch. 12]

The beginning is a parodic stylisation of high epic style. What follows is an enthusiastic glorification of Merdle, a chorus of his admirers in the form of the concealed speech of another (the italicised portion). The whole point here is to expose the real basis for such glorification, which is to unmask the chorus' hypocrisy: 'wonderful', 'great', 'master', 'endowed' can all be replaced by the single word 'rich'. This act of authorial unmasking, which is openly accomplished within the boundaries of a single simple sentence, merges with the unmasking of another's speech. The ceremonial emphasis on glorification is complicated by a second emphasis that is indignant, ironic, and this is the one that ultimately predominates in the final unmasking words of the sentence.

We have before us a typical double-accented, double-styled *hybrid construction*.

What we are calling a hybrid construction is an utterance that belongs, by its grammatical (syntactic) and compositional markers, to a single speaker, but that actually contains mixed within it two utterances, two speech manners, two styles, two 'languages', two semantic and axiological belief systems. We repeat, there is no formal – compositional and syntactic – boundary between these utterances, styles, languages, belief systems; the division of voices and languages takes place within the limits of a single syntactic whole, often within the limits of a simple sentence. It frequently happens that even one and the same word will belong simultaneously to two languages, two belief systems that intersect in a hybrid construction – and, consequently, the word has two contradictory meanings, two accents (examples below). As we shall see, hybrid constructions are of enormous significance in novel style.[1]

(4) But Mr Tite Barnacle was a buttoned-up man, and *consequently* a weighty one. [book 2, ch. 12]

The above sentence is an example of *pseudo-objective motivation*, one of the forms for concealing another's speech – in this example, the speech of 'current opinion'. If judged by the formal markers above, the logic motivating the sentence seems to belong to the author, i.e., he is formally at one with it; but in actual fact, the motivation lies within the subjective belief system of his characters, or of general opinion.

Pseudo-objective motivation is generally characteristic of novel style,[2] since it is one of the manifold forms for concealing another's speech in hybrid constructions. Subordinate conjunctions and link words ('thus', 'because', 'for the reason that', 'in spite of' and so forth), as well as words used to maintain a logical sequence ('therefore', 'consequently', etc.) lose their direct authorial intention, take on the flavour of someone else's language, become refracted or even completely reified.

1 For more detail on hybrid constructions and their significance, see ch. 4 of the present essay.
2 Such a device is unthinkable in the epic.

Such motivation is especially characteristic of comic style, in which someone else's speech is dominant (the speech of concrete persons, or, more often, a collective voice).[3]

(5) As a vast fire will fill the air to a great distance with its roar, so the sacred flame which the mighty Barnacles had fanned caused the air to resound more and more with the name of Merdle. It was deposited on every lip, and carried into every ear. There never was, there never had been, there never again should be, such a man as Mr Merdle. Nobody, as aforesaid, knew what he had done; but *everybody knew him to be the greatest that had appeared.* [book 2, ch. 13]

Here we have an epic, 'Homeric' introduction (parodic, of course) into whose frame the crowd's glorification of Merdle has been inserted (concealed speech of another in another's language). We then get direct authorial discourse; however, the author gives an objective tone to this 'aside' by suggesting that 'everybody knew' (the italicised portion). It is as if even the author himself did not doubt the fact.

(6) That illustrious man and great national ornament, Mr Merdle, con-tinued his shining course. It began to be widely understood that one who had done society the admirable service *of making so much money out of it*, could not be suffered to remain a commoner. A baronetcy was spoken of with confidence; a peerage was frequently mentioned. [book 2, ch. 24]

We have here the same fictive solidarity with the hypocritically ceremonial general opinion of Merdle. All the epithets referring to Merdle in the first sentences derive from general opinion, that is, they are the concealed speech of another. The second sentence – 'it began to be widely understood', etc. – is kept within the bounds of an emphatically objective style, representing not subjective opinion but the admission of an objective and completely indisputable fact. The epithet 'who had done society the admirable service' is com-pletely at the level of common opinion, repeating its official glorifi-cation, but the subordinate clause attached to that glorification ('of making so much money out of it') are the words of the author himself (as if put in parentheses in the quotation). The main sen-tence then picks up again at the level of common opinion. We have here a typical hybrid construction, where the subordinate clause is in direct authorial speech and the main clause in someone else's speech. The main and subordinate clauses are constructed in differ-ent semantic and axiological conceptual systems.

3 Cf. the grotesque pseudo-objective motivations in Gogol.

The whole of this portion of the novel's action, which centres around Merdle and the persons associated with him, is depicted in the language (or more accurately, the languages) of hypocritically ceremonial common opinion about Merdle, and at the same time there is a parodic stylisation of that everyday language of banal society gossip, or of the ceremonial language of official pronouncements and banquet speeches, or the high epic style or Biblical style. This atmosphere around Merdle, the common opinion about him and his enterprises, infects the positive heroes of the novel as well, in particular the sober Pancks, and forces him to invest his entire estate – his own, and Little Dorrit's – in Merdle's hollow enterprises.

(7) Physician had engaged to break the intelligence in Harley Street. Bar could not at once return to his inveiglements of the most enlightened and remarkable jury he had ever seen in that box, with whom, he could tell his learned friend, no shallow sophistry would go down, and no unhappily abused professional tact and skill prevail (this was the way he meant to begin with them); so he said he would go too, and would loiter to and fro near the house while his friend was inside. [Book 2, ch. 25, mistakenly given as ch. 15 in Russian text, tr.]

Here we have a clear example of hybrid construction where within the frame of authorial speech (informative speech) – the beginning of a speech prepared by the lawyer has been inserted, 'Bar could not at once return to his inveiglements . . . of the jury . . . so he said he would go too. . . .' etc. – while this speech is simultaneously a fully developed epithet attached to the subject of the author's speech, that is, 'jury'. The word 'jury' enters into the context of informative authorial speech (in the capacity of a necessary object to the word 'inveiglements') as well as into the context of the parodic-stylised speech of the lawyer. The author's word 'inveiglement' itself emphasises the parodic nature of the re-processing of the lawyer's speech, the hypocritical meaning of which consists precisely in the fact that it would be impossible to inveigle such a remarkable jury.

(8) It followed that Mrs Merdle, as a woman of fashion and good breeding *who had been sacrificed to wiles of a vulgar barbarian* (for Mr Merdle was found out from the crown of his head to the sole of his foot, the moment he was found out in his pocket), must be actively championed by her order for her order's sake. [book 2, ch. 33]

This is an analogous hybrid construction, in which the definition provided by the general opinion of society – 'a sacrifice to the wiles of a vulgar barbarian' – merges with authorial speech, exposing the hypocrisy and greed of common opinion.

So it is throughout Dickens' whole novel. His entire text is, in fact, everywhere dotted with quotation marks that serve to separate out little islands of scattered direct speech and purely authorial speech, washed by heteroglot waves from all sides. But it would have been impossible actually to insert such marks, since, as we have seen, one and the same word often figures both as the speech of the author and as the speech of another – and at the same time.

Another's speech – whether as storytelling, as mimicking, as the display of a thing in light of a particular point of view, as a speech deployed first in compact masses, then loosely scattered, a speech that is in most cases impersonal ('common opinion', professional and generic languages) – is at none of these points clearly separated from authorial speech: the boundaries are deliberately flexible and ambiguous, often passing through a single syntactic whole, often through a simple sentence, and sometimes even dividing up the main parts of a sentence. This varied *play with the boundaries of speech types*, languages and belief systems is one most fundamental aspects of comic style.

Comic style (of the English sort) is based, therefore, on the stratification of common language and on the possibilities available for isolating from these strata, to one degree or another, one's own intentions, without ever completely merging with them. *It is precisely the diversity of speech, and not the unity of a normative shared language, that is the ground of style.* It is true that such speech diversity does not exceed the boundaries of literary language conceived as a linguistic whole (that is, language defined by abstract linguistic markers), does not pass into an authentic heteroglossia and is based on an abstract notion of language as unitary (that is, it does not require knowledge of various dialects or languages). However a mere concern for language is but the abstract side of the concrete and active (i.e., dialogically engaged) understanding of the living heteroglossia that has been introduced into the novel and artistically organised within it.

In Dickens' predecessors, Fielding, Smollett and Sterne, the men who founded the English comic novel, we find the same parodic stylisation of various levels and genres of literary language, but the distance between these levels and genres is greater than it is in Dickens and the exaggeration is stronger (especially in Sterne). The parodic and objectivised incorporation into their work of various types of literary language (especially in Sterne) penetrates the deepest levels of literary and ideological thought itself, resulting in a parody of the logical and expressive structure of any ideological discourse as such (scholarly, moral and rhetorical, poetic) that is almost as radical as the parody we find in Rabelais.

Literary parody understood in the narrow sense plays a fundamental role in the way language is structured in Fielding, Smollett and Sterne (the Richardsonian novel is parodied by the first two, and almost all contemporary novel-types are parodied by Sterne). Literary parody serves to distance the author still further from language, to complicate still further his relationship to the literary language of his time, especially in the novel's own territory. The novelistic discourse dominating a given epoch is itself turned into an object and itself becomes a means for refracting new authorial intentions.

David Lodge: Analysis and Interpretation of the Realist Text: Ernest Hemingway's 'Cat in the Rain'

I

It is a commonplace that the systematic study of narrative was founded by Aristotle, and scarcely an exaggeration to say that little of significance was added to those foundations until the twentieth century. Narrative theory in the intervening period was mainly directed (or misdirected) at deducing from Aristotle's penetrating analysis of the system of Greek tragedy a set of prescriptive rules for the writing of epic. The rise of the novel as a distinctive and eventually dominant literary form finally exposed the poverty of neoclassical narrative theory, without for a long time generating anything much more satisfactory. The realistic novel set peculiar problems for any formalist criticism because it worked by disguising or denying its own conventionality. It therefore invited – and received – criticism which was interpretative and evaluative rather than analytical. It was not until the late nineteenth and early twentieth centuries that something like a poetics of fiction began to evolve from the self-conscious experiments of novelists themselves,

Reprinted from David Lodge, *Working with Structuralism: Essays and Reviews on Nineteenth- and Twentieth-Century Literature* (Boston, London and Henley, 1981), pp. 17–32. Line numbers refer to the Hemingway story as reprinted in this work (pp. 33ff.).

and was elaborated by literary critics. At about the same time, developments in linguistics, folklore and anthropology stimulated a more broad-ranging study of narrative, beyond the boundaries of modern literary fiction. For a long time these investigations were pursued on parallel tracks which seldom converged. In the last couple of decades, however, the Anglo-American tradition of formalist criticism, essentially empirical and text-based, theoretically rather underpowered but hermeneutically productive, has encountered the more systematic, abstract, theoretically rigorous and 'scientific' tradition of European structuralist criticism. The result has been a minor 'knowledge explosion' in the field of narrative theory and poetics of fiction.

The question I wish to raise in this essay is whether progress in theory and methodology means progress in the critical reading of texts. Is it possible, or useful to bring the whole battery of modern formalism and structuralism to bear upon a single text, and what is gained by so doing? Does it enrich our reading by uncovering depths and nuances of meaning we might not otherwise have brought to consciousness, help us to solve problems of interpretation and to correct misreadings? Or does it merely encourage a pointless and self-indulgent academicism, by which the same information is shuffled from one set of categories to another, from one jargon to another, without any real advance in appreciation or understanding? The analysis offered here of a short story by Ernest Hemingway is intended to support a positive answer to the first set of questions, a negative answer to the second set. But first it may be useful to remind ourselves of the range and variety of theories, methodologies and 'approaches' now available to the critic of fiction. I would group them into three categories, according to the 'depth' at which they address themselves to narrative structure.

1   *Narratology and Narrative Grammar* – i.e. the effort to discover the *langue* of narrative, the underlying system of rules and possibilities of which any narrative *parole* (text) is the realisation. With a few arguable exceptions – e.g. Northrop Frye's *Anatomy of Criticism* (1957) and Frank Kermode's *The Sense of an Ending* (1966) – this enterprise has been almost exclusively dominated by European scholars – Propp, Bremond, Greimas, Lévi-Strauss, Todorov and Barthes, among others. Crucial to this tradition of inquiry are the ideas of function and transformation. In the theory of Greimas, for instance, all narrative consists essentially of the transfer of an object or value from one '*actant*' to another. An actant performs a certain function in the story which may be classified as Subject or Object,

Sender or Receiver, Helper or Opponent, and is involved in doing things which may be classified as performative (tests, struggles, etc.), contractual (establishment and breaking of contracts) and disjunctional (departure and returns). These functions are not simply identifiable from the surface structure of a narrative text: for instance, several characters may perform the function of one actant, or one character may combine the functions of two actants. All concepts are semantically defined by a binary relationship with their opposites (e.g. Life/Death) or negatives (e.g. Life/Non-Life) yielding the basic semiotic model A:B :: –A:–B (e.g. Life:Death :: Non-Life:Non-Death), so that all narrative can be seen as the transformation into actants and actions of a thematic four-term homology.[1]

It is often said that this kind of approach is more rewarding when applied to narratives of a traditional, formulaic and orally transmitted type, rather than sophisticated literary narratives; and the exponents of narratology themselves frequently remind us that their aim is not the explication of texts but the uncovering of the system that allows narrative texts to be generated and competent readers to make sense of them. Narratology does, however, bring to the attention of the literary critic factors involved in reading narrative that are important, but in a sense so obvious that they tend to be overlooked. Roland Barthes has very fruitfully applied to the analysis of literary fictions the idea, derived from structuralist narratology, that narrative is divisible into sequences that open or close possibilities for the characters, and thus for the reader. The interest of these openings and closures may be either retrospective, contributing to the solution of some enigma proposed earlier in the text (the hermeneutic code), or prospective, making the audience wonder what will happen next (the proairetic code).[2] Curiosity and suspense are therefore the two basic 'affects' aroused by narrative, exemplified in a very pure form by the classic detective story and the thriller, respectively, as Tzvetan Todorov observes.[3] A story of any sophistication will also, as Kermode points out in *The Sense of an Ending*, make use of what Aristotle called peripeteia, or reversal, when a possibility is closed in a way that is unexpected and yet plausible and instructive. The reversal tends to produce an effect of irony, especially if it is anticipated by the audience.

Two problems arise in applying this kind of approach to realistic fiction. If we segment a text into its smallest units of information, how do we identify those which are functional on the basic narrative level, and what do we do with those units (the majority) which are not? Roland Barthes suggests one solution in his 'Introduction to the

Structural Analysis of Narratives' where, drawing his illustrations mainly from Ian Fleming's *Goldfinger*, he classifies the narrative units as either *nuclei* or *catalysers*. Nuclei open or close alternatives that are of direct consequence for the subsequent development of the narrative and cannot be deleted without altering the story. Catalysers are merely consecutive units which expand the nuclei or fill up the space between them. They can be deleted without altering the narrative, though not, in the case of realistic narrative, without altering its meaning and effect, since segments which connect not, or not only, with segments at the same level, but with some more generalised concept such as the psychological makeup of the characters, or the atmosphere of the story, function as *indices*, or (if merely factual) *informants*. Jonathan Culler has suggested that our ability to distinguish nuclei from catalysers intuitively and to rank them in order of importance is a typical manifestation of reader-competence, verified by the fact that different readers will tend to summarise the plot of a given story in the same way. The intuitive recognition or ranking of nuclei is 'governed by readers' desire to reach an ultimate summary in which plot as a whole is grasped in a satisfying form'.[4] In short, the structural coherence of narratives is inseparable from their meaning, and reading them is inseparable from forming hypotheses about their overall meaning.

2 *Poetics of Fiction* Under this head I include all attempts to describe and classify techniques of fictional representation. The great breakthrough in this field in the modern era was undoubtedly the Russian Formalists' distinction between *fabula* and *sjuzet*: on the one hand, the story in its most neutral, objective, chronological form – the story as it might have been enacted in real time and space, a seamless continuum of innumerable contiguous events; and on the other hand, the actual text in which this story is imitated, with all its inevitable (but motivated) gaps, elisions, emphases and distortions. Work along these lines in Europe, culminating in Gérard Genette's 'Discours du récit' (1972), established two principal areas in which *sjuzet* significantly modified *fabula*: time, and what is generally called 'point of view' in Anglo-American criticism – though Genette correctly distinguishes here between 'perspective' (who sees the action) and 'voice' (who speaks the narration of it). He also distinguishes most suggestively three different categories in the temporal organisation (or deformation) of the *fabula* by the *sjuzet*: order, duration and frequency. The first of these concerns the relation between the order of events in the *fabula*, which is always chronological, and the order of events in the *sjuzet*, which,

of course, need not be. The second category concerns the relation between the putative duration of events in the *fabula* and the time taken to narrate them (and therefore to read the narration) in the *sjuzet*, which may be longer, or shorter, or approximately the same. The third category concerns the relationship between the number of times an event occurs in the *fabula* and the number of times it is narrated in the *sjuzet*. There are four possibilities: telling once what happened once, telling *n* times what happened *n* times, telling *n* times what happened once, and telling once what happened *n* times.[5]

The choices made by the narrative artist at this level are in a sense prior to, or 'deeper' than his stylistic choices in composing the surface structure of the text, though they place important constraints upon what he can achieve in the surface structure. They are also of manifest importance in the realistic novel which, compared to other, earlier narrative forms, is characterised by a carefully discriminated, pseudo-historical treatment of temporality, and a remarkable depth and flexibility in its presentation of consciousness.

A good deal of Anglo-American critical theorising about the novel, from Percy Lubbock's *The Craft of Fiction* (1921) to Wayne Booth's *The Rhetoric of Fiction* (1961), was implicitly, if unconsciously, based on the same distinction between *fabula* and *sjuzet*, between 'story' and 'way of telling it'. The cross-fertilisation of the two critical traditions has produced much interesting and illuminating work, analysing and classifying novelistic techniques and covering such matters as tense, person, speech and indirect speech in fictional narrative; and we are now, it seems to me, within sight of a truly comprehensive taxonomy of fictional form at this level. Two recent books which have made particularly valuable contributions in this respect are Seymour Chatman's *Style and Discourse: Narrative Structure in Fiction and Film* (1978) and the more narrowly focused *Transparent Minds: Narrative Modes for Presenting Consciousness in Fiction* by Dorrit Cohn (1978).

3 *Rhetorical Analysis* By this I mean analysing the surface structure of narrative texts to show how the linguistic mediation of a story determines its meaning and effect. This is a kind of criticism in which Anglo-American tradition is comparatively strong, because of the close-reading techniques developed by the New Criticism. Mark Schorer's essays 'Technique as Discovery' (1948) and 'Fiction and the Analogical Matrix' (1949)[6] are classic statements of this approach. The stylistics that developed out of Romance Philology,

represented at its best by Spitzer and Auerbach,[7] also belongs in this category. When I wrote my first book of criticism, *Language of Fiction* (1966), this seemed the best route by which to achieve a formalist critique of the realistic novel.

The underlying aim of this criticism was to demonstrate that what looked like redundant or random detail in realistic fiction was in fact functional, contributing to a pattern of motifs with expressive and thematic significance. Much of this criticism was therefore concerned with tracing symbolism and keywords in the verbal texture of novels. Though very few of the New Critics were aware of the work of Roman Jakobson, he provided a theoretical justification for this kind of criticism in his famous definition of literariness, or the poetic function of language, as 'the projection of the principle of equivalence from the axis of selection to the axis of combination'.[8] What the New Critics called 'spatial form'[9] was precisely a pattern of paradigmatic equivalences concealed in the narrative syntagm. Furthermore, as I tried to show in my book *The Modes of Modern Writing* (1977), in his distinction between metaphor and metonymy,[10] Jakobson provided a key to understanding how the realistic novel contrives to build up a pattern of equivalences without violating its illusion of life.

Metaphor and metonymy (or synecdoche) are both figures of equivalence,[11] but generated by different processes, metaphor according to similarity between things otherwise different, metonymy according to contiguity or association between part and whole, cause and effect, thing and attribute, etc. Thus, if I transform the literal sentence 'Ships sail the sea' into 'Keels plough the deep', *plough* is equivalent to 'sail' because of the similarity between the movement of a plough through the earth and a ship through the sea, but *keel* is equivalent to 'ship' because it is part of a ship (synecdoche) and *deep* is equivalent to 'sea' because it is an attribute of the sea (metonymy). In fact, metonymy is a non-logical (and therefore foregrounded or rhetorical) condensation achieved by transformations of kernel sentences by deletion (*the keels of the ships* condensed to *keels* rather than *ships, deep sea* to *deep* rather than *sea*). Metonymy thus plays with the combination axis of language as metaphor plays with the selection axis of language, and together they epitomise the two ways by which any discourse connects one topic with another: either because they are similar or because they are contiguous. Jakobson's distinction thus allows the analyst to move freely between deep structure and surface structure.

Realistic fiction is dominantly metonymic: it connects actions that are contiguous in time and space and connected by cause and effect, but since it cannot describe exhaustively, the narrative *sjuzet* is always in a metonymic (or synecdochic) relation to the *fabula*. The narrative text necessarily selects certain details and suppresses or deletes others. The selected details are thus foregrounded by being selected, and their recurrence and interrelation with each other in the narrative text becomes aesthetically significant (what the Prague School calls systematic internal foregrounding). Furthermore, these details may carry connotations, building up a still denser pattern of equivalences, especially (though not exclusively) when they are described in figurative language, using the verbal tropes of metonymy or metaphor. This is usually (and rather loosely) called 'symbolism' in Anglo-American criticism. Barthes calls it connotation, the process by which one signified acts as the signifier of another signified not actually named. Jakobson's distinction enables us to distinguish four different ways in which it operates in literary texts, two of which are especially characteristic of realistic fiction:

A Metonymic Signified I metonymically evokes Signified II (e.g. the hearth fire in *Jane Eyre*, an invariably selected detail in any description of domestic interiors, signifying 'inhabited room', also symbolises comfort, intimacy, security, etc., cause evoking effect.)
B Metonymic Signified I metaphorically evokes Signified II (e.g. mud and fog at the beginning of *Bleak House*, signifying 'inclement weather', also symbolise the obfuscation and degradation of goodness and justice by the Law, because of the similarity between the effects of the elements and those of the institution).
C Metaphoric Signified I metonymically evokes Signified II (e.g. the description of the night in Llaregyb, in Dylan Thomas's *Under Milk Wood*, as 'bible-black', symbolises the Protestant chapel-going religious culture of the community; part, or attribute, standing for the whole).
D Metaphoric Signified I metaphorically evokes Signified II (e.g. in the opening lines of Yeats's poem, 'The Second Coming' –

> Turning and turning in the widening gyre
> The falcon cannot hear the falconer

where the metaphor *gyre* applied to the spiralling movement of the falcon also symbolises the cyclical movement of history).

Realistic fiction relies principally upon symbolism of types A and B, in which the primary signified is introduced into the discourse according to the metonymic principle of spatial or temporal contiguity with what has come before.

II

No choice of a text for illustrative purposes is innocent, and no analysis of a single text could possibly provide universally valid answers to the questions posed at the beginning of this essay. These questions will not be settled until we have a significant corpus of synthetic or pluralistic readings of narrative texts of various types. Two distinguished achievements of this kind come to mind: Barthes's *S/Z* and Christine Brooke-Rose's study of *The Turn of the Screw*.[12] The following discussion of Hemingway's short story 'Cat in the Rain' (1925) follows the model of the latter in taking the problem of interpretation as its starting-point, but it is necessarily much more modest in scope and scale than either. Two considerations prompted the choice of this story, apart from its convenient brevity. (1) A staff seminar on it in my own department at Birmingham revealed that it presents certain problems of interpretation, though without being quite so heavily encrusted with the deposits of previous readings and misreadings as *The Turn of the Screw*. (2) It is both realistic and modern, cutting across that historicist and tendentious distinction between the *lisible* and the *scriptible* which I personally find one of the less helpful features of the work of Barthes and his disciples.[13] The implied notion of *vraisemblance* on which Hemingway's story depends, the assumed relationship between the text and reality, is essentially continuous with that of classic bourgeois realism, yet in the experience of readers it has proved ambiguous, polyvalent and resistant to interpretative closure.

This is what Carlos Baker, in the standard critical work on Hemingway, had to say about 'Cat in the Rain' (he discusses it in the context of a group of stories about men-women relationships):

'Cat in the Rain', another story taken in part from the woman's point of view, presents a corner of the female world in which the male is only tangentially involved. It was written at Rapallo in May, 1923. From the window of a hotel room where her husband is reading and she is fidgeting, a young wife sees a cat outside in the rain. When she goes to get it, the animal (which somehow stands in her mind for comfortable bourgeois domesticity) has disappeared. This fact is very close to tragic because of the cat's association in her mind with many other things she longs for: long hair she can do in a knot at the back of her neck; a candle-lighted dining table where her own silver gleams; the season of spring and nice weather; and of course, some new clothes. But when she puts these wishes into words, her husband mildly advises her to shut up and find something to read. 'Anyway', says the young wife, 'I want a cat. I want a cat, I want a cat now. If I can't have long hair or any fun, I can have a cat.' The poor girl is the referee in a face-off between the actual and the possible. The actual is made of rain, boredom, a preoccupied husband, and irrational yearnings. The possible is made of silver, spring, fun, a new coiffure, and new dresses. Between the actual and the possible, stands the cat. It is finally sent up to her by the kindly old inn-keeper, whose sympathetic deference is greater than that of the young husband.[14]

There are several things to quibble with in this account of the story. Most important perhaps is Baker's assumption that the cat sent up by the hotel keeper at the end is the same as the one that the wife saw from her window. This assumption is consistent with Baker's sympathy with the wife as a character, implied by his reference to her as 'the poor girl' and his description of the disappearance of the cat as 'very close to tragic'. The appearance of the maid with a cat is the main reversal, in Aristotelian terms, in the narrative. If it is indeed the cat she went to look for, then the reversal is a happy one for her, and confirms her sense that the hotel keeper appreciated her as a woman more than her husband. In Greimas's terms, the wife is the subject of the story and the cat the object. The hotel-keeper and the maid enact the role of helper and George is the opponent. The story is disjunctive (departure and return) and concerns the transfer of the cat to the wife.

The description of the tortoise-shell cat as 'big', however, suggests that it is not the one to which the wife referred by the diminutive term 'kitty', and which she envisaged stroking on her lap. We might infer that the padrone, trying to humour a client, sends up the first cat he can lay hands on, which is in fact quite inappropriate to the wife's needs. This would make the reversal an ironic one at the wife's expense, emphasising the social and cultural abyss that separates her from the padrone, and revealing her quasi-erotic response to his professional attentiveness as a delusion.

I shall return to this question of the ambiguity of the ending. One more point about Baker's commentary on the story: he says that the cat 'somehow stands in [the wife's] mind for comfortable bourgeois domesticity', and speaks of its 'association in her mind with many other things she longs for'. In other words, he interprets the cat as a metonymic symbol of type A above. Indeed he sees the whole story as turning on the opposition between two groups of metonymies. 'The actual is made of rain, boredom, a preoccupied husband, and irrational yearnings. The possible is made of silver, spring fun, a new coiffure, and new clothes.'

John V. Hagopian gives a very different reading of this story. It is, he says, about 'a crisis in the marriage . . . involving the lack of fertility, which is symbolically foreshadowed by the public garden (fertility) dominated by the war monument (death)' in the first paragraph. These again are metonymic symbols of type A, effect connoting cause; but Hagopian's reading of the story hinges on the identification of the cat as a symbol of a wanted child, and of the man in the rubber cape (lines 52–3) as a symbol of contraception – symbolism of type B, in which a metonymic signified evokes a second signified metaphorically, i.e. by virtue of similarity.

As [the wife] looks out into the wet empty square, she sees a man in a rubber cape crossing to the café in the rain . . . The rubber cape is a protection from rain, and rain is a fundamental necessity for fertility and fertility is precisely what is lacking in the American wife's marriage. An even more precise interpretation is possible but perhaps not necessary here.[15]

What Hagopian is presumably hinting at is that 'rubber' is an American colloquialism for contraceptive sheath, and that the wife notices the man in the rubber cape because of the subconscious association – a piece of classic Freudian 'symbolism'. It is an ingenious interpretation and all the more persuasive because there seems to be no very obvious reason for introducing the man in the cape into the story – he is not an actant in the narrative but an item of the descriptive background, and his appearance does not tell us anything about the weather or the square that we do not know already. Admittedly, the cape does signify, by contrast, the wife's lack of protection from the rain, thus emphasising the padrone's thoughtfulness in sending the maid with the umbrella. But if we accept Hagopian's reading then the umbrella itself, opening with almost comical opportuneness and effortlessness behind her, becomes a symbol of how the wife's way of life comes between her and a vital, fertile relationship with reality. Her later demands for new clothes, a new hairstyle, a candle-lit dining-table are, according to Hagopian, expressions of a desire that never reaches full consciousness, for 'motherhood, a home with a family, an end to the strictly companionate marriage with George'. And the cat, he says, is by this stage in the story 'an obvious symbol for a child'.

Unlike Baker, Hagopian sees the final reversal in the story as ironic:

The girl's symbolic wish is grotesquely fulfilled in painfully realistic terms. It is George, not the padrone, by whom the wife wants to be fulfilled, but the padrone has sent up the maid with a big tortoise-shell cat, a huge creature that swings down against her body. It is not clear whether this is exactly the same cat as the one the wife had seen from the window – probably not; in any case, it will most certainly not do. The girl is willing to settle for a child-surrogate, but the big tortoise-shell cat obviously cannot serve that purpose.[16]

The reason why this story is capable of provoking these two very different interpretations might be expressed as follows: although it is a well-formed narrative, with a clearly defined beginning, middle and end, the primary action is not the primary vehicle of meaning. This can be demonstrated by testing upon the story Jonathan Culler's hypothesis that competent readers will tend to agree on what is and is not essential to the plot of a narrative text. Before the seminar at Birmingham University, participants were invited to summarise the action of the story in not more than thirty words of continuous prose.[17] All the contributors mentioned the wife, the cat, the rain, and the hotel manager; most mentioned the nationality of the wife and her failure to find the cat under the table; about half mentioned the husband, located the story in Italy, and made a distinction between the two cats. None mentioned the maid, or the bickering between husband and wife.

These omissions are particularly interesting. The non-appearance of the maid is easily explained: on the narrative level her function is indistinguishable from that of the manager – both are 'helpers' and the narrative would not be significantly altered *qua* narrative if the maid were deleted from the story and her actions performed by the manager himself. She does contribute to the symmetry of the story both numerically and sexually: it begins by pairing husband and wife, then pairs wife and manager, then wife and maid, then (in the wife's thoughts) maid and manager, then wife and manager again, then wife and husband again, and ends by pairing husband and maid. But this seems to be a purely formal set of equivalences with no significance in the hermeneutic or proairetic codes (such as would obtain if, for instance, there were some intrigue linking the husband with the maid and the manager, the kind of plotting characteristic of the *lisible* text). The main function of the maid in the story is to emphasise the status of the wife as a client and expatriate, and thus to act as a warning or corrective against the wife's tendency to attribute to the padrone a deeply personal interest in herself.

Both Baker and Hagopian agree that the rift between husband and wife is what the story is essentially about, even if they disagree about the precise cause. That none of the synopses should make any allusion to the bickering between the couple is striking evidence that the meaning of the story does not inhere in its basic action. In trying to preserve what is essential to that action in a very condensed summary – the quest for the cat, the failure of the quest, the reversal – one has to discard what seems most important in the story as read – the relationship between husband and wife. Adopting Barthes's terminology in 'The Structural Analysis of Narratives', there are only four nuclei in the story, opening possibilities which might be closed in different ways: will the wife or the husband go to fetch the cat? will the wife get the cat? will she get wet? who is at the door? There is perhaps another possibility tacitly opened around line 115, and closed, negatively, at line 131: namely, that George will put down his book and make love to his wife. All the rest of the story consists of catalysers that are indexical or informational, and since most of the information is given more than once, these too become indexical of mood and atmosphere (for instance, we are told more than once that it is raining). One might indeed describe the story generically as indexical: we infer its meaning indexically from its non-narrative components rather than hermeneutically or teleologically from its action. Another way of putting it would be to invoke Seymour Chatman's distinction between the resolved plot and the revealed plot:

> In the traditional narrative of resolution, there is a sense of problem solving . . . of a kind of ratiocinative or emotional teleology . . . 'What will happen?' is the basic question. In the modern plot of revelation, however, the emphasis is elsewhere, the function of the discourse is not to answer that question or even to pose it . . . It is not that events are resolved (happily or tragically) but rather that a state of affairs is revealed.[18]

Chatman offers *Pride and Prejudice* and *Mrs Dalloway* as examples of each kind of plot. 'Cat in the Rain' seems to share characteristics of both: it is, one might say, a plot of revelation (the relationship between husband and wife) disguised as a plot of resolution (the quest for the cat). The ambiguity of the ending is therefore crucial. By refusing to resolve the issue of whether the wife gets the cat she wants, the implied author indicates that this is not the point of the story.

There are several reasons why this ending is ambiguous. One, obviously, is that the story ends where it does, for if it continued for another line or two, or moment or two, it would become apparent from the wife's response whether the cat was the one she had seen from the window, whether she is pleased or disconcerted by its being brought to her, and so on. In other words, the *sjuzet* tantalisingly stops just short of that point in the *fabula* where we should, with our readerly desire for certainty, wish it to. In other respects there is nothing especially striking about the story's treatment of time, though we may admire the smooth transition in the first paragraph from summary of a state of affairs obtaining over a period of days or weeks to the state of affairs obtaining on a particular afternoon, and the subtle condensation of durational time in the final scene between husband and wife, marked by changes in the light outside the window. The order of events is strictly chronological (characteristic, Chatman observes, of the resolved plot). As regards what Genette calls frequency, the story tends towards reiteration rather than summary, telling *n* times what happened *n* times or *n* times what happened once rather than telling once what happened *n* times. This is important because it reinforces the definition of the characters according to a very limited repertoire of gestures. Thus the wife is frequently described as looking out of the window, the husband as reading, the manager as bowing (and the weather as raining).

The story of the quest for the cat involves four characters, and in theory could be narrated from four points of view, each quite distinct and different in import. The story we have is written from the point of view of the American couple rather than that of the Italian hotel staff, and from the wife's point of view rather than the husband's. We must distinguish here between what Genette calls voice and perspective. The story is narrated throughout by an authorial voice which refers to the characters in the third person and uses the past tense. This is the standard mode of authorial narration and by convention the narrator is authoritative, reliable and, within the fictional world of the discourse, omniscient. The authorial voice in this story, however, renounces the privilege of authorial omniscience in two ways, firstly by abstaining from any comment or judgment or explanation of motive regarding the behaviour of the characters, and secondly by restricting itself to the perspective of only two of the characters, and for part of the story to the perspective of only one. By this I mean that the narrator describes nothing that is not seen by either husband or wife or both. Yet it is not quite true to say that the narrator has no independent angle of vision: he has. As in a film, we sometimes see the wife from the husband's angle, and the husband sometimes from the wife's angle, but much of the time we see them both from some independent, impersonal angle.

The first paragraph adopts the common perspective of the American couple, making no distinction between them. With the first sentence of the second paragraph, 'The American wife stood at the window looking out', the narrative adopts her perspective but without totally identifying with it. Note the difference between '*her* husband' in line 30, which closely identifies the narration with her perspective, and 'the husband' in line 33, 'the wife' in line 36, which subtly reasserts the independence of the authorial voice. From this point onwards, however, for the next fifty lines the narration ident- ifies itself closely with the wife's perspective, following her out of the room and downstairs into the lobby, and reporting what she thinks as well as what she sees. The anaphoric sequence of sentences beginning 'She liked' (lines 45–50) affect us as being a transcription rather than a description of her thoughts because they could be transposed into monologue (first person/present tense) without any illogicality or stylistic awkwardness. Sentences in free indirect speech, 'The cat would be round to the right. Perhaps she could go along under the eaves' (54–5) and 'Of course, the hotel-keeper had sent her' (59), mark the maximum degree of identification of the narration with the wife's point of view. When she returns to the room the narration separates itself from her again. There is a lot of direct speech from now on, no report of the wife's thoughts, and occasionally the narration seems to adopt the husband's perspective alone, e.g. 'George looked up and saw the back of her neck, clipped close like a boy's' (109–10) and – very importantly:

Someone knocked on the door.
'Avanti,' George said. He looked up from his book.
In the doorway stood the maid. She held a big tortoise-shell cat . . . (142–4)

We can now fully understand why the ending of the story is so ambiguous: it is primarily because the narration adopts the hus- band's perspective at this crucial point. Since he did not rise from the bed to look out of the window at the cat sheltering from the rain, he has no way of knowing whether the cat brought by the maid is the same one – hence the non-committal indefinite article, 'a big tortoise-shell cat'. If, however, the wife's perspective had been adopted at this point and the text had read,

'Avanti,' the wife said. She turned round from the window.
In the doorway stood the maid. She held a big tortoise-shell cat . . .

then it would be clear that this was not the cat the wife had wanted to bring in from the rain (in which case the definite article would be used). It is significant that in the title of the story, there is no article before 'Cat', thus giving no support to either interpretation of the ending.

Carlos Baker's assumption that the tortoise-shell cat[19] and the cat in the rain are one and the same is therefore unwarranted. Hagopian's reading of the ending as ironic is preferable but his assumption that the wife's desire for the cat is caused by childlessness is also unwarranted. Here, it seems to me, the structuralist notion of language as a system of differences and of meaning as the product of structural oppositions can genuinely help to settle a point of interpretation. Hagopian's interpretation of the man in the rubber cape as a symbol of contraception depends in part on the association of rain with fertility. Now rain *can* symbolise fertility – when defined by opposition to drought. In this story, however (and incidentally, throughout Hemingway's work), it is opposed to 'good weather' and symbolises the loss of pleasure and joy, the onset of discomfort and ennui. Hagopian's comments on the disappearance of the painters, 'The rain, ironically, inhibits creativity,'[20] is a strained attempt to reconcile his reading with the text: there is no irony here unless we accept his equation, rain = fertility.

The cat as a child-surrogate is certainly a possible interpretation in the sense that it is a recognised cultural stereotype, but again Hagopian tries to enlist in its support textual evidence that is, if anything, negative. He comments on the description of the wife's sensations as she passes the hotel-keeper for the second time: ' "very small and tight inside . . . really important . . . of supreme importance" all phrases that might appropriately be used to describe a woman who is pregnant'.[21] But not, surely, to describe a woman who merely *wants* to be pregnant. Indeed, if we must have a gynaecological reading of the story it is much more plausible to suppose that the wife's whimsical craving for the cat, and for other things like new clothes and long hair, is the result of her *being* pregnant. There is, in fact, some extratextual support for this hypothesis. In his biography of Hemingway, Carlos Baker states quite baldly that 'Cat in the Rain' was about Hemingway, his wife Hadley and the manager and chambermaid at the Hotel Splendide in Rapallo, where the story was written in 1923. He also states, without making any connection between the two items, that the Hemingways had left the chilly thaw of Switzerland and gone to Rapallo because Hadley had announced that she was pregnant.[22]

At about the same time, Hemingway was evolving 'a new theory that you could omit anything if you knew what you omitted, and the omitted part would strengthen the story and make people feel something more than they understood'.[23] This is, I think, a very illuminating description by Hemingway of his application of the metonymic mode of classic realism to modernist literary purposes. Metonymy, as I said earlier, is a device of non-logical deletion. Hemingway's word is 'omission'. By omitting the kind of motivation that classic realistic fiction provided, he generated a symbolist polyvalency in his deceptively simple stories, making his readers 'feel more than they understood'. It would be a mistake, therefore, to look for a single clue, whether pregnancy or barrenness, to the meaning of 'Cat in the Rain'. That the wife's (and, for that matter, the husband's) behaviour is equally intelligible on either assumption is one more confirmation of the story's indeterminacy.

Hemingway's stories are remarkable for achieving a symbolist resonance without the use of rhetorical figures and tropes. Not only does 'Cat in the Rain' contain no metaphors and similes – it contains no metonymies and synecdoches either. The story is 'metonymic' in the structural sense defined above: its minimal semantic units are selected from a single context, a continuum of temporal and spatial contiguities, and all foregrounded simply by being selected, repeated and related to each other oppositionally. Consider, for example, the opening paragraph, which establishes the story's setting in diction that is apparently severely denotative, with no metaphors or metonymies, similes or synecdoches, no elegant variation or pathetic fallacies, yet is nevertheless highly charged with connotative meaning.

There were only two Americans stopping at the hotel. Americans opposed to other nationalities: index of cultural isolation.

They did not know any of the people they passed on the stairs on their way to and from their room. Index of social isolation and mutual dependence – vulnerability to breakdown in relationship.

Their room was on the second floor facing the sea. Culture faces nature.

It also faced the public garden and the war monument. Culture paired with nature (public: garden) and opposed to nature (monument: garden). Pleasure (garden) opposed to pain (war).

There were big palms and green benches in the public garden. Culture and nature integrated. Benches same colour as vegetation.

In the good weather there was always an artist with his easel. Artists liked the way the palms grew and the bright colors of the hotels facing the gardens and the sea. Culture and nature happily fused. Image of euphoria.

Italians came from a long way off to look up at the war monument. Euphoria qualified. War monument attracts the living but commemorates the dead. Looking associated with absence (of the dead). 'Italian' opposed to 'American'.

It was made of bronze and glistened in the rain. Inert mineral (bronze) opposed to organic vegetable (palm). Rain opposed to good weather. Euphoria recedes.

It was raining. Rain dripped from the palm trees. Euphoria recedes further. Weather uninviting.

Water stood in pools on the gravel paths. Image of stagnation.

The sea broke in a long line in the rain and slipped back down the beach to come up and break again in a long line in the rain. Excess of wetness. Monotony. Ennui.

The motor cars were gone from the square by the war monument. Across the square in the doorway of the café a waiter stood looking out at the square. Images of absence, loss, ennui.[24]

The first paragraph, then, without containing a single narrative nucleus, establishes the thematic core of the story through oppositions between nature and culture, joy and ennui. Joy is associated with a harmonious union of culture and nature, ennui is the result of some dissociation or discontinuity between culture and nature. The wife, looking out of the window at a scene made joyless by the rain, sees a cat with whose discomfort she emotionally identifies. Her husband, though offering to fetch it, implies his indifference to her emotional needs by not actually moving. The husband is reading, a 'cultural' use of the eyes. The wife is looking, a 'natural' use of the eyes. Her looking, through the window, expresses a need for communion. His reading of a book is a substitute for communion, and a classic remedy for ennui. It is worth noticing that he is reading on the bed – a place made for sleeping and making love; and the perversity of this behaviour is symbolised by the fact that he is lying on the bed the wrong way round. As the story continues, the contrast between looking and reading, both activities expressing the loss or failure of love, becomes more insistent. Denied the kitty, a 'natural' object (opposed to book) which she could have petted as a substitute for being petted, the wife looks in the mirror, pining for a more natural feminine self. Then she looks out of the window again, while her husband, who has not shifted his position (his immobility opposed to the padrone's punctilious bowing), reads on and impatiently recommends her to 'get something to read'. One could summarise this story in the style of Greimas, as follows: loving is to quarrelling as stroking a cat is to reading a book, a narrative transformation of the opposition between joy and ennui, thus:

Loving (Joy): Quarrelling (Ennui) :: stroking a cat (Non-joy, a giving but not receiving of pleasure): reading a book (Non-ennui).

Such a summary has this to recommend it, that it brings together the overt action of the story (the quest for the cat) with its implicit subject (the relationship between husband and wife). Whether it, and the preceding comments, enhance our understanding and appreciation of Hemingway's story, I leave others to judge.

Notes
(Note: books cited were published in London unless otherwise indicated.)

1. See A. J. Greimas, *Sémantique structurale* (Paris, 1966), *Du Sens* (Paris, 1970), and *Maupassant. La sémiologie du texte: exercices pratiques* (Paris, 1976). I am particularly indebted to Ann Jefferson's long review of this last work in *Poetics and Theory of Literature*, II (1977), pp. 579–88.

2. Roland Barthes, 'Introduction to the Structural Analysis of Narratives' in *Image-Music-Text*, ed. and trans. Stephen Heath (1977; first published 1966), and *S/Z*, trans. Richard Miller (1975; first published 1970).

3. Tzvetan Todorov, *The Poetics of Prose*, trans. Richard Howard (1977; first published 1971), p. 47.

4. Jonathan Culler, 'Defining Narrative Units' in *Style and Structure in Literature*, ed. Roger Fowler (Oxford, 1975), p. 139.

5. Gérard Genette, 'Discours du récit' in *Figures III* (Paris, 1972). An English translation of this treatise, entitled *Narrative Discourse*, has been published by Basil Blackwell (Oxford, 1979). For the sake of simplicity I have not introduced the terms (*récit, discours, histoire, narration*) in which Genette and other contemporary French critics have, with bewildering inconsistency, developed the Russian Formalists' *fabula/sjuzet* distinction. These terms, and Genette's theory of narrative in particular, are very elegantly elucidated in Shlomith Rimmon's 'A Comprehensive Theory of Narrative: Genette's *Figures III* and the Structuralist Study of Fiction' in *Poetics and Theory of Literature*, I (1976), pp. 32–62.

6. Mark Schorer, 'Technique as Discovery', *Hudson Review*, I (1948), pp. 67–87, and 'Fiction and the Analogical Matrix', *Kenyon Review*, XI (1949), pp. 539–60.

7. See Leo Spitzer, *Linguistics and Literary History: Essays in Stylistics* (Princeton, N J, 1948) and Eric Auerbach, *Mimesis* (Princeton, N J, 1953).

8. Roman Jakobson, 'Closing Statement: Linguistics and Poetics' in *Style and Language*, ed. Thomas A. Sebeok (Cambridge, Mass., 1960), p. 358.

9. Joseph Frank, 'Spatial Form in Modern Literature', *Sewanee Review*, LIII (1945), pp. 221–40, 433–56, 643–53.

10. Roman Jakobson, 'Two Aspects of Language and Two Types of Linguistic Disturbances', in *Fundamentals of Language* by Jakobson and Morris Halle (The Hague, 1956).

11. This point was blurred in my discussion of Jakobson's theory in the first edition of *The Modes of Modern Writing*. It is clarified in a Prefatory Note to the second impression of the book (a paperback edition published by Arnold in 1979).

12. Christine Brooke-Rose, 'The Squirm of the True', *Poetics and Theory of Literature*, I (1976), pp. 265–94 and 513–46, and II (1977), pp. 517–61

13. The distinction is made at the beginning of *S/Z*, whose English translator renders these terms as 'readerly' and 'writerly'. The classic realistic novel is 'readerly': it is based on logical and temporal order, it communicates along an uninterrupted chain of sense, we consume it,

passively, confident that all the questions it raises will be resolved. The modern text is in contrast 'writerly': it makes us not consumers but producers, because we write ourselves into it, we construct meanings for it as we read, and ideally these meanings are infinitely plural.

14. Carlos Baker, *Hemingway: The Writer as Artist* (Princeton, N J, 1963), pp. 135–6.

15. John V. Hagopian, 'Symmetry in "Cat in the Rain",' in *The Short Stories of Ernest Hemingway: Critical Essays*, ed. Jackson J. Benson (Durham, N C, 1975), p. 231.

16. *Ibid.*, p. 232.

17. My own effort was as follows: 'Bored young American staying with her husband at Italian hotel fails to rescue a cat seen sheltering from the rain but is provided with a cat by the attentive manager'.

18. Seymour Chatman, *Story and Discourse: Narrative Structure in Fiction and Film* (Ithaca, N Y, 1978), p. 48.

19. It has been pointed out to me that tortoise-shell cats are usually female and that since feminine pronouns are applied to the 'kitty' in lines 26–7, this suggests that it and the tortoise-shell cat are one and the same. I am doubtful whether so specialised a piece of knowledge should be allowed to disambiguate the conclusion, and in any case it is not conclusive evidence. It seems clear that if Hemingway had wanted to establish that the two cats were one and the same, he would have described the kitty as 'tortoise-shell'.

20. Hagopian, *op. cit.*, p. 230.

21. *Ibid.*, p. 231.

22. Carlos Baker, *Ernest Hemingway* (Harmondsworth, Middx, 1972), pp. 159 and 161.

23. *Ibid.*, p. 165.

24. The hotel in Rapallo at which the Hemingways stayed in 1923 still stands (now called the Hotel Riviera) and its outlook corresponds closely to the description in the first paragraph of 'Cat in the Rain' – with one interesting difference. The 'war monument' is, in fact, a statue of Christopher Columbus, erected in 1914 by grateful local businessmen who had made their fortunes in America and returned to enjoy their affluence in the homeland. As it is inconceivable that Hemingway should have mistaken the nature of the monument, one may legitimately conclude that he converted it into a war memorial for his own symbolic purposes. These, it should be said, are much more obvious to the reader when the story is read in its original context, the collection of stories and fragments *In Our Time* (1925), many of which are directly concerned with the war, and the experience of pain and death.

3   READER-RESPONSE

A major change in literary criticism of the past twenty-five years or so has been the emergence of the reader. Both Russian Formalism and the New Criticism had concentrated on the literary text as an object in itself and had devoted little or no attention to the reader. Indeed, a classic New Critical article is Wimsatt and Beardsley's 'The Affective Fallacy', which argued that the reader, like the question of authorial intention, did not warrant critical consideration.[1] The diversity of readers' interests and responses, it was argued, made it impossible to establish any secure or coherent critical position on the basis of reader response. To take account of the reader opened the door to a relativism that would undermine literary criticism as a discipline.

On the surface structuralism also had little interest in the reader, but it perhaps prepared the way for reader-based criticism. Structuralism showed that linguistic artifacts such as literary texts could exist only as a consequence of the performance of certain operations by the human mind. Literary texts were a kind of 'parole', to use Saussurean terminology, that is, forms of language that appeared to be independent and autonomous but which were in fact the product of a communicative system or 'langue' which human beings had to have mentally internalised if they were either to create such texts or to understand them. Thus though structuralists were not interested in the reader in an individual sense, they nevertheless shifted the focus from the text itself to its generation through the mental operations of the reader.

Reader-based criticism moves beyond the abstract or Kantian model of mind which governs structuralist thinking and focuses instead on the historical or psychological aspects of reading. In Reception Theory, for example, whose best known exponents are the German critics Hans Robert Jauss and Wolfgang Iser, the prime concern has been with the impact of literary texts on their readers and with how the reception of a particular text has changed since its original publication. For Jauss the concept of a 'horizon of expectations' is central: all readers of literature have certain expectations derived from reading other texts, but whereas works of little literary interest will tend to remain within the reader's horizon of expectations, the genuine literary work will tend to undermine or destablise that horizon. He believes that the modern reader of literary texts produced in the past has to make an effort to understand how and why these works were irreconcilable with or disrupted their original readers' horizon of expectations, if such works are to be experienced as literature by modern readers, for whom they may have been assimilated by the literary culture.

Iser's main concern has been more on the reading process than on historical reception. Rejecting the New Criticism's preoccupation with interpretation and meaning, he argues that any reading is only 'one of the possible realizations of a text' and that meanings 'are the product of a rather difficult interaction between text and reader and not qualities hidden in the text'.[2] The object of criticism, therefore, is to reveal the various norms and codes which the reader brings to the text but which the text itself may negate or call into question. Adapting the view of Roman Ingarden that a literary text is a 'schematised structure' which the reader needs to 'concretise' or fill out, Iser claims that such concretisation does not reveal unity or harmony but rather the existence of gaps and indeterminacies. Thus for him reading is a dynamic process in which the norms and codes that govern the reader's thinking and perception may be called into question by having to confront gaps and blanks in the text. One can see a link between Iser's theory and the Russian Formalist concept of defamiliarisation. For Iser this potential of literature to undermine or destabilise mental structures offers the possibility of liberation, though Marxist critics have objected that Iser's concept of liberation is only individual and not social.

Iser's work has been more influential than Jauss's in English-speaking countries, partly because his work has connections with American reader-response criticism and partly because he is a specialist in English literature and can therefore illustrate his theory from texts written in English, as can be seen here in his essay on Fielding's novel *Joseph Andrews*.

American reader-response has been more interested in the reader in an individual sense than reception theory. In his earlier career Stanley Fish was associated with 'affective stylistics', an approach which emphasised that reading is a temporal process and which rejected the New Critical view that form in literary texts is spatial. Fish argued, in contrast to the New Critics, that meanings are actualised in texts in the process of reading through the interaction between the text and 'the reader's expectations, projections, conclusions, judgments, and assumptions'.[3] Fish's earlier criticism resembles Iser's in that he preserves the separation of text and reader. More recently he has come to believe that such a separation cannot be defended since neither text nor reader has an independent existence: texts are brought into being by the reader's interpretative principles and strategies, though such strategies are not subjective in the narrow sense but are derived from 'interpretive communities' which share similar strategies of interpretation.

Fish goes so far as to argue that even what seem to be the most objective aspects of a text, such as rhyme and metre, are produced by interpretative principles and strategies, since such features could never be recognised unless the reader's mind had been conditioned in advance to apprehend such features. He rejects attacks which claim that his reader-based theory creates relativism on the grounds that interpretative strategies will be shared so that readers inevitably fall into groups in relation to their different interests. Recently he has become associated with 'new pragmatism', which argues that theory can never achieve a position outside of or separate from practice in such a way as to guide it. He emphasises the role of belief rather than theory since it is different beliefs – about, for example, what the value of reading or interpreting literature is – that underlie the formation of 'interpretive communities' and when theory wishes to engage in practice it inevitably hardens into belief.

Given these views, for Fish it is clearly pointless to engage in general literary interpretation that tries to arrive at a 'true' reading of the text. All one can do is either write for those readers and critics who are part of a particular 'interpretive community' or else change from interpreting texts to interpreting readers interpreting texts. This is what Fish chooses to do in the essay on Milton's *Paradise Lost* reprinted here. If one adopts the view that the text has no separate existence from the reader and from the interpretative principles and strategies the reader brings to the text, then interpretation should shift from the text to such principles and strategies, why they change causing interpretations to change, the cultural and ideological forces at work on readers and critics which lead to the emergence of new principles and strategies and therefore new interpretations.

Notes

1. See W. K. Wimsatt, Jr. *The Verbal Icon: Studies in the Meaning of Poetry* (New York, 1964).

2. Wolfgang Iser, 'Indeterminacy and the Reader's Response in Prose Fiction', in *Aspects of Narrative: Selected Papers from the English Institute* (New York, 1971), p. 4.

3. Stanley Fish, *Is There a Text in This Class? The Authority of Interpretive Communities* (Cambridge, Mass., 1980), p. 2.

Further Reading

Stanley Fish, *Self-Consuming Artifacts: The Experience of Seventeenth-Century Poetry* (Berkeley, 1972).
Wolfgang Iser, *Laurence Sterne: Tristram Shandy* (Cambridge, 1988).
Steven Mailloux, *Interpretive Conventions: The Reader in the Study of American Fiction* (Ithaca and London, 1982).

Wolfgang Iser: The Role of the Reader in Fielding's *Joseph Andrews*

I

'A new province of writing':[1] this is what Fielding called his novels. In what way new? Innovations as such in literature are very difficult to perceive; it is only when they are set against a familiar background that we can get some idea of their novelty. Once the new is distinguished from the old, there arises a certain tension, because we have lost the security of the familiar without knowing for sure the precise nature of the innovation. For what is new comes into being through changes in the reader's mind – the casting aside of old assumptions and preconceptions. It is difficult for Fielding as an author to define these changes, since he is concerned with presenting the new and not with merely changing the old.

For innovation itself to be a subject in a novel, the author needs direct cooperation from the person who is to perceive that innovation – namely, the reader. This is why it is hardly surprising that Fielding's novels, and those of the eighteenth century in general, are so full of direct addresses to the reader, which certainly have a rhetorical function, though this is by no means their only function. John Preston's book *The Created Self* is the first full-length study of these apostrophies, which he interprets in terms of rhetoric only: 'I

Reprinted from Wolfgang Iser, *The Implied Reader: Patterns of Communication from Bunyan to Beckett* (Baltimore, 1974), pp. 29–46.

make no attempt to provide a "rhetoric of reading", though no doubt this would be worth doing. Rather I trust that the rhetorical principles in question will provide a unifying point of view for these four novels (i.e. *Moll Flanders, Clarissa, Tom Jones,* and *Tristram Shandy*), and yet not seem unduly arbitrary or restrictive. And I should be glad to feel that such an approach might prompt other more radical enquiries into the nature of the reader's role in fiction.'[2]

This recommendation for a more radical enquiry can be taken as a starting-point for our discussion. The role which the Fielding novel assigns to its readers is not confined to a willingness to be persuaded. In the act of reading, we are to undergo a kind of transformation, such as W. Booth has described in connection with fiction in general: 'The author creates, in short, an image of himself and another image of his reader; he makes his reader, as he makes his second self, and the most successful reading is one in which the created selves, author and reader, can find complete agreement.'[3] But this transformation of the reader into the image created by the author does not take place through rhetoric alone. The reader has to be stimulated into certain activities, which may be guided by rhetorical signposts, but which lead to a process that is not merely rhetorical. Rhetoric, if it is to be successful, needs a clearly formulated purpose, but the 'new province of writing' that Fielding is trying to open up to his readers is in the nature of a promise, and it can only rouse the expectations necessary for its efficacy if it is not set out in words. The reader must be made to feel for himself the new meaning of the novel. To do this he must actively participate in bringing out the meaning and this participation is an essential precondition for communication between the author and the reader. Rhetoric, then, may be a guiding influence to help the reader produce the meaning of the text, but his participation is something that goes far beyond the scope of this influence. Northrop Frye has referred to an attack on Jakob Böhme which aptly describes the conditions leading to the reader's act of production: 'It has been said of Boehme that his books are like a picnic to which the author brings the words and the reader the meaning. The remark may have been intended as a sneer at Boehme, but it is an exact description of all works of literary art without exception.'[4]

Eighteenth-century novelists were deeply conscious of this interplay with the reader. Richardson once wrote – admittedly in a letter, and not in the novel itself – that the story must leave something for the reader to do.[5] Laurence Sterne, in *Tristram Shandy*, describes this vital process with the same unmistakable clarity with which he disclosed the principles of fiction as practiced in the novel during the first half of the eighteenth century. He writes in II, 11: 'no author, who understands the just boundaries of decorum and good-breeding, would presume to think all: The truest respect which you can pay to the reader's understanding, is to halve this matter amicably, and leave him something to imagine, in his turn, as well as yourself. For my own part, I am eternally paying him compliments of this kind, and do all that lies in my power to keep his imagination as busy as my own.'[6] The participation of the reader could not be stimulated if everything were laid out in front of him. This means that the formulated text must shade off, through allusions and suggestions, into a text that is unformulated though nonetheless intended. Only in this way can the reader's imagination be given the scope it needs; the written text furnishes it with indications which enable it to conjure up what the text does not reveal.

Fielding, too, often speaks of the offer of participation that must be made to the reader, if he is to learn to fulfil the promise of the novel. There is a clear reference to this in *Tom Jones*:

Bestir thyself on this occasion; for, though we will always lend thee proper assistance in difficult places, as we do not, like some others, expect thee to use the arts of divination to discover our meaning, yet we shall not indulge thy laziness where nothing but thy own attention is required; for thou art highly mistaken if thou dost imagine that we intended, when we began this great work, to leave thy sagacity nothing to do; or that, without sometimes exercising this talent, thou wilt be able to travel through our pages with any pleasure or profit to thyself.[7]

This typical appeal to the reader's 'sagacity' aimes at arousing a sense of discernment. This is to be regarded as a pleasure, because in this way the reader will be able to test his own faculties. It also promises to be profitable, because the need for discernment stimulates a process of learning in the course of which one's own sense of judgment may come under scrutiny. Here we have a clear outline of the role of the reader, which is fulfilled through the continual instigation of attitudes and reflections on those attitudes. As the reader is manoeuvred into this position, his reactions – which are, so to speak prestructured by the written text – bring out the meaning of the novel; it might be truer to say that the meaning of the novel only materialises in these reactions, since it does not exist per se.

II

This rough outline of the reader's role is something we can elaborate on, in more detail with reference to *Joseph Andrews* and *Tom Jones*, so that we can see more clearly the nature of the activity required of the reader as he produces the meaning of the novel. In the very first sentence of *Joseph Andrews*, the author mentions the fact that the 'mere English reader'[8] will certainly have different conceptions and also different expectations regarding the reading that lies ahead of him. For his reading habits are conditioned by epics, tragedies, and comedies, the underlying principles of which are called to mind so that the enterprise of our own author can be separated from them. Certainly the association of this novel with the hallowed forms of traditional literature was intended by Fielding, primarily, to raise the status of his tale in prose; but just as clear is the intention underlying his description of his work as a 'comic epic poem in prose'.[9] By listing his deviations from the classical models, he is drawing attention to the unique features of his enterprise. And so the 'classical reader'[10] will find pleasure in the 'parodies or burlesque imitations'[11] precisely because they conjure up the very 'genre' which they set out to transform.

This process can be linked with what Gombrich terms in esthetics 'schema and correction'.[12] Fielding calls to mind a whole repertoire of familiar literary 'genres', so that these allusions will arouse particular expectations from which his novel then proceeds to diverge. These subsequent divergences are the first step toward innovation.

In the preface, Fielding specifies the differences between his novel and classical predecessors, but these informative indications gradually disappear as the reader begins to fall in with the book. In the first of the initial essays of the novel, again he makes use of a familiar repertoire. But here the starting-point is contemporary rather than ancient literature. It is true that he alludes to classical and medieval Lives,[13] but his main concern here is with Colley Cibber's *Autobiography* and Richardson's *Pamela*, which both fit in perfectly with Fielding's intentions, since they each present a life-story.[14] But here it is no longer a question of Fielding showing the differences between his work and the models alluded to. Instead they are shown to be exemplary in a way that Fielding pretends he wants to emulate with his *Joseph Andrews*[15] – and this regardless of the fact that one biography is fictitious and the other real, though it is ironically pointed out that there is much fiction in the real one, and in the fictitious much that presumes to be exemplary for real life.

If the beginning of the introduction emphasised the divergences from the established repertoire, now the stress is laid on the similarities, so that the reader is left to discover the differences for himself – though these always remain clearly visible thanks to the ever-present irony.[16] *Joseph Andrews* is not to be read, then, as a glorification of the hero – in the mould of the Cibber *Autobiography* – or as a moral vade mecum for worldly success, like Richardson's novel. Here, too, schemata are corrected, though the correction is never formulated. As a result there appears a gap between the familiar repertoire in the novel and one's own observation of it.

These gaps heighten our awareness, and their effectiveness lies in the fact that they conceal something of vital importance. As we have seen, the reader is forced to discover for himself the divergences from the established repertoire, and at first sight this seems simple enough. The ironic style is sufficient to show us that the text means the opposite of what it says; but the situation becomes rather more complicated when we ask, 'What will the opposite of Richardson's *Pamela* and Colley Cibber's *Autobiography* look like?' The answer to this is far from obvious, and so the ironic allusions can no longer be regarded as a mere reversal of the written statement.

By negating the familiar, the irony indicates that now something is to be communicated of which hitherto there has been no proper conception. Our attention is drawn to the difficulty of deducing the exemplary from the private. Consequently, this negating irony drives us to seek the proper conception beyond the confines of the familiar models; and in this way, the nonfulfilment of those expectations aroused by the presence of the familiar, becomes the spur that pricks our imagination into action.

The repertoire of the familiar in *Joseph Andrews* is not confined to established literary patterns; it also incorporates various norms that were generally accepted in Fielding's day. The transplanting of these norms into the novel results in their transformation, for here they are presented in a different light from that in which they appeared at the time within the 'collective consciousness'[17] we call society. This aesthetic arrangement of social norms has certain consequences for the reader which can best be illustrated through the character of Abraham Adams, the real hero of the novel. The list of virtues that Fielding unfolds contains nearly all the qualities that would make up the perfect man. And yet it is his very possession of all these qualities that makes Adams totally incapable of dealing with this world, as Fielding actually points out.[18] The list of virtues is not seen from a Christian or a Platonic standpoint now, but from a worldly one, and from this totally different perspective the virtues appear to lose all their validity; they seem to belong to the past, for they are no longer capable of inspiring sensible conduct in the present. The question now arises as to whether this means that amoral conduct is best suited to this world. Or does it mean that we have to find a compromise relationship between norm and world? If this were so, surely any such compromise would be an intolerable strain, since the two factors – contemporary norms and worldly demands – would forever be tugging us in opposite directions. Virtues cannot be contemplated separately from the world, and the world cannot be viewed without the background of virtue. Is the conflict to be resolved? If so, how, and why? The answers are not given us. They are the gaps in the text. They give the reader the motivation and the opportunity to bring the two poles meaningfully together for himself.

Here, then, we have our first insight into the nature of the reader's active participation, as mobilised by the novel. The repertoire of the familiar – whether it be literary tradition, contemporary 'Weltanschauung', or social reality – forms the background of the novel. The familiar is reproduced in the text, but in its reproduction it seems different, for its component parts have been altered, its frame of reference has changed, its validity has, to a degree, been negated. But if the starting-point of the novel is a set of negations, then the reader is impelled to counterbalance these negations by seeking their positive potential, the alternate fulfilment of which we shall henceforth call the realisation of the text.

Fielding's preoccupation with this aspect of the reader's role can be traced from the remarks in the preface right through the initial essays in the novel. After drawing distinctions between his own novel and traditional writings, he continues:

Having thus distinguished Joseph Andrews from the productions of romance writers on the one hand and burlesque writers on the other, and given some few very short hints (for I intended no more) of this species of writing, which I have affirmed to be hitherto unattempted in our language; I shall leave to my good-natured reader to apply my piece to my observations.[19]

The reader, then, must apply the author's remarks to his novel, but the text will not tell him how to do this. The application will coincide largely with the realisation. In the preface, however, Fielding does outline the sphere in which this application is to take place, for he promises that the reader will have revealed to him the sources of the ridiculous which, he says, spring from the discovery of affectation and hypocrisy.[20] The intention of the novel, then, is not the presentation of affectation and hypocrisy, but the uncovering of their ridiculousness, which always occurs with the penetration of those false appearances that mask all social vices.

However, a discovery of this nature does not end with the unmasking of vice. Fielding simply says that the veil will fall from the ridiculous, without saying that this absurdity might carry with it some indication as to the proper way to conduct oneself. So far the reaction of the reader will signify no more than a feeling of superiority, and the question arises as to what lies behind this superiority evinced by our laughter. At best it is an awareness of the potential presence of what proper conduct should be, although we cannot discount the possibility that our superiority is also based on a misunderstanding. The reader, therefore, must not only see through the original false appearances; he must also set out even more intensively to discover the preconditions for model conduct, to make sure that this superiority, obtained through the unmasking of absurd vices, does not it in its turn become a false appearance. In this process, ridicule performs a very different function from its function in the literature of the past: it ceases to stigmatise the lower classes and instead stimulates the reader's mind into trying to formulate the potential morality contained in the unmasking. In order to set such a mental process into operation, the intention of the novel cannot be the subject of narration, for it is only by reconstructing for himself the unformulated part of the text – in this case, the correct mode of conduct – that the reader can experience this intention as a reality.

How this reality is constituted is indicated about half-way through *Joseph Andrews* in Fielding's final theoretical essay (III, 1). He would like to feel that the novel is a kind of mirror, in which the reader can see himself, as it were, through the characters he has been laughing at in apparent superiority. It is his purpose 'not to expose one pitiful wretch to the small and contemptible circle of his acquaintance; but to hold the glass to thousands in their closets, that they may contemplate their deformity, and endeavour to reduce it, and thus by suffering private mortification may avoid public shame'.[21]

If looking in the glass gives the reader the opportunity for self-correction, then the role assigned to him is clear. In taking this opportunity, he is bound to encounter sides of himself that he had not known about or – worse still – had not wanted to know about;

only then can he see that the correct mode of conduct first involves shaking off the familiar. However, it is obvious that correct conduct as such is only a potential thing, which will come into being in as many different ways as there are situations. Fielding makes his characters react almost mechanically and invariably, following the straight and narrow path of their own habits, and in this way the reader is called upon to replace the motivation presented by a motivation that will remove the imbalance of the characters' conduct.

The text, however, leaves out this corrective motivation, although it is not difficult to find. These omissions are repaired by the reader's own imagination. As the text invites him to imagine for himself what would be the right reaction to the given situation, he is bound to make the necessary adjustments consciously, and this process must in turn make him conscious of himself, of his own conduct, and of the customs and prejudices that condition it. This new awareness, Fielding hopes, will make the reader suddenly see himself as he really is, and so the role that he is to play in uncovering the hidden reality of the text will lead ultimately to his uncovering and correcting the hidden reality of himself.

III

Is this intention is to be realised, the process of change cannot be left entirely to the subjective discretion of the reader – he must, rather, be gently guided by indications in the text, though he must never have the feeling that the author wants to lead him by the nose. If he responds as the author wants him to, then he will play the part assigned to him, and in order to elicit the correct response, the author has certain strategems at his disposal. One of them we have already seen in connection with the repertoire of the familiar – namely, negation. Expectations aroused in the reader by allusions to the things he knows or thinks he knows are frustrated; through this negation, we know that the standards and models alluded to are somehow to be transcended, though no longer on their own terms. These now appear to be, as it were, things of the past; what follows cannot be stated, but has to be realised. Thus negation can be seen as the inducement to realisation – which is the reader's production of the meaning of the text. It initiates the act of imagination by which the reader makes the virtual actual, proceeding from the now obsolete norms of the past right through to the 'configurative' meaning of the newly formed present. This is why we often have the impression when reading that we are experiencing the story as an event in our own lives.

In order for such an experience to be possible, the distance between the story and the reader must at times be made to disappear, so that the privileged spectator can be made into an actor. A typical technique used for this purpose is to be seen right at the beginning of the novel, when Joseph has to resist the advances of Lady Booby and her maid. Lady Booby leads on her footman, whom she has got to sit on her bed, with all kinds of enticements, until the innocent Joseph finally recoils, calling loudly upon his virtue. Instead of describing the horror of his Potiphar, Fielding, at the height of this crisis, continues:

You have heard, reader, poets talk of the statue of Surprise; you have heard likewise, or else you have heard very little, how Surprise made one of the sons of Croesus speak, though he was dumb. You have seen the faces, in the eighteen-penny gallery, when, through the trap-door, to soft or no music, Mr Bridgewater, Mr William Mills, or some other of ghostly appearance, hath ascended, with a face all pale with powder, and a shirt all bloody with ribbons – but from none of these, nor from Phidias or Praxiteles, if they should return to life – no, not from the inimitable pencil of my friend Hogarth, could you receive such an idea of surprise as would have entered in at your eyes had they beheld the Lady Booby when those last words issued out from the lips of Joseph. 'Your virtue!' said the lady, recovering after a silence of two minutes; 'I shall never survive it!'[22]

As the narrative does not offer a description of Lady Booby's reaction, the reader is left to provide the description, using the directions offered him. Thus the reader must, so to speak, enter Lady Booby's bedroom and visualise her surprise for himself.

The directions contained in this passage are revealing in several ways. They direct attention to certain social differences between potential readers of the novel. As in the preface, Fielding differentiates between the 'mere English reader' and the 'classical reader'. The one can gear his imagination to the hair-raising shock tactics of well-known contemporary actors; the other can bring the scene to life through classical associations. But such passages also show that Fielding was not only concerned with catering for a varied public; he was also at pains to transcend the social or educational limitations of the individual, as his novel was to reveal human dispositions that were independent of all social strata.

This differentiation between possible types of reader also motiv-

ates the variety of directions enabling the reader to imagine Lady
Booby's surprise. These directions consist of a whole series of
'schematised views',[23] which present the same event from changing
standpoints. There are so many of these views that the means of
presentation seems to by-pass the thing presented – or in this case,
not presented – Lady Booby's surprise. In fact it is the very gap
between the 'schematised views' and their object that enables the
reader to understand the indescribability of that object, thus indica-
ting that he must now picture for himself what the given pictures
are incapable of conveying.

The nondescription of Lady Booby's surprise, and the insistence
on its inconceivability, create a gap in the text. The narrative breaks
off, so that the reader has room to enter into it. The 'schematised
views' then guide his imagination, but in order that they should
not be felt as restrictions, there follows the confession of their inadequacy. Thus the reader's imagination is left free to paint in the
scene. But instead of a concrete picture, the reader's imagination
is far more likely to create simply the impression of a living event,
and indeed this animation can only come about because it is not
restricted to a concrete picture. This is why the character suddenly
comes to life in the reader – he is creating instead of merely observing. And so the deliberate gaps in the narrative are the means by
which the reader is enabled to bring both scenes and characters to
life.

This process is not set in motion without careful forethought. In
this connection there are two observations that are worth making.
If the 'schematised views' of Lady Booby's reaction are all going
to fall short of their target, the question arises as to whether such
very precise indications are in fact totally irrelevant to the steering
of the reader's imagination. Classical references are interwoven with
contemporary, the former creating an effect of pathos, the latter of
comedy, if not of farce. The mixture of pathos and comedy tears
apart the false appearance with which Lady Booby tried to conceal
her lasciviousness. The result is an opportunity for discovery, and
the more the reader brings to life himself, the greater the discovery.

Our second observation is along the same lines. Before the scene
with Lady Booby, Fielding placed another similar scene, in which
Joseph was confronted by the passions of Slipslop. As in the Booby
affair, the reader is given a few directions as to how he is to picture
these 'attacks'.[24] Between these two scenes, Fielding says:

We hope, therefore, a judicious reader will give himself some pains to
observe, what we have so greatly laboured to describe, the different oper-

ations of this passion of love in the gentle and cultivated mind of the
Lady Booby, from those which it effected in the less polished and coarser
disposition of Mrs Slipslop.[25]

Fielding seems to suggest that the effects of love vary according to
social standing. And so we are led to anticipate that the scene with
Lady Booby will show how the passion of an aristocrat differs from
that of a maidservant. The more directly the reader can participate
in the removal of such distinctions, the more effective will be this
shattering of false expectations. Ideally, then, the reader should
take over production of the whole scene, so that the process of
animation will lead up to an enhanced awareness of all the implications. The technique mobilises the reader's imagination, not only
in order to bring the narrative itself to life but also – and even more
essentially – to sharpen his sense of discernment.

In *Joseph Andrews*, Fielding makes various observations about the
reader's role as producer. In the second theoretical essay, for example, he says that reading his book is like a journey, during which
the occasional reflections of the author are to be regarded as resting
places which will give the reader the chance to think back over
what has happened so far. As these chapters interrupt the narrative,
Fielding quite logically calls them 'vacant pages'.[26] Now these
'vacant pages' are themselves large-scale versions of vacancies that
occur right through the text, for instance in the Lady Booby scene.
And just as the reader is to 'reflect' during these 'vacant pages,' so
too must he reflect during all the other vacancies or gaps in the
text. The gaps, indeed, are those very points at which the reader
can enter into the text, forming his own connections and conceptions
and so creating the configurative meaning of what he is reading.
Thanks to the 'vacant pages', he can reflect, and through reflection
create the motivation through which he can experience the text as
a reality. He forms what we might call the 'gestalt' of the text, and
it is worth noting that this, too, is indicated by Fielding in *Joseph
Andrews*.

When, toward the end of the novel, Adams holds in his arms the
son whom he had presumed to be drowned, his overwhelming joy
causes him to forget the virtues of moderation and self-control that
he has always preached, regardless of what was going on around
him; but Fielding intervenes on his hero's behalf: 'No, reader; he
felt the ebullition, the overflowings of a full, honest, open heart,
towards the person who had conferred a real obligation, and of

which, if thou canst not conceive an idea within, I will not vainly endeavour to assist thee.'[27] The reader is shown the event and the outer appearance, but he is invited, almost exhorted, to penetrate behind that appearance, and finally to thrust it aside altogether, by conceiving the idea *within*. This is an almost direct statement of the role of the reader in this novel. From the given material he must construct his own conception of the reality and hence the meaning of the text.

This process can perhaps be seen most clearly in the character of Parson Adams and his contacts with the outside world. The vitality of his character is derived largely from the surprises he offers the reader. Even his name, Abraham Adams, suggests conflicting elements in him.[28] The unshakable faith of the biblical Abraham applies to all the parson's convictions, and yet at times these are thwarted by the Adam in him. These contrasting schemata encroach on each other, and one sometimes represses the other, so that the character cannot be regarded either as Abraham or as Adam; it seems, indeed, as if the character keeps freeing itself from its apparent characteristics. Through the conflict of schemata, the character takes on a definite individuality,[29] at times approaching caricature, and always full of potential surprises for the reader. Caricature depends for its effect on distortion, but distortion in turn depends for its effect on our conception of what is normal. Otherwise, how should we know something was being distorted? In the case of Parson Adams, the unshakable faith of Abraham is blended with the human weakness of Adam – Adam's pragmatic difficulties with Abraham's abstract resolution. These features are emphasised to the point of caricature, but it is for us to decide what the 'normal picture' should look like. At the same time, it is the very oddness of the picture presented that surprises us, and this unexpectedness stimulates those reactions that bring the character to life.

This bringing to life, however, is not an end in itself. It has the function of involving the reader in an action, the meaning of which he must discover for himself. The character is not aware of the conflicting schemata within himself, and the results of this ignorance are apparent right through the novel. Parson Adams, not knowing what he is, takes part in a variety of confrontations with the world, always reacting quite spontaneously, and nearly always reacting inappropriately. The reader, though, is 'in the picture'; not only is he aware of Adams's polarity but also, thanks to the author's numerous directions, he is aware of how inadequately Adams applies his ideal qualities in dealing with the world. Now what does the reader do with his knowledge? The episodes in the novel often become a test for the reader's own capabilities. He sees the world through the eyes of the hero, and the hero through the eyes of a pragmatic world. The result is conflicting views, linked only by their completely negative nature. From Adams's point of view, the worldly conduct of people seems underhand, selfish, and sordid; in the eyes of the world, Adams is ingenuous, narrow-minded, and naive. These two perspectives are completely dominant, and there is no indication whatsoever as to how people really *should* behave. This total absence of balance is intensified by the fact that the characters themselves remain quite unaware of the shamelessness of their so-called worldly wisdom or, in the case of Adams, the impracticality of his idealism.

And so the narrative itself has distinctly negative features, although one cannot go so far as to say that the text actually proclaims the sordidness of the world or the stupidity of virtue. The overprecision with which the two negative poles have been presented inevitably adumbrates the positive features that are not formulated in the text. The form, then, of this unwritten text, becomes apparent to the reader as he reads, and so he begins to uncover what we might call the virtual dimension of the text. Virtual, as it is not described in the text; a dimension, insofar as it balances even if it cannot reconcile the two conflicting, mutually negating poles. The virtual dimension is brought about through our forming the 'gestalt' of the text; here we establish consistency between contrasting positions; this is the configurative meaning of the text, where the unformulated becomes concrete; and finally this is the point at which the text becomes an experience for the reader.

At first sight, the configurative meaning may appear simple enough to find: the polarity shows all too clearly the inadequacy of Adams's virtuous conduct and the baseness of worldly behaviour. Adams should learn to adapt himself better to the world, and worldly people should realise the depravity of their vices. The reader sees the faults of both sides. However, on closer analysis, this apparent simplicity and symmetry will be seen to be misleading – a fact which enables our virtual dimension to take on a far more complex reality. The fact that Adams's steadfast virtue prevents him from adapting himself to the situations that arise, does not mean that the virtual balance would be found in continual adaptation to circumstances. For those characters who do adapt themselves to each new situation unmask their own worldly corruption.[30] And so although a balancing of the two poles will take place in the virtual dimension, this will not be in the sense of reconciling steadfastness with inconstancy, cunning with virtue; it will be a convergence at a point somewhere between or even above the two poles. It is possible simply because the reader has that which both poles lack and, in equal measure, need: insight into themselves. The acquisition of this insight is the aim that Fielding pursues, and the process of bringing characters and scenes to life is the means to this end.

As the reading process coincides with the establishment of the virtual dimension of the text, the impression might arise that the reader's balancing of the poles will gradually endow him with a degree of superiority over the characters. In the matter of overall observation, he *is* superior, but in another sense the superiority must be shown to be illusory or else the novel could not work as a glass reflecting the reader's own weaknesses – as Fielding intends it to do. Furthermore, it would be impossible to gain the right kind of insight, since this can only come about through awareness of one's own inadequacy and not in an affirmation of one's own superiority. And so the strategy of the novelist must be such that the reader, in bringing about the virtual dimension, is actually entangled in what he has produced. Only in this way does the reading process become something alive and dramatic, and this is vital since its meaning is not to be illustrated by the characters, but is to take place within the reader.

For this purpose, the author must employ strategems of various types, with a view to involving the reader on as many levels as possible. First, the reader must be given this feeling of superiority, and so the author takes care to supply him with knowledge that is unavailable to the characters. This privileged position is necessary because if the reader is to play the part intended for him, then for the duration of his reading he must be, so to speak, taken out of himself. The easiest way to entice him into opening himself up is to give him a grandstand view of all the proceedings. This is achieved by a simple strategem: putting Adams in a variety of situations that he cannot see through. For instance, even at the end, when he meets Peter Pounce, Lady Booby's steward, we read: 'Peter was a hypocrite, a sort of people whom Mr Adams never saw through'.[31] The very character who is possessed of the highest degree of integrity is devoid of the faculty emphasised in Fielding's preface as the intention of the novel: seeing through hypocrisy.

This defect in Adams runs through all the episodes of the novel in so unmistakable a fashion that the reader inevitably begins to look down on this, the novel's ambassador of morality. He feels that he has a far better grasp of Adams's situation than the parson himself, confined as he is within the limitations of his own steadfast convictions; the reader's feeling of superiority begins to grow. But his recognition of the unsuitability of Adams's mode of conduct has two sides, for it puts the reader in the position of the worldly wise, thrusting him closer to those characters to whom Adams seems ridiculous. In condemning Adams's lack of pragmatic sense, the reader unexpectedly finds himself on the side of those very people whose pretensions he should be seeing through and who can hardly represent the proper perspective from which he is to judge Adams.

And so the reader's insight becomes distinctly ambivalent. He cannot identify himself with the viewpoint of the worldly wise, for that would mean abandoning the insight he had gained in the unmasking of their hypocrisy. But when throughout a whole series of situations he finds himself sharing their views, which nevertheless he cannot allow to be his guide, then he is left in a state of suspense; his superiority becomes an embarrassment. The problems thus aroused are necessary to entangle him in the configurative meaning he is producing; only when this happens, can the effect of the novel really begin to work on the reader.

If Adams's conduct often strikes the reader as naive, such an impression naturally shows Adams in a negative light, and the question arises as to whether the reader is in a position to nullify this negative impression. The reason for what we regard as Adams's impracticality lies, after all, in his moral steadfastness; and this is what the reader comes up against in all those situations that reveal the impracticality. Is moral steadfastness to be regarded, then, as a condition for doing the wrong thing? Or does the reader now discover how small a part morality plays in the formation and application of his insight, even though he thinks he knows opportunism cannot be the criterion, either? At such moments he lacks orientation, which is something Adams has, without any self-doubts; he begins to fall from his position of superiority, and the configurative meaning of the novel becomes altogether richer. For now the moral conflict – of which the characters are generally relieved, thanks largely to the intervention of providence – takes place in the reader himself.

The conflict can only be resolved by the realisation of the virtual morality. This has already been prestructured by the strategems of the text insofar as the reader's acquired insight separates him from the society of the worldly wise and also shows him that his supposed superiority over Adams can only be based on a lack of moral steadfastness within himself. This is how the reader becomes trapped by his superiority. If he feels superior to the worldly wise, because he can see through them, then when he turns his attention to Adams, he is obliged to see through himself, because in the various situations he reacted differently from Adams. And if he wants to see through Adams, in order to maintain his superiority, then he is obliged to share the views of those whom he is continually unmasking. The worldly wise are lacking in morality, the moralist in self-awareness, and these two negative poles carry with them a virtual ideality against which the reader must measure himself; this ideality is the configurative meaning of the text, the product of the reader's own insight, creating standards below which he must not fall. This process, whereby the reader formulates the unwritten text, requires active participation on his part, and thus the formulated meaning becomes a direct product and a direct experience of the reader.

'A Book is a machine to think with.'[32] So said I. A. Richards, and it seems that *Joseph Andrews* is one of the first novels of the eighteenth century to which this description can be well and truly applied. We can see clearly from the role of the reader, as we have observed it, that the novel is no longer confined to the presentation of exemplary models, à la Richardson, inviting emulation; instead the text offers itself as an instrument by means of which the reader can make a number of discoveries for himself that will lead him to a reliable sense of orientation. A theme in *Joseph Andrews* that lends support to this conception of the novel is that of the relationship between book and world.

There are a number of situations in which Adams thinks he can settle the controversies and supply the urgently needed elucidations by referring to books – especially to Homer[33] and Aeschylus. For him, books and the world are the same thing; he still clings to the time-honoured view that the world is a book, and so the meaning of the world must be present in a book. For Adams it goes without saying that literature, as an imitation of Nature, is a great store-house of good conduct,[34] so that the actual deeds of men can only be measured against this criterion and are naturally always found wanting. This explicit affirmation of the value of literature involves implicitly imprisoning oneself in a fabric of phantasy and delusion. This in turn prevents one from making a correct assessment of empirical situations, since these are generally far too complex to be dealt with in accordance with one set formula. Very few issues are so cut-and-dried that they can be settled by reference to fictional example, and so Fielding's hero becomes quite absurd whenever he tries to supply a literary reduction of some empirical problem and believes that he has thus found the solution.

Occasionally, however, Adams seems to depart spontaneously from his models, for instance in the scene when he throws his beloved Aeschylus into the fire. In a different context, Mark Spilka says of this scene: 'Here Adams has literally stripped off an affectation while revealing his natural goodness – the book is a symbol, that is, of his pedantry, of his excessive reliance upon literature as a guide to life, and this is what is tossed aside during the emergency. Later on, when the book is fished out of the fire, it has been reduced to its simple sheepskin covering – which is Fielding's way of reminding us that the contents of the book are superficial, at least in the face of harsh experience.'[35] This spontaneous gesture is a manifestation of the incongruity of book and world, which Adams is not yet conscious of, even though he occasionally acts accordingly. The reader, however, is aware that the old equation of book and world has been negated and that the book has taken on a new function. Instead of representing the whole world, the novel illustrates points of access to the world; to do this it must offer the reader a kind of lens by means of which he will learn to see the world clearly and be able to adapt himself to it. Since the world is far greater in scope than the book can ever be, the book can no longer offer panacea-like models, but must open up representative approaches to which the reader must adjust for himself. This is the didactic basis of Fielding's novel, made necessary by the empiric variety of the world. The right mode of conduct can be extracted from the novel through the interplay of attitudes and discoveries; it is not presented explicitly. And so the meaning of the novel is no longer an independent, objective reality; it is something that has to be formulated by the reader. In the past, when book and world were regarded as identical, the book formulated its own exemplary meaning, which the reader had only to contemplate; but now that the reader has to produce the meaning for himself, the novel discloses its attitudes through degrees of negation, thwarting the reader's expectations and stimulating him to reflection which in turn creates a counterbalance to the negativity of the text. Out of this whole process emerges the meaning of the novel. Historically speaking, perhaps one of the most important differences between Richardson and Fielding lies in the fact that with *Pamela* the meaning is clearly formulated; in *Joseph Andrews* the meaning is clearly waiting to be formulated.

Notes

1. Henry Fielding, *Tom Jones* (Everyman's Library, London, 1957), II, 1, p. 39.
2. John Preston, *The Created Self. The Reader's Role in Eighteenth-Century Fiction* (London, 1970), p. 3.
3. Wayne C. Booth, *The Rhetoric of Fiction* (Chicago, 1963), p. 138.
4. Northrop Frye, *Fearful Symmetry. A Study of William Blake* (Princeton, 1967), pp. 427 f.
5. Cf. Samuel Richardson, *Selected Letters*, ed. J. Carroll (Oxford, 1964), p. 296.
6. Laurence Sterne, *Tristram Shandy* (Everyman's Library) (London, 1956, II, 11, p. 79.
7. *Tom Jones*, XI, 9, p. 95.
8. Henry Fielding, *Joseph Andrews* (Everyman's Library, London, 1948), Author's Preface: xxvii.
9. Ibid.
10. Ibid., p. xxviii.
11. Ibid.
12. Cf. E. H. Gombrich, *Art and Illusion* (London, 1962), p. 99.
13. Cf. *Joseph Andrews*, I, 1, p. 1.
14. Cf. ibid., p. 2.
15. Ibid.
16. Ibid.
17. In this essay, 'norm' is understood in the sense in which Jan Mukařovsky, *Kapitel aus der Ästhetik* (edition suhrkamp) (Frankfurt, 1970), pp. 43 ff., has defined it.
18. Cf. *Joseph Andrews*, I, 3, p. 5.
19. Ibid., Author's Preface, p. xxxii.
20. Cf. ibid., pp. xxx f.
21. Ibid., III, 1, p. 144.
22. Ibid., I, 8, p. 20.
23. For the specific connotation of this term cf. Roman Ingarden, *Das literarische Kunstwerk* (Tübingen, 1960), pp. 270 ff.
24. Cf. *Joseph Andrews*, I, 6, p. 14.
25. Ibid., I, 7, p. 15.
26. Ibid., II, 1, p. 60.
27. Ibid., IV, 8, p. 249.
28. Cf. Ian Watt, 'The Naming of Characters in Defoe, Richardson and Fielding,' *RES* 25 (1949): 335, who has given such an illuminating account of the component parts forming the name of Richardson's Pamela Andrews, but who does not seem to avail himself of his insight when he comes to dealing with names in *Joseph Andrews*.
29. For a detailed discussion of this problem in the medium of painting cf. Gombrich, *Art and Illusion*, pp. 279 ff., esp. pp. 302 f.
30. Cf. Irvin Ehrenpreis, 'Fielding's Use of Fiction. The Autonomy of

Joseph Andrews' in *Twelve Original Essays on Great English Novels*, ed. Charles Shapiro (Detroit, 1960), p. 23.

31. *Joseph Andrews*, III, 12, p. 212.

32. I. A. Richards, *Principles of Literary Criticism* (London, 1960, 1924), p. 1.

33. Cf. *Joseph Andrews*,II, 17, p. 138 ff.

34. Cf. ibid., II, 9: 100, and II, 2, p. 151 f.

35. Mark Spilka, 'Comic Resolution in Fielding's *Joseph Andrews*' in *Fielding. A Collection of Critical Essays* (Twentieth Century Views), ed. Ronald Paulson (Englewood Cliffs, 1962), p. 63.

Stanley Fish: Transmuting the Lump: 'Paradise Lost,' 1942–1982

In 1972 Raymond Waddington began an article on Books XI and XII of *Paradise Lost* in a way that is remarkable both for what it reveals and for what it conceals. What it reveals is that something has changed: 'Few of us today could risk echoing C. S. Lewis's condemnation of the concluding books of *Paradise Lost* as an "untransmuted lump of futurity." '[1] Waddington is taking note of the fact that Lewis's judgment has apparently been reversed and the concluding books of the poem are now held in more esteem than they once were. His view of that reversal (insofar as he could be said to have one) is not directly stated, but emerges inadvertently, as it were, in a footnote where the bibliographical reference to Lewis's book gives the date of publication as 1969. In fact, *A Preface to 'Paradise Lost'* was published in 1942. It is not that Waddington is inaccurate in any narrow technical sense; the edition he was consulting is a reprint or reissue, and he commits no scholarly error by citing its date. One can say then that it really doesn't matter, and obviously for Waddington it doesn't; but that is just the fact that calls out for explanation (the French would term it a 'scandal'), because in this and other sentences Waddington is reporting on the *history* of recent criticism, and it is, at the very least, a curious history that displays an unconcern with the dates of its events. The explanation, even more curious perhaps than the fact, is that Waddington doesn't really regard it as a history at all, that is, as a succession of developing norms, perspectives, possibilities, alternatives; rather he regards it simply as a change of states – from wrong to right – a change that might as well have occurred in an instant as in thirty years, and one that need not have occurred at all if only

Reprinted from *Literature and History: Theoretical Problems and Russian Case Studies*, ed. Gary Saul Morson (Stanford, 1986), pp. 33–56.

Lewis had been more discerning. 'Lewis's phrasing,' says Waddington in the very next sentence, 'emphasizes a failure to comprehend
structure.' It is not a failure that is time-bound, because it exists
in relation to a structure that was always there to be seen. Lewis
simply didn't see it (the reason he didn't see it is never inquired into;
both failures and successes are always mysterious or miraculous in
this view of things). The fact that others have seen it since is
important, but the precise date at which they saw it is not. Thus
Lawrence Sasek's 1962 article 'The Drama of *Paradise Lost*, Books
XI and XII' is cited in the anthologised version of 1965, and
Northrop Frye's remarks in *The Return of Eden* are dated 1966, no
mention being made of the fact that the substance of the book was
first presented as the Huron College Centennial Lectures in 1963.
The result is to obscure the extraordinary and apparently spontaneous proliferation of articles defending the concluding books in
the short period between 1958 and 1963. In his only gesture toward
historical understanding, Waddington observes that 'a generation
of readers has shared the conviction' that Lewis was mistaken in
his condemnation, but he leaves unasked and unanswered the question of what conviction the previous generation (1942–58) was sharing and why it was so slow to perceive what is now so clear to so
many.

Waddington's lack of interest in the historical conditions that
enabled the work of his predecessors goes hand in hand with a lack
of interest in the conditions that enable his own work. He is obviously doing something in these opening sentences, but he does not
pause to reflect on what he does because it never occurs to him
that one could do anything else; that is, the values, standards, goals,
and understood practices on which he relies are not regarded by
him as requiring explanation or defence; they are simply attendant
upon clear seeing. Thus, for example, he seems unaware that his
vocabulary is at once charged and ideological: 'Lewis's phrasing
emphasizes a failure to comprehend structure; and while an
occasional Broadbent or Martz will inveigh against the execution
of Books XI and XII, a generation of readers has shared the
conviction that, as in *Paradise Regained*, where the design also is
subtle and complex, structure and function are very firmly con-
trolled by the poet.' Words like 'design,' 'subtle,' 'complex,' 'structure,' 'function,' and 'control' are meaningful and meaningfully
honorific only within the assumption of a set of notions about
what constitutes poetry and poetic qualities. In general, these are
formalist notions, and for one who holds them, or is held by them,
'design' immediately means 'pattern' and not purpose or intended

goal, while 'function' refers to the relationship between the parts of an artifact and not to the role played by that artifact in a society, and 'control' is something that is exerted over the various elements of a structure (itself defined formally) rather than over the responses of a reader (although that is presumed to follow as a matter of course). A reader who understands these words as Waddington intends him to (an intention of which he is not consciously aware) will not reflect on them as he reads because they are not received as discrete bits of vocabulary, but form part of a system of understanding in which what could possibly be meant by this or that term is stipulated in advance. That system is not something that is brought to bear on a literary landscape; it *speaks* that landscape, and declares the shape of everything in it, including the entities that populate it and the questions that can properly be put to them. No term is ever innocently employed, not even the term 'poet', which is here as system-specific as any other, and is understood (implicitly) as 'poet-rather-than-moralist-or-philosopher'. That is, a formalist perspective on literary matters will deny the title 'poet' (and the category 'poem') to anyone else whose intentions are overtly didactic or political, a fact (also system-specific) that explains a great deal about the critical history of *Paradise Lost*, Books XI and XII.

Now Waddington knows all of this, but he knows it in an uncritical way; that is, he doesn't know it as something that could be otherwise, as knowledge that has been made possible by the institution of certain historical conditions. Rather he knows it as the simple truth, a truth that might have emerged at any time, but just happened to have emerged in the last generation. A case in point is the appearance in his very first sentence of the word 'risk': 'Few of us today could risk echoing C. S. Lewis's condemnation. . . .' From the point of view I will urge in this essay the word is a crucial one, because it indicates the extent to which what one can reasonably and prudently say is a function of assumptions currently in force in the profession. But to Waddington it indicates no such thing: it indicates simply that C. S. Lewis has been proved wrong and few of us (and they a very curious few) would want to risk being associated with error. Waddington has no real interest in the risk he points out (he doesn't think it interesting) even as he so carefully avoids it by aligning himself with 'the most influential readings'. He exercises professional prudence, but he doesn't seem to realise that by doing so he is choosing a strategy, a course of action with consequences that can be contrasted with the consequences of alternative courses; instead he regards himself as simply saying the obvious as it is dictated by facts that have been established for all time.

In a sense, then, Waddington writes against himself: he reports on a process – the process by which the details, large and small, of a literary topic are first established and then altered – but at the same time he discounts that process as something that has any real relationship either to his task or to its object. He quite self-consciously locates himself in a community, but presents himself as a single agent who just happens to be in agreement with other single agents who have come to see what he sees. His predecessors are presented as discrete workers each of whose conclusions provide '*independent* corroboration' of the assertions put forward by the others. In his sentences, Miltonists are always 'recognizing' this or 'becoming aware' of that; the dominant image is one of seeing, either clearly or through a glass darkly, and seeing is itself never seen as contextually determined, as an activity that is performed in accordance with the possibilities and options that are inherent in a particular historical moment. The result is literary history in a mode with which we are all familiar: a finite number of unchanging questions is addressed to a finite set of unchanging objects by persons whose perspicuity (or lack thereof) is the consequence of individual education and experience. I would like here to suggest the possibility of another kind of history, one that begins with the assumption that literary works are the products as well as the objects of our activity, that they are constituted by questions which are themselves meaningful only in relation to prevailing institutional conditions and that what makes convincing sense (of a kind that can be shared by a 'generation') is a function of the ideological and political situation of avowedly professional readers and writers who know very well (as Waddington himself knows) that what they can reasonably and profitably do depends very much on what has been done before them. Waddington's essay seems to me to be at once a document in, and an example of, this kind of history – we can call it history as persuasion – and in what follows I will take it (along with its predecessors and successors) more seriously than he does.

We can begin by simply stating the problem, although to do so is itself a contentious and polemical act. How is it that in 1942 it was possible to regard Books XI and XII of *Paradise Lose* as barely belonging to the poem, whereas in 1982 – and here I would instance Edward Tayler's fine book *Milton's Poetry: Its Development in Time*[2] – Books XI and XII are regarded as the poem's very centre? We will put aside, for the moment, the standard answer to that question –

in 1982 we are now in a position to see the truth – and look for an answer in the poem's critical history, regarded not as a record of discrete insights but as a linked and dynamic sequence of constitutive acts enabled by a set of specifiable conditions. The first thing to note is that the 'risk' of which Waddington speaks is attendant on every critical gesture and is therefore not irrelevant to the case of C. S. Lewis himself. Did Lewis take a risk when he said what he said? If so, what was it? If not, why not? Those questions should in turn be considered in terms of the more general question of the nature of risk in literary studies. How is it calculated? What is at stake? Of course, it is not calculated at all if by that word one means a self-conscious choice of this or that approach in relation to the probability of professional rewards; rather the choices that occur to one 'naturally' are already understood in terms of the needs of the profession and therefore come already calculated; one could not think of a course of action that was unrelated to conditions prevailing in the profession because those very conditions form the background – to be the all-pervasive but unarticulated context – within which thinking about possible courses of action goes on. Thus any reading one proposes will have a relationship – of confirmation, challenge, modifications, reversal – to previous readings, and this means that any reading one proposes will be political, since it will advance or retard someone's interest and declare itself on issues in relation to which sides have already been chosen.

This is not to say that the relationship between critical act and its predecessors is ever simple, or describable by a direct line of cause and effect. Untangling the filiations and antecedents of even a single assertion will lead not to an explanation (in the sense borrowed from the physical sciences) but to an awareness of the complexity that underlies the intelligibility and value of any critical gesture. Thus, for example, when Lewis condemns the concluding books of *Paradise Lost*, he is doing not a single thing, but several things, with varying degrees of self-consciousness. First of all, he is allying himself with a long tradition that is already in place by 1712 when Addison observes that Books XI and XII are 'not generally reckoned among the most shining Books of the poem' (*Spectator*, no. 363).[3] Addison comes to praise, and he defends the books by pointing out that without them the story of the fall of man 'would not have been complete, and consequently his Action would have been imperfect' (p. 216), but at the same time he establishes the basic line of complaint when he declares (p. 217) that 'if Milton's poem flags anywhere, it is in this Narration, where in some Places the

Author has been so attentive to his Divinity, that he has neglected his Poetry'.

The terms of Addison's qualified praise are exactly the terms of Lewis's qualified censure: the example of Virgil cited by both men; both point to particularly 'fine moments', and both are uneasy about the proportions of doctrine to poetry. But if on one level Lewis is merely reconfirming an old orthodoxy, on another level he is challenging a new one, the orthodoxy of anti-Miltonism, as it was represented in the writings of T. S. Eliot and F. R. Leavis. It was Leavis who had announced in 1933 that 'Milton's dislodgement, in the past decade, after his two centuries of predominance, was effected with remarkably little fuss'.[4] To our ears this sounds like either a premature or partial judgment or an effort to get away with an outrageous assertion by presenting it as a commonplace; but in fact what Douglas Bush was later to call 'these smug words'[5] (the question of who is smugger than whom in these controversies is a nice one) were more than a little justified when Leavis wrote, and as late as 1945 Bush feels compelled to devote the entire first chapter of '*Paradise Lost*' *in Our Time* to 'The Modern Reaction Against Milton'. The strength of that reaction is to be measured not by the numbers it embraced but by the names associated with it: in addition to Leavis, Ezra Pound, John Middleton Murry, Herbert Read, F. L. Lucas, Bonamy Dobrée, G. Wilson Knight, and, of course, Eliot. It is hard for us in a time when the absence of critical authority is lamented to imagine the influence attributed to Eliot in these discussions; but the attribution is made by all parties. Leavis, in the second sentence of his essay, declares that 'the irresistible argument was, of course, Mr Eliot's creative achievement' (the 'of course' tells its own story); twenty-five years later B. A. Wright is still complaining that 'young men and women go up to the universities to read Honours English without having read a line of Milton, for their teachers have told them that they need not bother about a poet of exploded reputation'.[6] 'Mr Eliot,' writes a historian of the period, 'was able to turn a generation of practitioners and readers of verse away from Milton toward Donne and the metaphysicals.'[7]

What is clear from these reports is that the weight of Eliot's judgment is a *political* fact rather than a fact that reflects the 'truth' (independently determined) of his opinions. Anyone who would advance another judgment, therefore, must make his case in the context of Eliot's authority. He must argue *about* Milton (as if Milton were an entity whose characteristics were a matter of public and obvious record), but against Eliot, and, ultimately, with the whole set of assumptions and presuppositions within which Milton emerges as a morally bad man whose poetry was insufficiently faithful to the felt complexities of human experience. Here then, in 1942, is a risk that Lewis must take, and the inescapably political (read 'historical') nature of critical debate is reflected in the care with which he orders his response to Eliot and the other anti-Miltonists. First he disposes of those (unnamed) who are of too gross a sensibility even to be answered (this is a strategy he borrows from the poet), critics 'who hate Milton through fear and envy'.[8] Next he considers 'a much more respectable class of readers' (p.131), those who find Milton's verse insufficiently in touch with the texture of felt human life. In this group Leavis is the chief figure, and he receives the respect due an equal: 'Dr Leavis does not differ from me about the properties of Milton's epic verse. . . . It is not that he and I see different things when we look at *Paradise Lost*. He sees and hates the very same that I see and love' (p. 130). When he comes to Eliot, however, Lewis's strategy changes. Rather than dismissing him, or simply agreeing to disagree, as equals always can, he first acknowledges his superiority and then makes it the grounds for discounting him. If some readers are not good enough for the poem, Eliot is *too* good for it; he has removed himself from its precincts 'in order to fast and pray in the wilderness' (p. 132). The act is a noble one, and Lewis says of Eliot 'I honour him', but it is finally an act too difficult for most men who 'live in merry middle earth' and find it 'necessary to have middle things' (p. 133).

Thus, Lewis himself takes a middle position, between Leavis's demand for 'a particular kind of realism' (p. 131) and Eliot's desire for an otherworldly purity, and in the context of that position his condemnation of Books XI and XII makes a different kind of sense than the sense made of it by Waddington and others. First of all, it is part of a *defence* of Milton in the face of the two-pronged attack on the abstractness of his verse and on the unacceptability of his religious ideas. Lewis handles the first or artistic objection by celebrating the ritual and formulaic qualities that Eliot and others deplore. The objection to Milton's theology is met, curiously enough, by denying the centrality of religion to his poem: 'I am not sure that *Paradise Lost* was intended to be a religious poem . . . and I am sure it need not be' (p. 128). Once again, Lewis has recourse to a traditional line of argument. Nineteenth-century Miltonists tended more and more to displace the burden of critical attention from Milton's ideas to his art – the negative form of this is well represented by Raleigh's famous pronouncement that '*Paradise Lost* is a monument to dead ideas'[9] – and for Lewis the art of *Paradise*

Lost, as apart from its theological content, resides in its plot. Of course, the contents of the plot are in some sense religious – Lewis is not making a case for ignorance of the theology – but our relationship to those contents does not and should not result in 'a religious exercise'. If it begins to feel like one, if 'we remember that we also have our places in this plot, that we also . . . are moving either towards the Messianic or towards the Satanic position, then we are entering the world of religion'. And when we do that, Lewis continues, 'our epic holiday is over; we rightly shut up our Milton'. Whereas in the religious life 'man faces God' directly, in our literary experience we are the observers of feigned encounters: 'We are not invited . . . to *enjoy* the spiritual life, but to *contemplate* the whole pattern within which the spiritual life arises.'

The assumptions that inform these statements are crucial for the entire history I hope to explore in this essay – indeed, it is when they have been dislodged that Books XI and XII will have been fully rehabilitated – but for the present it is enough to point out the justification they provide for Lewis's dismissal of those books. If the criterion of evaluation is structural – a matter of a functional relationship to the unfolding of a plot – then it follows that a lengthy rehearsal of theological doctrine, punctuated only now and then by any interaction between characters, is by definition 'inartistic' (p. 125). In making this judgment Lewis is able at once to affirm a basic principle of both Eliot's and Leavis's criticism – that literature must be evaluated as *literature* and not as something else (morality, religion, politics) – and to indicate that their application of that principle in the case of Milton is excessively draconian. One need not reject all of *Paradise Lost* because in some parts of it the poet has been so attentive to his divinity that he has neglected his poetry. In effect then, Books XI and XII of *Paradise Lost* are sacrificed by Lewis so that he can defend the rest of the poem in the face of its influential detractors. The gesture that Waddington sees as a failure to comprehend structure (that is, he sees it only in relationship to his own view of the matter) is, if understood historically, an attempt to *assert* structure, both as a principle of literary judgment and as a property of Milton's poem. Lewis is fighting a battle that has been won by the time that Waddington writes, and in fact Waddington is able to proceed within the assumption of the poem's greatness only because of what is begun in the very pages he deplores. (In 1972 there is still a 'Milton controversy', but it isn't the controversy that determines the significance of what Lewis does in 1942, although what Lewis does in 1942 finally makes it possible for Waddington to do what he does in 1972.)

In short, what looks from the vantage point of 1972 like an aberrant judgment, now happily corrected, is, in the context of its production, a perfectly understandable act that is politically astute and marvellously economical. It is also productive of its own eventual reversal: that is, it defines in a negative way the nature of the project that will end in the elevation of Books XI and XII to their present place of honour. That project will be guided by the terms of Lewis's dismissal. Those terms, as we have seen, are at once ideational and literary: the materials of these books are inappropriate to a literary work because they are doctrinal and didactic; and, moreover, 'the actual writing . . . is curiously bad' (p. 125), and it is bad because the books are insufficiently dramatic. Lewis delivers these strictures as if they represented discrete and independent judgments, but in fact, each judgment is a reflection of the others. If the content is didactic rather than 'poetic', the style will necessarily be bad because it will not reflect the subtle particulars of 'lived experience', and because it does not reflect those particulars, but has reference instead to static abstractions, the result will of course lack drama. The opposition of poetry and doctrine entails a bias for some styles and against others, and entails too a bias in favour of the vivid representation of action in the world. So long as this set of mutual entailments is firmly in place, there will be little that a would-be defender of Books XI and XII will be able to say.

I observed earlier that Waddington leaves unexplained the fact that fifteen years passed before there was any substantial challenge to Lewis's condemnation. Part of the explanation is to be found in the extent to which large features of the literary landscape would have to change before there could be any corresponding change in the arguments that could even be conceived (never mind heard) in the service of a possible defence. One sees this clearly in the early but ineffective effort of E. N. S. Thompson to redress the critical balance. The date is 1943 and Thompson himself knows how unpromising is the task he had undertaken: his very first sentence declares, 'A plea for the last two books of *Paradise Lost* will seem at the present time decidedly quixotic.'[10] He cites the 'incorrigibles' who object to 'all that Milton wrote', but he is even more dismayed 'to find a staunch supporter like Mr C. S. Lewis rendering an unfavorable judgment'. Nevertheless, Thompson is determined 'to put on record my impression that the details of this historical survey are poetically chosen and ordered effectively to the poet's chief end'. Notice what this statement of intention does *not* promise: it does not promise to defend the survey as history or as doctrine but to demonstrate that nevertheless it is employed poetically and contributes to a poetic end. Lewis's assumptions are left unchallenged, and Thompson is content to argue that this part of the poem exhibits many of the qualities generally admired in the earlier books ('the sentences are . . . no more cumbrous than Satan's first speech in Book II'). His strategy is two-pronged. He answers the stylistic objection by presenting isolated passages and praising them as 'finely etched pictures', and he answers the objection that these last books are structurally unrelated to the poem's plot by claiming that they are necessary to a psychological plot, the plot of Adam's education. Since Adam has had 'precious little personal experience' (p. 376), he needs the knowledge and wisdom conveyed to him by the succession of tableaus and commentary: 'Each scene adds something to Adam's fund of experience, just as the pictured scenes in the *Purgatorio* enlighten Dante toiling up the steep mountain path' (p. 378).

The emphasis on the psychology of education is hardly new. In 1734 Jonathan Richardson observes admiringly, 'tis Delightful to see how Finely Milton *observes* all the Growth of the New Man. Creation was all at Once, Regeneration is like the Natural Progression: we are Babes, and come by Degrees to be Strong Men in *Christ*'.[11] The difference is that Richardson's admiration is for a theological pattern whereas Thompson offers his reading in order to counter the charge that in these books the theology has crowded out the poetry. In Thompson's account the lessons Adam learns are not doctrinal but political and ethical, and the progress of his education is from the relatively simple lessons of Book XI to 'the more complex social and political problems' of Book XII. For Richardson the claims of the aesthetic and the theological do not pull against one another because the two categories are not mutually exclusive; but for Thompson, to defend the one is to devalue the other, and therefore he is forced to leave large sections of the text out of his account, an account that will have little chance of reversing the judgment so authoritatively made by Lewis.

Thompson's difficulty is seen in another form in the work of B. A. Rajan, who in 1947 also attempts something like a defence of Books XI and XII. Like Thompson, Rajan begins by conceding so much that there is very little left for him to defend. 'I myself,' he says, 'am not in love with the last books.'[12] 'They are bleak and barren and pessimistic.' 'The achievement falters' (p 85). 'Entire scenes do nothing' (p. 84). Milton is 'tired in spirit' (p. 92). 'There is no progression of poetic fervour to support the mechanical development of the epic.' Rajan has an explanation for these weaknesses, but it turns out to be a curious and finally damaging one. The

pessimism and dispiritedness, and the resulting flatness of the writing, are 'unmistakable' (p. 83), but 'they are not part and parcel
of Milton's poetic design' (p. 84); rather, they are 'intrusions in
that design . . . the clenched, spasmodic despair of the man who
will one day write *Samson Agonistes*, but intrusions nevertheless which
are in no way evidence of Milton's epic intention.' Milton, in short,
was out of control. 'The unevenness of the last two books reflects
a desperate attempt to find peace of mind' (p. 84), and by dramatis-
ing his own anxieties the poet violates the decorum of the epic
mode, forgetting that if self-exploration is your concern, 'there are
other forms of writing you can employ' (p. 85).

It is tempting to pause over this remarkable argument and examine its sources in contemporary theories of epic and lyric; but for
our purpose it is enough to point it out as an instance of the problem
facing anyone who would challenge the conventional wisdom about
Books XI and XII without first challenging the assumptions (about
what is and is not poetic) in the context of which that wisdom
seems inescapable. It will not be enough to produce instances of
'finely etched pictures' (thus countering Eliot's charge of visual
deficiency) or explain away large portions of the verse as irrelevant
to Milton's poetic intention; rather what is required is a redefinition
of the poetic that does not exclude the theological and a redefinition
of the theological that makes points of doctrine available for drama-
tisation. This is in fact exactly what happens in the period 1958–72,
and it happens in part because the argument from psychology – in
which the sweep of Books XI and XII is justified as a backdrop
for Adam's education – will also become the argument from theology, as that education is seen to be specifically religious, tied to
the states of regeneration as Milton describes them in his *On Christian Doctrine*. At the same time this double argument will be extended
to the reader, whose experience will be seen in a relationship of
symmetry and asymmetry to Adam's, and who will, in effect, by
incorporated into the poem as one of its characters. (This strategy
is already implicit in Richardson's observation, on p. 535, that at
the end of Book XII, Adam is brought 'into the Condition in Which
We Are, on *Even Ground* with Us'.)

Looking back, it is tempting to say that the components of this
unified reading are all present, and that Thompson and Rajan fail,
for a variety of reasons, to put them together; but in fact it would
have been impossible for them or for anyone else to put them
together because the intellectual framework, in which they are, in
a sense, already together, did not yet exist. The framework that did
exist rigorously separated poetry and theology, and refused to

extend the drama and tension of art to the lived experience of a reader who might then be moved to this or that decision about his obligations of responsibilities or proper course of action. That kind of reader response was, as Lewis so forcefully insisted, not appropriate to the aesthetic experience in which issues of choice and decision (in the sense of conversion) are encountered not directly but 'in profile'. Indeed, if someone were to have argued, in 1942 or 1947, that the excellence of Books XI and XII inhered in their capacity to provoke a self-examination of a specifically religious kind, he would in effect have been arguing that they weren't poetry.

The doctrine of poetic autonomy is so strong in the period that it rules quite different critical practices with the result that none of the competing schools is in a position to make an effective case for Books XI and XII. Rajan, like Thompson, is a historical critic, a follower of Lewis, although he would like to dissent from Lewis's verdict on the last two books. But even though he is committed to the recovery of a historical perspective (the title of his book is, after all, *'Paradise Lost' and the Seventeenth Century Reader*), his ruling principle is that 'there is nothing we can rely on except the poetry' (p. 36); and that principle prevents him from taking his historical materials seriously, that is, as having any bearing on the question of poetic quality. 'A preoccupation with doctrine,' he declares, 'will not help us.' The relationship between Milton's religious beliefs and his poetry is interesting, but 'I cannot see that it is aesthetically relevant'. It is hardly a surprise, then, when he cannot see that large parts of Books XI and XII are aesthetically relevant and falls to making excuses for them that are more damning than Lewis's censure.

The aesthetic irrelevance of Books XI and XII is even more assured in relation to the other dominant critical practice of the period, the close readings of New Criticism. For the New Critics the autonomy of poetry is at once an article of faith and the basis of a programme. That programme is one of exclusion: it is not simply that historical materials are to be considered only insofar as they further a poetic end; the New Critic (at least in his more doctrinaire moments) is afraid that the poetic end will be obscured if the historical materials receive any sustained consideration whatsoever. This is so because New Criticism defines the poetic end and poetry itself at once universally and narrowly, universally because the qualities that identify poetry are understood not to change over time, narrowly because those qualities are small in number and identical with those recently discovered to reside in the metaphysicals. Listen, for example, to this representative and authoritative statement by Cleanth Brooks:

> Our age rejoices in having recovered Donne; but in doing so we have recovered not just Donne's poetry, but poetry. This is so generally true that for many of us the quality of poetry – as distinguished from that of the more empty rhetorics – is bound up with functional metaphor, with dramatic tension, and with the fusion of thought and emotion – qualities which we associate with the poetry of Donne.[13]

The date is 1951 and the essay's title is 'Milton and the New Criticism.' As an admirer of Milton, Brooks's task is clear. He must rescue the poet from Eliot's praise of him as the builder of 'mazes of sounds' (for in such an account Milton becomes one 'of the more empty rhetorics'), and he must do so by demonstrating that his verse is characterised by functional metaphor, dramatic tension, and the fusion of thought and emotion. For as Brooks himself forthrightly declares in the very next sentence, 'We try to find these qualities . . . in the work of anyone to whom we give the name poet' (p. 3). What is at stake, then, is Milton's very right to be called a poet, and what follows, predictably, is a series of analyses, largely of similes from the early books of *Paradise Lost*, in which the requisite Donnean characteristics are duly discovered. Before the essay concludes, the poet of large and overarching designs (which may or may not falter in the execution) has been replaced by the poet of innumerable local effects, of complex and multiply resonant images, of a richness of texture that is inseparable from a richness of thought.

Brooks's performance is an impressive demonstration of the way in which a strongly held definition of poetry can become a strategy for turning particular poems into verse that has been rendered answerable to the definition. Significantly for our purposes the execution of that strategy does not involve any references to Books XI and XII. Nor is this surprising: if one is engaged in a defence of Milton which requires that his verse, at least in certain respects, be indistinguishable from Donne's, the last place one is going to look for support is a portion of the poem that has always been characterised as a stylistic 'falling off'. Not only does it make good sense for Brooks to ignore Books XI and XII when making his case; given the assumptions within which he works, he can ignore them with impunity. It is a tenet of New Critical theory that the essence of poetry involves a moment of lyric intensity; a long poem, then, is almost a contradiction in terms (and here of course the remarks of Poe are relevant), and one does not expect something the size of *Paradise Lost* to display at all points the qualities that mark it as poetic. Brooks is therefore under no obligation to take account of every moment in the poem because it is no part of his aesthetic to require a uniformity of texture or achievement. The situation is quite different in the case of the literary historian who is committed to finding in *Paradise Lost* the working out of a coherent and sustained design (whether that design be epic, or cosmological, or moral); he has the obligation to account for everything, and if something in the poem does not seem to contribute to the design or appears to be a fault in its execution, it must be explained or explained away. The result is the succession of excuses, rationalisations, and weak justifications that we have seen in the work of Lewis, Thompson, and Rajan, and the larger result is that, however opposed in aims and principles the new and historical critics may be, they are united in their inability to make anything admirable out of Books XI and XII of *Paradise Lost*. The only difference between them is that for the literary historian that inability is a cause for regret; he would like to be able to validate the merit of these books because to do so would be to strengthen his *general* account of Milton. Brooks has no such regrets since his defence of Milton requires only that he adduce a sufficient number of examples of the right kind of verse; and if Books XI and XII do not yield such examples, he will simply pass over them in silence.

It is now 1951 in our story, and if I were given to melodrama, I might say that 'things are looking bad for Books XI and XII of *Paradise Lost*'. The two dominant critical schools are either disinclined or unable to effect their rehabilitation; and if one were to measure the state of the art by James Thorpe's anthology of Milton criticism from four centuries (published in 1950), there would seem to be no reason to believe that there would soon be any change for the better. But in fact, the forces of change are already evident in the very documents that seem to argue against it. First of all, the recharacterisation of Books XI and XII has become a *project*: that is, it is on the list (invisible of course) of those things that need to be done. This was in part the result of Lewis's fortunately unfortunate phrasing – 'untransmuted lump of futurity' is a judgment in search of an argument – and in part the result of a general change in the basic mode of critical practice. The old mode called for two actions: one either first praised the beauties and then pointed out the deficiencies, or first pointed out the deficiencies and then praised the beauties. The assumption underlying the new mode, however, is that everything written by a poet is or should be equally poetic, and a corollary assumption that poets should be given the benefit of the doubt leads to a practice in which the understood task for criticism is to demonstrate that every rift is loaded with ore.

This new practice is nowhere announced as now beginning, but grows up alongside the ever more institutionalised practice of close reading of which it is a logical extension. If we think of close reading as a technique for bringing out the complexity of individual poetic moments, then the question of what to do with long poems can have two possible answers. Following the lead of Poe (whose pronouncements underlie much of New Critical theory), one can decide 'that a long poem does not exist . . . [it] is simply a flat contradiction in terms';[14] it would then be permissible to ignore those portions of a long work that did not seem truly poetic, just as so many critics took to ignoring the last two books of *Paradise Lost*. Or, alternatively, one can 'save' the long poem by regarding it as an extended short poem (a strategy Poe considers, but ironically), but deemphasising the narrative or sequential dimension and concentrating instead on the analysis of innumerable local effects. This is the course taken by New Criticism, which thus commits itself to finding poetic qualities (of tension, paradox, irony) in every corner of a work, however long. It might seem that such a programme runs the danger of turning poems into discontinuous fragments, held together only by the physical ligatures of paper and pages; but fragmentation is avoided by invoking another New Critical principle, the doctrine of organic unity: all the parts of a long poem are unified in their relation to a single theme or vision which informs them and of which they are the (repeated) expression. Consequently, sequence is once again legitimated, not, however, as the generator of meaning (as it is in the logic of narrative) but as a succession of spaces in which the same meaning is endlessly and variously displayed. This is the triumph of the New Critical privileging of the image: the long poem becomes an extended metaphor, a symbolic object whose structure does not so much develop as it exfoliates.

One could put this another way by observing that in extending its particular kind of attention to longer poems, New Critical practice spatialises time. It is thus itself an extension of modernism, of the tendency of modernist aesthetics to conceive of the work of art not as a series of propositions about an exterior reality but as a system of significations regulated by internal laws. The art object so conceived becomes a spatial field or gestalt in which every point is related to every other point, and while it is true that the relations between points can only be apprehended in time, the final and desired apprehension is one in which the temporal medium has been transcended and the network of internal references and cross-references can be grasped in a single moment of unified vision. When that happens, as Joseph Frank points out in 'Spatial Form in Modern Literature', 'past and present are seen spatially, locked in a timeless unity'. In place of the 'objective historical imagination' modern writers put the 'mythical imagination . . . the imagination that sees the actions and events of a particular time merely as the bodying forth of eternal prototypes', and these prototypes, Frank continues, 'are created by transmuting the time-world of history into the timeless world of myth'.[15]

It is finally no accident, I think, that Frank's formulation here is an uncanny prediction of the way in which the lump of *Paradise Lost*, Books XI and XII, will finally be redeemed: that apparently awkward history will, quite literally, be transmuted into the timeless world of myth. I am not suggesting any simple cause-and-effect relationship between Frank's essay, seminal and influential though it was, and the eventually happy fate of Milton's orphaned books. The relationship, while real, is a much more overdetermined one in that Frank is only one of many who are announcing, from a variety of perspectives, a shift from temporal to spatial ways of thinking: his use of the word 'myth' calls to mind another great spatialiser of the period, Northrop Frye, whose labours in *The Anatomy of Criticism* (1957) could also be well (and prophetically) described as a transmutation of the actions and events of a particular time into the timeless world of 'eternal prototypes'. Frye's prototypes are, of course, his archetypes, those large recurring patterns and images that together form an overarching and abiding grid in relation to which particular works (and if someone, not Frye, were so minded, particular lines) can be placed and understood: not understood, however, in their details – that is the work of a criticism devoted to explication – but understood as instances of a structure that makes them possible and intelligible. Frye, like the New Critics, is a formalist and a believer in the autonomy of literature, but for him literature means the general and generating literary structures, and the task of formal description is to get a proper account of them. In order to accomplish that task, as Frye points out, one does not take the 'close look' that defines New Critical practice; rather one 'stands back' so that the outlines of the 'archetypal organization' can come into view.[16] This standing back is obviously ahistorical and leads to the deemphasis on the succession of forms in favour of the enumeration of those forms that repeatedly appear. Nor are those forms exclusively literary, in any narrow sense. Frye is as committed as any New Critic to the study of literature *as* literature, but for him literature is not simply a collection of techniques, but an imaginative ordering, in words, of all the modes of being characteristic of human life. 'Literature neither reflects nor escapes from ordinary life: what it does is reflect the world as human imagination conceives it, in mythical, romantic, heroic and ironic as well as realistic and fantastic terms.'[17]

One effect of Frye's archetypal or mythic vision is to break down the barriers between the literary and other realism, not, however, by diluting or subordinating the literary (the great fear of twentieth-century aesthetics), but by appropriating for it everything that is centrally and essentially human. The same inclusiveness also characterises other 'mythologising' systems that were to become increasingly influential in the 1940s and 1950s: Cassirer's theory of symbolic forms, Jung's theory of archetypes, Freud's theory of the unconscious. These systems are of course very different from one another, but they are alike in their privileging of a primitive or original state in which subject/object and all the other distinctions rationality brings are not in force, and the entities we think of as already distributed in time and space exist together in a moment of simultaneity and primal fluidity, a moment in which the logic of metamorphosis has not yet given way to the logic of discreteness, and, as Cassirer puts it, 'everything may be turned into every-thing'.[18]

It follows that in each of these systems (although in varying degrees), the fall occurs with differentiation, with the dispersal into objectified space and irreversible time of what was once whole and unified; and it further follows that the tendency in these systems to value the 'edenic' or 'prerational' leads to the devaluing of the discursive and the sequential, that is, of narrative. In a passage that refers with approval to Jung and Cassirer, Frye contrasts the 'epiphanic moment, the flash of instantaneous apprehension with no direct reference to times' to the dilution of that moment in the 'forms of proverbs, riddles . . . and folk tales' where 'there already is a considerable element of narrative'.[19] The rhetoric here, as in the writings of the other great spatialisers, is the rhetoric of loss, and what is lost is an immediate and instantaneous apprehension of essence (be it mythic, archetypal, psychic, etc.), an apprehension that has been dulled or obscured by too close an immersion in the effects for which essence is ultimately responsible. For different reasons, the recovery of the instantaneous or epiphanic is associated by many of these same thinkers with the production and experience of poetry, and, more particularly, with poetic or metaphoric language, in which, it is asserted, the constraints and distortions of discursive temporalising language are loosened and, in moments of true vision, undone (one thinks here, for example, of Philip Wheelwright). This is thought to be more true of certain kinds of poetry than of other kinds. Lyric poetry, romance, and epic in the mode of the *Odyssey* or the *Orlando Furioso* are more likely to embody and induce the vision of wholeness than are the realistic novel, the political satire, or the more plot-centred epic mode of the *Aeneid* or *Jerusalem Delivered*; but of course it is always possible to reverse this judgment (sometimes made only implicitly or by acts of omission) by arguing that works that appear to be structured along lines of sequence and plot are in fact works in which those lines are repeatedly broken and blurred, so that attention is continually called to a timeless realm of underlying and constitutive truths (or archetypes, or myths).

Just such an argument was being made, in small and large ways, for *Paradise Lost* in the late 1950s. In 1958, both Geoffrey Hartman and Kingsley Widmer published essays in *English Literary History* that illustrate the way in which the technique of close reading was contributing to the spatialisation of Milton's epic. Hartman's 'Milton's Counterplot', a classic piece that has often been anthologised, anticipates in its brief compass much of the work that will be done in the next decade. In his argument the counterplot of *Paradise Lost* is found in those places where the apparent urgency of superficially dramatic moments (usually with Satan at their centre) is undercut by references to God's 'divine imperturbability' and his 'omnipotent knowledge that the creation will outlive death and sin'.[20] This counterplot, while expressed only in an 'indirect manner', is everywhere present: 'The root-feeling . . . for imperturbable Providence radiates from many levels of the text.' Hartman chooses in this essay to operate at the level of the simile, and he demonstrates, in a series of brilliant analyses, how at the centre of a Miltonic simile the restless activity of the diabolic host is often viewed from a vantage point of 'aesthetic distance' (p. 391), of 'a calm and cold radiance' (p. 390). The result is that 'a simile intended to sharpen our view of the innumerable stunned host of hell, just as it is about to be roused by Satan, at the same time sharpens our sense of the imperturbable order of the creation . . . and of the survival of man through Providence and his safe-shored will' (p. 391).

The counterplot, then, is a device or machine for arresting the forward action of narrative and directing us (insofar as it is possible) to God's 'Prospect high/Wherein past, present, future he beholds' (III, 77–8). The imperturbability of God's heavenly Prospect (like many of Milton's heroes, he sits) is contrasted to the busy restlessness of Satanic activity, and if one takes this contrast seriously, as criticism now begins to do, the very concept of action is redefined away from gestures of visible movement and toward the maintenance of a still, calm centre. Obviously, such a redefinition is an important part of the general effort to devalue plot and sequence in what had always been thought of a heroic poem, that is, a poem that celebrates heroics. It is a redefinition to which Widmer contributes in his essay 'The Iconography of Renunciation: The Miltonic Simile'.[21] What is being renounced in the similes and elsewhere, according to Widmer, is 'the flux . . . of worldly activity', which is, he asserts, essential evil, and in its place Milton elevates the 'unchanging and absolute good' of the divine. In the poems this new heroism is represented not by movement and energy but by 'the immutable Lord, the untemptable Christ, the renunciatory Samson, the poetic mind fixed only on a single revelation' (p. 84). Widmer's discussion traverses much of the same territory as Hartman's and yields a similar account of ironic reversals, double perspectives, and subversions of narrative progress. In the end, the entire poem, apparently so full of detail and dramatic gesture, has been transformed by Widmer into a 'fascinating and shocking master simile: the world as evil and virtue as renunciation' (p. 86).

This master simile is 'shocking' because it would seem to run counter to the then orthodox view of Milton as a Christian humanist, with the emphasis on the 'humanist', that is, 'upon the positive values of classical learning, religious and ethical moderation, and general reasonableness'. Widmer's Milton, on the other hand, is 'absolutist' (p. 75), unyielding, and dismissive of 'the texture of reality and plentitudinous human actuality' (p. 86). This is a noteworthy point because it is an early indication of another of the changes that will eventually lead to the rehabilitation of Books XI and XII. To the extent that Milton is thought of as holding *moderate* religious views – views that coexist harmoniously with the claims of humanism – it will be easy to regard Books XI and XII as a regrettable and uncharacteristic instance of immoderation in which human values are insufficiently acknowledged. ('The Author has been so attentive to his Divinity, that he has neglected his Poetry.') But once Milton's religious temper is recharacterised in the direction suggested by Widmer, the doctrinal emphasis of Books XI and XII will seem legitimate and central. This is precisely what will happen in the 1960s and 1970s, but it hasn't happened yet in 1959, although the way is being prepared by the spatialisation of the poem, which involves, as we have seen, a change from the celebration of infinite variety (regarded by earlier critics as one of Milton's glories) to a celebration of a single monolithic vision.

An important document in this change is Isabel MacCaffrey's *'Paradise Lost' as Myth*.[22] Published in 1959, MacCaffrey's book is the first self-conscious attempt to turn *Paradise Lost* into the kind of spatial object increasingly admired by modernist critics and readers. As myth, *Paradise Lost* records a prehistoric event from which all later realities are descended, 'and, therefore, the reality of occurrences in time . . . no longer *depends* on their recurrent manifestations; rather, their existence is made to depend on the prior reality of a metaphysical condition that is their cause' (pp. 15–16). It is Milton's achievement, MacCaffrey declares, 'to allow us temporarily to share a manner of seeing that will capture accurately the outlines of a peculiar kind of reality', and he does this by inventing 'a series of techniques profoundly original . . . and among them a style reverberatory . . . and a "spatial" structural pattern of interlocking, mutually dependent parts' (pp. 42–3). Consequently, MacCaffrey continues:

The 'normal' straightforward narrative patterns traditional to story-tellers will be inappropriate; suspense will be replaced by the tacit comment of interconnecting . . . threads. The mythical narrative slights chronology in favor of a folded structure which continually returns upon itself, or a spiral that circles about a single center; in this it reproduces the very shape of the myth itself which is circularly designed for resonance and cross-reference.

It follows that a poem constructed along these principles will not display a developing meaning – a meaning that is being processed by the events of a narrative – but will rather represent, again and again, a meaning that is as present in the first line as it is in the last. In *Paradise Lost*, 'meanings are deepened or heightened, but their direction and configuration [are] not essentially changed' (p. 51).

One can draw a direct line from this view of the poem to the eventual 'upgrading' of Books XI and XII, if only because the various rationales for leaving those books in the interpretive limbo they had come to occupy now become unavailable: one can no longer say, for example, that the poem is for all intents and purposes over at the end of Book X, and that, except for the last hundred lines or so, Books XI and XII are superfluous. One can no longer say that because as a judgment it is intelligible only within a strongly temporal reading, a reading in relation to which one asks of a line or a passage or a book, 'In what ways does it contribute

to the plot?' or 'What is its relevance to the poem's developing
meaning?' or (in a somewhat older tradition) 'How well does it
conform to a conventional epic practice?' (the visit to the under-
world, the catalogue of ships, the revelation to a hero of his future
history). These questions assume the independence from one
another of poetic 'components' as they are arranged along a
sequence, and within that assumption it makes sense to interrogate
those components separately and to pronounce one of them successful or unsuccessful. (And in some cases this pronouncement will be
made with reference to models *external* to the poem, to stylistic
models or to the model of 'the epic'.) But within the assumption of
a spatial or mythic poem of the sort MacCaffrey believes *Paradise
Lost* to be, there are no separable components, since every coordi-
nate of the spatial object displays the same significances and reson-
ances. One must therefore ask a new question: In what ways does
the line or passage or book realise the poem's single and all-pervasive vision? And that question will also be a programme: that is, to
ask it is to have assumed the shape of its answer, a shape in which
one portion of the text will be shown to have exactly the same
properties as every other portion. It is therefore not at all surprising
to find MacCaffrey asserting that the major and archetypal images
of Books I and II 'are continued into history in the final books of
Paradise Lost' (p. 175). Her reading of these books consists of finding
in every instance that a detail or an action is a version of something
we have seen innumerable times before: 'Each of the elements has
its mythical prototype in the books that have gone before, and the
evil fortune of the Egyptians is shown manifestly to be a product
of the same self-destructive power that brought the fallen angels to
their ill mansion' (pp. 176–7). The argument in short is that Books
XI and XII are just like Books I and II, and the significance of
the argument for the story I am telling can be seen in the fact that,
traditionally, one of the reasons for dismissing Books XI and XII
is that they weren't like Books I and II at all. (Later the argument
will go in the other direction, i.e., of making I and II, and all the
rest, just like the newly characterised XI and XII.)

By 1959, then, not only is the rehabilitation of Books XI and
XII a recognised and official project, it is a project of a very specific
kind; and the fact that it is now that kind of project means that
many of the obstacles to its success have already been removed,
although no one in particular has set out to remove them. Those
obstacles were contained, you will recall, in the charges usually
made against the books: they are insufficiently poetic; they do
not contribute to the unfolding of the plot; they are inert and

undramatic. The charge of poetic insufficiency has been answered by a shift in the mode of characterising the poetic texture: no longer does one look at isolated lines and passages and test them for the requisite qualities; rather, one notes the relationship between any local detail and a host of other details, all of which combine to form a single resonance. As MacCaffrey puts it, 'Not the thickness of individual denotation, but the density of endless implication, weights Milton's images' (p. 177). The charge of structural irrelevance has been answered by a reconceiving of the structure, which is no longer a succession of actions that follow one another in time, but a sustained projection of a single overriding and omnipresent master-meaning; and the charge that these books are undramatic is in the process of being answered by a redefinition of action, away from the theatrical and visible response to the pressure of occasions and toward the interior maintenance of a single unswerving position.

It is precisely at this moment that defences of Books XI and XII begin to appear all over the world – fortuitously, as far as we can tell from Waddington's account, but inevitably given the historical account I am here attempting. But this is also the moment of my having run out of time, barely into the middle of my story, and I can only tantalise you with a list of the coming attractions. They include:

1. The appearance as an interpretive strategy of *typology*, the perfect hermeneutic tool for the completion of the process begun by Frye and others.
2. The entry into the profession in increasing numbers of Jews and other minorities for whom the patterns of Christian thought are potentially as aesthetic as any other patterns.
3. The gradual weakening of the ideal of disinterested inquiry for which the Second World War was fought, and its replacement by an ethic of commitment in relation to which moderation and tolerance are bad words.
4. The transformation of Milton from a poet of democratic liberalism to a prophet of revolutionary absolutism.
5. The elaboration of a rhetoric of silence in which the best style is no style at all and heroes speak most forcefully when they refuse to say anything.

All of this and more I pledge you as a promissory note, but I should remind you once again of the project in whose service this evidence will be marshalled. It is an attempt to take the history of literary criticism seriously by demonstrating that the questions one can ask and therefore the answers one can receive, and therefore the details one can see and the accounts one can give, are the functions of conditions prevailing in the profession. The history of literary criticism, in short, is not a history of inexplicable successes and failures but a history of the categories of understanding that in each generation make available the objects of our attention. In place of Waddington's assumption that the complexity of Books XI and XII was there all the while for those with eyes clear enough to see, I would substitute the story of how that complexity – now as obvious and indisputable as Waddington says it is – came to be put there by the labours of men and women like you and me.

Notes

1. Raymond B. Waddington, 'The Death of Adam: Vision and Voice in Books XI and XII of *Paradise Lost*,' *Modern Philology*, 70 (1972): 9–21.

2. *Milton's Poetry: Its Development in Time* (Pittsburgh, Penn., 1972).

3. Quoted in John Shawcross, ed., *Milton: The Critical Heritage* (London, 1970), p. 216.

4. Quoted in C. A. Patrides, ed., *Milton's Epic Poetry* (Baltimore, Md., 1967); from F. R. Leavis, *Revaluation: Tradition and Development in English Poetry* (London, 1936), pp. 42–58; first published in *Scrutiny*, 2 (1933).

5. Douglas Bush, *'Paradise Lost' in Our Time* (Ithaca, N.Y., 1945), p. 8.

6. B. A. Wright, *Milton's 'Paradise Lost'* (New York, 1962).

7. K. L. Sharma, *Milton Criticism in the Twentieth Century* (New Delhi, 1971), p. 6.

8. C. S. Lewis, *A Preface to 'Paradise Lost'* (London, 1942), p. 130.

9. Sir Walter Raleigh, *Milton* (London, 1900).

10. E. N. S. Thompson, 'For *Paradise Lost*, XI-XII,' *Philological Quarterly*, 22 (1943): 376–82.

11. Jonathan Richardson, *Explanatory Notes and Remarks on Milton's 'Paradise Lost'* (London, 1734), p. 484.

12. B. A. Rajan, *'Paradise Lost' and the Seventeenth Century Reader* (London, 1947), p. 79.

13. 'Milton and the New Criticism,' *Sewanee Review*, 59 (1951): 3.

14. *The Portable Poe*, ed. Philip Van Doren Stern (New York, 1945), p. 568.

15. Joseph Frank, 'Spatial Form in Modern Literature,' in Mark Schorer, Josephine Miles, and Gordon McKenzie, eds, *Criticism: The Foundations of Modern Literary Judgment* (New York, 1948), pp. 379–92; first published in *Sewanee Review*, 53 (1945).

16. Northrop Frye, *Anatomy of Criticism* (Princeton, N.J., 1957), p. 140.

17. Northrop Frye, *The Well-Tempered Critic* (New York, 1963), p. 155.

18. 'The Archetypes of Literature,' in David Lodge, ed., *Twentieth Century Literary Criticism* (London, 1972), p. 429; first published in *Kenyon Review* 13 (1951).

20. 'Milton's Counterplot,' in Arthur E. Barker, ed., *Milton: Modern Essays in Criticism* (Oxford, 1965), p. 388; first published in *English Literary History*, 25 (1958).

21. 'The Iconography of Renunciation: The Miltonic Simile,' in *Critical Essays on Milton from ELH* (Baltimore, Md., 1969); first published in *English Literary History*, 25 (1958).

22. *'Paradise Lost' as Myth* (Cambridge, Mass., 1959).

4   POST-STRUCTURALISM

Post-structuralism has had a major impact on literary criticism, particularly in America. One of the main reasons for this was the influence of Jacques Derrida's writings on a group of critics based at Yale who became known as the 'Yale School' despite important differences between them. Some have argued that Derrida's work has been 'domesticated' by such critics in their efforts to adapt Derridean deconstruction to an American literary critical situation. It has been suggested, for example, that critics have tended to ignore the philosophical roots of Derrida's thinking and have adapted his ideas too freely in order to reconcile them with literary critical interests.

Derridean deconstruction emerged out of a critique of structuralism. Whereas Saussurean linguistics and the semiology derived from it emphasised the synchronic – the play of differences that define any system seen as existing at one point in time – at the expense of the diachronic or the changes that take place in any signifying system over time, Derrida questioned this synchronic model on the grounds that it assumes the existence of a centre which holds the structure together, a centre which is itself outside structurality. Derrida argues, in opposition to Saussure, that writing is the best model for understanding how language, and by implication any signifying system, works, since writing does not abolish the temporal dimension. Writing carries with it its past in terms of the meanings words had in previous contexts which can never be entirely banished, and it will continue to signify in an unlimited number of future contexts. Though writing cannot escape semiotics or being part of a system, the system itself can never achieve total stability.

Another reason for Derrida's influence was that, though a philosopher, he analysed texts in a manner similar to that of literary critics, especially critics such as those in the New Critical tradition who specialised in close textual analysis. But whereas the New Critics attempted to demonstrate that literary texts were finally unified even if that unity incorporated irony or apparent contradiction, Derrida deconstructed such unity by showing that, in a text by Rousseau, for example, elements that Rousseau wished to marginalise could nevertheless be interpreted as occupying the centre so that textual unity was destabilised. Paul de Man, however, the leading figure among the Yale critics, created a kind of reconciliation between Derrida and the New Criticism by reinterpreting an essay by Derrida on Rousseau in such a way as to suggest that Derrida's deconstruction of Rousseau had been performed by the text itself. Deconstruction, therefore, could be seen as incorporated within the literary text.

De Man's revision of Derrida has been a major influence on the criticism of J. Hillis Miller, probably the leading practitioner of deconstructionist criticism in America. Though best known as an interpreter of literary texts Hillis Miller has also written several theoretical essays, and in one of these he formulated a definition of deconstruction that sums up the approach of the Yale School of deconstruction:

> Deconstruction as a mode of interpretation works by a careful and circumspect entering of each textual labyrinth . . . The deconstructive critic seeks to find . . . the element in the system studied which is alogical, the thread in the text in question which will unravel it all, or the loose stone which will pull down the whole building.

For Miller the critic is a collaborator in the deconstructive process rather than merely a commentator who stands apart from the text:

> The critic cannot by any means get outside the text, escape from the blind alleys of language he finds in the work. He can only rephrase them in other, allotropic terms . . . The activity of deconstruction already performed and then hidden in the work must be performed again in criticism.[1]

This deconstructive approach is exemplified in the essay on Hardy's poem, 'The Torn Letter', reprinted here.

The kind of deconstructive criticism associated with de Man and Miller is not the only form of post-structuralist criticism practised in America. Some critics believe that the Yale School of criticism is apolitical and believe that deconstruction can be aligned with radical politics. Gayatri Chakrovorty Spivak, who translated Derrida's *Of Grammatology*, is one of the most prominent of such critics. Though she teaches in America, Spivak comes originally from India and believes that deconstruction is a tool that can be used to effect political change. As a non-white radical feminist with Marxist sympathies, her approach to deconstruction is thus very different from that of Yale school deconstructionists like Miller and de Man, as can be seen in her introduction to 'Draupadi', a short story by Mahasweta Devi, which she also translates from the Bengali.

Spivak's form of deconstructive criticism has a good deal in common with British post-structuralist criticism, though Derrida has been less influential with British critics than Foucault, Lacan, and the later Barthes, who along with Derrida are associated with the shift from structuralism to post-structuralism. Whereas a critic like Miller sees the text as collaborating with the deconstructive process, British post-structuralists tend to follow the model of Barthes in a work such as *S/Z* which accords the literary text much less respect. Thus novels in the realist tradition are accused by British post-structuralists of being 'classic realist texts', that is, works which inauthentically seek to establish a one-to-one relation between the language of the novel and the world.

Catherine Belsey is one of the leading British post-structuralists. Her criticism brings together a variety of theories: Althusserian Marxism, radical feminism, Foucauldian discourse theory, Lacanian psychoanalysis, elements of Derrida. She is particularly concerned with how the subject is constructed by ideology. Lacan's importance for her is that he used linguistic theory which stressed the primacy of language over the subject to decentre individual consciousness since the subject is constructed in language. Language and discourse are intrinsic to Lacan's 'symbolic order' which in turn creates ideology into which individuals are 'interpellated', that is, 'they "willingly" adopt the subject-positions necessary to their participation in the social formation'. Unconscious desire, however, enters into conflict with such interpellation so that the subject is the site of contradiction. In literary texts one sees language at its most persuasive, therefore it is one of the most powerful means of constructing the subject and promoting interpellation.

The role of criticism is to challenge this process: 'certain critical modes could be seen to challenge these concepts, and to call in question the particular complex of imaginary relations between individuals and the real conditions of their existence which helps to reproduce the present relations of class, race and gender'. A literary text, like the subject itself, is the site of contradiction: 'In its absences, in the collisions between its divergent meanings, the text implicitly criticizes its own ideology; it contains within itself the critique of its own values, in the sense that it is available for a new process of production of meaning by the reader.'[2] In the essay reprinted here, Belsey applies this critical approach to Milton's shorter poetry.

Lacan is only one element in British post-structuralism. A feature of modern criticism has been the emergence of a thoroughgoing psychoanalytic criticsm in which Freudian and Lacanian theory are accorded the central role. Shoshana Felman is a critic who has strong links with the Yale School of deconstruction, but her criticism has developed in a more Lacanian direction. The value of Lacan for her is that he 'embodies . . . a revolutionized interpretive stance and . . . a revolutionary theory of reading'. She claims that Lacan goes beyond the view that psychoanalysis is an interpretation of 'the excess in the patient's discourse':

Lacan's view is more radical than that. For the activity of reading is not just the analyst's, it is also the analysand's: interpreting is what takes place *on both sides* of the analytic situation . . . The unconscious . . . is not simply *that which must be read* but also, and perhaps primarily, *that which reads*. The unconscious is a reader. What this implies most radically is that whoever reads, interprets out of his unconscious, is an analysand, even when the interpreting is done from the position of the analyst.

In her essay on Poe she is concerned with 'the crucial question of the use-value of psychoanalysis'.[3] One cannot simply 'apply Freud or Lacan to a literary text, since for Lacan the ego of the psychoanalyst (or literary critic) is not a stable reference point. Thus psychoanalytic knowledge is not the discovery of something objective in the text but a process that is entered into with it in which psychoanalysis itself is threatened with being lost and has always to be recovered.

Notes

1. J. Hillis Miller, 'Stevens' Rock and Criticism as Cure, II', *Georgia Review*, 30 (1976), pp. 341, 331.
2. Catherine Belsey, 'Constructing the Subject: Deconstructing the Text', in *Feminist Criticism and Social Change*, eds Judith Newton and Deborah Rosenfelt (New York, 1985), pp. 49, 51, 57.
3. Shoshana Felman, *Jacques Lacan and the Adventure of Insight: Psychoanalysis in Contemporary Culture* (Cambridge, Mass., 1987), pp. 21-2, 10.

Further Reading

Catherine Belsey, *The Subject of Tragedy: Identity and Difference in Renaissance Drama* (London and New York, 1985).
Paul de Man, *Allegories of Reading: Figural Languages in Rousseau, Nietzsche, Rilke, and Proust* (New Haven, Conn., 1979).
Colin MacCabe, *James Joyce and the Revolution of the Word* (London, 1978).

Shoshana Felman, *Writing and Madness: (Philosophy/Psychoanalysis/Literature)* (Ithaca and London, 1985).

J. Hillis Miller, *Victorian Subjects* (Hemel Hempstead, 1990).

J. Hillis Miller: Thomas Hardy, Jacques Derrida, and the 'Dislocation of Souls'

My focus is a poem by Thomas Hardy, 'The Torn Letter'. As a way into this admirable poem, a passage from Kafka's *Letters to Milena* and a recent essay by Jacques Derrida will provide a line of communication. First Kafka:

The easy possibility of letter-writing must – seen merely theoretically – have brought into the world a terrible dislocation [*Zerrüttung*] of souls. It is, in fact, an intercourse with ghosts, and not only with the ghost of the recipient but also with one's own ghost which develops between the lines of the letter one is writing and even more so in a series of letters where one letter corroborates the other and can refer to it as a witness. How on earth did anyone get the idea that people can communicate with one another by letter! Of a distant person one can think, and of a person who is near one can catch hold – all else goes beyond human strength. Writing letters, however, means to denude oneself before the ghosts, something for which they greedily wait. Written kisses don't reach their destination, rather they are drunk on the way by the ghosts. It is on this ample nourishment that they multiply so enormously . . . The ghosts won't starve, but we will perish.[1]

Thinking and holding are here opposed to writing. The former belongs to 'the real world' of persons, bodies, and minds, of distance and proximity. If a person is near, one can touch him, hold him, kiss him (or her). If a person is distant one can think of that person. Such thinking relates one real 'soul' to another. It is as genuine a 'means of communication' as touch. The souls or selves pre-exist the thinking that joins then, as much as two bodies pre-exist their kiss. Writing is another matter. Nothing is easier than writing – a letter, for example. The writing of a poem, a story, a novel, is no more than an extension of the terrible power of dislocation involved in the simplest 'gesture' of writing a note to a friend. The dislocation is precisely a 'dislocation of souls'. Writing is a dislocation in the sense that it moves the soul itself of the writer, as well as of the

Reprinted from *Taking Chances: Derrida, Psychoanlysis, and Literature*, eds William Kerrigan and Joseph H. Smith (Baltimore, 1984), pp. 135–45.

recipient, beyond or outside of itself, over there, somewhere else. Far from being a form of communication, the writing of a letter dispossesses both the writer and the receiver of themselves. Writing creates a new phantom written self and a phantom receiver of that writing. There is correspondence all right, but it is between two entirely phantasmagorial or fantastic persons, ghosts raised by the hand that writes. Writing calls phantoms into being, just as the ghosts of the dead appear to Odysseus, to Aeneas, or to Hardy in his poem 'In Front of the Landscape'. In this case, however, the ghosts are also of the witnesses of those ghosts. The writer raises his own phantom and that of his correspondence. Kafka's ghosts, in his 'commerce with phantoms', drink not blood but written kisses. They flourish and multiply on such food, while the one who writes the kisses and the correspondent they do not reach die of hunger, eaten up by the very act through which they attempt to nourish one another at a distance.

Now Derrida: Some remarkable paragraphs in 'Télépathie' (1981) seem almost to have been written with 'second sight', that is, with prophetic foreknowledge that I would need to cite them here to support my reading of Hardy. In this essay Derrida speculates on the performative power a letter (in the epistolary sense) may have in order to bring into existence an appropriate recipient. If a letter happens to fall into my hands I may become the person that letter needs as its receiver, even though that new self is discontinous with the self I have been up till now. Derrida's argument is peripherally attached as an appendage to his polemic, in 'Le facteur de la vérité' (in *La carte postale*, 1980), against Jacques Lacan's idea that a letter always reaches its destination. For Derrida, in 'Télépathie', a letter reaches its destination all right, but not because the proper recipient, the self to which the letter corresponds, is waiting there for it, already in full-formed existence as a self. No, the letter creates the self appropriate to itself. It creates it by performing (in the strict Austinian sense of performative [see Austin, 1967], though with a twist) the utmost violence on the already existing self of the hapless person who accidentally reads the letter. The 'twist' lies in the fact that the performative power of the letter is not foreseen or intended. This is contrary to the strict concept of a performative utterance as defined by Austin, but it may be that Austin, here as in other aspects of his theory, was unsuccessfully attempting to limit the terrible and always to some degree unpredictable power of a performative utterance:

Why, [asks Derrida] do the theoreticians of the performative or of the pragmatic interest themselves so little, to my knowledge, in the effects of written things, notably in letters? What do they fear? If there is something performative in the letter, how is it that a letter can produce all sorts of these ends, foreseeable and unforeseeable, and in fact even produce its recipient? All of this, to be sure, according to a properly performative causality, if there is such a thing, and which is purely performative, not at all according to another sequence extrinsic to the act of writing. I admit that I do not fully know what I want to say by that; the unforeseen should not be able to be part of the performative structure in the strict sense, and yet . . . ['Télepathie,' p. 9; my translation]

As an example of this strange coercive and yet unpredictable power of the written word, Derrida has suggested on the previous page that someone might determine his whole life according to the 'programme' of a letter or of a postcard that he accidentally intercepts, a missive not even intended for him. The recipient becomes the self the letter invites him to be (but there is no 'him' before he receives the letter), just as poor Boldwood, in Thomas Hardy's novel *Far from the Madding Crowd*, becomes the bold lover Bathsheba's valentine seems to tell him he is:

I do not [says Derrida] make the hypothesis of a letter which would be the external occasion, in some way, of an encounter between two identifiable subjects – and which would be already determined. No, rather of a letter which after the fact seems to have been projected toward some unknown recipient at the moment it was written, predestined receiver unknown to himself or to herself, if that can be said, and who determines himself or herself, as you know so well how to do, on receipt of the letter; this is therefore an entirely different thing from the transfer of a message. Its content and its end no longer precede it. Here it is then: you identify yourself and you engage your life according to the programme of the letter, or perhaps better still of a postcard, a letter open, divisible, at once transparent and encrypted . . . Then you say: it is I, uniquely I who can receive this letter, not that it is meant especially for me, on the contrary, but I receive as a present the happenstance to which this card exposes itself. It chooses me. And I choose that it should choose me by chance, I wish to cross its trajectory, I wish to encounter myself there, I am able to do it and I wish to do it – its transit or its transfer. In short, by a gentle and yet terrifying choice you say: 'It was I.' . . . Others would conclude: a letter thus *finds* its recipient, he or she. No, one cannot say of the recipient that he exists before the letter. ['Télépathie,' pp. 7–8; my translation]

It almost seems, as I have said, that these sentences were written with a kind of retrospective prevision of their appropriateness as a commentary on Hardy's 'The Torn Letter', or as if 'The Torn Letter' had been written with foresight of Jacques Derrida's meditations on 9 July, 1979, though so far as I know Derrida had not then and has not yet read Hardy's poem. Even so, Hardy's poem, which is a 'letter' in the first person written to an unnamed 'you,' has found its proper recipient at last in the unwitting Derrida. Derrida has become its reader without even knowing it. He has been programmed by the poem to write an interpretation of it before, beside, or after the letter, so to speak, in displacement from any conscious encounter with it. He has become the person the poem-letter invites him to be, in a confirmation of his theories of which he is unaware.

Here is Hardy's poem:

The Torn Letter

I

I tore your letter into strips
  No bigger than the airy feathers
  That ducks preen out in changing weathers
Upon the shifting ripple-tips.

II

In darkness on my bed alone
  I seemed to see you in a vision,
  And hear you say: 'Why this derision
Of one drawn to you, though unknown?'

III

Yes, eve's quick need has run its course,
  The night had cooled my hasty madness;
  I suffered a regretful sadness
Which deepened into real remorse.

IV

I thought what pensive patient days
  A soul must know of grain so tender,
  How much of good must grace the sender
Of such sweet words in such brighter phrase.

V

Uprising then, as things unpriced
  I sought each fragment, patched and mended;
  The midnight whitened ere I had ended
And gathered words I had sacrificed.

VI

But some, alas, of those I threw
  Were past my search, destroyed for ever;

> They were your name and place; and never
> Did I regain those clues to you.

> VII
> I learnt I had missed, by rash unheed,
>   My track; that, so the Will decided,
>   In life, death, we should be divided,
> And at the sense I ached indeed.

> VIII
> That ache for you, born long ago,
>   Throbs on: I never could outgrow it.
>   What a revenge, did you but know it!
> But that, thank God, you do not know.

> [Hardy, 1976, pp. 313–14]

'The Torn Letter' contains several characteristic Hardyan ironic turns away from the straightforward notion that a letter may have a performative power to determine the self of its recipient. Derrida has the general idea of the letter-poem from Thomas Hardy right, but the message seems to have got garbled or overlaid with static and interference on the way. Some parts are twisted a bit or missing entirely, perhaps because somewhere along the line they have been switched or translated from Hardy's pungent and acerb English into Derrida's idiomatic French. In the latter, for example, the recipient of a letter is called its 'destinataire', with suggestions that the receiver is predestined, a latent fatality or doomed end point of the message. These overtones are missing in the equivalent English words, such as those I have used in my translation of 'Derrida's' ideas back into English.

'The Torn Letter' is spoken or written by someone who has received a letter from an unknown admirer, apparently a woman. Before concluding that the speaker-writer is 'Hardy' it must be remembered that Hardy claims most of his poems are 'personative', spoken or written by imaginary personages. The poem is addressed to the sender of the letter, but, paradoxically, the poem is posited on the assumption that she will never receive his message and therefore cannot learn how much her letter had made him suffer: 'But that, thank God, you do not know.' If the poem is thought of as spoken or perhaps as silently thought, then the woman will indeed never know. In fact it is written down (or how else could we be reading it?). The poem itself, in its physical existence, contradicts its own affirmation. It is always possible, perhaps even inevitable, that the poem will fall into the woman's hands and tell her what he says he thanks God she cannot know. If her 'revenge' on him for destroying her letter is the permanent ache of a remorse for not having kept it and answered it, his revenge on her is to let her know this in the act of saying she does not and cannot know. The poem is a version of that sort of mind-twisting locution, discussed elsewhere by Derrida,[2] which imposes disobedience to its own command: 'Do not read this', or 'Burn this without reading it.'

Ashamed or embarrassed at receiving such a letter from a stranger (though the reader is never told just what she said), the speaker-writer of the poem has turned her letter into strips, tiny unreadable fragments 'No bigger than the airy feathers / That ducks preen out in changing weathers / Upon the shifting ripple-tips.' The 'I' has divided and subdivided the letter until its bits are mere useless objects like moulted feathers. The scraps are no longer able to carry legible words or to communicate any message. The letter has been reduced to detached letters or fragments of words. The fragments are no longer able to form part of a whole and to 'fly', so to speak, in the sense of rising above the matter on which the message is written into the airy freedom of meaning. Unlike Farmer Boldwood, the 'I' here has such a violent resistance to receiving the letter, responding to it, becoming subject to its performative power, turning into the person it would by perlocution make him be, that he tries to destroy the letter and all its latent power. He wants to turn it back into senseless matter. This is a striking example of part at least of what Derrida may mean by the 'divisibility' of the letter. Derrida has in mind a letter's detachment from any single conscious emitting mind or self. He means also a letter's readiness to divide itself indiscriminately at the receiving end and to branch out to exert its power over any number of recipients, 'destinataires'. For Derrida, and for Hardy too, a letter or a poem is divisible, and divided, at its origin, in itself, and at its end. In 'The Torn Letter' the initial emphasis is on its physical divisibility. The letter by no means has the 'organic unity' that used to be attributed to the single text. It can be turned into a thousand tiny pieces.

It will surprise no reader of Hardy to discover that neither this theoretical divisibility, nor the fact that the 'I' turns theory into practice and fragments the letter, inhibits one bit its implacable performative power. To the contrary. The message is somehow distributed throughout the whole 'signifying chain,' like the proper name repeated beneath the text in one of Saussure's 'hypograms'.[3] The message can operate through any fragment of it, as a single cell contains the DNA message for reconstructing the whole organism of which it is a minute part, or as, in one of the more grotesque experiments of modern biology, one worm may learn behaviour from another worm that has been pulverised and fed to the first worm. The genetic code or imprint passes by ingestion.

The 'I' regrets his rash act. His 'regretful sadness' at his 'derision' 'of one drawn to him though unknown' deepens 'into real remorse' as the night wears on. He seems to see the writer of the letter 'in a vision', reproaching him. The letter has invoked this vision. It has raised the ghost or hallucination of the lady. It has operated as a prosopopoeia, a speech to the absent or dead. Or perhaps it would be better to say that the act of tearing the letter to pieces, reducing the letters to dead letters, so to speak, has made it act as a magic invocation, as a man might be haunted by the ghost of the woman he had killed, or as 'Hardy', in another poem, 'In Front of the Landscape', is haunted by the phantoms of those he has betrayed. The poet rises up collects the fragments of the letter, and pieces them together again.

The 'Hardyan twist' is that the speaker cannot find all the pieces of the torn letter. Those lost are the ones with the lady's name and address. The speaker's act, with a reversal of the sexes, is like that of Isis gathering up the fragments of the body of the Osiris she had murdered. In both cases something is missing, the phallus of Osiris in one case, the lady's identification in the other, head source of meaning in both cases. Once again, as in that strange myth, the story Hardy tells is of the dispersal, fragmentation, defacing, deper-sonification, or even unmanning of the self, since in the end the reader of the poem, as I shall argue, becomes not the speaker, receiver of the letter, but the unattainable woman to whom the poem is spoken. The speaker cannot, after all, write back to the lady. He cannot initiate a correspondence and a relationship in which he would, in spite of his initial resistance to doing so, become the self the letter invited him to be:

> I learnt I had missed, by rash unheed,
> My track; that, so the Will decided,
> In life, death, we should be divided,
> And at the sense I ached indeed.

The Will here is of course the Immanent Will, that unconscious energy within what is which, in Hardy's phrase, 'stirs and urges everything'.[4] The Will is Hardy's name for the fact that things happen as they do happen. This volition is will as force, not will as conscious intent. Its 'decisions' are the decisions of fortuity, the fact, for example, that the poet could not find the scraps with the woman's name and address. This means that the track he should have followed, the destiny that waited for him, remains untrodden. The divisibility of the letter means that he must remain divided from the correspondent, by a 'decision' that is another form of division, separating this possibility from that one, this track from that.

'I had missed, by rash unheed, / My track' – the phrasing is odd. On the one hand, the track was truly his. It was fated for him by the Will. The track pre-exists his taking it, and with the track the self appropriate to it also exists. This track is his destiny. How can a man avoid his destiny, even by the 'rash unheed' of not responding to the woman's call? On the other hand, 'the Will decided' that he should not, as punishment for his rash unheed, take the track that was nevertheless destined for him. It is as if he were two separate persons, or two superposed persons, the one who took the track and the one who did not take it, as in Borges's 'The Garden of the Forking Paths'.

Though the divisibility of the letter did not mean that its power could be destroyed, that power was partially inhibited, and so another form of division takes place, the poet's permanent division from the lady. On the other hand, the paradox of the poem, another wry ironic turn, is that by missing his track he only follows it more surely and securely. He becomes more deeply and more permanently marked by the letter just because he has lost the name and address of its sender and so cannot answer it back, follow out the track it lays out. The letter is detached from the real name and self of its sender and liberated to have an anonymous or universal power to make new selves and join them. Again as in Saussure's hypograms, what is 'proper' to the letter is not a proper name and place attached to it on the outside but a power distributed throughout its minutest parts, its letters, a power to bring into existence the phantom selves of both sender and destined receiver. The fact that the letter lacks the proper name and address is just what gives it its power of the dislocation of souls. This might be defined by saying that although the torn and then reconstructed letter operates as an apostrophe or prosopopoeia, the ghost that is invoked is that dislocated new self of the reader of the letter, the self the letter personified into existence, if such a transitive use of the word may be made. It is as though the letter were being written on my mind, inscribed there, thus giving that blank page a personality it did not have.

Had the speaker answered the letter the episode would have run its course, as always happens in Hardy. Warmth, intimacy, love perhaps, would have been followed by coolness, betrayal, the wrenching apart of a final division. For Hardy it is always the case that 'Love lives on propinquity, but dies of contact' (F. E. Hardy, 1965, p. 220). If he had followed the track he would ultimately have gone off the track and ceased forever to be the self the letter commands him to be. As it is the ache remains: 'That ache for you, born long ago, / Throbs on: I never could outgrow it'. For Hardy, the only relation to another person that can last is one that is in some way inhibited, prevented from moving on from propinquity to contact. In this case, the ache remains, like an unhealed and unhealable wound. One part of the 'I' does become and remain the self the letter 'performs' into existence. I say 'one part' because, as Derrida affirms, 'all is not recipient [*destinataire*] in a recipient, a part only which accommodates itself to the rest' ('Télépathie,' pp. 9–10; my translation). For Hardy, as for Derrida, or as for Nietzsche in paragraph 490 of *The Will to Power*[5] the divisibility of the self is not only along the diachronic track, but synchronically, in the moment. At any given time the 'self' is a commonwealth of many citizens. The self is the locus of many different selves dwelling uneasily with one another. Each struggles to dominate the others and to become the sole ruler, the single self within the domain of the self. For the speaker-writer in 'The Torn Letter', one of those selves will remain the self who would have answered the unknown woman's letter.

One more thing must be said of the significance of the missing name and address in 'The Torn Letter'. The fact that he cannot attach the letter to a proper name and to a specific place puts the 'I' of the poem in the same situation as the reader of this or of many other poems by Hardy. The reader is told precious little of the stories at which Hardy's poems hint. He is given a fragment only, usually lacking names, dates, and places. The poem is cut off from what came before and from what came after. It is the bare sketch of an episode. Vital facts are missing that would allow the reader to attach the poem with certainly to Hardy's biography or to actual places on a map of Dorset. Far from reducing the poems' power to haunt their readers, to stick in the mind and lodge there permanently, as an ache or throb the reader can never outgrow, the absence of these specifications multiplies the poems' powers over the reader a hundredfold. The poems produce something like that tantalising sense that there is a proper name one cannot quite remember. This incompletion gives the poems their power to dwell within the reader, like a ghost, or like an unrealised self, or like a parasite within its host. Each of Hardy's poems is an unsolved and unsolvable mystery. It is a track the reader cannot take or reach the end of, and so he remains fascinated by it. One part of the reader, too, becomes, by the law of multiple simultaneous selves, permanently the self the poem performatively creates.

As Derrida observes, it is not necessary for a letter that brings a new self into existence in me to contain detailed instructions about what that self should be. Far from it. The performative power of the letter works best if it remains a sketch, like Hardy's poems. If, as Derrida says, 'you identify yourself and engage your life according to the programme of the letter', it is also the case that 'the programme says nothing, it announces or enunciates nothing at all, not the least content, it does not even present itself as a programme. One cannot even say that it "works" as a programme, in the sense of appearing like one, but without looking like one, it *works*, it programmes' ('Télépathie,' p. 8; my translation). 'The Torn Letter' is a striking confirmation of this. Just because the poem is so bereft of details, like the torn letter itself, it is able to perform its magic on any reader who happenes to read it. It is as if he had accidentially come upon a letter intended for someone else. Reading the poem, I, you, or anyone becomes its addressee, since it has no name or specified destination. Hardy is forced to communicate with his lost correspondent by sending out a general letter to the world and publishing it in a book of poems, just as radio telescopists send out messages beamed into outer space in hopes they may be intercepted by some intelligent beings, somewhere: 'Is anybody there?'

The reader of 'The Torn Letter' becomes not so much, through a familiar kind of negative capability, the self of the speaker-writer of the poem, the 'I' who has received the letter and is haunted by it, as, by a far stranger form of metamorphosis, the 'you' to whom the poem is spoken or written. The reader becomes the woman who has caused the 'I' so much ache. The poem becomes a letter in its turn, a letter missing the name and address of its destined receiver, and so anyone who happens to read it is put in the place of that unnamed receiver and programmed ever after to be, a part of him or her at least, the self that letter-poem calls into being. If letters or postcards perform that fearful dislocation of souls of which Kafka speaks, putting a man beside himself, as it were, drinking his life in the creation of a phantom self and a phantom correspondent for that self, a phantom who intercepts the most passionate of written kisses so that they never reach their destination, works of literature enact a similar dispossession. A poem, too, may dislocate its reader. It may make him someone else somewhere else, perhaps without power ever to go back to himself.

Notes

1. Kafka, *Letters to Milena* (1954), p. 229, translation slightly altered; for the German, see Kafka, *Briefe an Milena* (1952), pp. 259–60.
2. For example, in 'Envois', *La carte postale* (1980)
3. See Starobinski (1971).
4. 'The Convergence of the Twain', *Complete Poems* (1976), p. 307.
5. Nietzsche, *The Will to Power* (1986), pp. 270–1; for the German see Nietzsche, *Werke* (1966), pp. 473–4.

References

Austin, J. L., *How To Do Things with Words* (Cambridge, Mass: Harvard University Press, 1967).

Derrida, J., *La carte postale* (Paris: Flammarion, 1980).

Derrida, J., 'Télépathie', *Furor*, February 1981, pp. 5–41.

Hardy, F. E., *The Life of Thomas Hardy: 1840–1928* (London: Macmillan, 1965).

Hardy, T., *The Complete Poems*, ed. by J. Gibson (London: Macmillan, 1976).

Kafka, F., *Letters to Milena*, ed. W. Hass, trans. T. and J. Stern (New York: Schocken Books, 1954). German edition: *Briefe an Milena*, ed. by W. Hass (New York: Schocken Books, 1952).

Nietzsche, F. W., *The Will to Power*, trans. W. Kaufmann and R. J. Hollingdale (New York: Vintage Books, 1968). German edition: *Werke* vol. 3. ed. K. Schlecta (Munich: Carl Hanser Verlag, 1966).

Starobinski, J., *Les mots sous les mots: Les anagrammes de Ferdinand de Saussure* (Paris Gallimard, 1971).

Gayatri Chakravorty Spivak: 'Draupadi' by Mahasweta Devi

Foreword

I translated this Bengali short story into English as much for the sake of its villain, Senanayak, as for its title character, Draupadi (or Dopdi). Because in Senanayak I find the closest approximation

Reprinted from Gayatri Chakravorty Spivak, *In Other Worlds: Essays in Cultural Politics* (London, 1987), pp. 179–96.

to the First-World scholar in search of the Third World, I shall speak of him first.

On the level of the plot, Senanayak is the army officer who captures and degrades Draupadi. I will not go so far as to suggest that, in practice, the instruments of First-World life and investigation are complicit with such captures and such a degradation.[1] The approximation I notice relates to the author's careful presentation of Senanayak as a pluralist aesthete. In *theory* Senanayak can identify with the enemy. But pluralist aesthetes of the First World are, willy-nilly, participants in the production of an exploitative society. Hence in *practice*, Senanayak must destroy the enemy, the menacing other. He follows the necessities and contingencies of what he sees as his historical moment. There is a convenient colloquial name for that as well: pragmatism. Thus his emotions at Dopdi's capture are mixed; sorrow (theory) and joy (practice). Correspondingly, we grieve for our Third-World sisters; we grieve and rejoice that they must lose themselves and become as much like us as possible in order to be 'free'; we congratulate ourselves on our specialists' knowledge of them. Indeed, like ours, Senanayak's project is interpretive: he looks to decipher Draupadi's song. For both sides of the rift within himself, he finds analogies in Western literature: Hochhuth's *The Deputy*, David Morrell's *First Blood*. He will shed his guilt when the time comes. His self-image for that uncertain future is Prospero.

I have suggested elsewhere that, when we wander out of our own academic and First-World enclosure, we share something like a relationship with Senanayak's doublethink.[2] When we speak for ourselves, we urge with conviction: the personal is also political. For the rest of the world's women, the sense of whose personal micrology is difficult (though not impossible) for us to acquire, we fall back on a colonialist theory of most efficient information retrieval. We will not be able to speak to the women out there if we depend completely on conferences and anthologies by Western-trained informants. As I see their photographs in women's-studies journals or on book jackets – indeed, as I look in the glass – it is Senanayak with his anti-Fascist paperback that I behold. In inextricably mingling historico-political specificity with the sexual differential in a literary discourse, Mahasweta Devi invites us to begin effacing that image.

My approach to the story has been influenced by 'deconstructive practice'. I clearly share an unease that would declare avant-garde theories of interpretation too elitist to cope with revolutionary feminist material. How, then, has the practice of deconstruction been helpful in this context?

The aspect of deconstructive practice that is best known in the United States is its tendency toward infinite regression.[3] The aspect that interests me most is, however, the recognition, within deconstructive practice, of provisional and intractable starting points in any investigative effort; its disclosure of complicities where a will to knowledge would create oppositions; its insistence that in disclosing complicities the critic-as-subject is herself complicit with the object of her critique; its emphasis upon 'history' and upon the ethicopolitical as the 'trace' of that complicity – the proof that we do not inhabit a clearly defined critical space free of such traces; and, finally, the acknowledgment that its own discourse can never be adequate to its example.[4] This is clearly not the place to elaborate each item upon this list. I should, however, point out that in my introductory paragraphs I have already situated the figure of Senanayak in terms of our own patterns of complicity. In what follows, the relationship between the tribal and classical characters of Draupadi, the status of Draupadi at the end of the story, and the reading of Senanayak's proper name might be seen as produced by the reading practice I have described. The complicity of law and transgression and the class deconstruction of the 'gentlemen revolutionaries', although seemingly minor points in the interpretation of the story as such, take on greater importance in a political context.

I cannot take this discussion of deconstruction far enough to show how Dopdi's song, incomprehensible yet trivial (it is in fact about beans of different colours), and ex-orbitant to the story, marks the place of that other that can be neither excluded nor recuperated.[5]

'Draupadi' first appeared in *Agnigarbha* ('Womb of Fire'), a collection of loosely connected, short political narratives. As Mahasweta points out in her introduction to the collection, 'Life is not mathematics and the human being is not made for the sake of politics. I want a change in the present social system and do not believe in mere party politics.'[6]

Mahasweta is a middle-class Bengali leftist intellectual in her fifties. She has a master's degree in English from Shantiniketan, the famous experimental university established by the bourgeois poet Rabindranath Tagore. Her reputation as a novelist was already well established when, in the late 1970s, she published *Hajar Churashir Ma* ('No. 1084's Mother'). This novel, the only one to be imminently published in English translation, remains within the excessively sentimental idiom of the Bengali novel of the last twenty-odd years.[7] Yet in *Aranyer Adhikar* ('The Rights [or, Occupation] of the Forest'), a serially published novel she was writing almost at the same time, a significant change is noticeable. It is a meticulously researched historical novel about the Munda Insurrection of 1899–1900. Here Mahasweta begins putting together a prose that is a collage of literary Bengali, street Bengali, bureaucratic Bengali, tribal Bengali, and the languages of the tribals.

Since the Bengali script is illegible except to the approximately 25 per cent literate of the about 90 million speakers of Bengali, a large number of whom live in Bangladesh rather than in West Bengali, one cannot speak of the 'Indian' reception of Mahasweta's work but only of its Bengali reception.[8] Briefly, that reception can be described as a general recognition of excellence; scepticism regarding the content on the part of the bourgeois readership; some accusations of extremism from the electoral Left; and admiration and a sense of solidarity on the part of the nonelectoral Left. Any extended reception study would consider that West Bengali has had a Left-Front government of the united electoral Communist parties since 1967. Here suffice it to say that Mahasweta is certainly one of the most important writers writing in India today.

Any sense of Bengal as a 'nation' is governed by the putative identity of the Bengali language.[9] (Meanwhile, Bengalis dispute if the purest Bengali is that of Nabadwip or South Calcutta, and many of the twenty-odd developed dialects are incomprehensible to the 'general speaker'.) In 1947, on the eve of its departure from India, the British government divided Bengal into West Bengal, which remained a part of India, and East Pakistan. Punjab was similarly divided into East Punjab (India) and West Pakistan. The two parts of Pakistan did not share ethnic or linguistic ties and were separated by nearly eleven hundred miles. The division was made on the grounds of the concentration of Muslims in these two parts of the subcontinent. Yet the Punjabi Muslims felt themselves to be more 'Arab' because they lived in the area where the first Muslim emperors of India had settled nearly seven hundred years ago and also because of their proximity to West Asia (the Middle East). The Bengali Muslims – no doubt in a class-differentiated way – felt themselves constituted by the culture of Bengal.

Bengal has had a strong presence of leftist intellectualism and struggle since the middle of the last century, before, in fact, the word 'Left' entered our political shorthand.[10] West Bengal is one of three Communist states in the Indian Union. As such, it is a source of considerable political irritation to the central government of India. (The individual state governments have a good deal more autonomy under the Indian Constitution than is the case in the US.) Although officially India is a Socialist state with a mixed economy, historically it has reflected a spectrum of the Right, from military dictatorship to nationalist class benevolence. The word 'democracy' becomes highly interpretable in the context of a largely illiterate, multilingual, heterogeneous, and unpoliticised electorate.

In the spring of 1967, there was a successful peasant rebellion in the Naxalbari area of the northern part of West Bengal. According to Marcus Franda, 'unlike most other areas of West Bengal, where peasant movements are led almost solely by middle-class leadership from Calcutta, Naxalbari has spawned an indigenous agrarian reform leadership led by the lower classes, including tribal culti- vators.[11] This peculiar coalition of peasant and intellectual sparked off a number of Naxalbaris all over India.[12] The target of these movements was the long-established oppression of the landless peas- antry and itinerant farm worker, sustained through an unofficial government-landlord collusion that too easily circumvented the law. Indeed, one might say that legislation seemed to have an eye to its own future circumvention.

It is worth remarking that this coalition of peasant and intellec- tual – with long histories of apprenticeship precisely on the side of the intellectual – has been recuperated in the West by both ends of the polarity that constitutes a 'political spectrum'. Bernard-Henri Lévy, the ex-Maoist French 'New Philosopher', has implicitly com- pared it to the May 1968 'revolution' in France, where the students joined the workers.[13] In France, however, the student identity of the movement had remained clear, and the student leadership had not brought with it sustained efforts to undo the privilege of the intellectual. On the other hand, 'in much the same manner as many American college presidents have described the protest of American students, Indian political and social leaders have explained the Naxalites (supporters of Naxalbari) by referring to their sense of alienation and to the influence of writers like Marcuse and Sartre which has seemingly dominated the minds of young people through- out the world in the 1960s.'[14]

It is against such recuperations that I would submit what I have called the theme of class deconstruction with reference to the young gentlemen revolutionaries in 'Draupadi'. Senanayak remains fixed within his class origins, which are similar to those of the gentlemen revolutionaries. Correspondingly, he is contained and judged fully within Mahasweta's story; by constrast, the gentlemen revolutionaries remain latent, underground. Even their leader's voice is only heard formulaically within Draupadi's solitude. I should like to think that it is because they are so persistently engaged in undoing class containment and the opposition between reading (book learning) and doing – rather than keeping the two aesthetically forever separate – that they inhabit a world whose authority and outline no text – including Mahasweta's – can encompass.

In 1970, the implicit hostility between East and West Pakistan flamed into armed struggle. In 1971, at a crucial moment in the struggle, the armed forces of the government of India were deployed, seemingly because these were alliances between the Naxalites of West Bengal and the freedom fighters of East Bengal (now Bangladesh). 'If a guerrilla-style insurgency had persisted, their forces would undoubtedly have come to dominate the politics of the movement. It was this trend that the Indian authorities were determined to pre-empt by intervention.' Taking advantage of the general atmosphere of jubilation at the defeat of West Pakistan, India's 'principal national rival in South Asia'[15] (this was also the first time India had 'won a war' in its millennial history), the Indian prime minister was able to crack down with exceptional severity on the Naxalites, destroying the rebellious sections of the rural population, most significantly the tribals, as well. The year 1971 is thus a point of reference in Senabayak's career.

This is the setting of 'Draupadi'. The story is a moment caught between two deconstructive formulas: on the one hand, a law that is fabricated with a view to its own transgression, on the other, the undoing of the binary opposition between the intellectual and the rural struggles. In order to grasp the minutiae of their relationship and involvement, one must enter a historical micrology that no foreword can provide.

Draupadi is the name of the central character. She is introduced to the reader between two uniforms and between two versions of her name, Dopdi and Draupadi. It is either that as a tribal she cannot pronounce her own Sanskrit name (Draupadi), or the tribalised form, Dopdi, is the proper name of the ancient Draupadi. She is on a list of wanted persons, yet her name is not on the list of appropriate names for the tribal women.

The ancient Draupadi is perhaps the most celebrated heroine of the Indian epic *Mahabharata*. The *Mahabharata* and the *Ramayana* are the cultural credentials of the so-called Aryan civilisation of India. The tribes predate the Aryan invasion. They have no right to heroic Sanskrit names. Neither the interdiction nor the significance of the name, however, must be taken too seriously. For this pious, domesticated Hindu name was given Dopdi at birth by her mistress, in the usual mood of benevolence felt by the oppressor's wife toward the tribal bond servant. It is the killing of this mistress's husband that sets going the events of the story.

And yet on the level of the text, this elusive and fortuitous name does play a role. To speculate upon this role, we might consider the *Mahabharata* itself in its colonialist function in the interest of the so-called Aryan invaders of India. It is an accretive epic, where the 'sacred' geography of an ancient battle is slowly expanded by succeeding generations of poets so that the secular geography of the expanding Aryan colony can present itself as identical with it and thus justify itself.[16] The complexity of this vast and anonymous project makes it an incomparably more heterogeneous text than the *Ramayana*. Unlike the *Ramayana*, for example, the *Mahabharata* contains cases of various kinds of kinship structure and various styles of marriage. And in fact it is Draupadi who provides the only example of polyandry, not a common system of marriage in India. She is married to the five sons of the impotent Pandu. Within a patriarchal and patronymic context, she is exceptional, indeed 'singular' in the sense of odd, unpaired, uncoupled.[17] Her husbands, since they are husbands rather than lovers, are legitimately pluralised. No acknowledgement of paternity can secure the Name of the Father for the child of such a mother. Mahasweta's story questions this 'singularity' by placing Dopdi first in a comradely, activist, monogamous marriage and then in a situation of multiple rape.

In the epic, Draupadi's legitimised pluralisation (as a wife among husbands) in singularity (as a possible mother or harlot) is used to demonstrate male glory. She provides the occasion for a violent transaction between men, the efficient cause of the crucial battle. Her eldest husband is about to lose her by default in a game of dice. He had staked all he owned, and 'Draupadi belongs within that all' (*Mahabharata* 65:32). Her strange civil status seems to offer grounds for her predicament as well: 'The Scriptures prescribed one husband for a woman; Draupadi is dependent on many husbands; therefore she can be designated a prostitute. There is nothing improper in bringing her, clothed or unclothed, into the assembly' (65:35–6). The enemy chief begins to pull at Draupadi's *sari*.

Draupadi silently prays to the incarnate Krishna. The idea of Sustaining Law (Dharma) materialises itself as clothing, and as the king pulls and pulls at her *sari* there seems to be more and more of it. Draupadi is infinitely clothed and cannot be publicly stripped. It is one of Krishna's miracles.

Mahasweta's story rewrites this episode. The men easily succeed in stripping Dopdi – in the narrative it is the culmination of her political punishment by the representative of the law. She remains publicly naked at her own insistence. Rather than save her modesty through the implicit intervention of a benign and divine (in this case it would have been godlike) comrade, the story insists that this is the place where male leadership stops.

It would be a mistake, I think, to read the modern story as a refutation of the ancient. Dopdi is (as heroic as) Draupadi. She is also what Draupadi – written into the patriarchal and authoritative sacred text as proof of male power – could not be. Dopdi is at once a palimpsest and a contradiction.

There is nothing 'historically implausible' about Dopdi's attitudes. When we first see her, she is thinking about washing her hair. She loves her husband and keeps political faith as an act of faith toward him. She adores her fore*fathers* because they protected their women's honour. (It should be recalled that this is thought in the context of American soldiers breeding bastards.) It is when she crosses the sexual differential into the field of what could *only happen to a woman* that she emerges as the most powerful 'subject', who, still using the language of sexual 'honour', can derisively call herself 'the object of your search', whom the author can describe as a terrifying superobject – 'an unarmed target'.

As a tribal, Dopdi is not romanticised by Mahasweta. The decision makers among the revolutionaries are, again, 'realistically', bourgeois young men and women who have oriented their book learning to the land and thus begun the long process of undoing the opposition between book (theory or 'outside') and spontaneity (practice or 'inside'). Such fighters are the hardest to beat, for they are neither tribal nor gentlemen. A Bengali reader would pick them out by name among the characters: the one with the aliases who bit off his tongue; the ones who helped the couple escape the army cordon; the ones who neither smoke nor drink tea; above all, Arijit. His is a fashionable first name, tinsel Sanskrit, with no allusive paleonymy and a meaning that fits the story a bit too well: victorious over enemies. Yet it *is* his voice that gives Dopdi the courage to save not herself but her comrades.

Of course, this voice of male authority also fades. Once Dopdi enters, in the final section of the story, the postscript area of lunar flux and sexual difference, she is in a place where she will finally act *for* herself in *not* 'acting', in challenging the man to (en)counter her as unrecorded or misrecorded objective historical monument. The army officer is shown as unable to ask the authoritative onto- logical question, What is this? In fact, in the sentence describing Dopdi's final summons to the *sahib*'s tent, the agent is missing. I can be forgiven if I find in this an allegory of the woman's struggle within the revolution in a shifting historical moment.

As Mahasweta points out in an aside, the tribe in question is the Santal, not to be confused with the at least nine other Munda tribes that inhabit India. They are also not to be confused with the so- called untouchables, who, unlike the tribals, are Hindu, though probably of remote 'non-Aryan' origin. In giving the name *Harijan* ('God's people') to the untouchables, Mahatma Gandhi had tried to concoct the sort of pride and sense of unity that the tribes seem to possess. Mahasweta has followed the Bengali practice of calling each so-called untouchable caste by the name of its menial and unclean task within the rigid structural functionalism of institution- alised Hinduism.[18] I have been unable to reproduce this in my translation.

Mahasweta uses another differentiation, almost on the level of caricature: the Sikh and the Bengali. (Sikhism was founded as a reformed religion by Guru Nanak in the late fifteenth century. Today the roughly nine million Sikhs of India live chiefly in East Punjab, at the other end of the vast Indo-Gangetic Plain from Bengal. The tall, muscular, turbanned, and bearded Sikh, so unlike the slight and supposedly intellectual Bengali, is the stereotyped butt of jokes in the same way as the Polish community in North America or the Belgian in France.) Arjan Singh, the diabetic Sikh captain who falls back on the *Granthsahib* (the Sikh sacred book – I have translated it 'Scripture') and the 'five Ks' of the Sikh religion, is presented as all brawn and no brains; and the wily, imaginative, corrupt Bengali Senanayak is of course the army officer full of a Keatsian negative capability.[19]

The entire energy of the story seems, in one reading, directed toward breaking the apparently clean gap between theory and prac- tice in Senanayak. Such a clean break is not possible, of course. The theoretical production of negative capability is a practice; the practice of mowing down Naxalites brings with it a theory of the historical moment. The assumption of such a clean break in fact depends upon the assumption that the individual subject who theor- ises and practices is in full control. At least in the history of the

Indo-European tradition in general, such a sovereign subject is also the legal or legitimate subject, who is identical with his stable patronymic.[20] It might therefore be interesting that Senanayak is not given the differentiation of a first name and surname. His patronymic is identical with his function (not of course by the law of caste): the common noun means 'army chief'. In fact, there is the least hint of a doubt if it is a proper name or a common appellation. This may be a critique of the man's apparently self-adequate identity, which sustains his theory-practice juggling act. If so, it goes with what I see as the project of the story: to break this bonded identity with the wedge of an *unreasonable* fear. If our certitude of the efficient-information-retrieval and talk-to-the-accessible approach toward Third-World women can be broken by the wedge of an unreasonable uncertainty, into a feeling that what we deem gain might spell loss and that our practice should be forged accordingly, then we would share the textual effect of 'Draupadi' with Senanayak.

The italicised words in the translation are in English in the original. It is to be noticed that the fighting words on both sides are in English. Nation-state politics combined with multinational economies produce war. The language of war – offence *and* defence – is international. English is standing in here for that nameless and heterogeneous world language. The peculiarities of usage belong to being obliged to cope with English under political and social pressure for a few centuries. Where, indeed, is there a 'pure' language? Given the nature of the struggle, there is nothing bizarre in 'Comrade Dopdi'.[21] It is part of the undoing of opposites – intellectual-rural, tribalist-internationalist – that is the wavering constitution of 'the underground', 'the wrong side' of the law. On the right side of the law, such deconstructions, breaking down national distinctions, are operated through the encroachment of king-emperor or capital.

The only exception is the word '*sahib*'. An Urdu word meaning 'friend', it came to mean, almost exclusively in Bengali, 'white man'. It is a colonial word and is used today to mean 'boss'. I thought of Kipling as I wrote 'Burra Sahib' for Senanayak.

In the matter of 'translation' between Bengali and English, it is again Dopdi who occupies a curious middle space. She is the only one who uses the word 'counter' (the 'n' is no more than a nasalisation of the diphthong 'ou'). As Mahasweta explains, it is an abbreviation for 'killed by police in an encounter', the code description for death by police torture. Dopdi does not understand English, but she understands this formula and the word. In her use of it at the end, it comes mysteriously close to the 'proper' English usage. It is the menacing appeal of the objectified subject to its politico-sexual enemy – the provisionally silenced master of the subject-object dialetic – to encounter – 'counter' – her. What is it to 'use' a language 'correctly' without 'knowing' it?

We cannot answer because we, with Senanayak, are in the opposite situation. Although we are told of specialists, the meaning of Dopdi's song remains undisclosed in the text. The educated Bengali does not know the languages of the tribes, and no political coercion obliges him to 'know' it. What one might falsely think of as a political 'privilege' – knowing English properly – stands in the way of a deconstructive practice of language – using it 'correctly' through a political displacement, or operating the language of the other side.

It follows that I have had the usual 'translator's problems' only with the peculiar Bengali spoken by the tribals. In general we educated Bengalis have the same racist attitude toward it as the late Peter Sellers had toward our English. It would have been embarrassing to have used some version of the language of D. H. Lawrence's 'common people' or Faulkner's blacks. Again, the specificity is micrological. I have used 'straight English', whatever that may be.

Rather than encumber the story with footnotes, in conclusion I shall list a few items of information:

Page 149: The 'five Ks' are *Kes* ('unshorn hair'); *kachh* ('drawers down to the knee'); *karha* ('iron bangle'); *kirpan* ('dagger'); *kanga* ('comb'; to be worn by every Sikh, hence a mark of identity).

Page 151: 'Bibidha Bharati' is a popular radio programme, on which listeners can hear music of their choice. The Hindi film industry is prolific in producing pulp movies for consumption in India and in all parts of the world where there is an Indian, Pakistani, and West Indian labour force. Many of the films are adaptations from the epics. Sanjeev Kumar is an idolised actor. Since it was Krishna who rescued Draupadi from her predicament in the epic, and, in the film the soldiers watch, Sanjeev Kumar encounters Krishna, there might be a touch of textual irony here.

Page 152: 'Panchayat' is a supposedly elected body of village self-government.

Page 155: 'Champabhumi' and 'Radhabhumi' are archaic names for certain areas of Bengal. 'Bhumi' is simply 'land'. All of Bengal is thus 'Bangabhumi'.

Page 155: The jackal following the tiger is a common image.

Page 156: Modern Bengali does not distinguish between 'her' and 'his'. The 'her' in the sentence beginning 'No comrade will . . .' can therefore be considered an interpretation.[22]

Page 157: A *sari* conjures up the long, many-pleated piece of cloth, complete with blouse and underclothes, that 'proper' Indian women wear. Dopdi wears a much-abbreviated version, without blouse or underclothes. It is referred to simply as 'the cloth'.

Draupadi

Name Dopdi Mejhen, age twenty-seven, husband Dulna Majhi (deceased), domicile Cherakhan, Bankrahjarh, information whether dead or alive and/or assistance in arrest, one hundred rupees . . .

An exchange between two liveried *uniforms*.

FIRST LIVERY: What's this, a tribal called Dopdi? The list of names I brought has nothing like it! How can anyone have an unlisted name?

SECOND: Draupadi Mejhen. Born the year her mother threshed rice at Surja Sahu (killed)'s at Bakuli. Surja Sahu's wife gave her the name.

FIRST: These officers like nothing better than to write as much as they can in English. What's all this stuff about her?

SECOND: *Most notorious* female. *Long wanted in many* . . .

Dossier: Dulna and Dopdi worked at harvests, *rotating* between Birbhum, Burdwan, Murshidabad, and Bankura. In 1971, in the famous *Operation* Bakuli, when three villages were *cordonned off* and *machine gunned*, they too lay on the ground, faking dead. In fact, they were the main culprits. Murdering Surja Sahu and his son, occupying upper-caste wells and tubewells during the drought, not surrendering those three young men to the police. In all this they were the chief instigators. In the morning, at the time of the body count, the couple could not be found. The blood-sugar level of Captain Arjan Singh, the *architect* of Bakuli, rose at once and proved yet again that diabetes can be a result of anxiety and depression. Diabetes has twelve husbands – among them anxiety.

Dulna and Dopdi went underground for a long time in a *Neanderthal* darkness. The Special Forces, attempting to pierce that dark by an armed search, compelled quite a few Santals in the various districts of West Bengal to meet their Maker against their will. By the Indian Constitution, all human beings, regardless of caste or creed, are sacred. Still, accidents like this do happen. Two sorts of reasons: (1), the underground couple's skill in self-concealment; (2), not merely the Santals but all tribals of the Austro-Asiatic Munda tribes appear the same to the Special Forces.

In fact, all around the ill-famed forest of Jharkhani, which is under the jurisdiction of the police station at Bankrajharh (in this India of ours, even a worm is under a certain police station), even in the southeast and southwest corners, one comes across hair-raising details in the eyewitness records put together on the people who are suspected of attacking police stations, stealing guns (since the snatchers are not invariably well educated, they sometimes say 'give up your *chambers*' rather than give up your gun), killing grain brokers, landlords, moneylenders, law officers, and bureaucrats. A black-skinned couple ululated like police *sirens* before the episode. They sang jubilantly in a savage tongue, incomprehensible even to the Santals. Such as:

> Samaray hijulenako mar goekope

and,

> Hendre rambra keche keche
> Pundi rambra keche keche

This proves conclusively that they are the cause of Captain Arjan Singh's diabetes.

Government procedure being as incomprehensible as the Male Principle in Sankhya philosophy or Antonioni's early films, it was Arjan Singh who was sent once again on *Operation Forest* Jharkhani. Learning from Intelligence that the above-mentioned ululating and dancing couple was the escaped corpses, Arjan Singh fell for a bit into a *zombie*like state and finally acquired so irrational a dread of black-skinned people that whenever he saw a black person in a ball-bag, he swooned, saying 'they're killing me', and drank and passed a lot of water. Neither uniform nor Scriptures could relieve that depression. At long last, under the shadow of a *premature and forced retirement*, it was possible to present him at the desk of Mr Senanayak, the elderly Bengali specialist in combat and extreme-Left politics.

Senanayak knows the activities and capacities of the opposition better than they themselves do. First, therefore, he presents an encomium on the military genius of the Sikhs. Then he explains further: Is it only the opposition that should find power at the end of the barrel of a gun? Arjan Singh's power also explodes out of the *male organ* of a gun. Without a gun even the 'five Ks' come to nothing in this day and age. These speeches he delivers to all and sundry. As a result, the fighting forces regain their confidence in the *Army Handbook*. It is not a book for everyone. It says that the most despicable and repulsive style of fighting is guerrilla warfare with primitive weapons. Annihilation at sight of any and all prac-tioners of such warfare is the sacred duty of every soldier. Dopdi and Dulna belong to the *category* of such fighters, for they too kill by means of hatchet and scythe, bow and arrow, etc. In fact, their fighting power is greater than the gentlemen's. Not all gentlemen become experts in the explosion of 'chambers'; they think the power will come out on its own if the gun is held. But since Dulna and Dopdi are illiterate, their kind have practised the use of weapons generation after generation.

I should mention here that, although the other side make little of him, Senanayak is not to be trifled with. Whatever his *practice*, in *theory* he respects the opposition. Respects them because they could be neither understood nor demolished if they were treated with the attitude, 'It's nothing but a bit of impertinent game-playing with guns'. *In order to destroy the enemy, become one.* Thus he understood them by (*theoretically*) becoming one of them. He hopes to write on all this in the future. He has also decided that in his written work he will demolish the gentlemen and *highlight* the message of the harvest workers. These mental processes might seem complicated, but actually he is a simple man and is as pleased as his third great-uncle after a meal of turtle meat. In fact, he knows that, as in the old popular song, turn by turn the world will change. And in every world he must have the credentials to survive with honour. If necessary he will show the future to what extent he alone under-stands the matter in its proper perspective. He knows very well that what he is doing today the future will forget, but he also knows that if he can change colour from world to world, he can represent the particular world in question. Today he is getting rid of the young by means of '*apprehension and elimination*', but he knows people will soon forget the memory and lesson of blood. And at the same time, he, like Shakespeare, believes in delivering the world's *legacy* into youth's hands. He is Prospero as well.

At any rate, information is received that many young men and women, *batch by batch* and on jeeps, have attacked police station after police station, terrified and elated the region, and disappeared into the forest of Jharkhani. Since after escaping from Bakuli, Dopdi and Dulna have worked at the house of virtually every landowner, they can efficiently inform the killers about their targets and announce proudly that they too are soldiers, *rank and file*. Finally the impenetrable forest of Jharkhani is surrounded by real soldiers, the *army* enters and splits the battlefield. Soldiers in hiding guard the falls and springs that are the only source of drinking water; they are still guarding, still looking. On one such search, army informant Dukhiram Gharari saw a young Santal man lying on his stomach on a flat stone, dipping his face to drink water. The soldiers shot him as he lay. As the .303 threw him off spread-eagled and brought a bloody foam to his mouth, he roared 'Ma – ho' and then went limp. They realised later that it was the redoubtable Dulna Majhi.

What does 'Ma – ho' mean? Is this a violent slogan in the tribal language? Even after much thought, the Department of Defence could not be sure. Two tribal-specialist types are flown in from Calcutta, and they sweat over the dictionaries put together by worthies such as Hoffmann-Jeffer and Golden-Palmer. Finally the omniscient Senanayak summons Chamru, the water carrier of the *camp*. He giggles when he sees the two specialists, scratches his ear with his 'bidi,' and says, the Santals of Maldah did say that when they began fighting at the time of King Gandhi! It's a battle cry. Who said 'Ma – ho' here? Did someone come from Maldah?

The problem is thus solved. Then, leaving Dulna's body on the stone, the soldiers climb the trees in green camouflage. They embrace the leafy boughs like so many great god Pans and wait as the large red ants bite their private parts. To see if anyone comes to take away the body. This is the hunter's way, not the soldier's. But Senanayak knows that these brutes cannot be dispatched by the approved method. So he asks his men to draw the prey with a corpse as bait. All will come clear, he says. I have almost deciphered Dopdi's song.

The soldiers get going at his command. But no one comes to claim Dulna's corpse. At night the soldiers shoot at a scuffle and, descending, discover that they have killed two hedgehogs copulating on dry leaves. Improvidently enough, the soldiers' jungle scout Dukhiram gets a knife in the neck before he can claim the reward for Dulna's capture. Bearing Dulna's corpse, the soldiers suffer shooting pains as the ants, interrupted in their feast, begin to bite them. When Senanayak hears that no one has come to take the corpse, he slaps his *anti-Fascist paperback* copy of *The Deputy* and shouts, '*What?*' Immediately one of the tribal specialists runs in with a joy as naked and transparent as Archimedes' and says, 'Get up, *sir*! I have discovered the meaning of that "hende rambra" stuff. It's Mundari *language*.'

Thus the search for Dopdi continues. In the forest *belt* of Jharkhani, the *Operation* continues – will continue. It is a carbuncle on the government's backside. Not to be cured by the tested ointment, not to burst with the appropriate herb. In the first place, the fugitives, ignorant of the forest's topography, are caught easily, and by the law of confrontation they are shot at the taxpayer's expense. By the law of confrontation, their eyeballs, intestines, stomachs, hearts, genitals, and so on become the food of fox, vulture, hyena, wildcat, ant, and worm, and the untouchables go off happily to sell their bare skeletons.

They do not allow themselves to be captured in open combat in the next phase. Now it seems that they have found a trustworthy courier. Ten to one it's Dopdi. Dopdi loved Dulna more than her blood. No doubt it is she who is saving the fugitives now.

'They' is also a *hypothesis*.

Why?

How many went *originally*?

The answer is silence. About that there are many tales, many books in press. Best not to believe everything.

How many killed in six years' confrontation?

The answer is silence.

Why after confrontations are the skeletons discovered with arms broken or severed? Could armless men have fought? Why do the collarbones shake, why are legs and ribs crushed?

Two kinds of answer. Silence. Hurt rebuke in the eyes. Shame on you! Why bring this up? What will be will be . . .

How many left in the forest? The answer is silence.

A *legion*? Is it *justifiable* to maintain a large battalion in that wild area at the taxpayer's expense?

Answer: *Objection*. 'Wild area' in incorrect. The battalion is provided with supervised nutrition, arrangements to worship according to religion, opportunity to listen to 'Bibidha Bharati' and to see Sanjeev Kumar and the Lord Krishna face-to-face in the movie *This is Life*. No. The area is not wild.

How many are left?

The answer is silence.

How many are left? Is there anyone *at all*?

The answer is long.

Item: *Well, action* still goes on. Moneylenders, landlords, grain brokers, anonymous brothel keepers, ex-informants are still terrified. The hungry and naked are still defiant and irrepressible. In some *pockets* the harvest workers are getting a *better wage*. Villages sympathetic to the fugitives are still silent and hostile. These events cause one to think . . .

Where in this picture does Dopdi Mejhen fit?

She must have connections with the fugitives. The cause for fear is elsewhere. The ones who remain have lived a long time in the primitive world of the forest. They keep company with the poor harvest workers and the tribals. They must have forgotten book learning. Perhaps they are *orienting* their book learning to the soil they live on and learning new combat and survival techniques. One can shoot and get rid of the ones whose only recourse is extrinsic book learning and sincere intrinsic enthusiasm. Those who are working practically will not be exterminated so easily.

Therefore *Operation* Jharkhani *Forest* cannot stop. Reason: the words of warning in the *Army Handbook*.

2.

Catch Dopdi Mejhen. She will lead us to the others.

Dopdi was proceeding slowly, with some rice knotted into her belt. Mushai Tudu's wife had cooked her some. She does so occasionally. When the rice is cold, Dopdi knots it into her waist-cloth and walks slowly. As she walked, she picked out and killed the lice in her hair. If she had some *kerosene*, she'd rub it into her scalp and get rid of the lice. Then she could wash her hair with baking *soda*. But the bastards put traps at every bend of the falls. If they smell *kerosene* in the water, they will follow the scent.

Dopdi!

She doesn't respond. She never responds when she hears her own name. She has seen in the Panchayat office just today the notice for the reward in her name. Mushai Tudu's wife had said, 'What are you looking at? Who is Dopdi Mejhen! Money if you give her up!'

'How much?'

'Two – hundred!'

Oh God!

Mushai's wife said outside the office: 'A lot of preparation this time. A-ll new policemen.'

Hm.

Don't come again.

Why?

Mushai's wife looked down. Tudu says that Sahib has come again. If they catch you, the village, our huts . . .

They'll burn again.

Yes. And about Dukhiram . . .

The Sahib knows?

Shomai and Budhna betrayed us.

Where are they?

Ran away by train.

Dopdi thought of something. Then said, Go home. I don't know what will happen, if they catch me don't know me.

Can't you run away?

No. Tell me, how many times can I run away? What will they do if they catch me? They will *counter* me. Let them.

Mushai's wife said, We have nowhere else to go.

Dopdi said softly, I won't tell anyone's name.

Dopdi knows, has learned by hearing so often and so long, how one can come to terms with torture. If mind and body give way under torture, Dopdi will bite off her tongue. That boy did it. They countered him. When they counter you, your hands are tied behind you. All your bones are crushed, your sex is a terrible wound. *Killed by police in an encounter . . . unknown male . . . age twenty-two . . .*

As she walked thinking these thoughts, Dopdi heard someone calling, Dopdi!

She didn't respond. She doesn't respond if called by her own name. Here her name is Upi Mejhen. But who calls?

Spines of suspicion are always furled in her mind. Hearing 'Dopdi' they stiffen like a hedgehog's. Walking, she *unrolls the film* of known faces in her mind. Who? No Shomra, Shomra is on the run. Shomai and Budhna are also on the run, for other reasons. Not Golok, he is in Bakuli. Is it someone from Bakuli? After Bakuli, her and Dulna's names were Upi Mejhen, Matang Majhi. Here no one but Mushai and his wife knows their real names. Among the young gentlemen, not all of the previous *batches* knew.

That was a troubled time. Dopdi is confused when she thinks about it. *Operation* Bakuli in Bakuli. Surja Sahu arranged with Biddibabu to dig two tubewells and three wells within the compound of his two houses. No water anywhere, drought in Birbhum. Unlimited water at Surja Sahu's house, as clear as a crow's eye.

Get your water with canal tax, everything is burning.

What's my profit in increasing cultivation with tax money?

Everything's on fire.

Get out of here. I don't accept your Panchayat nonsense. Increase cultivation with water. You want half the paddy for sharecropping.

Everyone is happy with free paddy. Then give me paddy at home, give me money, I've learned my lesson trying to do you good.

What good did you do?

Have I not given water to the village?

You've given it to your kin Bhagunal.

Don't you get water?

No. The untouchables don't get water.

The quarrel began there. In the drought, human patience catches easily. Satish and Jugal from the village and that young gentleman, was Rana his name?, said a landowning moneylender won't give a thing, put him down.

Surja Sahu's house was surrounded at night. Surja Sahu had brought 'out his gun. Surja was tied up with cow rope. His whitish eyeballs turned and turned, he was incontinent again and again. Dulna had said, I'll have the first blow, brothers. My greatgrandfather took a bit of paddy from him, and I still give him free labour to repay that debt.

Dopdi had said, His mouth watered when he looked at me. I'll put out his eyes.

Surja Sahu. Then a *telegraphic message* from Shiuri. *Special train. Army. The jeep* didn't come up to Bakuli. *March-march-march.* The *crunch-crunch-crunch* of gravel under hobnailed boots. *Cordon up. Commands* on the *mike.* Jugal Mandal, Satish Mandal, Rana *alias* Prabir *alias* Dipak, Dulna Majhi-Dopdi Mejhen *surrender surrender surrender. No surrender surrender. Mow-mow-mow down the village.* Putt-putt putt-putt – *cordite* in the air – putt-putt – *round the clock* – putt-putt. *Flame thrower. Bakuli is burning. More men and women, children . . . fire – fire. Close canal approach. Over-over-over by nightfall.* Dopdi and Dulna had crawled on their stomachs to safety.

They could not have reached Paltakuri after Bakuli. Bhupati and Tapa took them. Then it was decided that Dopdi and Dulna would work around the Jharkhani *belt.* Dulna had explained to Dopdi, Dear, this is best! We won't get family and children this way. But who knows? Landowner and moneylender and policemen might one day be wiped out!

Who called her from the back today?

Dopdi kept walking. Villages and fields, bush and rock – *Public Works Department* markers – sound of running steps in back. Only one person running. Jharkhani *Forest* still about two miles away. Now she thinks of nothing but entering the forest. She must let them know that the *police* have set up *notices* for her again. Must tell them that that bastard Sahib has appeared again. Must change *hideouts.* Also, the *plan* to do to Lakkhi Bera and Naran Bera what they did to Surja Sahu on account of the trouble over paying the field hands in Sandara must be cancelled. Shomai and Budhna knew everything. There was the *urgency* of great danger under Dopdi's ribs. Now she thought there was no shame as a Santal in Shomai and Budhna's treachery. Dopdi's blood was the pure unadulterated black blood of Champabhumi. From Champa to Bakuli the rise and set of a million moons. Their blood could have been contaminated; Dopdi felt proud of her forefathers. They stood guard over their women's blood in black armour. Shomai and Budhna are half-breeds. The fruits of the war. Contributions to Radhabhumi by the American soldiers stationed at Shiandanga. Otherwise, crow would eat crow's flesh before Santal would betray Santal.

Footsteps at her back. The steps keep a distance. Rice in her belt, tobacco leaves tucked at her waist. Arijit, Malini, Shamu, Mantu – none of them smokes or even drinks tea. Tobacco leaves and limestone powder. Best medicine for scorpion bite. Nothing must be given away.

Dopdi turned left. This way is the *camp*. Two miles. This is not the way to the forest. But Dopdi will not enter the forest with a cop at her back.

I swear by my life. By my life Dulna, by my life. Nothing must be told.

The footsteps turn left. Dopdi touches her waist. In her palm the comfort of a half-moon. A baby scythe. The smiths at Jharkhani are fine artisans. Such an edge we'll put on it Upi, a hundred Dukhirams – Thank God Dopdi is not a gentleman. Actually, perhaps they have understood scythe, hatchet, and knife best. They do their work in silence. The lights of the *camp* at a distance. Why is Dopdi going this way? Stop a bit, it turns again. Huh! I can tell where I am if I wander all night with my eyes shut. I won't go in the forest, I won't lose him that way. I won't outrun him. You fucking jackal of a cop, deadly afraid of death, you can't run around in the forest. I'd run you out of breath, throw you in a ditch, and finish you off.

Not a word must be said. Dopdi has seen the new *camp*, she has sat in the *bus station*, passed the time of day, smoked a 'bidi' and found out how many *police convoys* had arrived, how many *radio vans*. Squash four, onions seven, peppers fifty, a straightforward account. This information cannot now be passed on. They will understand Dopdi Mejhen has been countered. Then they'll run. Arijit's voice. If anyone is caught, the others must catch the *timing* and *change* their *hideout*. If *Comrade* Dopdi arrives late, we will not remain.

There will be a sign of where we've gone. No *comrade* will let the others be destroyed for her own sake.

Arijit's voice. The gurgle of water. The direction of the next *hideout* will be indicated by the tip of the wooden arrowhead under the stone.

Dopdi likes and understands this. Dulna died, but, let me tell you, he didn't lose anyone else's life. Because this was not in our heads to begin with, one was countered for the other's trouble. Now a much harsher rule, easy and clear. Dopdi returns – good; doesn't return – bad. *Change hideout.* The clue will be such that the opposition won't see it, won't understand even if they do.

Footsteps at her back, Dopdi turns again. These three and a half miles of land and rocky ground are the best way to enter the forest. Dopdi has left that way behind. A little level ground ahead. Then rocks again. The *army* could not have struck *camp* on such rocky terrain. This area is quiet enough. It's like a maze, every hump looks like every other. That's fine. Dopdi will lead the cop to the burning 'ghat'. Patitpaban of Saranda had been sacrificed in the name of Kali of the Burning Ghats.

Apprehend!

A lump of rock stands up. Another. Yet another. The elderly Senanayak was at once triumphant and despondent. *If you want to destroy the enemy, become one.* He had done so. As long as six years ago he could anticipate their every move. He still can. Therefore he is elated. Since he has kept up with the literature, he has read *First Blood* and seen approval of his thought and work.

Dopdi couldn't trick him, he is unhappy about that. Two sorts of reasons. Six years ago he published an article about information storage in brain cells. He demonstrated in that piece that he supported this struggle from the point of view of the field hands. Dopdi is a field hand. *Veteran fighter. Search and destroy.* Dopdi Mejhen is about to be *apprehended*. Will be *destroyed*. Regret.

Halt!

Dopdi stops short. The steps behind come around to the front. Under Dopdi's ribs the *canal* dam breaks. No hope. Surja Sahu's brother Rotoni Sahu. The two lumps of rock come forward. Shomai and Budhna. They had not escaped by train.

Arijit's voice. Just as you must know when you've won, you must also acknowledge defeat and start the activities of the next *stage.*

Now Dopdi spreads her arms, raises her face to the sky, turns toward the forest, and ululates with the force of her entire being. Once, twice, three times. At the third burst the birds in the trees at the outskirts of the forest awake and flap their wings. The echo of the call travels far.

3.

Draupadi Mejhen was apprehended at 6:53 P.M. It took an hour to get her to *camp*. Questioning took another hour exactly. No one touched her, and she was allowed to sit on a canvas camp stool. At 8:57 Senanayak's dinner hour approached, and saying, 'Make her. *Do the needful*', he disappeared.

Then a billion moons pass. A billion lunar years. Opening her eyes after a million light years, Draupadi, strangely enough, sees sky and moon. Slowly the bloodied nailheads shift from her brain. Trying to move, she feels her arms and legs still tied to four posts. Something sticky under her ass and waist. Her own blood. Only the gag has been removed. Incredible thirst. In case she says 'water' she catches her lower lip in her teeth. She senses that her vagina is bleeding. How many came to make her?

Shaming her, a tear trickles out of the corner of her eye. In the muddy moonlight she lowers her lightless eye, sees her breasts, and understands that, indeed, she's been made up right. Her breasts are bitten raw, the nipples torn. How many? Four-five-six-seven – than Draupadi had passed out.

She turns her eyes and sees something white. Her own cloth. Nothing else. Suddenly she hopes against hope. Perhaps they have abandoned her. For the foxes to devour. But she hears the scrape of feet. She turns her head, the guard leans on his bayonet and leers at her. Draupadi closes her eyes. She doesn't have to wait long. Again the process of making her begins. Goes on. The moon vomits a bit of light and goes to sleep. Only the dark remains. A compelled spread-eagled still body. Active *pistons* of flesh rise and fall, rise and fall over it.

Then morning comes.

Then Draupadi Mejhen is brought to the tent and thrown on the straw. Her piece of cloth is thrown over her body.

Then, after *breakfast*, after reading the newspaper and sending the radio message 'Draupadi Mejhen apprehended', etc., Draupadi Mejhen is ordered brought in.

Suddenly there is trouble.

Draupadi sits up as soon as she hears 'Move!' and asks, Where do you want me to go?

To the Burra Sahib's tent.

Where is the tent?

Over there.

Draupadi fixes her red eyes on the tent. Says, Come. I'll go.

The guard pushes the water pot forward.

Draupadi stands up. She pours the water down on the ground. Tears her piece of cloth with her teeth. Seeing such strange behaviour, the guard says, She's gone crazy, and runs for orders. He can lead the prisoner out but doesn't know what to do if the prisoner behaves incomprehensibly. So he goes to ask his superior.

The commotion is as if the alarm had sounded in a prison. Senanayak walks out surprised and sees Draupadi, naked, walking toward him in the bright sunlight with her head high. The nervous guards trail behind.

What is this? He is about to cry, but stops.

Draupadi stands before him, naked. Thigh and pubic hair matted with dry blood. Two breasts, two wounds.

What is this? He is about to bark.

Draupadi comes closer. Stands with her hand on her hip, laughs and says, The object of your search, Dopdi Mejhen. You asked them to make me up, don't you want to see how they made me?

Where are her clothes?

Won't put them on, *sir*. Tearing them.

Draupadi's black body comes even closer. Draupadi shakes with an indomitable laughter that Senanayak simply cannot understand. Her ravaged lips bleed as she begins laughing. Draupadi wipes the blood on her palm and says in a voice that is as terrifying, sky splitting, and sharp as her ululation, What's the use of clothes? You can strip me, but how can you clothe me again? Are you a man?

She looks around and chooses the front of Senanayak's white bush shirt to spit a bloody gob at and says, There isn't a man here that I should be ashamed. I will not let you put my cloth on me. What more can you do? Come on, *counter* me – come on, *counter* me –

Draupadi pushes Senanayak with her two mangled breasts, and for the first time Senanayak is afraid to stand before an unarmed *target*, terribly afraid.

Notes

1. For elaborations upon such a suggestion, see Jean-François Lyotard, *La Condition post-moderne: Rapport sur le savoir* (Paris, 1979).

2. See my 'Three Feminist Readings: McCullers, Drabble, Habermas,' *Union Seminary Quarterly Review* 1–2 (Fall-Winter 1979–80), and 'French Feminism in an International Frame', *In Other Worlds*, pp. 134–53.

3. I develop this argument in my review of Jacques Derrida's *Memoires in boundary* 2 forthcoming.

4. This list represents a distillation of suggestions to be found in the work of Jacques Derrida: see, e.g., 'The Exorbitant. Question of Method', *Of Grammatology*, trans. Spivak (Baltimore: Johns Hopkins University Press, 1976); 'Limited Inc,' trans. Samuel Weber, *Glyph* 2 (1977); 'Ou commence et comment finit un corps enseignant', in *Politiques de la philosophie*, ed. Dominique Grisoni (Paris: B. Grasset, 1976); and my 'Revolutions That as Yet Have No Model: Derrida's "Limited Inc"', *Diacritics* 10 (Dec. 1980), and 'Sex and History in Wordsworth's *The Prelude* (1805) IX-XIII', *In Other Worlds*, pp.46–76.

5. It is a sign of E. M. Forster's acute perception of India that *A Passage to India* contains a glimpse of such an ex-orbitant tribal in the figure of the punkha puller in the courtroom.

6. Mahasweta, *Agnigarbha* (Calcutta, 1978), p. 8.

7. For a discussion of the relationship between academic degrees in English and the production of revolutionary literature, see my 'A Vulgar Inquiry into the Relationship between Academic Criticism and Literary Production in West Bengal' (paper delivered at the Annual Convention of the Modern Language Association, Houston, 1980).

8. These figures are an average of the 1971 census in West Bengal and the projected figure for the 1974 census in Bangladesh.

9. See Dinesh Chandra Sen, *History of Bengali Language and Literature* (Calcutta, 1911). A sense of Bengali literary nationalism can be gained from the (doubtless apocryphal) report that, upon returning from his first investigative tour of India, Macaulay remarked: 'The British Crown presides over two great literatures: the English and the Bengali.'

10. See Gautam Chattopadhyay, *Communism and the Freedom Movement in Bengal* (New Delhi, 1970).

11. Marcus F. Franda, *Radical Politics in West Bengal* (Cambridge: MIT Press, 1971), p. 153. I am grateful to Michael Ryan for having located this accessible account of the Naxalbari movement. There now exists an excellent study by Sumanta Banerjee, *India's Simmering Revolution: The Naxalite Uprising* (London: Zed Press, 1984).

12. See Samar Sen, et al., eds, *Naxalbari and After: A Frontier Anthology*, 2 vols (Calcutta, 1978).

13. See Bernard-Henri Lévy, *Bangla Desh: Nationalisme dans la révolution* (Paris, 1973).

14. Tranda, *Radical Politics*, pp. 163–4. See also p. 164, n.22.

15. Lawrence Lifschultz, *Bangladesh: The Unfinished Revolution* (London: Zed Press, 1979), pp. 25, 26.

16. For my understanding of this aspect of the *Mahabharata*, I am indebted to Romila Thapar of Jawaharlal Nehru University, New Delhi.

17. I borrow this sense of singularity from Jacques Lacan, 'Seminar on "The Purloined Letter",' trans. Jeffrey Mehlman, *Yale French Studies* 48 (1972): 53, 59.

18. As a result of the imposition of the capitalist mode of production and the Imperial Civil Service, and massive conversions of the lowest castes to Christianity, the invariable identity of caste and trade no longer holds. Here, too, there is the possiblity of a taxonomy micrologically deconstructive of the caste-class opposition, functioning heterogeneously in terms of the social hierarchy.

19. If indeed the model for this character is Ranjit Gupta, the notorious inspector general of police of West Bengal, the delicate textuality, in the interest of a political position, of Senanayak's delineation in the story takes us far beyond the limits of a reference *à clef*. I am grateful to Michael Ryan for suggesting the possibility of such a reference.

20. The relationship between phallocentrism, the patriarchy, and clean binary oppositions is a pervasive theme in Derrida's critique of the metaphysics of presence. See my 'Unmaking and Making in *To the Lighthouse*', *In Other Worlds*, pp. 30–45.

21. 'My dearest Sati, through the walls and the miles that separate us I can hear you saying, "In Sawan it will be two years since Comrade left us". The other women will nod. It is you who have taught them the meaning of Comrade' (Mary Tyler, 'Letter to a Former Cell-Mate,' in *Naxalbari and After*, 1:307; see also Tyler, *My Years in an Indian Prison* [Harmondsworth: Penguin, 1977]).

22. I am grateful to Soumya Chakravarti for his help in solving occasional problems of English synonyms and archival research.

Catherine Belsey: Milton's Shorter Poems

The project

This book is not about John Milton. Readers anxious to treat Milton's writing as a means of access to something beyond itself, the 'mind' of a long-dead individual, may prefer to consult a critical biography of the author.[1] Here 'Milton' marks a moment in English textual history, and this book is about that moment in its history and its textuality.

Reprinted from Catherine Belsey, *John Milton: Language, Gender, Power* (Oxford, 1988), pp. 5–10, 23–34.

I do not mean to suggest, of course, that John Milton did not exist as an individual, that he did not write Milton's texts, or that this process of production was in any way negligible. But I want to resist the conventional critical assumption that Milton himself is available, ready to be invoked as the ultimate explanation of his writing. My reading of his texts is not necessarily one that John Milton would have recognised or acknowledged. Interpretation is not – cannot be – an activity of reconstructing an intended meaning which preceded the writing process. This traditional quarry of criticism is always a phantom – not merely elusive and probably illusory, but also dead. The author's intended meaning died in the moment that the text came into being, and the text is necessarily more than the author conceived or knew. The interpretation I want to offer does not seek out an apparition; instead it attends to an appearance, the signifying surface of the text, not an essence concealed by the words, but the textuality of the words themselves.

Words are not entirely under our control. Neither authors nor readers give them their meanings. On the contrary, it is the process of learning their meanings which releases the possibility of writing or reading, meaning or understanding. And meaning, in turn, is an effect of difference, finding its cause not in a prior substance or a concept, but in a relationship which is also an absence, the spacing between one signifier and another.

In Jacques Derrida's analysis the difference which makes meaning possible is linked in the term 'difference' with the deferment of what is meant.[2] Meaning is not only what is differed, differentiated, but also what is deflected by the signifier, and in that sense what is always and inevitably absent. Writing, then, is a process of substitution which is also one of relegation. In a double and antithetical movement it both conjures up meaning and supplants it. Reading in its conventional understanding and practice has been deeply imbued with a metaphysical desire for meaning as presence, for access to the relegated, supplanted 'thought', intention or idea, which common sense so often locates 'behind' the text itself. But the spatial metaphor betrays the impossibility of the project: the meaning is elsewhere and is thus inaccessible. Only the signifier is within reach.

Reading can therefore be no more than attention to the signifier. This does not imply that we cannot talk about meaning(s). The claim that the *opposition* between signifier and signified is metaphysical does not eliminate the *difference* between them.[3] Signifiers do signify, do differentiate. But because the signifier cannot be anchored to a fixed, anterior presence 'behind' it, meaning is always unstable, plural, dispersed and disseminated.

Nor does the proposition that reading attends to the signifier imply that meaning is no longer an issue, that criticism concentrates on 'form' as distinct from 'content'. That distinction is itself metaphysical, reaffirming the notion that form is a kind of decorative but translucent container for an idea, an intention, an intelligibility, which could equally exist in some other form, or independently. Pure meaning does not exist on its own, independent of the signifier. But although meaning, absolute and unconditional, does not exist, it does not follow that nothing means anything. On the contrary, precisely on account of difference, meanings do exist – in their materiality and their effectivity. They are, however, an effect of interpretation, not its origin.

An interpretation is also a text. It is not a replica of the first text (Milton's). Nor is it a transcription of the phantom intention. It is not, in fact, a transcription of anything outside language, but a set of signifiers concerning another set of signifiers. There are cases where drawings, or gestures or music have been offered as interpretations of written texts, but these too are signifying practices. There is no interpretation and no understanding outside signifying practice.

My interpretation of Milton's plural, disseminated texts lays claim, then, to no special authority. I have no access to the meaning, absolute and unconditional, of these writings or any others. Does it follow that anything goes, that any interpretation is as good as any other, that 'it's all subjective', as they say?

Not at all. Meaning is no more located in the subjectivity of the reader than in the mind of the writer. The identification of meaning as subjective reaffirms the metaphysical notion of pure intelligibility independent of the signifier, meaning as an idea which precedes the signifying difference. Meaning in its plurality and its dissemination is public, linguistic and conventional: what it is possible for those (differential) signifiers to mean or to have meant.

But since the plurality remains, why this interpretation rather than any other? There are already plenty of readings of Milton around. And why Milton? There are in my view two answers to the latter question. The first is worth a paragraph and the second will take the rest of this book. There are two answers because the question is (of course) plural. In so far as it asks why *Milton*'s texts, why this grouping of texts marked by the name of the author, my answer is that the English examination syllabus still all too frequently arranges the material for study under authors' names, at least to the extent that it continues to share the nineteenth-century assumption that the works signed by an author must in some continuous way express, and so make present, not only the phantom intention which lies behind the text, but the even more spectral subjectivity which is its origin. Students are still required to write essays about authors. And one way of trying to intervene in this state of affairs is to start from where things are. For that reason, too, I shall tend to concentrate on the familiar texts.

But in so far as the question asks why *Lycidas*, or *Samson Agonistes* or *Paradise Lost*, my answer is more complex. These texts, readily available in modern editions, are part of a continuing history. They chart, I shall argue, some of the struggles and transformations which brought into being the world we now inhabit. They also constitute an intervention in those struggles and transformations. They record and participate in the historical turning-point which marks the installation of the modern epoch.

There is a close relationship between power and meaning. Despotic regimes have always attempted to take control of meaning, to fix it in their own interests, outlawing alternatives by making them literally unthinkable. In democratic societies the contest for meaning is also a struggle for power. If it were possible to pin down the single, authorised, guaranteed meaning of, say, masculine and feminine, or literature, freedom, or democracy itself, it would in consequence be possible to delimit those categories, excluding or repudiating as inadmissible whatever did not fit the definition. Social institutions reproduce and extend their own power by arresting the inevitable play of meaning.

In the Middle Ages it was probably the Catholic Church that made the most unremitting efforts to take institutional control of meaning. While God held in place the real meaning of good and truth, evil and heresy were excommunicated, burned and relegated to hell. It is not surprising, therefore, that in the cause of advancing the interests of the English nation-state and the absolute power of the Tudor monarchy, Henry VIII declared himself head of the Church of England. Evidently it was imperative to lay claim to the Church's power of determining meaning and truth. But the unforeseen price of Reformation was also the decentring of the Church as an institution. Protestant truth found its differentiating, defining others not only in popery, but also in the array of separatist sects, which challenged the power of the sovereign over their consciences, their religious and social practices and ultimately, if they still refused to conform, their bodies. The 'resolution' of these conflicts was also the founding moment of the modern world.

The sects reread the Scriptures and proclaimed themselves the true interpreters of the sacred text. In the twentieth century the institution of English, far less powerful than the medieval Church, but by no means negligible in its influence, assumes command of meaning in the compulsory school discipline of English language, and struggles to control of the range of admissible readings of texts through the apparatus of literary criticism. It fails, of course. In the event Milton has been read for and against theocentrism, for and against humanism, for and against sexism. The project in many of these instances has been to enlist the author, a great writer, a genius, Milton, in support of a cause. Alternatively, and notoriously in Milton's case, the poet is condemned for his bad verses, which means that there is no need to pay any attention to his radical political views.

Thus interpretation, like writing itself, constitutes an affirmation of values, an intervention in the struggle for meaning. My own interpretation is no exception. But I shall be less concerned than most earlier critics with Milton's genius (or lack of it), the unity of his texts (for better or worse), and the singularity of his wisdom (or wickedness). On the contrary, my interest is precisely in the plurality of the texts and the contests for meaning played out within them. Milton's writings, as I read them, demonstrate the conflicts between heaven and earth, authority and freedom, man and woman, which were ostensibly resolved in the creation of the modern world. In the twentieth century it is no longer obvious that all those conflicts were resolved to our satisfaction. In addition, the texts display a struggle to master meaning itself, and their failure demonstrates the triumph of language in its creativity. All these issues, identifiable in Milton's writing, are perhaps in a special way issues for us now. For that reason the texts seem to me worth rereading.

Differance

Meaning is always an effect of difference between signifiers. And since meaning does not find its cause in a substance or a concept, but only in difference itself, there is also a difference within the signified, the trace of otherness within the self-same, a result of the inevitable allusion to difference itself, and so to the meanings that are excluded. But meaning is also a deferment, a distancing by the signifier, which is always a detour, of the concept or the substance it offers to represent. Signification suspends the referent; re-presentation separates the present or presence, however minutely, from itself. Derrida's term 'différance' points to both difference and deferment, and to their consequence. The signifier cannot make present, even in imagination, a single, full, masterable meaning-which-is-truth. It cannot incarnate the Logos. At the same time there is no meaning (and no Logos) outside signification. Differance 'maintains our relationship with that which we necessarily misconstrue, and which exceeds the alternative of presence and absence'.[4]

This melancholy recognition, or something like it, became available as the seventeenth-century Protestant church splintered into sects, each claiming access to salvation on the basis of the Word of God. With no single, central institution to guarantee the meaning of the Scriptures, authority was dispersed among a range of voices, each competing to promise redemption. But if the Word could not make present a single, masterable meaning-which-was-truth, that must be because the Logos had left the earth. The Fall, the moment of division between human and divine, therefore prised open in this period as never before the gap between signification and truth, earth and heaven.

This is the gap which begins to be glimpsed in 'The Nativity Ode' and is more clearly apparent in 'At a Solemn Music'. In each case the problem is evident in the question of voice. To lay claim to the truth is to speak with the voice of God from a position of divine omniscience. But to do so is to repudiate the human voice of the poet, and thus to widen the gap between heaven and earth, when the project is to close it by affirming redemption as a human reality. It is as a solution to this problem that 'sphere-borne' song can act as a pledge of heaven's joy in 'At a Solemn Music', but it is a consequence of it that 'we' cannot be certain of our ability to join in without discord.

In Dziga Vertov's film, *Man with a Movie Camera* (1928), the camera triumphantly swoops and glides from place to place, presenting the audience with long-shots and close-ups, showing familiar objects from unusual angles, and recording events which the human eye cannot possibly be in a position to see. The voice in 'The Nativity Ode' behaves in a rather similar way – and effects something like the same celebration of signifying power. The poet, who is not simply an omniscient third-person narrator, but speaks for 'us', does so from within the stable and from the cosmos, from the present and the past, laying claim to a knowledge of the future which implies divine authority, and acknowledging a human limitation on what can be known. But as I have suggested, it is exactly this triumphant versatility, this difference within the voice of the poet/prophet, that calls in question the authority of the text and begins the Fall into differance.

Milton's poetry continues to be haunted by the problem of voices which query presence even while they construct it. Sonnet XVI, 'On his Blindness' confronts the issue directly by isolating the doubting voice of the human speaker from the authoritative voice of virtue:

> When I consider how my light is spent,
>   Ere half my days, in this dark world and wide,
>   And that one talent which is death to hide,
>   Lodged with me useless, though my soul more bent
> To serve therewith my maker, and present
>   My true account, lest he returning chide,
>   Doth God exact day-labour, light denied,
>   I fondly ask. But Patience to prevent
> That murmur, soon replies, God doth not need
>   Either man's work or his own gifts. Who best
>   Bear his mild yoke, they serve him best. His state
> Is kingly: thousands at his bidding speed
>   And post o'er land and ocean without rest;
>   They also serve who only stand and wait.[5]

The two voices of the text are in marked contrast to each other. The first speaker, no longer the generalised 'we' of the earlier poems, is identified as a specific individual, a subjectivity struggling to make sense of the world amid a welter of subordinate clauses. Patience is authoritative, clear and paratactic. The Sonnet is thus dramatic as the previous texts are not. It solves the problem of voice in formal terms. We have no reason to doubt the authenticity of the 'I', who does no more than formulate a question (with whatever syntactic difficulty, and however 'fondly' – foolishly, as well as eagerly). But what guarantees the authority of Patience? Very little, except the syntax. The ringing main clauses in the second half of the Sonnet do not invite discussion or debate. Who would feel qualified to dispute the force of these emphatic assertions, culminating in a line which sounds like a piece of the proverbial wisdom (and has become so since)? Patience's position also has a broad scriptural authority, of course, though it quite alters the usual reading of the parable of the talents (Matthew xxv, 14–30). But 'On his Blindness' is a great deal more modest in its pretensions than 'The Nativity Ode', which claims the authority to make present the Logos. If the Sonnet offers meaning-which-is-truth, it does

so as a matter of rhetoric, without anchoring the truth in any extratextual source.

Comus (A Masque Presented at Ludlow Castle) (1634), is fully dramatic, and the problem of the authority of the speaker is here made
explicit. The *Masque* displays an encounter between vice and virtue,
rapacious enchanter and innocent lady. Comus employs the full
resources of rhetoric to persuade the Lady to drink his magic potion,
but she counters his 'wit' and 'dazzling fence' (lines 789–90) with
a plain argument for temperance and an assertion of the value of
chastity. Comus responds, but not to her words themselves:

> She fables not, I feel that I do fear
> Her words set off by some superior power;
> And though not mortal, yet a cold shuddering dew
> Dips me all o'er, as when the wrath of Jove
> Speaks thunder.
>
> (799–803)

The presence, the superior power which guarantees the truth of
the Lady's words, is elsewhere. The text no longer fully trusts to
the effectiveness of its own signifying processes. Nor does it trust
its audience to distinguish rhetoric from truth, but feels it necessary
to authorise in this way one of the conflicting voices. The villain
explicitly concedes the case. In practice the precaution turns out to
have been more than justified; despite Comus's response, a number
of twentieth-century critics have still preferred to be convinced by
the sensuous particularity of his earlier speeches, and to repudiate
the egalitarian politics of the Lady's. But the inclusion in the text
of Comus's comment ironically acknowledges what criticism has
so amply demonstrated, that truth cannot be sealed finally and
incontrovertibly into words, and that interpretation always takes
place from a position, on the basis of existing assumptions, presuppositions and values.

In hell the fallen angels seek the distraction in a number of
pursuits. Some find it in 'song', singing to the accompaniment of
the harp the story of their own heroic deeds and their tragic fall.

> Their song was partial, but the harmony
> (What could it less when spirits immortal sing?)
> Suspended hell, and took with ravishment
> The thronging audience.
>
> (*Paradise Lost* II, 552–5)

The song is 'partial' (polyphonic as well as biased), but it has a
magic power to distance hell. Others among the fallen angels take
comfort in philosophy, a still more pleasing pastime, 'For eloquence

the soul, song charms the sense' (line 556). The philosophy, of course, is false, 'Yet with a pleasing sorcery could charm/Pain for a while' (lines 566–7). The imagery (sorcery, charms) is of enchantment. Are song and eloquence therefore suspect? Or are *this* song and *this* eloquence magic only because they are false? The generalised nature of the comment suggests not: 'For eloquence the soul, song charms the sense'. But it implies a hierarchy in which eloquence (intellectual debate, philosophy) appeals to the higher faculty.

Comus the enchanter uses charms to ensnare the Lady (lines 757, 852), and she succumbs, at least to the extent that she follows him to his palace. The charms he displays for the audience are most evidently the 'Shakespearean' imagery of his rhetoric ('millions of spinning worms,/That in their green shops weave the smooth-haired silk' (lines 714–15).[6] But the suspicion that charms are confined to evil enchanters, and indeed the implication of the quotation from *Paradise Lost* that poetry is inferior to philosophy, are both dispelled in *Comus* in an engaging moment of recognition by the Second Brother (played by Thomas Egerton, aged nine). The Elder Brother describes the sun-clad power of chastity in verse which is marginally less Shakespearean than Comus's, but still gratifying full of ghosts and goblins, charnels and perilous wilds. The younger boy exclaims,

> How charming is divine philosophy!
> Not harsh, and crabbed as dull fools suppose,
> But musical as is Apollo's lute,
> And a perpetual feast of nectared sweets.
>
> (475–8)

The enchantment is there and the sensual delight too, in an instance of authorised 'eloquence' which is both poetry and philosophy. The power of 'song' is reaffirmed.

But if the 'charm' of song is at once the property of hell, of wicked enchanters and of divine philosophy alike, how can the reader or the audience be sure to distinguish one from the other? How is delusion to be avoided? How can a poet be certain 'to imbreed and cherish . . . the seeds of virtue'?

Comus attempts to solve the problem by authorising one of its voices. In *Lycidas* the problem of voice becomes critical; and so does the problem of poetry. The claims made in *Lycidas* on behalf of poetry are as high as ever. The whole text centres on the question of song. In accordance with the pastoral mode of the poem, the dead Lycidas was a shepherd. Shepherds conventionally sing (and play their oaten reeds). The text itself will be a song for a poet:

> Who would not sing for Lycidas? he knew
> Himself to sing, and build the lofty rhyme.
>
> (10–11)

But it is also to be the song of a shepherd-poet: 'For we were nursed upon the self-same hill,/Fed the same flock' (lines 23–4). Thus the shepherd-speaker too may merit an elegy in due course (19–22).

The delicacy of the imagery should not be allowed to obscure the seriousness of the project. In a section which startlingly discards all delicacy the poem denounces bad shepherds and their 'lean and flashy songs' (line 123), which are no more than 'wind' and 'rank mist' (line 126). The passage differentiates those songs from this, the text itself, and in doing so offers to specify the limits beyond which poetry no longer cherishes virtue.

When *Lycidas* was printed for the second time in 1645, Milton included a headnote explaining that the poem 'by occasion foretells the ruin of our corrupted clergy then in their height'. This may have been a politic move in 1645, but it has tended to cloud for subsequent criticism the continuity and the complexity of the shepherd imagery which runs all the way through the text. In 1637, when the poem first appeared without the headnote, it would have been more readily apparent that the bad shepherds were bad poets as well as bad clergy. Throughout Milton's writing there is a parallel between the two. Poetry works 'beside the office of a pulpit' to cherish virtue. The prophetic character of the poet and the poetic quality of the Scriptures hold the link in place. The bad shepherds of *Lycidas* betray the sheep. They are

> Blind mouths! that scarce themselves know how to hold
> A sheep-hook, or have learned aught else the least
> That to the faithful herdman's art belongs!
>
> (119–21)

Their 'lean and flashy songs' are an echo of the 'new-fangled toys and trimming slight' characteristic of fashionable verse in 'At a Vacation Exercise' (1628), and perhaps too of Comus's 'dear wit, and gay rhetoric' (*Comus*, line 789).

Edward King, the Lycidas of the poem, as a Fellow of Christ's College, Cambridge, was in holy orders. He was also a poet. And the unnamed Shepherd who authorises both vocations, origin and guarantee of the utterances of all good shepherds, is of course Christ himself.

But although in *Lycidas* poetry has lost none of its importance and has surrendered none of its high claims, and although the delusive charms of bad poetry are denounced more vehemently than ever before, the poem seems nevertheless to betray an uncertainty about the power of poetry which is not finally resolved. This hesitation begins with an allusion to Calliope, the muse of epic and the mother of a poet:

> What could the muse herself that Orpheus bore,
> The muse herself for her enchanting son
> Whom universal nature did lament,
> When by the rout that made the hideous roar,
> His gory visage down the stream was sent?
>
> (58–62)

In classical legend the song of Orpheus had the power to charm beasts and plants. In the moralised version of the story, common from the Middle Ages onwards, a parallel was drawn between Orpheus and the biblical poet, author of the Psalms, whose music was able to comfort the melancholy King Saul. In the humanist interpretation of the legend, which begins to appear in the sixteenth century, the music of Orpheus is able to control wild things because it is in tune with the universal harmony, the music of the spheres.[7] According to *Lycidas*, 'enchanting' Orpheus was torn to pieces by disordered and frenzied creatures whose own wild utterance was a 'hideous roar'. The muse could not save him.

Is it possible that bad poetry drives out good? Or that meaningless noise drives out poetry altogether? If so, is the herdman's art worth learning? At once the poem continues,

> Alas! What boots it with uncessant care
> To tend the homely slighted shepherd's trade,
> And strictly meditate the thankless muse?
>
> (64–6)

If fame is the motive, the speaker goes on, the death of Lycidas (and Orpheus, of course) demonstrates that a poet might not live to enjoy it. But Apollo, himself a poet, intervenes: 'Fame is no plant that grows on mortal soil' (line 78). Fame belongs in heaven, where 'all-judging Jove' makes the final assessment of poetic merit (line 82).

The crisis is averted and the conclusion of the poem anticipated: good poetry is recognised in heaven, if not on earth; Lycidas is in heaven, where he hears the saints, 'That sing, and singing in their glory move' (line 180). But it is striking that in this text God has become the *judge* of true poetry. He is no longer its author, as he was in 'The Nativity Ode'.

After the denunciation of the bad poets there follows, as if to demonstrate what can and should be done, a passage of perfect pastoral delicacy. Primroses and violets, cowslips and daffodils are summoned to strew the 'laureate' hearse of Lycidas (laurelled – for a poet). The surprise of what follows calls into question the confidence of the demonstration:

> For so to interpose a little ease,
> Let our frail thoughts dally with a false surmise.

(152–3)

Lycidas has no hearse: he was drowned and the body was not recovered. The flower passage is a cheat, escapism, its charms pure wind and mist, frail thoughts dallying with a false surmise.

Nevertheless, Lycidas is now in heaven, where he hears 'the unexpressive nuptial song' which surrounds the throne of God (line 176). 'Unexpressive' is familiar from 'The Nativity Ode' where it characterises the song of the angels both as inexpressible and also as an instance of full presence, not an expression of something else, but the thing itself, 'unexpressive' in that it obliterates the differance of representation. In the 'Ode', however, the angels' song constitutes the bond between heaven and earth, and signifies the miracle of redemption. By contrast, in the economy of the later text it belongs in heaven, audible there only. Presence has left the earth. There remains in this world only a textuality from which the certainty of truth has fled, enchantment which may prove to be a 'false surmise'.

The prophetic utterance is single and single-minded, monologic, guaranteed as it is by the Word whose word it represents. *Lycidas* is composed of a range of voices. As in 'On his Blindness', one of these is a questioning, doubting subject-speaker. Antony Easthope has argued persuasively that the iambic pentameter became the dominant mode of English verse from the sixteenth century onwards, as the project of poetry was increasingly to simulate the individual speaking voice. The effect is a verse form which helps to construct the illusion of an identifiable individual spontaneously expressing his or her subjective experience.[8] In a discussion specifically of 'On his Blindness', Easthope also points to the way that in this poem the syntax rides across the rhyme scheme:

> And that one talent which is death to hide,
> Lodged with me useless, though my soul more bent

> To serve therewith my maker, and present
> My true account . . .
>
> (3–6)

The effect, Easthope argues, is relatively to efface the signifier, the materiality of the verse itself, metre, rhyme and rhythm, in favour of the construction of an individual voice speaking, struggling, feeling.[9]

A similar strategy is developed in a slightly different way in *Lycidas*. Here the verse form is a freer version of the *canzone*, a mode considerably adapted and modified in sixteenth-century Italy. The *canzone* consists of a repeated long stanza with a complex rhyme scheme, and a shorter concluding stanza. The further modification of this form in *Lycidas* develops a tendency to counterpoint between rhyme scheme and sentence structure, so that the syntactic pauses frequently do not coincide with the ends of the couplets. In other words, where the rhyme points to closure, the syntax does not, except at the end of each verse paragraph. The resulting impression is of an intensity of feeling which is barely contained.[10]

> I come to pluck your berries harsh and crude,
> And with forced fingers rude,
> Shatter your leaves before the mellowing year.
> Bitter constraint, and sad occasion dear,
> Compels me to disturb your season due:
> For Lycidas is dead, dead ere his prime,
> Young Lycidas, and hath not left his peer:
> Who would not sing for Lycidas? he knew
> Himself to sing, and build the lofty rhyme.
>
> (3–11)

'Year' is disjoined from 'dear', even though lines 5 and 6 are also held together formally by a half-rhyme at the beginning; lines 6 and 7 are joined syntactically but they do not rhyme; lines 8 and 9 begin with a repeated pattern ('For Lycidas', 'Young Lycidas'). The syntax breaks line 10 in the middle and runs lines 10 and 11 together. Here the sense would lead us to expect a couplet but the rhymes refer back to lines 7 and 8. The effect is of feeling transgressing the austere discipline of the verse form, and the reader's attention is focused on the speaker's grief, which is brought under control with such difficulty. We are invited to attend in consequence to the subjectivity which thus marshals its feelings, the 'I' of line 3.

This 'I' is the main voice of the text. For much of the poem it is a doubtful questioning voice. The occasion for a poem has come too soon. Why did no one intervene to save Lycidas? What is the value of poetry? Is it worth the struggle? Finally, however, the voice acquires authority. 'Weep no more, woeful shepherds weep no more' (line 165). The rhythmic echo of the opening line ('Yet once more, O ye laurels, and once more') declares this the moment of resolution. Lycidas is in heaven, where he hears the song of the saints.

But at the instant when, believing that we have been reading the direct utterance of the poet, encountering a subjectivity, Milton, we seem to share the triumph of his new-found confidence, 'Milton' slips away: 'Thus sang the uncouth swain . . .' (line 186). Another quite impersonal enunciating subject takes the place of the 'I' in the text, this time the author of a fiction in which an uncouth swain is the main speaker. An anonymous third-person narrative suddenly comes to frame the text we have read, turning it into a dramatic monologue, releasing the possibility of layers of irony. Where now is the (authorised) voice of *Lycidas*?

Meanwhile, there have been other voices, perhaps possessed of greater authority than the shepherd-speaker's. Phoebus Apollo speaks of true poetic fame. Quite apart from the Christian orthodoxy of his views, and his status as god of poetry, the weight and the finality of his concluding couplet convince us that he must surely be right:

> As he pronounces lastly on each deed,
> Of so much fame in heaven expect thy meed.
>
> (83–4)

And the denunciation of bad poets by the 'dread voice' (line 132) of the pilot of the Galilean lake must certainly be right too, since his concluding couplet is even more solemnly resonant (whatever it means):

> But that two-handed engine at the door,
> Stands ready to smite once, and smite no more.
>
> (130–1)

Who, then, is speaking in *Lycidas*? An uncouth swain struggling with the question of vocation? An increasingly confident Christian poet divinely endorsed by Apollo and St. Peter? A modern subjectivity desiring the Lacanian other (*objet a*) –

> To sport with Amaryllis in the shade,
> Or with the tangles of Neaera's hair?
>
> (68–9)

Or perhaps an author desiring the Lacanian Other: longing to be the origin of language, the source of meaning and truth, to be able to inscribe the Word in the word, for ever in quest of presence, but haunted by the lack which ensures differance?

Notes

1. The standard biography is W. R. Parker, *Milton* (2 vols, Oxford: Clarendon Press, 1968).

2. Jacques Derrida, 'Différance', in *Margins of Philosophy*, trans. Alan Bass (Brighton: Harvester, 1982), pp. 1–27. Much of Derrida's theory of language is available in relatively accessible form in three interviews he gave between 1967 and 1971; see *Positions* trans. Alan Bass (London: Athlone Press, 1987).

3. Derrida, *Positions*, p. 20.

4. Jacques Derrida, 'Différance', in *Margins of Philosophy*, trans. Alan Bass (Brighton: Harvester, 1982), p. 20.

5. I have modernised the punctuation of this poem for the sake of the syntax.

6. F. R. Leavis, 'Milton's Verse' (1933), in *Revaluation: Tradition and Development in English Poetry* (London: Penguin, 1964), pp.42–61, see pp. 46–7.

7. John Hollander, *The Untuning of the Sky* (Princeton: Princeton University Press, 1961), pp.163–73.

8. Antony Easthope, *Poetry as Discourse* (London: Methuen, 1983), pp. 69–77.

9. Antony Easthope, 'Towards the Autonomous Subject in Poetry: Milton's "On his Blindness" ', in *Post-structuralist Readings of English Poetry*, ed. Richard Machin and Christopher Norris (Cambridge: Cambridge University Press, 1987),pp. 122–33, see pp. 128–9.

10. F. T. Prince, *The Italian Element in Milton's Verse* (Oxford: Clarendon Press, 1954), pp. 84–8.

Shoshana Felman: The Case of Poe: Applications/Implications of Psychoanalysis

Lacan's first collection of published essays, the *Ecrits*, opens with a chapter entitled 'The Seminar on *The Purloined Letter*'. This so-called 'Seminar' is the written account of a year-long course devoted to the exploration of a short literary text, one of Edgar Allen Poe's *Extraordinary Tales*, 'The Purloined Letter'. The Seminar was offered to trainees in psychoanalysis. Why did Lacan choose to devote a whole year of teaching to this tale? What is the significance of the

Reprinted from Shoshana Felman, *Jacques Lacan and the Adventure of Insight: Psychoanalysis in Contemporary Culture* (Cambridge, Mass., 1987), pp. 27–32, 39–51.

strategic decision to place this 'Seminar' at the opening of the *Ecrits*, as a key work in Lacan's endeavour?

I will approach these questions indirectly, by meditating first on the 'case of Poe' in the literary investigations of psychology and psychoanalysis before Lacan. I will then attempt to analyse both the difference that Lacan has made in the psychoanalytical approach to reading and the way in which the lesson Lacan derived from Poe is a lesson in psychoanalysis.

To account for poetry in psychoanalytical terms has traditionally meant to analyse poetry as a symptom of a particular poet. I would here like to reverse this approach, and to analyse a particular poet as a symptom of poetry.

Perhaps no poet has been so highly acclaimed and, at the same time, so violently disclaimed as Edgar Allan Poe. One of the most controversial figures on the American literary scene, 'perhaps the most thoroughly misunderstood of all American writers',[1] 'a stumbling block for the judicial critic',[2] no other poet in the history of criticism has engendered so much disagreement and so many critical contradictions. It is my contention that this critical disagreement is itself symptomatic of a *poetic effect*, and that the critical contradictions to which Poe's poetry has given rise are themselves indirectly significant of the nature of poetry.

The Poe-etic Effect: A Literary Case History

No other poet has been so often referred to as a 'genius', in a sort of common consensus shared even by his detractors. Joseph Wood Krutch, whose study tends to belittle Poe's stature and to disparage the value of his artistic achievement, nevertheless entitles his monograph *Edgar Allan Poe: A Study in Genius*.[3] So do many other critics, who acknowledge and assert Poe's 'genius' in the very titles of their essays.[4] 'It happens to us but few times in our lives,' writes Thomas Wentworth Higginson, 'to come consciously into the presence of that extraordinary miracle we call genius. Among the many literary persons whom I have happened to meet . . . there are not half a dozen who have left an irresistible sense of this rare quality; and among these few, Poe.'[5] The English poet Swinburne speaks of 'the special quality of [Poe's] strong and delicate genius'; the French poet Mallarmé describes his translations of Poe as 'a monument to the genius who . . . exercised his influence in our country'; and the American poet James Russell Lowell, one of Poe's harshest critics, who, in his notorious versified verdict, judged Poe's poetry to include 'two fifths sheer fudge', nonetheless asserts, 'Mr. Poe has that indescribable something which men have agreed to call *genius* . . . Let talent writhe and contort itself as it may, it has no such magnetism. Larger of bone and sinew it may be, but the wings are wanting.'[6]

However suspicious and unromantic the critical reader might wish to be with respect to 'that indescribable something which men have agreed to call genius', it is clear that Poe's poetry produces what might be called a *genius effect:* the impression of some undefinable but compelling force to which the reader is subjected. To describe 'this power, *which is felt*',[7] as one reader puts it, Lowell speaks of 'magnetism'; other critics speak of 'magic'. 'Poe,' writes Bernard Shaw, 'constantly and inevitably produced magic where his greatest contemporaries produced only beauty.'[8] T. S. Eliot quite reluctantly agrees: 'Poe had, to an exceptional degree, the feeling for the incantatory element in poetry, of that which may, in the most nearly literal sense, be called "the magic of verse".'[9]

Poe's 'magic' is thus ascribed to the ingenuity of his versification, to his exceptional technical virtuosity. And yet the word *magic*, 'in the most nearly literal sense', means much more than just the intellectual acknowledgment of an outstanding technical skill; it connotes the effective action of something that exceeds both the understanding and the control of the person who is subjected to it; it connotes a force to which the reader has no choice but to submit. 'No one could tell us what it is,' writes Lowell, still in reference to Poe's genius, 'and yet there is none who is not inevitably aware of . . . its power' (p. 11). 'Poe,' said Shaw, 'inevitably produced magic.' Something about Poe's poetry is experienced as inevitable, unavoidable (and not just as irresistible). What is more, once this poetry is read, its inevitability is there to stay; it becomes lastingly inevitable: 'it will stick to the memory of every one who reads it,' writes P. Pendleton Cooke (p. 23). And Eliot: 'Poe is the author of a few . . . short poems . . . which do somehow stick in the memory' (pp. 207–8).

This is why Poe's poetry can be defined, and indeed has been, as a poetry of influence par excellence, in the sense emphasised by Harold Bloom: 'to inflow', or to have power over another. The case of Poe in literary history could in fact be accounted for as an extreme and complex case of 'the anxiety of influence', of the anxiety unwittingly provoked by the 'influence' irresistibly emanating from this poetry. What is unique, however, about Poe's influence, as about the magic of his verse, is the extent to which its action is unaccountably insidious, exceeding the control, the will, and the awareness of those who are subjected to it. Eliot writes:

Poe's influence is . . . puzzling. In France the influence of his poetry and of his poetic theories has been immense. In England and America it seems almost negligible . . . And yet one cannot be sure that one's own writing has *not* been influenced by Poe. (p. 205; original italics)

Studying Poe's influence on Baudelaire, Mallarmé, and Valéry, Eliot goes on to comment:

Here are three literary generations, representing almost exactly a century of French poetry. Of course, these are poets very different from each other . . . But I think we can trace the development and descent of one particular theory of the nature of poetry through these three poets and it is a theory which takes its origin in the theory . . . of Edgar Poe. And the impression we get of the influence of Poe is the more impressive, because of the fact that Mallarmé, and Valéry in turn, did not merely derive from Poe through Baudelaire: each of them subjected himself to that influence directly, and has left convincing evidence of the value which he attached to the theory and practice of Poe himself. (p. 206)

Curiously enough, while Poe's worldwide importance and effective influence is beyond question, critics nonetheless continue to protest and to proclaim, as loudly as they can, that Poe is unimportant, that Poe is *not* a major poet. Taxing Poe with 'vulgarity', Aldous Huxley argues:

Was Edgar Allan Poe a major poet? It would surely never occur to any English-speaking critic to say so. And yet, in France, from 1850 till the present time, the best poets of each generation – yes, and the best critics, too; for, like most excellent poets, Baudelaire, Mallarmé, Paul Valéry are also admirable critics – have gone out of their way to praise him. . . . We who are speakers of English . . . , we can only say, with all due respect, that Baudelaire, Mallarmé and Valéry were wrong and that Poe is not one of our major poets. (*Recognition*, p. 160)

Poe's detractors seem to be unaware, however, of the paradox that underlies their enterprise: it is by no means clear why anyone should take the trouble to write – at length – about a writer of no importance. Poe's most systematic denouncer, Yvor Winters, thus writes:

The menace lies not, primarily, in his impressionable admirers among literary people of whom he still has some, even in England and in America, where a familiarity with his language ought to render his crudity obvious, for these individuals in the main do not make themselves permanently very effective: it lies rather in the impressive body of scholarship . . . When a writer is supported by a sufficient body of scholarship, a very little philosophical elucidation will suffice to establish him in the scholarly world as a writer whose greatness is self-evident. (*Recognition*, p. 177)

The irony here is that, in writing his attack on Poe, what the attacker is in fact doing is adding still another study to the bulk of 'the impressive body of scholarship' in which, in his own terms, 'the menace lies'; so that, paradoxically enough, through Winters' study, the menace – that is, the possibility of taking Poe's 'greatness as a writer' as 'self-evident' – will indeed increase. I shall argue that, regardless of the value-judgment it may pass on Poe, this impressive bulk of Poe scholarship, the very quantity of the critical literature to which Poe's poetry has given rise, is itself an indication of its effective poetic power, of the strength with which it drives the reader to an *action*, compels him to a *reading act*. The elaborate written denials of Poe's value, the loud and lengthy negations of his importance, are therefore very like psychoanalytical negations. It is clear that if Poe's text in effect were unimportant, it would not seem so important to proclaim, argue, and prove that he is unimportant. The fact that it so much *matters* to proclaim that Poe *does not matter* is but evidence of the extent to which Poe's poetry is, in effect, a poetry that matters.

Poe might thus be said to have a *literary case history*, most revealing in that it incarnates, in its controversial forms, the paradoxical nature of a strong poetic effect: the very poetry that, more than any other, is experienced as *irresistible* has also proved to be, in literary history, the poetry most *resisted*, the one that, more than any other, has provoked resistances.

This apparent contradiction, which makes of Poe's poetry a unique case in literary history, clearly partakes of the paradoxical nature of an *analytical effect*. The enigma it presents us with is the enigma of the analytical par excellence, as stated by Poe himself, whose amazing intuitions of the nature of what he calls 'analysis' are strikingly similar to the later findings of psychoanalysis. 'The mental features discoursed of as the analytical are, in themselves, but little susceptible of analysis. We appreciate them only in their effects.'[10]

Because of the very nature of its strong effects, of the reading-acts that it provokes, Poe's text (and not just Poe's biography of his personal neurosis) is clearly an analytical case in the history of literary criticism, a case that suggests something crucial to understand in psychoanalytic terms. It is therefore not surprising that

Poe has been repeatedly singled out for psychoanalytical research, has persistently attracted the attention of psychoanalytic critics.

Lacan: The Approach of Textual Problematization

'The Purloined Letter', as is well known, is the story of the double theft of a compromising letter, originally sent to the queen. Surprised by the unexpected entrance of the king, the queen leaves the letter on the table in full view of any visitor, where it is least likely to appear suspicious and therefore to attract the king's attention. Enter the Minister D who, observing the queen's anxiety and the play of glances between her and the unsuspicious king, analyses the situation, figures out, recognising the addressor's handwriting, what the letter is about, and steals it – by substituting for it another letter he takes from his pocket – under the very eyes of the challenged queen, who can do nothing to prevent the theft without provoking the king's suspicions. The queen then asks the prefect of police to search the minister's apartment and person for the letter. The prefect uses every conceivable secret-police technique to search every conceivable hiding place on the minister's premises, but to no avail.

Having exhausted his resources, the prefect consults Auguste Dupin, the famous 'analyst', as Poe calls him (i.e., an amateur detective who excels in solving problems by means of deductive logic), to whom he tells the whole story. (It is, in fact, from this narration of the prefect of police to Dupin and in turn reported by the first-person narrator, Dupin's friend, who is also present, that we, the readers, learn the story.)

On a second encounter, Dupin, to the great surprise of the prefect and of the narrator, produces the purloined letter out of his drawer and hands it to the prefect in return for a large amount of money. The prefect leaves, and Dupin explains to the narrator how he found the letter: he deduced that the minister, knowing that his premises would be thoroughly combed by the police, has concluded that the best principle of concealment would be to leave the letter in the open, in full view; the letter would not be discovered precisely because it would be too self-evident. On this assumption, Dupin called on the minister in his apartment and, glancing around, soon located the letter carelessly hanging from the mantelpiece in a card rack. A little later, a disturbance in the street provoked by a man in Dupin's employ drew the minister to the window, at which moment Dupin quickly replaced the letter with a facsimile.

What Lacan is concerned with at this point of his research is the psychoanalytic problematics of the 'repetition compulsion',[11] as elaborated in Freud's speculative *Beyond the Pleasure Principle*. The thrust of Lacan's endeavor, with respect to Poe, is thus to point out the way in which the story's plot, its sequence of events (as, for Freud, the sequence of events in a life-story), is contingent on, overdetermined by, a principle of repetition that governs it and inadvertently structures its dramatic and ironic impact. 'There are two scenes,' remarks Lacan, 'the first of which we shall straightway designate the primal scene . . . since the second may be considered its repetition in the very sense we are considering today' (p. 41).[12] The primal scene takes place in the queen's boudoir: it is the theft of the letter from the queen by the minister; the second scene – its repetition – is the theft of the letter from the minister by Dupin.

What constitutes repetition for Lacan, however, is not the mere thematic resemblance of the double theft, but the whole structural situation in which the repeated theft takes place: in each case, the theft is the outcome of an intersubjective relationship between three terms; in the first scene, the three participants are the police, the minister, and Dupin. In much the same way as Dupin takes the place of the minister in the first scene (the place of the letter's robber), the minister in the second scene takes the place of the queen in the first (the dispossessed possessor of the letter); whereas the police, for whom the letter remains invisible, take the place formerly occupied by the king. The two scenes thus mirror each other, in that they dramatise the repeated exchange of 'three glances, borne by three subjects, incarnated each time by different characters'. What is repeated, in other words, is not a psychological act committed as a function of the individual psychology of a character, but three functional *positions in a structure* which, determining three different viewpoints, embody three different relations to the act of seeing – of seeing, specifically, the purloined letter.

The first is a glance that sees nothing: the King and the Police.
The second, a glance which sees that the first sees nothing and deludes itself as to the secrecy of what it hides: the Queen, then the Minister.
The third sees that the first two glances leave what should be hidden exposed to whomever would seize it: the Minister, and finally Dupin.

(p. 44)

I have devised the following diagram as an attempt to schematise Lacan's analysis and to make explicit the synchronic, structural perceptions he proposes of the temporal, diachronic unfolding of the drama.

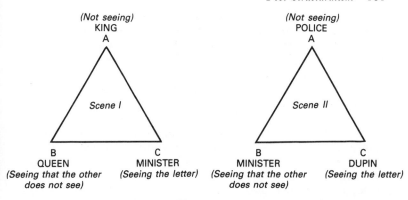

FIGURE 1

Although Lacan does not elaborate upon the possible ramifications of this structure, the diagram is open to a number of terminological translations, reinterpreting it in the light of Freudian and Lacanian concepts. Here are two such possible translations:

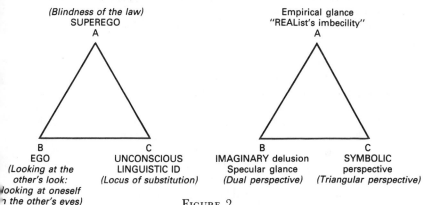

FIGURE 2

'What interests us today,' insists Lacan,

is the manner in which the subjects relay each other in their displacement during the intersubjective repetition.

We shall see that their displacement is determined by the place which a pure signifier – the purloined letter – comes to occupy in their trio. And that is what will confirm for us its status as repetition automatism.

(p. 45)

The purloined letter, in other words, becomes itself – through its insistence in the structure – a symbol or a signifier of the unconscious, to the extent that it is destined 'to signify the annulment of what it signifies' – the necessity of its own repression, of the repression of its message: 'It is not only the meaning but the text of the message which it would be dangerous to place in circulation' (p. 56). But in much the same way as the repressed *returns* in the *symptom*, which is its repetitive symbolic substitute, the purloined letter ceaselessly returns in the tale – as a signifier of the repressed – through its repetitive displacements and replacements. 'This is indeed what happens in the repetition compulsion,' says Lacan (p. 60). Unconscious desire, once repressed, survives in displaced symbolic media that govern the subject's life and actions without his ever being aware of their meaning or of the repetitive pattern they structure:

If what Freud discovered and rediscovers with a perpetually increasing sense of shock has a meaning, it is that the displacement of the signifier determines the subjects in their acts, in their destiny, in their refusals, in their blindnesses, in their end and in their fate, their innate gifts and social acquisitions notwithstanding, without regard for character or sex, and that, willingly or not, everything that might be considered the stuff of psychology, kit and caboodle, will follow the path of the signifier.

(p. 60)

In what sense, then, does the second scene in Poe's tale, while repeating the first scene, nonetheless differ from it? In the sense, precisely, that the second scene, through the repetition, allows for an understanding, for an *analysis* of the first. This analysis through repetition is to become, in Lacan's ingenious reading, no less than an *allegory of psychoanalysis*. The intervention of Dupin, who restores the letter to the queen, is thus compared to the intervention of the analyst, who rids the patient of the symptom. The analyst's effectiveness, however, does not spring from his intellectual strength but – insists Lacan – from his position in the repetitive structure. By virtue of his occupying the third position – that is, the *locus* of the unconscious of the subject as a place of substitution of letter for letter (of signifier for signifier) – the analyst, through transference, allows at once for a repetition of the trauma and for a symbolic substitution, and thus effects the drama's denouement.

It is instructive to compare Lacan's study of the psychoanalytical repetition compulsion to Poe's text to Marie Bonaparte's study of Poe's repetition compulsion through his text.[13] Although the two analysts study the same author and focus on the same psychoanalytic concept, their approaches are strikingly different. To the extent that Bonaparte's study of Poe has become a classic, a model of applied psychoanalysis, I would like, in pointing out the differences in Lacan's approach, to suggest the way in which those differences at once put in question the traditional approach and offer an alternative to it.

1. *What does a repetition compulsion repeat? Interpretation of difference as opposed to interpretation of identity.* For Marie Bonaparte, what is compulsively repeated through the variety of Poe's texts is the same unconscious fantasy: Poe's sadonecrophiliac desire for his dead mother. For Lacan, what is repeated in the text is not the content of a fantasy but the symbolic displacement of a signifier through the insistence of a signifying chain; repetition is not of *sameness* but of *difference*, not of independent terms or of analogous themes but of a structure of differential interrelationships,[14] in which what *returns* is always *other*. Thus, the triangular structure repeats itself only through the difference of the characters who successively come to occupy the three positions; its structural significance is perceived only *through* this difference. Likewise, the significance of the letter is situated in its displacement, that is, in its repetitive movements toward a different place. And the second scene, being, for Lacan, an allegory of analysis, is important not just in that it *repeats* the first scene, but in the way this repetition (like the transferential repetition of a psychoanalytical experience) *makes a difference:* brings about a solution to the problem. Thus, whereas Bonaparte analyses repetition as the insistence of identity, for Lacan any possible insight into the reality of the unconscious is contingent on a perception of repetition, not as a confirmation of identity, but as the insistence of the indelibility of a difference.

2. *An analysis of the signifier as opposed to an analysis of the signified.* In the light of Lacan's reading of Poe's tale as itself an allegory of the psychoanalytic reading, it might be illuminating to define the difference in approach between Lacan and Bonaparte in terms of the story. If the purloined letter can be said to be a sign of the unconscious, for Bonaparte the analyst's task is to uncover the letter's content, which she believes – as do the police – to be hidden somewhere in the real, in some secret biographical depth. For Lacan, on the other hand, the analyst's task is not to read the letter's hidden referential content, but to situate the superficial indication of its external movement, to analyse the paradoxically invisible symbolic evidence of its displacement, its structural insistence, in a signifying chain. 'There is such a thing,' writes Poe, 'as being too profound. Truth is not always in a well. In fact, as

regards the most important knowledge, I do believe she is invariably superficial.'[15] Espousing Poe's insight, Lacan makes the principle of symbolic evidence the guideline for an analysis not of the signified but of the signifier – for an analysis of the unconscious (the repressed) not as hidden but on the contrary as *exposed* – in language – through a significant (rhetorical) displacement.

This analysis of the signifier, the model of which can be found in Freud's interpretation of dreams, is nonetheless a radical reversal of the traditional expectations involved in the common psychoanalytical approach to literature and its invariable search for hidden meanings. Indeed, not only is Lacan's reading of 'The Purloined Letter' subversive of the traditional model of psychoanalytic reading: it is, in general, a type of reading that is methodologically unprecedented in the history of literary criticism. The history of reading has accustomed us to the assumption – usually unquestioned – that reading is finding meaning, that interpretation can dwell only on the meaningful. Lacan's analysis of the signifier opens up a radically new assumption, an assumption that is an insightful logical and methodological consequence of Freud's discovery: that what *can* be read (and perhaps what *should* be read) is not just meaning but the lack of meaning; that significance lies not just in consciousness but, specifically, in its disruption; that the signifier can be analysed in its effects without its signified being known; that the lack of meaning – the discontinuity in conscious understanding – can and should be interpreted as such, without necessarily being transformed into meaning. 'Let's take a look,' writes Lacan:

We shall find illumination in what at first seems to obscure matters: the fact that the tale leaves us in virtually total ignorance of the sender, no less than of the contents, of the letter.

(p. 57)

The signifier is not functional. . . . We might even admit that the letter has an entirely different (if no more urgent) meaning for the Queen than the one understood by the Minister. The sequence of events would not be noticeably affected, not even if it were strictly incomprehensible to an uninformed reader.

(p. 56)

But that this is the very effect of the unconscious in the precise sense that we teach that the unconscious means that man is inhabited by the signifier.

(p. 66)

Thus, for Lacan, what is analytical par excellence is not (as is the case for Bonaparte) the readable but the unreadable and the effects of the unreadable. What calls for analysis is the insistence of the unreadable in the text.

Poe, of course, has said it all in his comment on the nature of what he too – amazingly enough, before the fact – called 'the analytical': 'The mental features discoursed of as the analytical are, in themselves, but little susceptible of analysis. We appreciate them only in their effects.' But, oddly enough, what Poe himself had said so strikingly about the analytical had itself remained totally unanalysed, indeed unnoticed, by psychoanalytic scholars before Lacan, perhaps because it, too, according to its own analytical logic, had been 'a little too self-evident' to be perceived.

3. *A textual as opposed to a biographical approach.* The analysis of the signifier implies a theory of textuality for which Poe's biography, or his so-called sickness, or his hypothetical personal psychoanalysis, become irrelevant. The presupposition – governing enterprises like that of Marie Bonaparte – that poetry can be interpreted only as autobiography is obviously limiting and limited. Lacan's textual analysis for the first time offers a psychoanalytical alternative to the previously unquestioned and thus seemingly exclusive biographical approach.

4. *The analyst/author relation: a subversion of the master/slave pattern and of the doctor/patient opposition.* Let us remember how many readers were unsettled by the humiliating and sometimes condescending psychoanalytic emphasis on Poe's 'sickness', as well as by an explanation equating the poetic with the psychotic. There seemed to be no doubt in the minds of psychoanalytic readers that if the reading situation could be assimilated to the psychoanalytic situation, the poet was to be equated with the sick patient, with the analysand on the couch. Lacan's analysis, however, subverts not only this clinical status of the poet, but along with it the 'bedside' security of the interpreter. If Lacan is not concerned with Poe's sickness, he is quite concerned nonetheless with the figure of the poet in the tale, and with the hypotheses made about his specific competence and incompetence. Both the minister and Dupin are said to be poets, and it is their *poetic* reasoning that the prefect fails to understand and that thus enables both to outsmart the police. 'D—, I presume, is not altogether a fool,' comments Dupin early in the story, to which the prefect of police replies:

'Not altogether a fool . . . but then he's a poet, which I take to be only one remove from a fool.'

'True,' said Dupin, after a long and thoughtful whiff from his meerschaum, 'although I have been guilty of certain doggerel myself.'

(p. 334)

A question Lacan does not address could be raised by emphasising still another point that would normally tend to pass unnoticed, since, once again, it is both so explicit and so ostentatiously insignificant: Why does Dupin say that he too is *guilty* of poetry? In what way does the status of the poet involve guilt? In what sense can we understand the guilt of poetry?

Dupin, then, draws our attention to the fact that both he and the minister are poets, a qualification to which the prefect is condescending. Later, when Dupin explains to the narrator the prefect's defeat, he again insists upon the prefect's blindness to a logic or to a 'principle of concealment' which has to do with poets and thus (it might be assumed) is specifically poetic:

This functionary has been thoroughly mystified; and the remote source of his defeat lies in the supposition that the Minister is a fool, because he has acquired renown as a poet. All fools are poets; this the Prefect feels, and he is merely guilty of a *non distributio medii* in thence inferring that all poets are fools.

(pp. 341–2)

In Baudelaire's translation of Poe's tale into French, the word *fool* is rendered, in its strong, archaic sense, as *fou*, 'mad'. Here, then, is Lacan's paraphrase of this passage in the story:

After which, a moment of derision [on Dupin's part] at the Prefect's error in deducing that because the Minister is a poet, he is not far from being mad, an error, it is argued, which would consist . . . simply in a false distribution of the middle term, since it is far from following from the fact that all madmen are poets.

Yes indeed. But we ourselves are left in the dark as to the poet's superiority in the art of concealment.

(p. 52)

Both this passage in the story and this comment by Lacan seem to be marginal, incidental. Yet the hypothetical *relationship between poetry and madness* is significantly relevant to the case of Poe and to the other psychoanalytical approaches we have been considering. Could it not be said that the error of Marie Bonaparte (who, like the prefect, engages in a search for hidden meaning) lies precisely in the fact that, like the prefect once again, she simplistically equates the poetic with the psychotic, and so, blinded by what she takes to be the poetic *incompetence*, fails to see or understand the specificity of poetic *competence?* Many psychoanalytic investigations diagnosing the poet's sickness and looking for his poetic secret in his person (as do the prefect's men) are indeed very like police investigations;

and like the police in Poe's story, they fail to find the letter, fail to see the textuality of the text.

Lacan, of course, does not say all this – this is not what is at stake in his analysis. All he does is open up still another question where we believed we had come into possession of some sort of answer:

Yes indeed. But we ourselves are left in the dark as to the poet's superiority in the art of concealment.

This seemingly lateral question, asked in passing and left unanswered, suggests, however, the possibility of a whole different focus or perspective of interpretation in the story. If 'The Purloined Letter' is specifically the story of 'the poet's superiority in the art of concealment', then it is not just an allegory of psychoanalysis but also, at the same time, an allegory of poetic writing. And Lacan is himself a poet to the extent that a thought about poetry is what is superiorly concealed in his Seminar.

In Lacan's interpretation, however, the poet's superiority can only be understood as the structural superiority of the third position with respect to the letter: the minister in the first scene, Dupin in the second, both poets. But the third position is also – this is the main point of Lacan's approach, the status of the poet is no longer that of the sick patient, but, if anything, that of the analyst. If the poet is still the object of the accusation of being a fool, his folly – if it does exist (which remains an open question) – would at the same time be the folly of the analyst. The clear-cut opposition between madness and health, or between doctor and patient, is unsettled by the odd functioning of the purloined letter of the unconscious, which no one can possess or master. 'There is no metalanguage', says Lacan: there is no language in which interpretation can itself escape the effects of the unconscious; the interpreter is not more immune than the poet to unconscious delusions and errors.

5. *Implication, as opposed to application, of psychoanalytic theory.* Lacan's approach no longer falls into the category of what has been called 'applied psychoanalysis', since the concept of application implies a relation of exteriority between the applied science and the field it is supposed, unilaterally, to inform. Since, in Lacan's analysis, Poe's text serves to reinterpret Freud just as Freud's text serves to interpret Poe; since psychoanalytic theory and the literary text mutually inform – and displace – each other; since the very position of the interpreter – of the analyst – turns out to be not outside but inside the text, there is no longer a clear-cut opposition or a

well-defined border between literature and psychoanalysis: psychoanalysis can be intraliterary just as much as literature is intrapsychoanalytic. The methodological stake is no longer that of the *application* of psychoanalysis *to* literature but, rather, of their *interimplication in* each other.

If I have dealt at length with Lacan's innovative contribution and with the different methodological example of his approach, it is not so much to set this example up as a new model for imitation, but rather to indicate the way in which it suggestively invites us to go beyond itself (as it takes Freud beyond itself), the way in which it opens up a whole new range of as yet untried possibilities for the enterprise of reading. Lacan's importance in my eyes does not, in other words, lie specifically in any new dogma his 'school' may propose, but in his outstanding demonstration that *there is more than one way* to implicate psychoanalysis in literature; that *how to* implicate psychoanalysis in literature is itself a question for interpretation, a challenge to the ingenuity and insight of the interpreter, and not a *given* that can be taken in any way for granted; that what is of analytical relevance in a text is not necessarily and not exclusively 'the unconscious of the poet', let alone his sickness or his problems in life; that to situate in a text the analytical as such – to situate the object of analysis or the textual point of its implication – is not necessarily to recognise a *known*, to find an answer, but also, and perhaps more challengingly, to locate an *unknown*, to find a question.

The Poe-etic Analytical

Let us now return to the crucial question we left in suspension earlier, after having raised it by reversing Freud's reservation concerning Marie Bonaparte's type of research: Can psychoanalysis give us an insight into the specificity of the poetic? We can now supplement this question with a second one: where can we situate the analytical with respect to Poe's poetry?

The answers to these questions might be sought in two directions. (1) In a direct reading of a poetic text by Poe, trying to locate in the poem itself a signifier of poeticity and to analyse its functioning and its effects; to analyse, in other words, how poetry as such works through signifiers (to the extent that signifiers, as opposed to meanings, are always signifiers of the unconscious); (2) in an analytically informed reading of literary history itself, since its treatment of Poe obviously constitutes a literary *case history*. Such a reading has never, to my knowledge, been undertaken with respect to any writer: never has literary history itself been viewed as an analytical object, as a subject for a psychoanalytic interpretation.[16] And yet it is overwhelmingly obvious, in a case like Poe's, that the discourse of literary history itself points to some unconscious determinations that structure it but of which it is not aware. What is the unconscious of literary history? Can the question of *the guilt of poetry* be relevant to that unconscious? Could literary history be in any way considered a repetitive unconscious *transference* of the guilt of poetry?

Literary history, or more precisely the critical discourse surrounding Poe, is indeed one of the most visible ('self-evident') effects of Poe's poetic signifier, of his text. Now, how can the question of the peculiar effect of Poe be dealt with analytically? My suggestion is: by locating what seems to be unreadable or incomprehensible in this effect; by situating the most prominent discrepancies or discontinuities in the overall critical discourse concerning Poe, the most puzzling critical contradictions, and by trying to interpret those contradictions as symptomatic of the unsettling specificity of the Poe-etic effect, as well as of the contingence of such an effect on the unconscious.

According to its readers' contradictory testimonies, Poe's poetry, let it be recalled, seemed to be at once the most *irresistible* and the most *resisted* poetry in literary history. Poe is felt to be at once the most unequalled master of conscious art *and* the most tortuous unconscious case, as such doomed to remain 'the perennial victim of the *idée fixe*, and of amateur psychoanalysis'.[17] Poetry, I would thus argue, is precisely the effect of a deadly struggle between consciousness and the unconscious; it has to do with resistance and with what can neither be resisted nor escaped. Poe is a symptom of poetry to the extent that poetry is both what most resists a psychoanalytical interpretation and what most depends on psychoanalytical effects.

But this, paradoxically enough, is what poetry and psychoanalysis have in common. They both exist only insofar as they resist our reading. When caught in the act, both are always already, once again, purloined.

Notes

1. 'Although Poe was not the social outcast Baudelaire conceived him to be, he was, and still is, perhaps the most thoroughly misunderstood of all American writers.' Floyd Stovall, *Edgar Poe the Poet: Essays New and Old on the Man and His Work* (Charlottesville: University of Virginia Press, 1969).

2. T. S. Eliot's famous statement on Poe in his study, 'From Poe to Valéry', *Hudson Review*, Autumn 1949; reprinted in *The Recognition of Edgar Allan Poe: Selected Criticism since 1829*, ed. Eric W. Carlson (Ann Arbor: University of Michigan Press, 1966), p. 205. This collection of critical essays will hereafter be cited as *Recognition*, with individual essays abbreviated as follows: P. P. Cooke, 'Edgar A. Poe' (1848); T. S. Eliot, 'From Poe to Valéry' (1949); T. W. Higginson, 'Poe' (1879); Aldous Huxley, 'Vulgarity in Literature' (1931); J. R. Lowell, 'Edgar Allan Poe' (1845); C. M. Rourke, 'Edgar Allan Poe' (1931); G. B. Shaw, 'Edgar Allan Poe' (1909); Edmund Wilson, 'Poe at Home and Abroad' (1926); Yvor Winters, 'Edgar Allan Poe: A Crisis in American Obscurantism' (1937).

3. J. W. Krutch, *Edgar Allan Poe: A Study in Genius* (New York: Knopf, 1926).

4. J. M. S. Robertson, 'The Genius of Poe', *Modern Quarterly*, 3 (1926); Camille Mauclair, *Le Génie d'Edgar Poe* (Paris, 1925); John Dillon, *Edgar Allan Poe: His Genius and His Character* (New York, 1911); John R. Thompson, *The Genius and Character of Edgar Allan Poe* (privately printed, 1929); Jeannet A. Marks, *Genius and Disaster: Studies in Drugs and Genius* (New York, 1925); Jean A. Alexander, 'Affidavits of Genius: French Essays on Poe', *Dissertation Abstracts*, 22 (September 1961).

5. Higginson, 'Poe', *Recognition*, p. 67.

6. Swinburne, letter to Sara Sigourney Rice, 9 November 1875, *Recognition*, p. 63. Mallarmé, 'Scolies', in *Oeuvres complètes*, ed. H. Mondor and G. Jean-Aubry (Paris: Pléiade, 1945), p. 223; my translation. Lowell, 'Edgar Allan Poe', *Recognition*, p. 11.

7. Cooke, quoting Elizabeth Barrett, in 'Edgar A. Poe', *Recognition*, p. 23; original italics.

8. Shaw, 'Edgar Allan Poe', *Recognition*, p. 98.

9. Eliot, 'From Poe to Valéry', *Recognition*, p. 209.

10. 'The Murders in the Rue Morgue', in *Edgar Allan Poe: Selected Writings*, ed. David Galloway (New York: Penguin, 1967), p. 189; hereafter cited as *Poe*.

11. For a remarkable analysis of the way repetition is enacted in the problematics of reading set in motion by Lacan's text, see Barbara Johnson's 'The Frame of Reference: Poe, Lacan, Derrida', in *The Critical Difference: Essays in the Rhetoric of Contemporary Criticism* (Baltimore: Johns Hopkins University Press, 1980).

12. Lacan, 'Le Séminaire sur *La Lettre volée*,' in *Ecrits* (Paris: Seuil, 1966); first translated by Jeffrey Mehlman in 'French Freud', *Yale French Studies*, 48 (1972). All references here to Lacan's Poe Seminar are to the *Yale French Studies* translation.

13. Bonaparte, *Edgar Poe* (Paris: Denöel et Steele, 1933). English edition: *Life and Works of Edgar Allan Poe*, trans. John Rodker (London: Imago, 1949). All references to Marie Bonaparte will be to the English editions.

14. 'Need we emphasize the similarity of these two sequences? Yes, for the resemblance we have in mind is not a simple collection of traits chosen only in order to delete their difference. And it would not be enough to retain those common traits at the expense of the others for the slightest truth to result. It is rather the intersubjectivity in which the two actions are motivated that we wish to bring into relief, as well as the three terms through which it structures them. The special status of these terms results from their corresponding simultaneously to the three logical moments through which the decision is precipitated and to the three places it assigns to the subjects among whom it constitutes a choice ... Thus three moments, structuring three glances, borne by three subjects, incarnated each time by different characters.' 'Seminar on *The Purloined Letter*', pp. 43–4.

15. 'The Murders in the Rue Morgue', *Poe*, p. 204.

16. I have attempted, however, an elementary exploration of such an approach with respect to Henry James in my essay, 'Turning the Screw of Interpretation', in *Writings and Madness: Literature/Philosophy/Psychoanalysis* (Ithaca: Cornell University Press, 1985).

17. The formula is David Galloway's (*Poe*, p. 24).

5 GENDER AND RACE

Feminist criticism and theory have become a force in modern literary criticism only within the last thirty years. The first critics to make an impact were the 'images of women' group who focussed on how women were depicted in works written by men. Their main concern was, as Josephine Donovan puts it, 'to determine the degree to which sexist ideology controls the text'.[1] Later feminists tended to believe that this approach was too negative and that it gave too much emphasis to the work of men. These feminist critics shifted the focus to women's writing. They argued that there was a specifically female tradition of writing. Elaine Showalter coined the term 'gynocritics' to categorise this form of feminist criticism.

Showalter was at first suspicious of attempts to align feminist criticism with contemporary theories which, she wrote, 'have offered literary critics the opportunity to demonstrate that the work they do is as manly and aggressive as nuclear physics – not intuitive and feminine, but strenuous, rigorous, impersonal and virile'.[2] In her later criticism, however, she has adopted a more sympathetic position towards theory. Obviously theory is necessary if feminists who reject, as Showalter does, the view that the imagination is genderless are to support their position not only against traditional opponents but also against materialists who accuse them of essentialism on the grounds that female identity is assumed to be capable of transcending social and historical determinants.

In a recent essay Showalter argues that in the 1980s gynocriticism 'has been sufficiently large, undogmatic, and flexible to have accommodated many theoretical revisions and criticisms'. She sees Gilbert and Gubar's study, *The Madwoman in the Attic*, as 'pivotal' in offering 'a detailed revisionist reading of Harold Bloom's theory of the anxiety of influence, transforming his Freudian paradigm of Oedipal struggle between literary fathers and sons into a feminist theory of influence which describes the nineteenth-century woman writer's anxieties within a patriarchal literary culture'. In the essay included here, however, Showalter moves from gynocriticism to 'gynesis', a term coined by Alice Jardine and which Showalter defines as 'the exploration of the textual consequences and representations of "the feminine" in Western thought'.[3] Focussing on Ophelia 'brings to the foreground the issues in an ongoing theoretical debate about the cultural links between femininity, female sexuality, insanity, and representation'.

In Showalter, one sees a feminist critic who at first had little sympathy with theory, interpreting it in terms of aggressive maleness, moving towards a position that takes account of post-structuralist and psychoanalytic theory. Barbara Johnson, in contrast, was initially associated with the Yale school of deconstructive criticism and her criticism had little obvious feminist dimension. Her recent writing, however, has moved in a feminist direction, while still preserving its connections with post-structuralism and psychoanalysis, as can be seen in the essay included here which discusses three texts – by Hawthorne, Charlotte Perkins Gilman, and Freud – concerned with failed attempts by doctors to cure women.

Though not yet as powerful a presence as gender in contemporary criticism and theory, race is a factor that cannot be left out of account. To a large extent black criticism has followed the same pattern as feminism. Earlier criticism in denying a specific place for the female dimension, in the same way denied both black writers and black readers special consideration. Texts by women or by black writers had to satisfy general critical standards which in principle paid no attention to questions of gender or race. Similarly the reader was not considered in specific sexual or racial terms but as human in a general sense. Feminist and black critics would argue that in practice critical standards were determined by white males and that the generalised human reader also was conceived as being white and male. As feminists exposed these assumptions in relation to the representation of women and women's writing, black critics likewise saw literature as dominated by whites with non-whites represented in stereotypical terms. As with feminism, black criticism emerged out of a political struggle. Before the black power movement of the 1960s, black writers had adhered to an integrationist philosophy that assumed that black writing should submit itself to the same standards of criticism as white writing. With the rise of the black power movement, radicals both insisted that black forms of expression were unique and therefore required a special form of interpretation and assessment, and also asserted that white standards were not as disinterested as they claimed to be.

As feminist critics eventually had to come to terms with developments in critical theory, so black criticism has also developed in a similar direction. Younger black critics began to make use of post-structuralist theory in writing about black forms of expression. Henry Louis Gates Jr is probably the most important of these critics. As feminists such as Gilbert and Gubar focussed almost exclusively on women's writing, Gates saw his province as black writing not only in the USA but in Africa and the Caribbean also. And whereas earlier criticism had tended to interpret black writing in social or anthropological terms, thus emphasising its documentary interest rather than its claims as art, Gates applied a variety of critical theories to black texts: 'The black literary tradition now demands, for sustenance and for growth, the sorts of reading which it is the especial province of the literary critic to render.'[4]

But is the language of theory, being a white product, not a distorting element when applied to black art? Do black critics not need to create a distinctive critical language that is black in its basis? Gates's recent writing moves in this direction. Critical discourses based on structuralism, post-structuralism, Marxism, feminism, new historicism, he claims, arise 'from a specific set of texts within the Western tradition', and as black criticism and theory develop 'we shall invent our own theories . . . We must learn to read a black text within a black formal cultural matrix'. But Gates still believes that this black cultural matrix can be combined with critical theory: '. . . by learning to read a black text within a black formal cultural matrix, and explicating it with the principles of criticism at work in *both* the Euro-American and African-American traditions, I believe that we critics can produce richer structures of meaning than are possible otherwise'.

Gates describes the method he adopts in relation to texts written by blacks as follows: 'I have tried to utilize contemporary theory to *defamiliarize* the texts of the black tradition, to create a distance between this black reader and our black texts, so that I may more readily *see* the formal workings of those texts.' In the essay included here we see this approach applied to the first chapter of Frederick Douglass's autobiography.

Notes

1. Josephine Donovan, 'Beyond the Net: Feminist Criticism as a Moral Criticism', *Denver Quarterly*, 17 (1983), p. 43.

2. Elaine Showalter, 'Towards a Feminist Poetics', in *Twentieth-Century Literary Theory: A Reader*, ed K. M. Newton (Basingstoke and London, 1989), pp. 270–1.

3. Elaine Showalter, 'A Criticism of Our Own', in *The Future of Literary Theory*, ed. Ralph Cohen (New York, 1989), pp. 363–4, 364, 365.

4. Quoted in Showalter, 'A Criticism of Our Own', p. 354.

5. Henry Louis Gates, Jr, 'Authority, (White) Power, and the (Black) Critic; or, it's all Greek to me', in *The Future of Literary Theory*, ed. Cohen, pp. 329, 334–5, 335.

Further Reading

Judith Fetterley, *The Resisting Reader: A Feminist Approach to American Fiction* (Bloomington, Indiana, 1978).

Henry Louis Gates, Jr, *The Signifying Monkey: The Theory of Afro-American Criticism* (New York, 1988).

Mary Jacobus, *Reading Women: Essays in Feminist Criticism* (London, 1986).

The New Feminist Criticism: Essays on Women, Literature, and Theory, ed. Elaine Showalter (London, 1986).

Elaine Showalter: Representing Ophelia: women, madness, and the responsibilities of feminist criticism

'As a sort of a come-on, I announced that I would speak today about that piece of bait named Ophelia, and I'll be as good as my word.' These are the words which begin the psychoanalytic seminar on *Hamlet* presented in Paris in 1959 by Jacques Lacan. But despite his promising come-on, Lacan was *not* as good as his word. He goes on for some forty-one pages to speak about Hamlet, and when he does mention Ophelia, she is merely what Lacan calls 'the object Ophelia' – that is, the object of Hamlet's male desire. The etymology of Ophelia, Lacan asserts, is 'O-phallus,' and her role in the drama can only be to function as the exteriorised figuration of what Lacan predictably and, in view of his own early work with psychotic women, disappointingly suggests is the phallus as transcendental signifier.[1] To play such a part obviously makes Ophelia 'essential', as Lacan admits; but only because, in his words, 'she is linked forever, for centuries, to the figure of Hamlet'.

The bait-and-switch game that Lacan plays with Ophelia is a

Reprinted from *Shakespeare and the Question of Theory*, eds Patricia Parker and Geoffrey Hartman (New York and London, 1985), pp. 77–94.

....

cynical but not unusual instance of her deployment in psychiatric and critical texts. For most critics of Shakespeare, Ophelia has been an insignificant minor character in the play, touching in her weakness and madness but chiefly interesting, of course, in what she tells us about Hamlet. And while female readers of Shakespeare have often attempted to champion Ophelia, even feminist critics have done so with a certain embarrassment. As Annette Kolodny ruefully admits: 'it is after all, an imposition of high order to ask the viewer to attend to Ophelia's sufferings in a scene where, before, he's always so comfortably kept his eye fixed on Hamlet.'[2]

Yet when feminist criticism allows Ophelia to upstage Hamlet, it also brings to the foreground the issues in an ongoing theoretical debate about the cultural links between femininity, female sexuality, insanity, and representation. Though she is neglected in criticism, Ophelia is probably the most frequently illustrated and cited of Shakespeare's heroines. Her visibility as a subject in literature, popular culture, and painting, from Redon who paints her drowning, to Bob Dylan, who places her on Desolation Row, to Cannon Mills, which has named a flowery sheet pattern after her, is in inverse relation to her invisibility in Shakespearean critical texts. Why has she been such a potent and obsessive figure in our cultural mythology? Insofar as Hamlet names Ophelia as 'woman' and 'frailty', substituting an ideological view of femininity for a personal one, is she indeed representative of Woman, and does her madness stand for the oppression of women in society as well as in tragedy? Furthermore, since Laertes calls Ophelia a 'document in madness', does she represent the textual archetype of woman *as* madness or madness *as* woman? And finally, how should feminist criticism represent Ophelia in its own discourse? What is our responsibility towards her as character and as woman?

Feminist critics have offered a variety of responses to these questions. Some have maintained that we should represent Ophelia as a lawyer represents a client, that we should become her Horatia, in this harsh world reporting her and her cause aright to the unsatisfied. Carol Neely, for example, describes advocacy – speaking *for* Ophelia – as our proper role: 'As a feminist critic,' she writes, 'I must "tell" Ophelia's story.'[3] But what can we mean by Ophelia's story? The story of her life? The story of her betrayal at the hands of her father, brother, lover, court, society? The story of her rejection and marginalisation by male critics of Shakespeare? Shakespeare gives us very little information from which to imagine a past for Ophelia. She appears in only five of the play's twenty scenes; the pre-play course of her love story with Hamlet is known only by a few ambiguous flashbacks. Her tragedy is subordinated in the play; unlike Hamlet, she does not struggle with moral choices or alternatives. Thus another feminist critic, Lee Edwards, concludes that it is impossible to reconstruct Ophelia's biography from the text: 'We can imagine Hamlet's story without Ophelia, but Ophelia literally has no story without Hamlet.'[4]

If we turn from American to French feminist theory, Ophelia might confirm the impossibility of representing the feminine in patriarchal discourse as other than madness, incoherence, fluidity, or silence. In French theoretical patriarchal language and symbolism, it remains on the side of negativity, absence, and lack. In comparison to Hamlet, Ophelia is certainly a creature of lack. 'I think nothing, my lord,' she tells him in the Mousetrap scene, and he cruelly twists her words:

Hamlet: That's a fair thought to lie between maids' legs.
Ophelia: What is, my lord?
Hamlet: Nothing.

(III.ii.117–19)

In Elizabethan slang, 'nothing' was a term for the female genitalia, as in *Much Ado About Nothing*. To Hamlet, then, 'nothing' is what lies between maids' legs, for, in the male visual system of representation and desire, women's sexual organs, in the words of the French psychoanalyst Luce Irigaray, 'represent the horror of having nothing to see'.[5] When Ophelia is mad, Gertrude says that 'Her speech is nothing', mere 'unshaped use'. Ophelia's speech thus represents the horror of having nothing to say in the public terms defined by the court. Deprived of thought, sexuality, language, Ophelia's story becomes the Story of O – the zero, the empty circle or mystery of feminine difference, the cipher of female sexuality to be deciphered by feminist interpretation.[6]

A third approach would be to read Ophelia's story as the female subtext of the tragedy, the repressed story of Hamlet. In this reading, Ophelia represents the strong emotions that the Elizabethans as well as the Freudians thought womanish and unmanly. When Laertes weeps for his dead sister he says of his tears that 'When these are gone,/The woman will be out' – that is to say, that the feminine and shameful part of his nature will be purged. According to David Leverenz, in an important essay called 'The Woman in *Hamlet*', Hamlet's disgust at the feminine passivity in himself is translated into violent revulsion against women, and into his brutal behaviour towards Ophelia. Ophelia's suicide, Leverenz argues, then becomes 'a microcosm of the male world's banishment of the female, because "woman" represents everything denied by reasonable men'.[7]

It is perhaps because Hamlet's emotional vulnerability can so readily be conceptualised as feminine that this is the only heroic male role in Shakespeare which has been regularly acted by women, in a tradition from Sarah Bernhardt to, most recently, Diane Venora, in a production directed by Joseph Papp. Leopold Bloom speculates on this tradition in *Ulysses*, musing on the Hamlet of the actress Mrs Bandman Palmer: 'Male impersonator. Perhaps he was a woman? Why Ophelia committed suicide?'[8]

While all of these approaches have much to recommend them, each also presents critical problems. To liberate Ophelia from the text, or to make her its tragic centre, is to re-appropriate her for our own ends; to dissolve her into a female symbolism of absence is to endorse our own marginality; to make her Hamlet's anima is to reduce her to a metaphor of male experience. I would like to propose instead that Ophelia *does* have a story of her own that feminist criticism can tell; it is neither her life story, nor her love story, nor Lacan's story, but rather the *history* of her representation. This essay tries to bring together some of the categories of French feminist thought about the 'feminine' with the empirical energies of American historical and critical research: to yoke French theory and Yankee knowhow.

Tracing the iconography of Ophelia in English and French painting, photography, psychiatry, and literature, as well as in theatrical production, I will be showing first of all the representational bonds between female insanity and female sexuality. Secondly, I want to demonstrate the two-way transaction between psychiatric theory and cultural representation. As one medical historian has observed, we could provide a manual of female insanity by chronicling the illustrations of Ophelia; this is so because the illustrations of Ophelia have played a major role in the theoretical construction of female insanity.[9] Finally, I want to suggest that the feminist revision of Ophelia comes as much from the actress's freedom as from the critic's interpretation.[10] When Shakespeare's heroines began to be played by women instead of boys, the presence of the female body and female voice, quite apart from details of interpretation, created new meanings and subversive tensions in these roles, and perhaps most importantly with Ophelia. Looking at Ophelia's history on and off the stage, I will point out the contest between male and female representations of Ophelia, cycles of critical repression and feminist reclamation of which contemporary feminist criticism is only the most recent phase. By beginning with these data from cultural history, instead of moving from the grid of literary theory, I hope to conclude with a fuller sense of the responsibilities of feminist criticism, as well as a new perspective on Ophelia.

'Of all the characters in *Hamlet*,' Bridget Lyons has pointed out, 'Ophelia is most persistently presented in terms of symbolic meanings.'[11] Her behaviour, her appearance, her gestures, her costume, her props, are freighted with emblematic significance, and for many generations of Shakespearean critics her part in the play has seemed to be primarily iconographic. Ophelia's symbolic meanings, moreover, are specifically feminine. Whereas for Hamlet madness is metaphysical, linked with culture, for Ophelia it is a product of the female body and female nature, perhaps that nature's purest form. On the Elizabethan stage, the conventions of female insanity were sharply defined. Ophelia dresses in white, decks herself with 'fantastical garlands' of wild flowers, and enters, according to the stage directions of the 'Bad' Quarto, 'distracted' playing on a lute with her 'hair down singing'. Her speeches are marked by extravagant metaphors, lyrical free associations, and 'explosive sexual imagery'.[12] She sings wistful and bawdy ballads, and ends her life by drowning.

All of these conventions carry specific messages about femininity and sexuality. Ophelia's virginal and vacant white is contrasted with Hamlet's scholar's garb, his 'suits of solemn black'. Her flowers suggest the discordant double images of female sexuality as both innocent blossoming and whorish contamination; she is the 'green girl' of pastoral, the virginal 'Rose of May' and the sexually explicit madwoman who, in giving away her wild flowers and herbs, is symbolically deflowering herself. The 'weedy trophies' and phallic 'long purples' which she wears to her death intimate an improper and discordant sexuality that Gertrude's lovely elegy cannot quite obscure.[13] In Elizabethan and Jacobean drama, the stage direction that a woman enters with dishevelled hair indicates that she might either be mad or the victim of a rape; the disordered hair, her offence against decorum, suggests sensuality in each case.[14] The mad Ophelia's bawdy songs and verbal licence, while they give her access to 'an entirely different range of experience' from what she is allowed as the dutiful daughter, seem to be her one sanctioned form of self-assertion as a woman, quickly followed, as if in retribution, by her death.[15]

Drowning too was associated with the feminine, with female

fluidity as opposed to masculine aridity. In his discussion of the 'Ophelia complex', the phenomenologist Gaston Bachelard traces the symbolic connections between women, water, and death. Drowning, he suggests, becomes the truly feminine death in the dramas of literature and life, one which is a beautiful immersion and submersion in the female element. Water is the profound and organic symbol of the liquid woman whose eyes are so easily drowned in tears, as her body is the repository of blood, amniotic fluid, and milk. A man contemplating this feminine suicide understands it by reaching for what is feminine in himself, like Laertes, by a temporary surrender to his own fluidity – that is, his tears; and he becomes a man again in becoming once more dry – when his tears are stopped.[16]

Clinically speaking, Ophelia's behaviour and appearance are characteristic of the malady the Elizabethans would have diagnosed as female love-melancholy, or erotomania. From about 1580, melancholy had become a fashionable disease among young men, especially in London, and Hamlet himself is a prototype of the melancholy hero. Yet the epidemic of melancholy associated with intellectual and imaginative genius 'curiously bypassed women'. Women's melancholy was seen instead as biological, and emotional in origins.[17]

On the stage, Ophelia's madness was presented as the predictable outcome of erotomania. From 1660, when women first appeared on the public stage, to the beginnings of the eighteenth century, the most celebrated of the actresses who played Ophelia were those whom rumour credited with disappointments in love. The greatest triumph was reserved for Susan Mountfort, a former actress at Lincoln's Inn Fields who had gone mad after her lover's betrayal. One night in 1720 she escaped from her keeper, rushed to the theatre, and just as the Ophelia of the evening was to enter for her mad scene, 'sprang forward in her place . . . with wild eyes and wavering motion'.[18] As a contemporary reported, 'she was in truth *Ophelia herself*, to the amazement of the performers as well as of the audience – nature having made this last effort, her vital powers failed her and she died soon after'.[19] These theatrical legends reinforced the belief of the age that female madness was a part of female nature, less to be intimidated by an actress than demonstrated by a deranged woman in a performance of her emotions.

The subversive or violent possibilities of the mad scene were nearly eliminated, however, on the eighteenth-century stage. Late Augustan stereotypes of female love-melancholy were sentimentalised versions which minimised the force of female sexuality, and made female insanity a pretty stimulant to male sensibility. Actresses such as Mrs Lessingham in 1772, and Mary Bolton in 1811, played Ophelia in this decorous style, relying on the familiar images of the white dress, loose hair, and wild flowers to convey a polite feminine distraction, highly suitable for pictorial reproduction, and appropriate for Samuel Johnson's description of Ophelia as young, beautiful, harmless, and pious. Even Mrs Siddons in 1785 played the mad scene with stately and classical dignity. For much of the period, in fact, Augustan objections to the levity and indecency of Ophelia's language and behaviour led to censorship of the part. Her lines were frequently cut, and the role was often assigned to a singer instead of an actress, making the mode of representation musical rather than visual or verbal.

But whereas the Augustan response to madness was a denial, the romantic response was an embrace.[20] The figure of the madwoman permeates romantic literature, from the gothic novelists to Wordsworth and Scott in such texts as 'The Thorn' and *The Heart of Midlothian*, where she stands for sexual victimisation, bereavement, and thrilling emotional extremity. Romantic artists such as Thomas Barker and George Shepheard painted pathetically abandoned Crazy Kates and Crazy Anns, while Henry Fuseli's 'Mad Kate' is almost demonically possessed, an orphan of the romantic storm.

In the Shakespearean theatre, Ophelia's romantic revival began in France rather than England. When Charles Kemble made his Paris debut as Hamlet with an English troupe in 1827, his Ophelia was a young Irish ingénue named Harriet Smithson. Smithson used 'her extensive command of mime to depict in precise gesture the state of Ophelia's confused mind'.[21] In the mad scene, she entered in a long black veil, suggesting the standard imagery of female sexual mystery in the gothic novel, with scattered bedlamish wisps of straw in her hair. Spreading the veil on the ground as she sang, she spread flowers upon it in the shape of a cross, as if to make her father's grave, and mimed a burial, a piece of stage business which remained in vogue for the rest of the century.

The French audiences were stunned. Dumas recalled that 'it was the first time I saw in the theatre real passions, giving life to men and women of flesh and blood'.[22] The twenty-three-year-old Hector Berlioz, who was in the audience on the first night, fell madly in love, and eventually married Harriet Smithson despite his family's frantic opposition. Her image as the mad Ophelia was represented in popular lithographs and exhibited in bookshop and printshop windows. Her costume was imitated by the fashionable, and a coiffure 'à la folle', consisting of a 'black veil with wisps of straw tastefully interwoven' in the hair, was widely copied by the Parisian beau monde, always on the lookout for something new.[23]

Although Smithson never acted Ophelia on the English stage, her intensely visual performance quickly influenced English productions as well; and indeed the romantic Ophelia – a young girl passionately and visibly driven to picturesque madness – became the dominant international acting style for the next 150 years, from Helena Modjeska in Poland in 1871, to the eighteen-year-old Jean Simmons in the Laurence Olivier film of 1948.

Whereas the romantic Hamlet, in Coleridge's famous dictum, thinks too much, has an 'overbalance of the contemplative faculty' and an overactive intellect, the romantic Ophelia is a girl who *feels* too much, who drowns in feeling. The romantic critics seem to have felt that the less said about Ophelia the better; the point was to *look* at her. Hazlitt, for one, is speechless before her, calling her 'a character almost too exquisitely touching to be dwelt upon'.[24] While the Augustans represent Ophelia as music, the romantics transform her into an *objet d'art*, as if to take literally Claudius's lament, 'poor Ophelia/Divided from herself and her fair judgment,/Without the which we are pictures'.

Smithson's performance is best recaptured in a series of pictures done by Delacroix from 1830 to 1850, which show a strong romantic interest in the relation of female sexuality and insanity.[25] The most innovative and influential of Delacroix's lithographs is *La Mort d'Ophélie* of 1843, the first of three studies. Its sensual languor, with Ophelia half-suspended in the stream as her dress slips from her body, anticipated the fascination with the erotic trance of the hysteric as it would be studied by Jean-Martin Charcot and his students, including Janet and Freud. Delacroix's interest in the drowning Ophelia is also reproduced to the point of obsession in later nineteenth-century painting. The English Pre-Raphaelites painted her again and again, choosing the drowning which is only described in the play, and where no actress's image had preceded them or interfered with their imaginative supremacy.

In the Royal Academy show of 1852, Arthur Hughes's entry shows a tiny waif-like creature – a sort of Tinker Bell Ophelia – in a filmy white gown, perched on a tree trunk by the stream. The overall effect is softened, sexless, and hazy, although the straw in her hair resembles a crown of thorns. Hughes's juxtaposition of childlike femininity and Christian martyrdom was overpowered, however, by John Everett Millais's great painting of Ophelia in the same show. While Millais's Ophelia is sensuous siren as well as victim, the artist rather than the subject dominates the scene. The division of space between Ophelia and the natural details Millais had so painstakingly pursued reduces her to one more visual object; and the painting had such a hard surface, strangely flattened perspective, and brilliant light that it seems cruelly indifferent to the woman's death.

These Pre-Raphaelite images were part of a new and intricate traffic between images of women and madness in late nineteenth-century literature, psychiatry, drama, and art. First of all, superintendents of Victorian lunatic asylums were also enthusiasts of Shakespeare, who turned to his dramas for models of mental aberration that could be applied to their clinical practice. The case study of Ophelia was one that seemed particularly useful as an account of hysteria or mental breakdown in adolescence, a period of sexual instability which the Victorians regarded as risky for women's mental health. As Dr John Charles Bucknill, president of the Medico-Psychological Association, remarked in 1859, 'Ophelia is the very type of a class of cases by no means uncommon. Every mental physician of moderately extensive experience must have seen many Ophelias. It is a copy from nature, after the fashion of the Pre-Raphaelite school'.[26] Dr John Conolly, the celebrated superintendent of the Hanwell Asylum, and founder of the committee to make Stratford a national trust, concurred. In his *Study of Hamlet* in 1863 he noted that even casual visitors to mental institutions could recognise an Ophelia in the wards: 'the same young years, the same faded beauty, the same fantastic dress and interrupted song'.[27] Medical textbooks illustrated their discussions of female patients with sketches of Ophelia-like maidens.

But Conolly also pointed out that the graceful Ophelias who dominated the Victorian stage were quite unlike the women who had become the majority of the inmate population in Victorian public asylums. 'It seems to be supposed,' he protested, 'that it is an easy task to play the part of a crazy girl, and that it is chiefly composed of singing and prettiness. The habitual courtesy, the partial rudeness of mental disorder, are things to be witnessed. . . . An actress, ambitious of something beyond cold imitation, might find the contemplation of such cases a not unprofitable study.'[28]

Yet when Ellen Terry took up Conolly's challenge, and went to an asylum to observe real madwomen, she found them 'too *theatrical*' to teach her anything.[29] This was because the iconography of the romantic Ophelia had begun to infiltrate reality, to define a style for mad young women seeking to express and communicate their distress. And where the women themselves did not willingly throw themselves into Ophelia-like postures, asylum superintendents, armed with the new technology of photography, imposed the costume, gesture, props, and expression of Ophelia upon them. In England, the camera was introduced to asylum work in the 1850s by Dr Hugh Welch Diamond, who photographed his female patients at the Surrey Asylum and at Bethlem. Diamond was heavily influenced by literary and visual models in his posing of the female subjects. His pictures of madwomen, posed in prayer, or decked with Ophelia-like garlands, were copied for Victorian consumption as touched-up lithographs in professional journals.[30]

Reality, psychiatry, and representational convention were even more confused in the photographic records of hysteria produced in the 1870s by Jean-Martin Charcot. Charcot was the first clinician to install a fully-equipped photographic atelier in his Paris hospital, La Salpêtrière, to record the performances of his hysterical stars. Charcot's clinic became, as he said, a 'living theatre' of female pathology; his women patients were coached in their performances for the camera, and, under hypnosis, were sometimes instructed to play heroines from Shakespeare. Among them, a fifteen-year-old girl named Augustine was featured in the published volumes called *Iconographies* in every posture of *la grande hystérie*. With her white hospital gown and flowing locks, Augustine frequently resembles the reproductions of Ophelia as icon and actress which had been in wide circulation.[31]

But if the Victorian madwoman looks mutely out from men's pictures, and acts a part men had staged and directed, she is very differently represented in the feminist revision of Ophelia initiated by newly powerful and respectable Victorian actresses, and by women critics of Shakespeare. In their efforts to defend Ophelia, they invent a story for her drawn from their own experiences, grievances, and desires.

Probably the most famous of the Victorian feminist revisions of the Ophelia story was Mary Cowden Clarke's *The Girlhood of Shakespeare's Heroines*, published in 1852. Unlike other Victorian moralising and didactic studies of the female characters of Shakespeare's plays, Clarke's was specifically addressed to the wrongs of women, and especially to the sexual double standard. In a chapter on Ophelia called 'The rose of Elsinore', Clarke tells how the child

Ophelia was left behind in the care of a peasant couple when Polonius was called to the court at Paris, and raised in a cottage with a foster-sister and brother, Jutha and Ulf. Jutha is seduced and betrayed by a deceitful knight, and Ophelia discovers the bodies of Jutha and her still-born child, lying 'white, rigid, and still' in the deserted parlour of the cottage in the middle of the night. Ulf, a 'hairy loutish boy', likes to torture flies, to eat songbirds, and to rip the petals off roses, and he is also very eager give little Ophelia what he calls a bear-hug. Both repelled and masochistically attracted by Ulf, Ophelia is repeatedly cornered by him as she grows up; once she escapes the hug by hitting him with a branch of wild roses; another time, he sneaks into her bedroom 'in his brutish pertinacity to obtain the hug he had promised himself', but just as he bends over her trembling body, Ophelia is saved by the reappearance of her real mother.

A few years later, back at the court, she discovers the hanged body of another friend, who has killed herself after being 'victimized and deserted by the same evil seducer'. Not surprisingly, Ophelia breaks down with brain fever – a staple mental illness of Victorian fiction – and has prophetic hallucinations of a brook beneath willow trees where something bad will happen to her. The warnings of Polonius and Laertes have little to add to this history of female sexual trauma.[32]

On the Victorian stage, it was Ellen Terry, daring and unconventional in her own life, who led the way in acting Ophelia in feminist terms as a consistent psychological study in sexual intimidation, a girl terrified of her father, of her lover, and of life itself. Terry's debut as Ophelia in Henry Irving's production in 1878 was a landmark. According to one reviewer, her Ophelia was 'the terrible spectacle of a normal girl becoming hopelessly imbecile as the result of overwhelming mental agony. Hers was an insanity without wrath or rage, without exaltation or paroxysms'.[33] Her 'poetic and intellectual performance' also inspired other actresses to rebel against the conventions of invisibility and negation associated with the part.

Terry was the first to challenge the tradition of Ophelia's dressing in emblematic white. For the French poets, such as Rimbaud, Hugo, Musset, Mallarmé and Laforgue, whiteness was part of Ophelia's essential feminine symbolism; they call her *'blanche Ophélia'* and compare her to a lily, a cloud, or snow. Yet whiteness also made her a transparency, an absence that took on the colours of Hamlet's moods, and that, for the symbolists like Mallarmé, made her a blank page to be written over or on by the male imagination. Although Irving was able to prevent Terry from wearing black in the mad scene, exclaiming, 'My God, Madam, there must be only *one* black figure in this play, and that's Hamlet!' (Irving, of course, was playing Hamlet), nonetheless actresses such as Gertrude Eliot, Helen Maude, Nora de Silva, and in Russia Vera Komisarjevskaya, gradually won the right to intensify Ophelia's presence by clothing her in Hamlet's black.[34]

By the turn of the century, there was both a male and a female discourse on Ophelia. A. C. Bradley spoke for the Victorian male tradition when he noted in *Shakespearean Tragedy* (1906) that 'a large number of readers feel a kind of personal irritation against Ophelia; they seem unable to forgive her for not having been a heroine'.[35] The feminist counterview was represented by actresses in works such as Helena Faucit's study of Shakespeare's female characters, and *The True Ophelia*, written by an anonymous actress in 1914, which protested against the 'insipid little creature' of criticism, and advocated a strong and intelligent woman destroyed by the heartlessness of men.[36] In women's paintings of the *fin de siècle* as well, Ophelia is depicted as an inspiring, even sanctified emblem of righteousness.[37]

While the widely read and influential essays of Mary Cowden Clarke are now mocked as the epitome of naive criticism, these Victorian studies of the girlhood of Shakespeare's heroines are of course alive and well as psychoanalytic criticism, which has imagined its own prehistories of oedipal conflict and neurotic fixation; and I say this not to mock psychoanalytic criticism, but to suggest that Clarke's musings on Ophelia are a pre-Freudian speculation on the traumatic sources of a female sexual identity. The Freudian interpretation of *Hamlet* concentrated on the hero, but also had much to do with the re-sexualisation of Ophelia. As early as 1900, Freud had traced Hamlet's irresolution to an Oedipus complex, and Ernest Jones, his leading British disciple, developed this view, influencing the performances of John Gielgud and Alec Guinness in the 1930s. In his final version of the study, *Hamlet and Oedipus*, published in 1949, Jones argued that 'Ophelia should be unmistakably sensual, as she seldom is on stage. She may be "innocent" and docile, but she is very aware of her body'.[38]

In the theatre and in criticism, this Freudian edict has produced such extreme readings as that Shakespeare intends us to see Ophelia as a loose woman, and that she has been sleeping with Hamlet. Rebecca West has argued that Ophelia was not 'a correct and timid virgin of exquisite sensibilities', a view she attributes to the popularity of the Millais painting; but rather 'a disreputable young woman'.[39] In his delightful autobiography, Laurence Olivier, who made a special pilgrimage to Ernest Jones when he was preparing his *Hamlet* in the 1930s, recalls that one of his predecessors as actor-manager had said in response to the earnest question, 'Did Hamlet sleep with Ophelia?' – 'In my company, always'.[40]

The most extreme Freudian interpretation reads *Hamlet* as two parallel male and female psychodramas, the counterpointed stories of the incestuous attachments of Hamlet and Ophelia. As Theodor Lidz presents this view, while Hamlet is neurotically attached to his mother, Ophelia has an unresolved oedipal attachment to her father. She has fantasies of a lover who will abduct her from or even kill her father, and when this actually happens, her reason is destroyed by guilt as well as by lingering incestuous feelings. According to Lidz, Ophelia breaks down because she fails in the female developmental task of shifting her sexual attachment from her father 'to a man who can bring her fulfillment as a woman'.[41] We see the effects of this Freudian Ophelia on stage productions since the 1950s, where directors have hinted at an incestuous link between Ophelia and Laertes. Trevor Nunn's production with Helen Mirren in 1970, for example, made Ophelia and Laertes flirtatious doubles, almost twins in their matching fur-trimmed doublets, playing duets on the lute with Polonius looking on, like Peter, Paul, and Mary. In other productions of the same period, Marianne Faithfull was a haggard Ophelia equally attracted to Hamlet and Laertes, and, in one of the few performances directed by a woman, Yvonne Nicholson sat on Laertes' lap in the advice scene, and played the part with 'rough sexual bravado'.[42]

Since the 1960s, the Freudian representation of Ophelia has been supplemented by an antipsychiatry that represents Ophelia's madness in more contemporary terms. In contrast to the psychoanalytic representation of Ophelia's sexual unconscious that connected her essential femininity to Freud's essays on female sexuality and hysteria, her madness is now seen in medical and biochemical terms, as schizophrenia. This is so in part because the schizophrenic woman has become the cultural icon of dualistic femininity in the mid-twentieth century as the erotomaniac was in the seventeenth and the hysteric in the nineteenth. It might also be traced to the work of R. D. Laing on female schizophrenia in the 1960s. Laing argued that schizophrenia was an intelligible response to the experience of invalidation within the family network, especially to the conflicting emotional messages and mystifying double binds experienced by daughters. Ophelia, he noted in *The Divided Self*, is an empty space. 'In her madness there is no one there. . . . There is no integral selfhood expressed through her actions or utterances.

Incomprehensible statements are said by nothing. She has already died. There is now only a vacuum where there was once a person.'[43]

Despite his sympathy for Ophelia, Laing's readings silence her, equate her with 'nothing', more completely than any since the Augustans; and they have been translated into performances which only make Ophelia a graphic study of mental pathology. The sickest Ophelias on the contemporary stage have been those in the productions of the pathologist-director Jonathan Miller. In 1974 at the Greenwich Theatre his Ophelia sucked her thumb; by 1981, at the Warehouse in London, she was played by an actress much taller and heavier than the Hamlet (perhaps punningly cast as the young actor Anton Lesser). She began the play with a set of nervous tics and tuggings of hair which by the mad scene had become a full set of schizophrenic routines – head banging, twitching, wincing, grimacing, and drooling.[44]

But since the 1970s too we have had a feminist discourse which has offered a new perspective on Ophelia's madness as protest and rebellion. For many feminist theorists, the madwoman is a heroine, a powerful figure who rebels against the family and the social order; and the hysteric who refuses to speak the language of the patriarchal order, who speaks otherwise, is a sister.[45] In terms of effect on the theatre, the most radical application of these ideas was probably realised in Melissa Murray's agitprop play *Ophelia*, written in 1979 for the English women's theatre group 'Hormone Imbalance'. In this blank verse retelling of the Hamlet story, Ophelia becomes a lesbian and runs off with a woman servant to join a guerrilla commune.[46]

While I've always regretted that I missed this production, I can't proclaim that this defiant ideological gesture, however effective politically or theatrically, is all that feminist criticism desires, or all to which it should aspire. When feminist criticism chooses to deal with representation, rather than with women's writing, it must aim for a maximum interdisciplinary contextualism, in which the complexity of attitudes towards the feminine can be analysed in their fullest cultural and historical frame. The alternation of strong and weak Ophelias on the stage, virginal and seductive Ophelias in art, inadequate or oppressed Ophelias in criticism, tells us how the representations have overflowed the text, and how they have reflected the ideological character of their times, erupting as debates between dominant and feminist views in periods of gender crisis and redefinition. The representation of Ophelia changes independently of theories of the meaning of the play or the Prince, for it depends on attitudes towards women and madness. The decorous

and pious Ophelia of the Augustan age and the postmodern schizophrenic heroine who might have stepped from the pages of Laing
can be derived from the same figure; they are both contradictory
and complementary images of female sexuality in which madness
seems to act as the 'switching-point, the concept which allows the
co-existence of both sides of the representation'.[47] There is no 'true'
Ophelia for whom feminist criticism must unambiguously speak,
but perhaps only a Cubist Ophelia of multiple perspectives, more
than the sum of all her parts.

But in exposing the ideology of representation, feminist critics
have also the responsibility to acknowledge and to examine the
boundaries of our own ideological positions as products of our
gender and our time. A degree of humility in an age of critical
hubris can be our greatest strength, for it is by occupying this
position of historical self-consciousness in both feminism and criticism that we maintain our credibility in representing Ophelia, and
that, unlike Lacan, when we promise to speak about her, we make
good our word.

Notes

1. Jacques Lacan, 'Desire and the interpretation of desire in *Hamlet*', in
Literature and Psychoanalysis: The Question of Reading: Otherwise, ed. Shoshana
Felman (Baltimore, 1982), pp. 11, 20, 23. Lacan is also wrong about the
etymology of Ophelia, which probably derives from the Greek for 'help' or
'succour'. Charlotte M. Yonge suggested a derivation from 'ophis', 'serpent'. See her *History of Christian Names* (1884, republished Chicago, 1966),
pp. 346–7. I am indebted to Walter Jackson Bate for this reference.
2. Annette Kolodny, 'Dancing through the minefield: some observations
on the theory, practice, and politics of feminist literary criticism' (*Feminist
Studies* 6, (1980)), p. 7.
3. Carol Neely, 'Feminist modes of Shakespearean criticism' (*Women's
Studies*, 9 (1981)), p. 11.
4. Lee Edwards, 'The labors of Psyche' (*Critical Inquiry*, 6 (1979)),
p. 36.
5. Luce Irigaray: see *New French Feminisms*, ed. Elaine Marks and Isabelle
de Courtivron (New York, 1982), p. 101. The quotation above, from III.ii,
is taken from the Arden Shakespeare, *Hamlet*, ed. Harold Jenkins (London
and New York, 1982), p. 295. All quotations from *Hamlet* are from this
text.
6. On images of negation and feminine enclosure, see David Wilbern,

'Shakespeare's "nothing" ', in *Representing Shakespeare: New Psychoanalytic Essays*, ed. Murray M. Schwartz and Coppélia Kahn (Baltimore, 1981).

7. David Leverenz, 'The woman in *Hamlet*: an interpersonal view' (*Signs*, 4 (1978)), p. 303.

8. James Joyce, *Ulysses* (New York, 1961) p. 76.

9. Sander L. Gilman, *Seeing the Insane* (New York, 1981), p. 126.

10. See Michael Goldman, *The Actor's Freedom: Toward a Theory of Drama* (New York, 1975), for a stimulating discussion of the interpretative interaction between actor and audience.

11. Bridget Lyons, 'The iconography of Ophelia' (*English Literary History*, 44 (1977), p. 61.

12. See Maurice and Hanna Charney, 'The language of Shakespeare's madwomen' (*Signs*, 3 (1977)), pp. 451, 457; and Carroll Camden, 'On Ophelia's madness' (*Shakespeare Quarterly* (1964)), p. 254.

13. See Margery Garber, *Coming of Age in Shakespeare* (London, 1981), 155–7; and Lyons, op. cit. pp. 65, 70–2.

14. On dishevelled hair as a signifier of madness or rape, see Charney and Charney, op. cit., pp. 452–3, 457; and Allan Dessen, *Elizabethan Stage Conventions and Modern Interpreters* (Cambridge, 1984), pp. 36–8. Thanks to Allan Dessen for letting me see advance proofs of his book.

15. Charney and Charney, op. cit., p. 456.

16. Gaston Bachelard, *L'Eau et les rêves* (Paris, 1942) p. 109–25. Se also Brigitte Peucker, 'Dröste-Hulshof's Ophelia and the recovery of voice' (*The Journal of English and Germanic Philology* (1983)), pp. 374–91.

17. Vieda Skultans, *English Madness: Ideas on Insanity 1580–1890* (London, 1977), pp. 79–81. On historical cases of love-melancholy, see Michael MacDonald, *Mystical Bedlam* (Cambridge, 1982).

18. C. E. L. Wingate, *Shakespeare's Heroines on the Stage* (New York, 1895), pp. 283–4, 288–9.

19. Charles Hiatt, *Ellen Terry* (London, 1898), p. 11.

20. Max Byrd, *Visits to Bedlam: Madness and Literature in the Eighteenth Century* (Columbia, 1974), p. xiv.

21. Peter Raby, *Fair Ophelia: Harriet Smithson Berlioz* (Cambridge, 1982), 63.

22. Ibid., p. 68.

23. Ibid., pp. 72, 75.

24. Quoted in Camden, op. cit. p. 247.

25. Raby, op cit., p. 182.

26. J. C. Bucknill, *The Psychology of Shakespeare* (London, 1859, reprinted New York, 1970) p. 110. For more extensive discussions of Victorian psychiatry and Ophelia figures, see Elaine Showalter, *The Female Malady: Women, Madness and English Culture* (New York, 1985).

27. John Conolly, *Study of Hamlet* (London, 1863), p. 177.

28. Ibid., pp. 177–8, 180.

29. Ellen Terry, *The Story of My Life* (London, 1908), p. 154.

30. Diamond's photographs are reproduced in Sander L. Gilman, *The*

Face of Madness: Hugh W. Diamond and the Origin of Psychiatric Photography (New York, 1976).

31. See Georges Didi-Huberman, *L'Invention de l'hystérie* (Paris, 1982), and Stephen Heath, *The Sexual Fix* (London, 1983), p. 36.

32. Mary Cowden Clarke, *The Girlhood of Shakespeare's Heroines* (London, 1852). See also George C. Cross, 'Mary Cowden Clarke, *The Girlhood of Shakespeare's Heroines,* and the sex education of Victorian women' (*Victorian Studies,* 16 (1972)), pp. 37–58, and Nina Auerbach, *Woman and the Demon* (Cambridge, Mass., 1983), pp. 210–15.

33. Hiatt, op. cit., p. 114. See also Wingate, op. cit. pp. 304–5.

34. Terry, op cit., pp. 155–6.

35. Andrew C. Bradley, *Shakespearean Tragedy* (London, 1906), p. 160.

36. Helena Faucit Martin, *On Some of Shakespeare's Female Characters* (Edinburgh and London, 1891), pp. 4, 18; and *The True Ophelia* (New York, 1914), p. 15.

37. Among these paintings are the Ophelias of Henrietta Rae and Mrs F. Littler. Sarah Bernhardt sculpted a bas relief of Ophelia for the Women's Pavilion at the Chicago World's Fair in 1893.

38. Ernest Jones, *Hamlet and Oedipus* (New York, 1949), p. 139.

39. Rebecca West, *The Court and the Castle* (New Haven, 1958), p. 18.

40. Laurence Olivier, *Confessions of an Actor* (Harmondsworth, 1982), pp. 102, 152.

41. Theodor Lidz, *Hamlet's Enemy: Madness and Myth in Hamlet* (New York, 1975), pp. 88, 113.

42. Richard David, *Shakespeare in the Theatre* (Cambridge, 1978), p. 75. This was the production directed by Buzz Goodbody, a brilliant young feminist radical who killed herself that year. See Colin Chambers, *Other Spaces: New Theatre and the RSC* (London, 1980), especially pp. 63–7.

43. R. D. Laing, *The Divided Self* (Harmondsworth, 1965), p. 195n.

44. David, op. cit. pp. 82–3; thanks to Marianne DeKoven, Rutgers University, for the description of the 1981 Warehouse production.

45. See, for example, Hélène Cixous and Catherine Clément, *La Jeune Née* (Paris, 1975).

46. For an account of this production, see Micheline Wandor, *Understudies: Theatre and Sexual Politics* (London, 1981), p. 47.

47. I am indebted for this formulation to a critique of my earlier draft of this paper by Carl Friedman, at the Wesleyan Center for the Humanities, April 1984.

Barbara Johnson: Is Female to Male as Ground Is to Figure?

No women, then, if I have read correctly. With the notable exception of the mother, of course. But this makes up part of the system, for the mother is the faceless, unfigurable figure of a *figurante*. She creates a place for all the figures by losing herself in the background.

Jacques Derrida, 'All Ears: Nietzsche's Otobiography'

We must be cured of it by a cure of the ground . . .
New senses in the engenderings of sense.

Wallace Stevens, 'The Rock'

As a way of discussing the relations between feminism and psychoanalysis, I would like to bring together three well-known texts, each of which tells the story of a failed cure: Nathaniel Hawthorne's 'Birthmark', Charlotte Perkins Gilman's 'Yellow Wallpaper', and Sigmund Freud's 'Fragment of an Analysis of a Case of Hysteria'.[1] While the three cases fail in very different ways, they are alike in presenting a female patient subject to the therapeutic ambitions of a male doctor. In all three cases, in fact, the initiative toward therapy comes not from the patient herself but from a man she has in some sense discommoded – which is not to say the woman does not suffer.

The question asked by my title is a rephrasing of Sherry Ortner's famous title 'Is Female to Male as Nature Is to Culture?'[2] The terms *figure* and *ground*, which refer to a certain distribution of outline and attention, are of course drawn from the visual arts.[3] That origin is not irrelevant here, since the question of the woman in the texts I will discuss is as much aesthetic as it is medical – or, rather, since the texts reveal a profound complicity between aesthetics and medicine.

For a preliminary description of the figure-ground relationship, I turn to a quotation from Douglas Hofstadter's *Gödel, Escher, Bach*, which I inflect in terms of psychoanalysis and sexual difference:

When a figure or 'positive space' [call this 'the male child' or simply 'the child' or 'Oedipus'] is drawn inside a frame [call this frame 'psychoanalytic theory'], an unavoidable consequence is that its complementary shape – also called the 'ground,' or 'background,' or 'negative space' [call this the

Reprinted from *Feminism and Psychoanalysis*, eds. Richard Feldstein and Judith Root (Ithaca and London, 1989), pp. 255–68.

'girl' or the 'other'] – has also been drawn. In most drawings, however, this figure-ground relationship plays little role. The artist is much less interested in the ground than in the figure. But sometimes an artist will take interest in the ground as well.

Let us now officially distinguish between two kinds of figures: *cursively drawable* ones, and *recursive* ones. . . . A *cursively drawable* figure is one whose ground is merely an accidental by-product of the drawing act. [Later, Hofstadter refers to this as a 'recognizable form whose negative space is not any recognizable form'.] A *recursive* figure is one whose ground can be seen as a figure in its own right . . . The 're' in 'recursive' represents the fact that both foreground *and* background are cursively drawable – the figure is 'twice-cursive.' Each figure-ground boundary in a recursive figure is a double-edged sword.[4]

The dream of psychoanalysis is of course to represent sexual difference as a recursive figure, a figure in which both figure and ground, male and female, are recognisable, complementary forms. This dream articulates itself through the geometry of castration in Freud, in which the penis is the figure, or positive space, and the vagina the ground, or negative space. But there are limits to how recursive Freud wishes this figure to be: he wants to stop short of something analogous to M. C. Escher's drawing hands, with male and female each drawing the other. Indeed, the expression 'double-edged sword' occurs in the form of a 'knife that cuts both ways', which Freud, in a footnote to his essay 'Female Sexuality', uses to dismiss the undecidability of his own psychoanalytic authority when the drawing of the male-female relationship threatens to become truly recursive. Having just discussed the difficulties experienced by the woman in accepting 'the fact of her castration', Freud notes:

It is to be anticipated that male analysts with feminist sympathies, and our woman analysts also, will disagree with what I have said here. They will hardly fail to object that such notions have their origins in the man's 'masculinity complex,' and are meant to justify theoretically his innate propensity to disparage and suppress women. But this sort of psychoanalytic argument reminds us here, as it so often does, of Dostoevsky's famous 'knife that cuts both ways.' The opponents of those who reason thus will for their part think it quite comprehensible that members of the female sex should refuse to accept a notion that appears to gainsay their eagerly coveted equality with men. The use of analysis as a weapon of controversy obviously leads to no decision.[5]

In a footnote to Joel Fineman's response to Neil Hertz's discussion of male hysteria, which is where I came across Freud's footnote, an additional note is cited: 'The editor [of the *Standard Edition*] notes that "The actual simile used by Freud and in the Russian original is 'a stick with two ends' ".'[6] Out of this regression of footnotes, the basic question is clear: is the figure of sexual difference in psychoanalytic theory cursive or recursive?

The literary equivalent of the visual image of woman as ground has been richly evoked by Susan Gubar in the form of the blank page, the raw material on which the pen-penis of male creativity inscribes its figures, the negative space surrounding what is presented as truly interesting.[7] When woman does appear as a figure in a text, notes Gubar, she is generally mute, passive, or inert, an idealised object of male desire.

The Isak Dinesen story from which Gubar takes the title of her essay offers one displacement of this figure-ground relationship. The story involves a museum of fine white sheets hung up to display the blood stains produced on the wedding night of royal brides. One of these sheets is blank. Gubar sees both the blood and the blank as figures for female writing – females as the subjects of writing, not merely as its objects. Both figure and ground become figure here, but the blank sheet is more recursive than the stained because it proclaims both ground and figure to be open to interpretation, whereas the stained sheets are produced with the proclamation, 'We declare her to have been a virgin'.

With these considerations in mind, I will now pursue the conjunction between the aesthetics of the figure-ground relationship and the therapeutics of the male-female relationship by juxtaposing 'The Birthmark' and 'The Yellow Wallpaper'. In the Hawthorne story, a passionate scientist, Aylmer, attempts to remove a crimson birthmark from the white cheek of his wife Georgiana, in order 'that the world might possess one living specimen of ideal loveliness without the semblance of a flaw' (205). He succeeds in removing the mark but, in the process, kills Georgiana. In the Gilman story, a woman is confined by her husband, a doctor, to a country house for a rest cure. She begins to focus obsessively on the ugliness of the wallpaper until, in the end, she seems to have become a part of it. The superficial symmetry between the two stories is obvious and suggestive. In both, the therapeutic is underwritten by a strong aesthetic investment. In the male writer's story, the birthmark is an overinvested *figure* inscribed on a page that should be blank. In the female writer's story, the wallpaper is an overinvested *ground*. In the first, the figure *on* the woman-ground is erased, in the second, the woman-figure merges *into* the ground. In both cases, the lady vanishes.

To what extent can these stories be read as allegories of psychoanalysis? At first sight, they seem to be examples not of a talking cure but of a silencing cure. Yet if we take as a subtext the third failed

treatment of a female patient, Freud's case of Dora, we find that
Dora, too, has recourse to silence, not only in breaking off treatment
but in ceasing her denial: 'And Dora disputed the fact no longer'
(125). In all three stories, it is the male observer who identifies
something about the woman as a symptom and who determines the
nature of the treatment: Aylmer calls Georgiana's birthmark a
defect, John calls Gilman's narrator 'slightly hysterical', and Dora's
father hands his daughter over to Freud, hoping that she will adjust
to *his* version of reality. She adjusts neither to his nor to Freud's.

Let us look, then, at the shifting relations between ground and
figure in Hawthorne and Gilman, beginning with Hawthorne's first
description of Georgiana's mark:

> In the center of Georgiana's left cheek there was a singular mark, deeply
> interwoven, as it were, with the texture and substance of her face. In the
> usual state of her complexion – a healthy though delicate bloom – the mark
> wore a tint of deeper crimson, which imperfectly defined its shape amid
> the surrounding rosiness. When she blushed, it gradually became more
> indistinct, and finally vanished amid the triumphant rush of blood that
> bathed the whole cheek with its brilliant glow. But if any shifting motion
> caused her to turn pale, there was the mark again, a crimson stain upon
> the snow, in what Aylmer sometimes deemed an almost fearful distinctness.
> Its shape bore not a little similarity to the human hand, though of the
> smallest pygmy size. Georgiana's lovers were wont to say that some fairy
> at her birth hour had laid her tiny hand upon the infant's cheek, and left
> this impress there in token of the magic endowments that were to give her
> such sway over all hearts. Many a desperate swain would have risked life
> for the privilege of pressing his lips to the mysterious hand. It must not be
> concealed, however, that the impression wrought by this fairy sign manual
> varied exceedingly, according to the difference of temperament in the
> beholders.
>
> (204–5)

The mark on Georgiana's cheek is a mark of intersubjectivity: it is
interpreted differently by different beholders, and it interprets *them*
in response. This 'fairy sign manual' is what Lacan might call 'a
signifier that represents a subject for another signifier'. It is the
relation between figure and ground that shifts in response to another,
but the ground is what responds while the figure remains constant.
It is perhaps this point of autonomy that does not *simply* reflect (the
woman as 'pas toute') which makes the mark so irritating to
Aylmer. If the cheek is ground and the birthmark figure (figure of
being born a woman as well as being of woman born), then what
Aylmer wishes to do in erasing the mark is to erase the difference
– to erase sexual difference – by reducing woman to 'all', to ground,

to blankness.[8] And he does indeed succeed in consigning this woman to the ground.

In Gilman's 'Yellow Wallpaper,' the female narrator has been confined for treatment by her physician husband, a man of science like Aylmer, a man who 'scoffs openly at any talk of things not to be felt and seen and put down in figures'. As has often been noted, the first use of the word *paper* refers to the paper (called the 'dead paper') on which the narrator is writing her journal (which at first coincides with the story we are reading), even though her husband has forbidden her to write.[9] It is clear, therefore, that the paper that comes alive on the walls is related to the dead paper on which the narrator is forbidden to write. The following passages demonstrate the gradual animation of the paper through a shift in the figure-ground relationship.

At first, the design is unified:

I never saw a worse paper in my life. One of those sprawling, flamboyant patterns committing every artistic sin.

(p. 5)

Then a figure begins to take shape *in the ground*:

This wallpaper has a kind of sub-pattern in a different shade, a particularly irritating one, for you can only see it in certain lights, and not clearly then.

But in the places where it isn't faded and where the sun is just so – I can see a strange, provoking, formless sort of figure that seems to skulk about behind that silly and conspicuous front design.

(p. 8)

The figure in the ground begins to look like a woman:

Behind that outside pattern the dim shapes get clearer every day.

It is always the same shape, only very numerous.

And it is like a woman stooping down and creeping about behind that pattern.

(p. 11)

The ground begins to rebel against the dominant figure:

The faint figure behind seemed to shake the pattern, just as if she wanted to get out.

(p. 11)

I lay there for hours trying to decide whether that front pattern and the back pattern really did move together or separately.

(p. 12)

Suddenly, we are not sure which side of the paper the narrator is on:

By daylight she is subdued, quiet. I fancy it is the pattern that keeps her so still. It is so puzzling.

It keeps me quiet by the hour.

(p. 13)

I think that woman gets out in the daytime!

(p. 15)

Finally, the crossing is complete:

I don't like to look out of the windows even – there are so many of those creeping women, and they creep so fast.

I wonder if they all came out of that wallpaper as I did?

I don't want to go outside.

For outside you have to creep on the ground.

(p. 18)

If at first it seems that the woman projected into the paper is trying to move from ground to figure, by the end of the story the narrator has moved *herself* past the outside, upper figure into a ground that cannot be located in real space. To escape figuration in the patriarchal conception of the real (the upper pattern), she has relocated elsewhere. But this alternative real can be figured only as madness, the erasure of the figure/ground distinction. The cursively drawable figure becomes recursive with a vengeance, turning the narration itself into a double-edged sword. In the end we don't know which side of the paper she is on, and hence, we no longer know quite where to locate *ourselves*. Hawthorne's story, too, becomes recursive – 'twice told' – with even more catastrophic results. The moment the figure/ground distinction is erased, it self-destructs. This can be read as a story of 'failed idealism' only by readers who cannot see its recursiveness.[10]

Freud's attempt to draw the geometry of castration into a narrative of female development offers a similar set of complexities. Freud knows where the story starts (the mother) and where the story 'must' end (Freud's 'must'), but the narrative of how the woman converts the 'fact of her castration' into something desirable is a real challenge, even to a storyteller as gifted as Freud.

He begins with the known figure – the male – and seeks the specificity of the female by comparison.

There is another, far more specific motive for the turning away from the mother, arising out of the effect of the castration-complex on the little creature without a penis. Some time or other the little girl makes the discovery of her organic inferiority, of course earlier and more easily if she has brothers or other boy companions. We have already noted the three paths which diverge from this point: (a) that which leads to the suspension

of the whole sexual life, (b) that which leads to the defiant over-emphasis of her own masculinity, and (c) the first steps towards definitive femininity.
(FS pp. 200–1)

The turning-away from the mother is a most important step in the little girl's development: it is more than a mere change of object. We have already described what takes place and what a number of motives are alleged for it; we must now add that we observe, hand in hand with it, a marked diminution in the active and an augmentation of the passive sexual impulses. . . . The transition to the father-object is accomplished with the assistance of the passive tendencies so far as these have escaped overthrow.
(FS pp. 207–8)

What the Hawthorne and Gilman stories show is the *cost* of adopting the third choice, the choice of 'definitive femininity'. These stories are stories of an education in passivity: Georgiana is an excellent student, Gilman flunks. It is her teacher who lies motionless on the floor at the end of the story.

Yet both stories are narratives of the woman's growing complicity in her own destruction. Georgiana learns suicide as masochistic self-effacement, while Gilman's narrator learns madness as masochistic self-assertion. How does the complicity work? The stories point to a number of answers.

In both cases, the husband seems to have organised the world around his love for his wife and his concern for her problem. Aylmer stakes his scientific pride on success at removing the birthmark; John rents a house in the country and organises family life around his wife's illness. This concern makes it impossible for the woman to protest, since she cannot do so without seeming ungrateful or at least without losing her centrality in her husband's world. Both Georgiana and Gilman's narrator are prisoners of an idealisation. The cost of their attaining a valued status in the world is to become an object in someone else's reality and, hence, to have, in fact, *no* status in the world. If woman's value is only assured by the place assigned to her by patriarchy, then the alternatives can only be u-topian. The symptom that both Aylmer and John are trying to remove is the mark of femininity itself as both more and less than what is required of women by patriarchal structures. Femininity, in other words, is by nature a 'normal ill'.[11]

Both the 'mark' and the 'paper' can be seen as figures for women's writing. Georgiana's 'bloody hand,' a kind of *écriture féminine* that is both corporal and cheeky, throbs to its own rhythms in response to the world until she is taught to feel so ashamed of it that she is ready to die rather than live with her horrible deformity. Gilman's narrator, too, learns to renounce her writing: 'I did write for a while in spite of them; but it *does* exhaust me a good deal – having to be so sly about it, or else meet with heavy opposition' (p. 4). Both women, in other words, internalise the rejection of their writerly self.

What this internalisation indicates is that the repression of writing is related to a repression of ambivalence. The woman is not allowed to have mixed feelings, to be 'composite' or 'interwoven'. She must renounce everything about which she has negative feelings, even when those feelings are internalised from the opinions of others. Ultimately, the thing about which she feels ambivalent, and which she renounces, is herself.

In Freud, too, the 'composite' nature of the woman is what is not allowed to stand. Frustrated in what Luce Irigaray has called the 'dream of symmetry',[12] Freud discovers not that woman *is* the second sex, but that she *has* a second sex:

It will help our exposition if, as we go along, we compare the course of female development with that of the male.

First of all, there can be no doubt that the bisexual disposition which we maintain to be characteristic of human beings manifests itself much more plainly in the female than in the male. The latter has only one principal sexual zone – only one sexual organ – whereas the former has two: the vagina, the true female organ, and the clitoris, which is analogous to the male organ. . . . The sexual life of the woman is regularly split up into two phases, the first of which is of a masculine character, whilst only the second is specifically feminine. Thus in female development there is a process of transition from the one phase to the other, to which there is nothing analogous in males. A further complication arises from the fact that the clitoris, with its masculine character, continues to function in later female sexual life in a very variable manner, which we certainly do not as yet fully understand.

(FS p. 197)

The irritation Freud feels at this excess organ comes out in his triumphant revelation of Dora's supposed secret: her masturbation.

When I set myself the task of bringing to light what human beings keep hidden within them . . . by observing what they say and what they show, I thought the task was a harder one than it really is. He that has eyes to see and ears to hear may convince himself that no mortal can keep a secret. If his lips are silent, he chatters with his finger-tips; betrayal oozes out of him at every pore. . . .

The reproaches against her father for having made her ill, together with the self-reproach underlying them, the leucorrhoea, the playing with the reticule, the bed-wetting after her sixth year, the secret which she would not allow the physicians to tear from her – the circumstantial evidence of her having masturbated in childhood seems to me complete and without a flaw.

(*Dora* pp. 96–7)

In this notoriously fragmented and incomplete case history, Freud's pleasure at an interpretation that is 'complete and without a flaw' is striking. Also striking is the parallel between Freud's scientific jubilation and the triumph anticipated by Aylmer as he prepares to render his wife 'complete and without a flaw'. Indeed, that throbbing birthmark, that hand already upon Georgiana's body, that 'little mark', as Georgiana describes it, 'which I cover with the tips of two small fingers', may perhaps be read as the displacement upward precisely of that troublingly excessive female organ. Precedent for such a displacement can be found in the continuation of the passage I have just quoted from *Dora*:

In the present case I had begun to suspect the masturbation when she had told me of her cousin's gastric pains . . . and had then identified herself with her by complaining for days together of similar painful sensations. It is well known that gastric pains occur especially often in those who masturbate. According to a personal communication made to me by W. Fliess, it is precisely gastralgias of this character which can be interpreted by an application of cocaine to the 'gastric spot' discovered by him in the nose, and which can be cured by the cauterization of the same spot. (97)

It is hard not to see the scientific energies deployed by Aylmer, Freud, and Fliess in the face of this wandering spot as a sign of patriarchal befuddlement at the multiformity of female sexuality. 'The Birthmark', indeed, can be read as a story of fatal clitoridectomy.

This is not to substitute a clitorocentric universe for a phallocentric one but rather to take the clitoris, as Gayatri Spivak and Naomi Schor have both suggested, as a synecdoche for the possibility that the world could be articulated differently, that resistance is always the sign of a counterstory, that the 'knife that cuts both ways' does so not because the stories are symmetrical but because each of them is differently situated, serves different ends, and accounts for different things.[13] There is no guarantee that the figures in a *truly* recursive figure would fit together at all.

Freud's story of female sexuality, like Hawthorne's, is a story of renunciation required by the needs of symmetry: 'In women the development of sexuality is complicated by the task of *renouncing* that genital zone which was originally the principal one, namely, the clitoris, in favor of a new zone – the vagina' (FS 194). But as Freud's own repeated analysis shows, this renunciation is never any

more 'complete and without a flaw' than another renunciation
Freud considers equally necessary: 'We have, after all, long since
given up any expectation of a neat parallelism between male and
female sexual development.' (FS p. 195) What is at stake in the
relationship between psychoanalysis and feminism can indeed be
summed up in this relationship between renunciation *for* symmetry
and renunciation *of* symmetry.

Having now reached a point of closure in my argument, I would
like to end by examining how closure is marked in each of the three
texts I have been discussing. I find such a gesture most emphatically
inscribed in 'The Birthmark'. Early in the text, we are promised a
'deeply impressive moral'. Hawthorne does not fail to deliver what
bears all the stylistic marks of an authoritative conclusion. Yet in
attempting to capitalise morally upon the failed hubris of science,
the narrator actually repeats the error he has just documented. The
plea for interwovenness and incompletion is couched in a language
that attempts to achieve the same type of objective mastery its
message is designed to demystify.

As the last crimson tint of the birthmark – that sole token of human
imperfection – faded from her cheek, the parting breath of the now perfect
woman passed into the atmosphere, and her soul, lingering a moment near
her husband, took its heavenward flight. Then a hoarse, chuckling laugh
was heard again! Thus ever does the gross fatality of earth exult in its
invariable triumph over the immortal essence which, in this dim sphere of
half development, demands the completeness of a higher state. Yet, had
Aylmer reached a profounder wisdom, he need not thus have flung away
the happiness which would have woven his mortal life of the selfsame
texture with the celestial. The momentary circumstance was too strong for
him; he failed to look beyond the shadowy scope of time, and, living once
for all in eternity, to find the perfect future in the present.

What is astonishing about this passage is that it wants to have its
interwovenness and deny it, too. The multiplication of contradictory
categories is contained within a grammar of moral certainty. The
meaning of these assertions is open to doubt, their claim-to-mean
is not.

'I did not succeed in mastering the transference in good time,'
writes Freud at a similar point in his story. These descriptions of
failure are couched in the language of *narrative* control. From whose
perspective does one say 'Thus ever . . .'? Georgiana is dead, Dora
is still somatizing alone, and Hawthorne and Freud have gone into
high oratorical gear. Whatever the damage done by their finished
or unfinished business, the story must have its proper ending, its
concluding scientific postscript:

Years have gone by since her visit. In the meantime the girl has married, and indeed – unless all the signs mislead me – she has married the young man who came into her associations at the beginning of the analysis of the second dream. Just as the first dream represented her turning away from the man she loved to her father – that is to say, her flight from life into disease – so the second dream announced that she was about to tear herself free from her father and had been reclaimed once more by the realities of life.

(p. 144)

'The perfect future in the present', 'the realities of life': each story ends by pledging its allegiance to a larger story, a larger sense of coherence, a larger set of myths. In contrast, Gilman ends with the very voice of inconclusiveness:

'I've got out at last,' said I, 'in spite of you and Jane. And I've pulled off most of the paper, so you can't put me back!'
Now why should that man have fainted? But he did, and right across my path by the wall, so that I had to creep over him every time! (20)

While the figure of the patriarchal story lies senseless on the floor, the escaped story creeps wildly around in circles. Gilman's ending could not be more different from Freud's or Hawthorne's. Or could it? Twenty years later, Gilman published a sequel titled 'Why I Wrote "The Yellow Wallpaper" ', which documents the therapeutic effects of the story on other women suffering from the rest cure and concludes, 'It was not intended to drive people crazy, but to save people from being driven crazy, and it worked' (p. 20). The impulse to put the story to work therapeutically is equally irresistible to all three authors, as it has, no doubt, been to me. Feminism is structured no less therapeutically than the normalising patriarchal therapies it is designed to combat. The suspicion arises, however, that it is precisely the therapeutic haste toward closure that works in a countertherapeutic way.

In all three cases, then, the text concludes with a coda that takes the story itself as its object. Each author stands back from the story as *its reader*, salvaging from the wreckage of its characters the therapeutic coherence of a moral. Transference here is transference onto the story itself as value-object. A quotation from Dinesen's 'Blank Page' can perhaps serve to underscore this transference onto story as the moral of *our* transference onto all three tales: 'Where the story-teller is loyal, eternally and unswervingly loyal to the story, there, in the end, silence will speak. Where the story has been betrayed, silence is but emptiness. But we, the faithful, when we have spoken our last word, will hear the voice of silence.'[14]

Loyalty to the story does not, however, guarantee any unproblematic relation to silence. I would like to conclude by sounding a dimension of silence that may have been going unheard in my remarks. Freud, Hawthorne, and Gilman all write about middle-class white men and women. The very equation of the woman's body with the blank page implies that woman's body is white (indeed, of a whiteness no actual bodies possess). And the concept of femininity as passivity is applicable only to a certain class of women, even within the texts we have been reading. Are there, perhaps, other figures trapped in the ground of these literary carpets?

In the Gilman and Hawthorne stories, several figures are standing in the background – Mary, who cares for the children; Jennie, the housekeeper; and Aminadab, the personification of matter and physical work, placed beside the sorcerer Aylmer as Caliban is beside Prospero. This background role is often played, in white Western literature, by non-white characters. (In pointing this out, I am, of course, prolonging the colonial gesture of *equating* race and class.) The two most-cited capsule descriptions of black characters in white American fiction, I think, are that of Topsy, who 'just grew', and of Dilsey, who 'endured'. This is another way of denying a character the status of figure and confining him or her to ground. Topsy has no origin; Dilsey has no end; they have no story, no history, nothing to put into figure. Anne Tyler, in her novel *Searching for Caleb*, plays upon the invisibility – the purloined-letter status – of the black characters that occupy the ground of much white American literature. In that novel, a white family, searching for a son who has disappeared, is never able to trace him until someone finally thinks to ask the black couple working for the family, who knew all along but were never asked.

In short, there are many other invisible men and women trapped in the wallpaper of the Western canon or caught in the divisions of labour that neither psychoanalytic nor feminist theory has taken sufficiently into account – figures that have often remained consigned to the background of discussions of feminism and psychoanalysis. Could some of these figures be discerned through a reading of another birthmark, the birthmark imprinted on the face of Toni Morrison's Sula? Perhaps, but that would have to be the subject of another essay.

Notes

1. Page references, given in the text, are to Nathaniel Hawthorne, *The Celestial Railroad and Other Stories* (New York: Signet, 1963); *The Charlotte Perkins Gilman Reader,* ed. Ann J. Lane (New York: Pantheon, 1980); and Sigmund Freud, *Dora: An Analysis of a Case of Hysteria* (New York: Collier, 1963), abbreviated, where necessary, as *Dora*. See also *The Standard Edition of the Complete Psychological Works*, ed. and trans. James Strachey (London: Hogarth, 1953–74), vol. 7. My reading of *Dora* has been greatly illuminated by Charles Bernheimer and Claire Kahane's anthology *In Dora's Case: Freud, Hysteria, Feminism* (New York: Columbia University Press, 1985).

2. Sherry Ortner, 'Is Female to Male as Nature Is to Culture?' in *Woman, Culture, and Society*, ed. Michelle Zimbalist Rosaldo and Louise Lamphere (Stanford: Stanford University Press, 1974).

3. It might at first sight appear that my question ought to be asked the other way around, particularly with regard to the visual arts, where the 'figure' of the woman is often at the centre of a representation as the very image of beauty. I would say that the centrality of the female figure in such cases is not an indication of true gynocentrism but is, rather, structured like a fetish, i.e., the woman as idealised *object* is really a substitute for the phallus. See Susan Gubar, ' "The Blank Page" and the Issues of Female Creativity', in *Writing and Sexual Difference*, ed. Elizabeth Abel (Chicago: University of Chicago Press, 1982). Whether woman is seen as ground – the place upon or within which what is interesting stands out – or as figure – a detachable object of degradation or desire – the relations between the sexes seem commonly to have found figuration, at any rate, in various versions of the figure-ground relationship.

4. Douglas Hofstadter, *Gödel, Escher, Bach* (New York: Vintage Books, 1980) p. 67.

5. Sigmund Freud, 'Female Sexuality', in *Sexuality and the Psychology of Love* (New York: Collier, 1963), p. 199, henceforth abbreviated as FS.

6. Joel Fineman, *Representations* 4 (Fall 1983), 70. Neil Hertz's essay is titled 'Medusa's Head: Male Hysteria under Political Pressure'. It appeared in the same issue as Fineman's reply.

7. Gubar, ' "The Blank Page" and the Issues of Female Creativity'.

8. Many readers have seen Aylmer's response to the birthmark as a response to female sexuality. It is instructive, however, to see the terms in which they gloss this. Simon O. Lesser, for instance, suggests that the mark 'may represent female sexuality – that is, be a castration symbol'. *Fiction and the Unconscious* (Boston: Beacon Press, 1957) p. 88. If the figure is not read as recursive, female sexuality can only be read as castration.

9. See, for example, Annette Kolodny, 'A Map for Rereading', in *The New Feminist Criticism*, ed. Elaine Showalter (New York: Pantheon, 1985); and Paula Treichler, 'Escaping the Sentence,' *Tulsa Studies in Women's Literature* 3 (Spring/Fall 1984).

10. For a truly recursive ('resisting') reading of 'The Birthmark,' see

Judith Fetterley, *The Resisting Reader* (Bloomington: Indiana University Press, 1978), pp. 22–33.

11. It is hardly necessary to recall that the conference for which this essay was written took place in Normal, Ill.

12. Luce Irigaray, *Speculum* (Paris: Minuit, 1974).

13. See Gayatri Chakravorty Spivak, 'French Feminism in an International Frame', and Naomi Schor, 'Female Paranoia', both in *Feminist Readings: French Texts/ American Contexts, Yale French Studies* 62 (1981).

14. Isak Dinesen, 'The Blank Page', *The Norton Anthology of Literature by Women* ed. Sandra Gilbert and Susan Gubar (New York: Norton, 1985), p. 1419.

Henry Louis Gates, Jr: Binary Oppositions in Chapter One of *Narrative of the Life of Frederick Douglass an American Slave Written by Himself*

I was not hunting for my liberty, but also hunting for my name.

William Wells Brown

Whatever may be the ill or favored condition of the slave in the matter of mere personal treatment, it is the chattel relation that robs him of his manhood.

James Pennington

The white race will only respect those who oppose their usurpation, and acknowledge as equals those who will not submit to their rule. . . . We must make an issue, create an event and establish for ourselves a position. This is essentially necessary for our effective elevation as a people, directing our destiny and redeeming ourselves as a race.

Martin R. Delany

Autobiographical forms in English and in French assumed narrative priority toward the end of the eighteenth century; they shaped themselves principally around military exploits, court intrigues, and spiritual quests. As one scholar has outlined,

Elizabethan sea dogs and generals of the War of the Spanish Succession wrote of the strenuous campaigns, grand strategy, and gory battles. The memoirs of Louis XIV's great commander, the Prince of Conde, for example, thrilled thousands in Europe and America, as did the 'inside stories' of the nefarious, clandestine doings of the great European courts. The

Reprinted from Henry Louis Gates, Jr, *Figures in Black: Words, Signs, and the 'Racial' Self* (New York, 1987), pp. 80–97.

memoirs of the Cardinal de Retz, which told of the Machiavellian intrigues of French government during Louis XIV's minority and of the cabal behind the election of a Pope, captivated a large audience. Even more titillating were personal accounts of the boudoir escapades of noblemen and their mistresses. Nell Gwyn, Madame Pompadour, and even the fictitious Fanny Hill were legends if not idols in their day. More edifying but no less marvelous were the autobiographies of spiritual pilgrimage – such as the graphic accounts of Loyola, John Bunyan, and the Quaker George Fox. Their mystical experiences and miraculous deliverances filled readers with awe and wonder.[1]

It is no surprise, then, that the narratives of the escaped slave became, during the three decades before the Civil War, the most popular form of written discourse in the country. Its audience was built to order. And the expectations created by this peculiar autobiographical convention, as well as by two other literary traditions, had a profound effect on the shape of discourse in the slave narrative. I am thinking here of the marked (but generally unheralded) tradition of the sentimental novel and, more especially, of the particularly American transmutation of the European picaresque. The slave narrative, I suggest, is a countergenre, a mediation between the novel of sentiment and the picaresque, oscillating somewhere between the two in a bipolar moment, set in motion by the mode of the confession. (Indeed, as we shall see, the slave narrative spawned its formal negation, the plantation novel.)

Claudio Guillen's seminal typology of the picaresque, outlined in seven 'characteristics' of that form and derived from numerous examples in Spanish and French literature, provides a curious counterpoint to the morphology of the slave narratives and aids remarkably in delineating what he has proved to be an elusive but recurring narrative structure.

The picaro, who is after all a type of character, only becomes one at a certain point in his career, just as a man or woman 'becomes' a slave only at a certain (and structurally crucial) point of perception in his or her 'career'. Both the picaro and the slave narrators are orphans; both, in fact, are outsiders. The picaresque is a pseudo-autobiography, whereas the slave narratives often tend toward quasi-autobiography. Yet, in both, 'life is at the same time revived and judged, presented and remembered'. In both forms, the narrator's point of view is partial and prejudiced, although the total view of both is 'reflective, philosophical, and critical on moral or religious grounds'. In both, there is a general stress on the material level of existence or indeed of subsistence, sordid facts, hunger, money. There is in the narration of both a profusion of objects and detail. Both the picaro and the slave, as outsiders, comment on, if not parody, collective social institutions.[2] Moreover, both, in their odysseys, move horizontally through space and vertically through society.

If we combine these resemblances with certain characteristics of the sentimental novel such as florid asides, stilted rhetoric, severe piety, melodramatic conversation, destruction of the family unit, violation of womanhood, abuse of innocence, punishment of assertion, and the rags-to-riches success story, we can see that the slave narrative grafted together the conventions of two separate literary traditions and became its own form, utilising popular conventions to affect its reader in much the same way as did cheap popular fiction. Lydia Child, we recall, was not only the amanuensis for escaped slave Harriet Jacobs, but also a successful author in the sentimental tradition. (That the plantation novel was the antithesis or negation of the slave narrative becomes apparent when we consider its conventions. From 1824, when George Tucker published *The Valley of the Shenandoah*, the plantation novel concerned itself with aristocratic, virtuous masters; beast-like, docile slaves; great manor houses; squalid field quarters; and idealised, alabaster womanhood – all obvious negations of themes common to the slave narratives. Indeed, within two years of the publication in 1852 of Harriet Beecher Stowe's *Uncle Tom's Cabin*, at least fourteen plantation novels appeared.)

It should not surprise us, then, that the narratives were popular, since the use of well-established and well-received narrative conventions was meant to ensure commercial and hence political success. By at least one account, the sales of slave narratives reached such high proportions that a critic was moved to complain that the 'shelves of booksellers groan under the weight of Sambo's woes, done up in covers! . . . We hate this niggerism, and hope it may be done away with. . . . If we are threatened with any more negro stories – here goes.' These 'literary nigritudes' [sic] were 'stories' whose 'editions run to hundreds of thousands'.[3] Marion Wilson Starling recalls Gladstone's belief that not more than about 5 per cent of the books published in England had a sale of more than five hundred copies; between 1835 and 1863, no fewer than ten of these were slave narratives.[4] So popular were they in England that a considerable number were published at London or Manchester before they were published in America, if at all. Nor should it surprise us that, of these, the more popular were those that defined the genre structurally. It was Frederick Douglass's *Narrative* of 1845 that exploited the potential and came to determine the shape of language in the slave narrative.

Douglass's *Narrative*, in its initial edition of five thousand copies, was sold out in four months. Within a year, four more editions of two thousand copies each were published. In the British Isles, five editions appeared, two in Ireland in 1846 and three in England in 1846 and 1847. Within the five years after its appearance, a total of some thirty thousand copies of the *Narrative* had been published in the English-speaking world. By 1848, a French paperback edition was being sold in the stalls. *Littells Living Age*, an American periodical, gave an estimate of its sweep in the British Isles after one year's circulation: 'Taking all together, not less than one million persons in Great Britain and Ireland have been excited by the book and its commentators.'[5]

Of the scores of reviews of the *Narrative*, two especially discuss the work in terms of its literary merits. One review, published initially in the *New York Tribune* and reprinted in *The Liberator*, attempts to place the work in the larger tradition of the narrative tale as a literary form:

Considered merely as a narrative, we have never read one more simple, true, coherent, and warm with genuine feeling. It is an excellent piece of writing, and on that score to be prized as a specimen of the powers of the black race, which prejudice persists in disputing. We prize highly all evidence of this kind, and it is becoming more abundant.[6]

Even more telling is the review from the *Lynn Pioneer* reprinted in the same issue of *The Liberator*; this review was perhaps the first to attempt to attach a priority to the *Narrative*'s form and thereby place Douglass directly in a major literary tradition:

It is evidently drawn with a nice eye, and the coloring is chaste and subdued, rather than extravagant or overwrought. Thrilling as it is, and full of the most burning eloquence, it is yet simple and unimpassioned.

Although its 'eloquence is the eloquence of truth' and so 'is as simple and touching as the impulses of childhood', yet its 'message' transcends even its superior moral content: 'There are passages in it which would brighten the reputation of any author, – while the book, as a whole, judged as a mere work of art, would widen the fame of Bunyan or De Foe.'[7] Leaving the matter of 'truth' to the historians,[8] these reviews argue correctly that despite the intention of the author for his autobiography to be a major document in the abolitionist struggle and regardless of Douglass's meticulous attempt at documentation, the *Narrative* falls into the larger class of the heroic fugitive with some important modifications that are related to the confession and the picaresque forms (hence, Bunyan and Defoe), a peculiar blend that would mark Afro-American fiction at least until the publication of James Weldon Johnson's *Autobiography of an Ex-Coloured Man*.

These resemblances between confession and picaresque informed the narrative shape of Afro-American fiction in much the same way as they did that of the English and American novel. As Robert Scholes and Robert Kellogg maintain,

> the similarity in narrative stance between picaresque and confession enables the two to blend easily, making possible an entirely fictional narrative which is more in the spirit of the confession than the picaresque, such as *Moll Flanders* and *Great Expectations*.

But this same blend makes possible a different sort of sublime narrative, 'one that is picaresque in spirit but which employs actual materials from the author's life, such as [Wells's] Tono-Bungay'. Into this class fall slave narratives, the polemical Afro-American first-person form, the influence of which would shape the development of point of view in black fiction for the next hundred years, precisely because

> by turning the direction of the narrative inward the author almost inevitably presents a central character who is an example of something. By turning the direction of the narrative outward the author almost inevitably exposes weaknesses in society. First-person narrative is thus a ready vehicle for ideas.[9]

It is this first-person narration, utilised precisely in this manner, that is the first great shaping characteristic of the slave narratives. But there is another formal influence on the slave narratives whose effect is telling: the American romance. Stephen Butterfield[10] makes this argument tellingly, and I shall paraphrase it closely.

Like Herman Melville's marvellous romance, *Pierre*, the slave narratives utilise as a structural principle the irony of seeming innocence. Here in American society, both say, is to be found as much that is contrary to moral order as could be found in pre-revolutionary Europe. The novelty of American innocence is, however, the refusal or failure to recognise evil while participating in that evil. As with other American romantic modes of narration, the language of the slave narratives remains primarily an expression of the self, a conduit for particularly personal emotion. In this sort of narrative, language was meant to be merely a necessary but unfortunate instrument. In the slave narratives, this structuring of the self couples with the minute explication of gross evil and human depravity, and does so with such sheer intent as to make for a tyranny of point. If the matter of the shaping of the self can come only after the slave is free, in the context of an autobiograpical narrative where the slave first posits that full self, then slavery indeed dehumanises and must in no uncertain terms be abolished, by violence if necessary, since it is by nature a violent institution. The irony here is tyrannically romantic: illusion and substance are patterned antitheses.

As with other examples of romance, the narratives turn on an unconsummated love. The slave and the ex-slave are the dark ladies of the new country destined to expire for unrequited love. Yet the leitmotif of the journey north and the concomitant evolution of consciousness within the slave – from an identity as property and object to a sublime identity as human being and subject – display in the first person the selfsame spirit of the New World's personal experience with titanic nature that Benjamin Franklin's *Autobiography* has come to symbolise. The author of the slave narrative, in his or her flight through the wilderness (recreated in vivid detailed descriptions of the relationship between man and land on the plantation and off), seems to be arguing strongly that one can 'study nature' to know oneself. The two great precepts – the former Emersonian and the latter Cartesian – in the American adventure become one. Further, as with the American symbolists, the odyssey is a process of becoming. Walt Whitman, for instance, is less concerned with explorations of emotion than with exploration as a mode of consciousness. Slave narratives not only describe the voyage but also enact the voyage so that their content is primarily a reflection of their literary method. Theirs is a structure in which the writer and the subject merge into the stream of language. Language indeed is primarily a perception of reality. Yet, unlike the American symbolists, these writers of slave narratives want not so much to adopt a novel stance from which the world assumes new shapes as to impose a new form onto the world. There can be no qualification regarding the nature of slavery; there can be no equivocation.

Butterfield explicates this idea rather well by contrasting the levels of diction in the slave narrative *The Life of John Thompson*[11] with a remarkably similar passage from Herman Melville's *Moby-Dick*. The first is from Thompson:

The harpoon is sharp, and barbed at one end, so that when it has once entered the animal, it is difficult to draw it out again, and has attached to its other end a pole, two inches thick and five feet long. Attached to this is a line 75 to 100 fathoms in length, which is coiled into the bow of the boat.

Melville follows:

Thus the whale-line folds the whole boat in its complicated coils, twisting and writhing about it in almost every direction. All the oarsmen are involved in its perilous contortions; so that to the timid eye of the landsman they seem as festooning their limbs.

There is a difference here of rhetorical strategies that distinguishes the two. Melville's language is symbolic and weighted with ambiguous moral meanings: the serpentine rope allows for no innocence; 'all the oarsmen' are involved, even those who have nothing to do with coiling the rope in the tub; the crew lives with the serpent and by the serpent, necessarily for their livelihood, unaware of the nature of the coil yet contaminated and imperilled by its inherent danger. Melville thus depicts the metaphysical necessity of evil.

Thompson's language is distinguished formally from the concrete and symbolistic devices in Melville. Thompson allows the imagery of a whaling voyage to carry moral and allegorical meanings, yet he means his narration to be descriptive and realistic; his concern is with verisimilitude. There can be nothing morally ambiguous about the need to abolish slavery, and there can be little ambiguity about the reason for the suffering of the slave. 'The slave narrative,' Butterfield concludes, 'does not see oppression in terms of a symbol-structure that transforms evil into a metaphysical necessity. For to do so would have been to locate the source of evil outside the master-slave relationship, and thus would have cut the ideological ground from under the entire thrust of the abolitionist movement.'[12] Thompson means not so much to narrate as to convey a message, a value system; as with the black sermon, the slave's narrative functions as a single sign. And the nature of Frederick Douglass's rhetorical strategy directly reflects this sentiment through the use of what rhetoricians have called antitheses and of what the structuralists have come to call the binary opposition.

In the act of interpretation, we establish a sign relationship between the description and a meaning. The relations most crucial to structural analysis are functional binary oppositions. Roman Jakobson and Morris Halle argue in *Fundamentals of Language* that binary oppositions are inherent in all languages, that they are, indeed, a fundamental principle of language formation itself.[13] Many structuralists, seizing on Jakobson's formulation, hold the binary opposition to be a fundamental operation of the human mind, basic to the production of meaning. Lévi-Strauss, who turned topsy-turvy the way we examine mythological discourse, describes the binary opposition as 'this elementary logic which is the smallest common denominator of all thought'.[14] Lévi-Strauss's model of opposition and mediation, which sees the binary opposition as an underlying structural pattern as well as a method of revealing that pattern, has in its many variants become a most satisfying mechanism for retrieving almost primal social contradictions, long ago 'resolved' in the mediated structure itself.[15] Perhaps it is not irresponsible or premature to call Lévi-Strauss's contribution to human understanding a classic one.

Fredric Jameson, in *The Prison-House of Language*, maintains that

the binary opposition is . . . at the outset a heuristic principle, that instrument of analysis on which the mythological hermeneutic is founded. We would ourselves be tempted to describe it as a technique for stimulating perception, when faced with a mass of apparently homogeneous data to which the mind and the eyes are numb: a way of forcing ourselves to perceive difference and identity in a whole new language the very sounds of which we cannot yet distinguish from each other. It is a decoding or deciphering device, or alternately a technique of language learning.

How does this 'decoding device' work as a tool for practical criticism? When any two terms are set in opposition to each other, the reader is forced to explore qualitative similarities and differences, to make some connection, and, therefore, to derive some meaning from points of disjunction. If one opposes A to B, for instance, and X to Y, the two cases become similar as long as each involves the presence and absence of a given feature. In short, two terms are brought together by some quality that they share and are then opposed and made to signify the absence and presence of that quality. The relationship between presence and absence, positive and negative signs, is the simplest form of the binary opposition. These relationships, Jameson concludes, 'embody a tension "in which one of the two terms of the binary opposition is apprehended as positively having a certain feature while the other is apprehended as deprived of the feature in question." '[16]

Frederick Douglass's *Narrative* attempts with painstaking verisimilitude to reproduce a system of signs that we have come to call plantation culture, from the initial paragraph of the first chapter:

I was born in Tuckahoe, near Hillsborough, and about twelve miles from Easton, in Talbot County, Maryland. I have no accurate knowledge of my age, never having seen any authentic record containing it. By far the larger part of the slaves know as little of their ages as horses know of theirs, and it is the wish of most masters within my knowledge to keep their slaves thus ignorant. I do not remember to have ever met a slave who could tell of his birthday, they seldom come nearer to it than planting-time, harvest-time, cherry-time, spring-time, or fall-time. A want of information concerning my own was a source of unhappiness to me even during childhood. The white children could tell their ages, I could not tell why I ought to be deprived of the same privilege. I was not allowed to make any inquiries of my master concerning it. He deemed such inquiries on the part of a slave improper and impertinent, and evidence of a restless spirit. The nearest estimate I can give makes me now between twenty-seven and twenty-eight years of age. I come to this, from hearing my master say, sometime during 1835, I was about seventeen years old.[17]

We see an ordering of the world based on a profoundly relational type of thinking, in which a strict barrier of difference or opposition forms the basis of a class rather than, as in other classification schemes, an ordering based on resemblances or the identity of two or more elements. In the text, we can say that these binary oppositions produce through separation the most inflexible of barriers: that of meaning. We, the readers, must exploit the opposition and give them a place in a larger symbolic structure.

Douglass's narrative strategy seems to be this: He brings together two terms in special relationships suggested by some quality that they share; then, by opposing two seemingly unrelated elements, such as the sheep, cattle, or horses on the plantation and the specimen of life known as slave, Douglass's language is made to signify the presence and absence of some quality – in this case, humanity.[18] Douglass uses this device to explicate the slave's understanding of himself and of his relation to the world through the system of the perceptions that defined the world the planters made. Not only does his *Narrative* come to concern itself with two diametrically opposed notions of genesis, origins, and meaning itself, but its structure actually turns on an opposition between nature and culture as well. Finally and, for our purposes, crucially, Douglass's method of complex mediation – and the ironic reversals so peculiar to his text – suggests overwhelmingly the completely arbitrary relationship between description and meaning, between signifier and signified, between sign and referent.

Douglass uses these oppositions to create a unity on a symbolic level, not only through physical opposition but also through an opposition of space and time. The *Narrative* begins, 'I was born in Tuckahoe, near Hillsborough, and about twelve miles from Easton, in Talbot County, Maryland.' Douglass knows the physical circumstances of his birth: Tuckahoe, we know, is near Hillsborough and is twelve miles from Easton. Though his place of birth is fairly definite, his date of birth is not for him to know: 'I have no accurate knowledge of my age,' he admits, because 'any authentic record containing it' would be in the possession of his master. Indeed, this opposition, or counterpoint, between that which is knowable in the world of the slave and that which is not abounds throughout this chapter. Already we know that the world of the master and the world of the slave are separated by an inflexible barrier of meaning. The knowledge the slave has of his circumstances he must deduce from the earth; a quantity such as time, our understanding of which is cultural and not natural, derives from a nonmaterial source, let us say the heavens. How do we know a white child from a black child? Douglass's response is brilliant in its simplicity: 'The white children could tell their ages. I could not.'

The deprivation of the means to tell the time is the very structural centre of this initial paragraph, in which he defines what it means to become aware of one's own enslavement: 'A want of information concerning my own [birthday] was a source of unhappiness to me even during childhood.' This state of disequilibrium – this absence of choice – motivates the slave's search for his humanity as well as Douglass's search for his text, the text that will come to stand for his life in the form of an autobiography. This deprivation has created that gap in the slave's imagination between self and other, between lord and bondsman, between black and white. What is more, this deprivation of time has created an apparent likeness between the slave and the plantation's animals. 'By far,' Douglass confesses, 'the large part of slaves know as little of their ages as horses know of theirs.' This deprivation is not accidental; it is systematic: 'it is the wish of most masters within my knowledge to keep their slaves thus ignorant.' Douglass, in his subtle juxtaposition here of 'masters' and 'knowledge' and of 'slaves' and 'ignorance', again introduces homologous terms. 'I do not remember to have ever met a slave,' Douglass emphasises, 'who could tell of his birthday.' Slaves, he seems to conclude, are those who cannot plot their course by and who stand outside of the linear progression of the calendar. And precisely here Douglass summarises the symbolic code of this world, which makes the slave's closest blood relations the horses and which makes his or her very notion of time a cyclical one, diametrically opposed to the master's linear conception: 'They [the slaves] seldom come nearer to [the notion of time] than plant-ing-time, harvest-time, cherry-time, spring-time, or fall-time.' The slave had arrived, but not in time to partake at the welcome table of human culture.

For Douglass, the bonds of blood kinship are the primary meta-phors of human culture.[19] As an animal would know its mother, so Douglass knows his. 'My mother was named Harriet Bailey. She was the daughter of Isaac and Betsey Bailey,' both of whom were 'colored', Douglass notes, 'and quite dark.' His mother 'was of a darker complexion' even than either grandparent. His father, on the other hand, is some indefinite 'white man,' suggested through innuendo to be his master: 'The opinion was also whispered,' he says, 'that my master was my father.' His master was his father; his father his master. 'Of the correctness of this opinion,' Douglass concludes, 'I know nothing,' only and precisely because 'the means of knowing was withheld from me.' Two paragraphs below, having reflected on the death of his mother, Douglass repeats this peculiar unity twice again. 'Called thus suddenly away,' he commences, 'she left me without the slightest intimation of who my father was.' Yet Douglass repeats 'the whisper that my father was my master' as he launches into a description of the rank odiousness of a system 'that slaveholders have ordained, and by law established', in which the partrilineal succession of the planter has been forcibly replaced by a matrilineal succession for the slave: 'the children of slave women shall in all cases follow the condition of their mothers'. The planters therefore make of the 'gratification of their wicked desires', spits Douglass, a thing 'profitable as well as pleasurable'. Further, the end result of 'this cunning arrangement' is that 'the slaveholder, in cases not a few, sustains to his slaves the double relation of master and father'. 'I know of such cases,' he opens his sixth paragraph, using a declaration of verisimilitude as a transition to introduce another opposition, this one between the fertile slave-lover-mother and the planter's barren wife.

The profound ambiguity of this relationship between father and son and master and slave persists, if only because the two terms 'father' and 'master' are here embodied in one, with no mediation between them. It is a rather grotesque bond that links Douglass to his parent, a bond that embodies 'the distorted and unnatural relationship endemic to slavery'.[20] It is as if the usually implied primal tension between father and son is rendered apparent in the daily contact between father-master-human and son-slave-animal, a contact that occurs, significantly, only during the light of day.

Douglass's contact with his mother ('to know her as such', he qualifies) never occurred 'more than four or five times in my life'. Each of these visits, he recalls, 'was of short duration', and each, he repeats over and over, took place 'at night'. Douglass continues: '[My mother] made her journey to see me in the night, travelling the whole distance,' he mentions as if an afterthought, 'on foot.' 'I do not recollect of ever seeing my mother,' he repeats one sentence later, 'by the light of day. She was with me in the night.' Always she returned to a Mr Stewart's plantation, some twelve miles away, 'long before I waked', so as to be at the plantation before dawn, since she 'was a field hand, and a whipping is the penalty of not being in the field at sunrise'. The slaves metaphorically 'owned' the night, while the master owned the day. By the fourth paragraph of the narrative, the terms of our homology – the symbolic code of this world – are developed further to include relations of the animal, the mother, the slave, the night, the earth, the matrilineal succession, and nature opposed to relations of the human being, the father, the master, the daylight, the heavens, patrilineal succession, and culture. Douglass, in short, opposes the absolute and the eternal to the mortal and the finite. Our list certainly could be expanded to include oppositions between spiritual/material, aristocratic/ base, civilized/barbaric, sterile/fertile, enterprise/sloth, force/principle, fact/imagination, linear/cyclical, thinking/feeling, rational/ irrational, chivalry/cowardice, grace/brutishness, pure/cursed, and human/beastly.

Yet the code, Douglass proceeds to show, stands in defiance of the natural and moral order. Here Douglass commences as mediator and as trickster to reverse the relations of the opposition. That the relationship between the slave-son and master-father was an unnatural one and even grotesque, as are the results of any defilement of order, is reflected in the nature of the relationship between the plantation mistress and the planter's illegitimate offspring. 'She is ever disposed to find fault with them,' laments Douglass; 'she is never better pleased than when she sees them under the lash.' Indeed, it is the white mistress who often compels her husband, the master, to sell 'this class of his slaves, out of deference to the feelings of his white wife'. But it is the priority of the economic relation over the kinship tie that is the true perversion of nature in this world: 'It is often the dictate of humanity for a man to sell his own children to human flesh-mongers,' Douglass observes tellingly. Here we see the ultimate reversal: it is now the mistress, the proverbial carrier of culture, who demands that the master's son be delivered up to the 'human flesh-mongers' and traded for consumption. Douglass has here defined the American cannibalism, a consumption of human flesh dictated by a system that could only be demonic.

Douglass's narrative demonstrates not only how the deprivation of the hallmarks of identity can affect the slave but also how the slaveowner's world negates and even perverts those very values on which it is built. Deprivation of a birthdate, a name, a family structure, and legal rights makes of the deprived brute a subhuman, says Douglass, until he comes to a consciousness of these relations; yet, it is the human depriver who is the actual barbarian structuring his existence on the consumption of human flesh. Just as the mulatto son is a mediation between two opposed terms, man and animal, so too has Douglass's text become the complex mediator between the world as the master would have it and the world as the slave knows it really is. Douglass has subverted the terms of the code he was meant to mediate; he has been a trickster. As with all mediations, the trickster is a mediator and his mediation is a trick – only a trick – for there can be no mediation in this world. Douglass's narrative has aimed to destroy the symbolic code that created the false oppositions themselves. The oppositions, all along, were only arbitrary, not fixed.

Douglass first suggests that the symbolic code created in this text is arbitrary and not fixed, human-imposed and not divinely ordained, in an ironic aside on the myth of the curse of Ham, which comes in the very centre of the seventh paragraph of the narrative and is meant to be an elaboration of the ramifications of 'this class of slaves' who are the fruit of the unnatural liaison between animal and man. If the justification of this order is the curse on Ham and his tribe, if Ham's tribe signifies the black African, and if this prescription for enslavement is scriptural, then, Douglass argues, 'it is certain that slavery at the south must soon become unscriptural; for thousands are ushered into the world, annually, who, like myself, owe their existence to white fathers, and those fathers,' he repeats for the fourth time, are 'most frequently their own masters.'

As if to underscore the falsity of this notion of an imposed, inflexibly divine order, Douglass inverts a standard Christian symbol, that of the straight and narrow gate to Paradise. The severe beating of his Aunt Hester, who, Douglass advises us parenthetically, 'happened to be absent when my master desired her presence', is the occasion of this inversion. 'It struck me with awful force,' he remembers. 'It was the blood-stained gate, the entrance to the hell of slavery, through which I was about to pass. It was,' he concludes, 'a most terrible spectacle.' This startling image suggests that of the archetypal necromancer, Faustus, in whose final vision the usual serene presence of the Cross is stained with warm and dripping blood.

Douglass has posited the completely arbitrary nature of the sign. The master's actions belie the metaphysical suppositions on which is based the order of his world. It is an order ostensibly imposed by the father of Adam, yet one in fact exposed by the sons of Ham. It is a world whose oppositions have generated their own mediator, Douglass himself. This mulatto son, half-animal, half-man, writes a text (which is itself another mediation) in which he can expose the arbitrary nature of the signs found in this world, the very process necessary to the destruction of this world. 'You have seen how a man was made a slave,' Douglass writes at the structural centre of his *Narrative*, 'you shall see how a slave was made a man.'[21] As with all mediation, Douglass has constructed a system of perception that becomes the plot development in the text but results in an inversion of the initial state of the oppositions through the operations of the mediator himself, as indicated in this diagram:

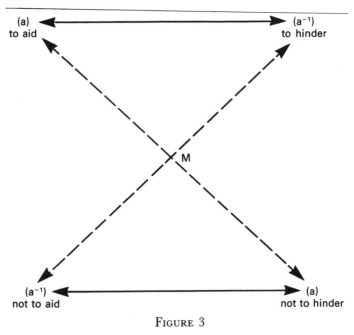

FIGURE 3

With this narrative gesture alone, slave has become master, creature has become man, object has become subject. What more telling embodiment of Emersonian idealism and its capacity to transubstantiate a material reality! Not only has an idea made subject of object, but creature has assumed self, and the assumption of self has created a race. For, as with all myths of origins, the relation of self to race is a relation of synecdoche. As Michael Cooke maintains concerning the characteristics of black autobiography,

the self is the source of the system of which it is a part, creates what it discovers, and although (as Coleridge realized) it is nothing unto itself, it is the possibility of everything for itself. Autobiography is the coordination of

the self as content – everything available in memory, perception, understanding, imagination, desire – and the self as shaped, formed in terms of
a perspective and pattern of interpretation.[22]

If we step outside the self-imposed confines of Douglass's first
chapter to seek textual evidence, the case becomes even stronger.
The opposition between culture and nature is clearly contained in
a description of a slave meal, found in Chapter V.[23]

We were not regularly allowanced. Our food was coarse corn meal boiled.
This was called *mush*. It was put into a large wooden tray or trough, and
set down upon the ground. The children were then called, like so many
pigs, and like so many pigs they would come and devour the mush; some
with oyster-shells, others with pieces of shingle, some with naked hands,
and none with spoons. He that ate fastest got most; he that was strongest
secured the best place; and few left the trough satisfied.

The slave, we read, did not eat food; he ate mush. He did not eat
with a spoon; he ate with pieces of shingle, or on oyster shells, or
with his naked hands. Again we see the obvious culture-nature
opposition at play. When the slave, in another place, accepts the
comparison with and identity of a 'bad sheep', he again has inverted
the terms, supplied as always by the master, so that the unfavour-
able meaning this has for the master is supplanted by the favourable
meaning it has for the slave. There is in this world the planter has
made, Douglass maintains, an ironic relationship between appearance and reality. 'Slaves sing most,' he writes at the end of Chapter
II, 'when they are most unhappy. . . . The singing of a man cast
away upon a desolate island might be as appropriately considered
as evidence of contentment and happiness, as the singing of a slave;
the songs of the one and of the other are prompted by the same
emotion.'

Douglass concludes his second chapter with a discourse on the
nature of interpretation, which we could perhaps call the first chart-
ing of the black hermeneutical circle and which we could take again
as a declaration of the arbitrary relationship between a sign and its
referent, between the signifier and the signified. The slaves, he
writes, 'would compose and sing as they went along, consulting
neither time nor tune. The thought that came up, came out – if not
in the word, [then] in the sound; – and as frequently in the one as
in the other.'[24] Douglass describes here a certain convergence of
perception peculiar only to members of a very specific culture: the
thought could very well be embodied nonverbally, in the sound if
not in the word. What is more, sound and sense could very well
operate at odds to create through tension a dialectical relation.

Douglass remarks: 'They would sometimes sing the most pathetic sentiment in the most rapturous tone, and the most rapturous sentiment in the most pathetic tone. . . . They would thus sing as a chorus to words which to many would seem unmeaning jargon, but which, nevertheless, were full of meaning to themselves.' Yet the decoding of these cryptic messages did not, as some of us have postulated, depend on some sort of mystical union with their texts. 'I did not, when a slave,' Douglass admits, 'understand the deep meaning of those rude and apparently incoherent songs.' Meaning, on the contrary, came only with a certain aesthetic distance and an acceptance of the critical imperative. 'I was myself within the circle,' he concludes, 'so that I neither saw nor heard as those without might see and hear.' There exists always the danger, Douglass seems to say, that the meanings of nonlinguistic signs will seem natural; one must view them with a certain detachment to see that their meanings are in fact merely the products of a certain culture, the result of shared assumptions and conventions. Not only is meaning culture-bound and the reference of all signs an assigned relation, Douglass tells us, but *how* we read determines *what* we read, in the truest sense of the hermeneutical circle.

Notes

1. See Marion Wilson Starling's *The Slave Narrative* (Boston: G. K. Hall, 1981); and William L. Andrews, *To Tell a Free Story: The First Century of Afro-American Autobiography, 1760–1865* (Urbana: University of Illinois Press, 1986) for the fullest treatments of the slave's narrative.

2. Claudio Guillen, *Literature As System: Essays Toward the Theory of Literary History* (Princeton University Press, 1971), pp. 71–106 and especially pp. 135–58. Quotations are from p. 81.

3. George R. Graham, 'Black Letters; or Uncle Tom-Foolery in Literature', *Graham's Illustrated Magazine of Literature, Romance, Art, and Fashion* 42 (February 1853): 209.

4. Marion Wilson Starling, *'The Slave Narrative: Its Place in American Literary History'*, dissertation New York University, 1946, pp. 47–48.

5. 'Narrative of Frederick Douglass', *Littell's Living Age* (April 1, 1846): p. 47.

6. *New York Tribune*, 10 June 1845, p. 1; reprinted in *The Liberator*, 30 May 1845, p. 97.

7. *Lynn Pioneer*; reprinted in *The Liberator*, 30 May 1845, p. 86 .

8. See especially John Blassingame, 'Black Autobiography as History

and Literature,' *Black Scholar* 5, no. 4 (December 1973-January 1974): 2-9; and his *Slave Testimony: Two Centuries of Letters, Speeches, Interviews, and Autobiographies* (Baton Rouge: Louisiana State University Press, 1977).

9. Robert Scholes and Robert Kellogg, *The Nature of Narrative* (New York: Oxford University Press, 1966), p. 76.

10. Stephen Butterfield, *Black Autobiography in America* (Amherst: University of Massachusetts Press, 1974), p. 36.

11. John Thompson, *The Life of John Thompson, a Fugitive Slave, Containing His History of Twenty-Five Years in Bondage and His Providential Escape* (Worcester, 1856), p. 113.

12. Butterfield, *Black Autobiography*, p. 37.

13. Roman Jakobson and Morris Halle, *Fundamentals of Language* (The Hague: Mouton, 1971), pp. 4, 47-9.

14. Claude Lévi-Strauss, *Totemism* (New York: Penguin, 1969), p. 130.

15. What has this rather obvious model of human thought to do with the study of mundane literature generally and with the study of Afro-American literature specifically? It has forced us to alter irrevocably certain long-held assumptions about the relationship between sign and referent, between signifier and signified. It has forced us to remember what queries we intended to resolve when we first organised a discourse in a particular way. What's more, this rather simple formulation has taught us to recognise texts where we find them and to read these texts as they demand to be read. Yet we keepers of black critical activity have yet to graft fifty years of systematic thinking about literature onto the consideration of our own. The study of Afro-American folklore, for instance, remains preoccupied with unresolvable matters of genesis or with limitless catalogues and motif indices. Afraid that Brer Rabbit is merely a trickster or that Anansi spiders merely spin webs, we reduce these myths to their simplest thematic terms – the perennial relationship between the wily, persecuted black and the not-too-clever, persecuting white. This reduction belies our own belief in the philosophical value of these mental constructs. We admit, albeit inadvertently, a nagging suspicion that these are the primitive artifacts of childish minds, grappling with a complex Western world and its languages, three thousand years and a world removed. These myths, as the slave narratives would, did not so much narrate as they did convey a value system; they functioned, much like a black sermon, as a single sign. The use of binary opposition, for instance, allows us to perceive much deeper meanings than a simplistic racial symbolism allows. Refusal to use sophisticated analysis on our own literature smacks of a symbolic inferiority complex as blatant as the use of skin lighteners and hair straighteners.

16. Fredric Jameson, *The Prison-House of Language: A Critical Account of Structuralism and Russian Formalism* (Princeton: Princeton University Press, 1972), pp. 113, 115, citing Troubetskoy's *Principes de phonologie*. See also Jonathan Culler, *Structuralist Poetics: Structuralism, Linguistics, and the Study of Literature* (Ithaca: Cornell University Press, 1975), pp. 93, 225-7; Roland Barthes, *S/Z, An Essay*, trans. Richard Miller (New York: Hill and Wang, 1975), p. 24.

17. Frederick Douglass, *Narrative* (Boston: Anti-Slavery Office, 1845), p. 1. All subsequent quotes, unless indicated, are from pp. 1–7.

18. There is overwhelming textual evidence that Douglass was a consummate stylist who, contrary to popular myth, learned the craft of the essayist self-consciously. The importance of Caleb Bingham's *The Columbian Orator* (Boston: Manning and Loring, 1797) to Douglass's art is well established. John Blassingame is convinced of Douglass's use of Bingham's rhetorical advice in his writing, especially of antitheses. (Personal interview with John Blassingame, 7 May 1976.) For an estimation of the role of language in political struggle of antebellum blacks, see Alexander Crummell, 'The English Language in Liberia', in his *The Future of Africa* (New York: Scribners, 1862), pp. 9–57.

19. See also Nancy T. Clasby, 'Frederick Douglass's *Narrative: A* Content Analysis', *CLA Journal 14* (1971): 244.

20. Clasby, p. 245.

21. Douglass, p. 77.

22. Michael Cooke, 'Modern Black Autobiography in the Tradition', in *Romanticism, Vistas, Instances, and Continuities*, ed. David Thorburn and Geoffrey Hartman (Ithaca: Cornell University Press, 1973), p. 258.

23. Douglass, pp. 13–15.

24. Douglass, p. 30.

6 POLITICS AND HISTORY

Marxist literary criticism has a relatively long history but it is only comparatively recently that it has become widely accepted that Marxism should be seen as at the centre of critical discussion and debate. Earlier Marxist criticism – so-called 'vulgar' Marxism – tended to be viewed by those uncommitted to Marxist politics as reductive, since literary texts were interpreted in reflective terms as being directly determined by socio-economic forces, and though a critic such as Georg Lukács was widely respected and could not be dismissed as a vulgar Marxist, his work was mainly influential within the Marxist tradition. Contemporary Marxism has questioned traditional dogma and has been prepared to enter into engagement with developments in modern theory. Thus what Jacques Derrida has termed a more 'open Marxism' has emerged.[1]

Two key figures in modern Marxism are Louis Althusser and Pierre Macherey. Althusser's writings provided the basis for a radical revision of the reflection model that dominated earlier Marxist criticism. He brought together structuralist thinking and Marxism in his interpretation of society or the 'social formation' by moving from a causal model to a relational one. Thus he attacked a traditional Marxian concept like mediation, the idea that all levels of the superstructure are essentially similar in structure since they are reflections of the economic base. Economic determinism was largely discarded and the various levels of the superstructure, such as art, were allowed to have a degree of autonomy, what he called 'relative autonomy'. Works of art have to be seen as 'overdetermined', a term he borrowed from Freud, rather than being the product of socio-economic forces in any simple sense. Macherey, a colleague of Althusser, developed a Marxist literary theory that had strong connections with structuralism and anticipated post-structuralism in certain respects. He argued that literary texts possessed a multiplicity of meanings and should therefore be seen as 'decentred'. The relation between ideology and history is crucial for Macherey. Adopting a Freudian model, he sees history as the unconscious which can be apprehended only indirectly by focussing on the contradictions within ideology. Ideology aims at completeness but gaps and fissures inevitably emerge and reality or history is to be discerned through these gaps. Literary texts in giving form to ideology enable ideology 'to speak of its *own absences*' and make it possible 'to escape from the false consciousness of self, of history, and of time'.[2]

Terry Eagleton, the leading British Marxist critic, was strongly influenced by Althusser and Macherey. In his book *Criticism and Ideology* he saw the object of criticism as the 'unconsciousness' of the text, the space which is articulated by ideology being put to work within a text. However, Eagleton does not feel able, like Althusserian Marxism, to discard causality and mediation. To focus also only on gaps and silences in the text is for him too negative a conception of a text's relation to history. He believes one can deal with the division between the ideology of the text and history in a more direct way than Macherey thinks possible. In *Criticism and Ideology*, therefore, Eagleton seeks to reconcile traditional and Althusserian Marxism. Since writing it he has moved on critically to create new alignments with, for example, feminism and deconstruction, an indication that modern Marxist criticism is continually developing. The essay on Conrad reprinted here, however, comes from *Criticism and Ideology* and argues that Conrad's fiction is caught up in the contradictions of bourgeois ideology since it is part of 'a tradition which offered an idealist critique of bourgeois social relations, coupled with a consecration of the rights of capital'.[3]

Marxist criticism tends not to deal very specifically with the detail of history. In the past twenty years or so a materialist criticism has emerged which directs its attention much more closely to history while at the same time drawing on a wide range of theory, both literary and cultural. In America this development has been called new historicism. Its best known practitioner is Stephen Greenblatt. He has tended to concentrate on practice rather than theory but he has voiced certain critical principles. His aim is to create 'a more cultural or anthropological criticism' which will be 'conscious of its own status as interpretation and intent upon understanding literature as a part of the system of signs that constitutes a given culture'. Literary criticism and cultural critique are integrated, with the critic's role being to investigate 'both the social presence to the world of the literary text and the social presence of the world in the literary text'.[4]

It is clear that, unlike traditional historical critics, Greenblatt believes the critic cannot and should not desire to escape from the hermeneutic circle of interpretation which would implicate the critic in that which he or she interprets. Thus modern preoccupations with ideology, power relations, and the politics of imperialism are apparent in his criticism. In contrast to most modern critics he does not see literature as necessarily promoting liberation. In one of his

most influential essays he argues that in Renaissance texts elements
that appear to resist or subvert prevailing ideologies function rather
to immunise ideological discourse from being seriously undermined
since subversion is both generated and contained by the dominant
ideology.[5] In many of his essays Greenblatt begins by interpreting
a non-literary text before going on to discuss a canonic text. He
adopts this method in the essay on *King Lear* which is reprinted
here.

The equivalent to new historicism in Britain is what has been
called cultural materialism. Whereas the dominant influences on
new historicism were the cultural theory of Foucault and the social
anthropology of Clifford Geertz, cultural materialists were most
strongly influenced by Althusser, the writings of Raymond Williams
and cultural studies in Britain. Their criticism is also more directly
political than that of most new historicists. Unlike Greenblatt, they
tend to see the 'resistances' in literary texts more positively as
destabilising ideology so that literature and criticism have a more
direct role to play in promoting social and political change. Alan
Sinfield and his colleague Jonathan Dollimore believe that cultural
materialist criticism 'registers its commitment to the transformation
of a social order which exploits people on grounds of race, gender,
and class'.[6] In his essay on *Macbeth* Sinfield proclaims his commitment to 'an oppositional criticism' but it is clear that he would also
claim that his reading is not merely imposed for political purposes
but more valid in interpretative terms than traditional readings.

A critic who has attempted to create a criticism that brings
together theory and politics in a way that diverges from the critics
discussed above is Edward Said. Unlike most new historicists and
cultural materialists, Said is directly involved in a political struggle,
being an exiled Palestinian, and as well as publishing literary criticism and theory he has also written a major work of cultural critique
with his book *Orientalism*. For literary criticism to play a significant
role in modern culture it must be able to confront such cultural
and historical phenomena as imperialism and colonialism. Said,
however, has been mainly associated with post-structuralist criticism in his writing on literary texts but he has attacked the apolitical
nature of most post-structuralist criticism. He believes that a concern with textuality must not become dissociated from history and
contemporary politics. Contemporary critical theory needs to 'rein-
vest critical discourse with something more than contemplative
effort or an appreciative technical reading method for texts as unde-
cidable objects'. Yet Said also believes strongly that 'method and
system' in criticism should not be abandoned, and unlike some

critics who share his cultural concerns he shows no inclination to jettison canonic texts. The problem for criticism is rather to do justice to major works of the canon in the manner of textualist modes of criticism while also showing that 'even when they appear to deny it, they are nevertheless a part of the social world, human life, and of course of the historical moments in which they are located and interpreted'.[7] In the essay on Jane Austen's *Mansfield Park* reprinted here he argues that the geography of the novel is not 'a neutral fact' but 'a politically charged one' which relates to both imperialism and colonialism and which prefigures later works dealing more directly with these issues.

Notes

1. See James Kearns and Ken Newton, 'An Interview with Jacques Derrida', *Literary Review*, 14, 1980, pp. 21–2.

2. Pierre Macherey, *A Theory of Literary Production*, trans. Geoffrey Wall (London, 1978), p. 132.

3. Terry Eagleton, *Criticism and Ideology: A Study in Marxist Literary Theory* (London, 1976), p. 102.

4. Stephen Greenblatt, *Renaissance Self-Fashioning: From More to Shakespeare* (Chicago, 1980), pp. 4, 5.

5. See Greenblatt, 'Invisible Bullets: Renaissance Authority and Its Subversion', *Glyph*, 8 (1981), pp. 40–61.

6. *Political Shakespeare: New Essays in Cultural Materialism*, eds Jonathan Dollimore and Alan Sinfield (Manchester, 1985), p. viii.

7. Edward W. Said, *The World, the Text, the Critic* (London, 1984) pp. 224, 4.

Further Reading

Jonathan Dollimore, *Radical Tragedy: Religion, Ideology and Power in the Drama of Shakespeare and his Contemporaries* (Brighton, 1984).

Terry Eagleton, *Myths of Power: A Marxist Study of the Brontës* (London, 1975).

Stephen Greenblatt, *Shakespearean Negotiations: The Circulation of Energy in Renaissance England* (Oxford, 1988).

Peter Hulme, *Colonial Encounters: Europe and the Native Caribbean 1492–1797* (London, 1986).

Edward W. Said, 'Yeats and Decolonization', in *Literature and the Modern World*, ed. Dennis Walder (Oxford, 1990).

Terry Eagleton: Ideology and Literary Form: Joseph Conrad

It would be a predictable error to trace the development of organicism in nineteenth-century literature from George Eliot to that later petty-bourgeois novelist of rural life, Thomas Hardy. Yet though Hardy inherits an ideology of organic social evolution (he writes, echoing Eliot, of the human race as 'one great network or tissue . . . like a spider's web'),[1] his fiction is essentially preoccupied with those structural conflicts and tragic contradictions in rural society which Eliot's novels evade. I have argued in the previous chapter that Hardy's movement towards a fully-developed critical realism was laborious and uneven; it is the peculiar *impurity* of his literary forms (pastoral, melodrama, social realism, naturalism, myth, fable, classical tragedy) which is most striking. Ambiguously placed within both his own declining rural enclave and the social formation at large, exploring 'Wessex' with realist internality yet viewing it also through the immobilising perspectives of myth, Hardy's situation as a literary producer was ridden with contradictions. They are contradictions inseparable from his fraught productive relation to the metropolitan audience whose spokesmen rejected his first, abrasively radical work. His use of pastoral and mythological forms occasionally reflects an anxious pact with that readership's flat patronage of the 'bucolic'; but he also deploys the 'universalising' frames of fable, ballad and classical tragedy to confer major status on fictional material liable to be dismissed as of merely provincial import. The formal problem of how to reconcile these conflicting literary modes – is Alec D'Urberville bourgeois *arriviste*, pantomime devil, melodramatic villain, symbol of Satanic evil? – is the product of Hardy's unusually complex mode of insertion into the dominant ideological formation and its span of possible literary forms. Yet by the time of *Jude the Obscure*, 'reconciliation' has been effectively abandoned: that novel is less an offering to its audience than a calculated assault on them. What have been read as its 'crudities' are less the consequences of some artistic incapacity than of an

Reprinted from Terry Eagleton, *Criticism and Ideology: A Study in Marxist Literary Theory* (London, 1976), pp. 130–40.

astonishing raw boldness on Hardy's part, a defiant flouting of 'verisimilitude' which mounts theatrical gesture upon gesture in a driving back of the bounds of realism. It is not fortuitous that the book's epigraph is 'The letter killeth': crammed with lengthy quotations from other texts, thematically obsessed with the violence of literary culture, laced with typological devices, *Jude* contrasts the murderous inertia of the *letter* with that alternative image of artistic production which is material craftsmanship. The models, forms, moulds and productive practices over which the text broods are themselves images of its own construction – of that montage of 'seemings' ('*productions* of this pen', in Hardy's revealing phrase) whose 'permanency' or 'consistency' is beside the point. Within the radical *provisionality* of Hardy's productive practice is inscribed a second, more fundamental provisionality – the desired un-closure of social forms themselves (epitomised in sexuality), forms which in their received shape the novel 'explodes' in the act of 'exploding' the letter of its own text. Throughout the novel, hallowed manuscripts – the Nicean creed, the Book of Job – are violently transformed by Jude into angry oral assaults on an unresponsive audience – assaults through which the novel mimes its own displaced position within the literary social relations of its time. Hardy claimed that the bigoted public response to *Jude* cured him of novel-writing for ever; but whether a producer of Hardy's status stops writing merely on account of bad reviews is surely questionable. The truth is that after *Jude* there was nowhere for Hardy to go; having 'exploded' the organic forms of fiction, he was forced to disembark.

The organicist tradition in the *fin-de-siècle*, then passes not to the rural Englishman Hardy, but to the Polish *émigré* Conrad. With the entry into the English literary arena of Joseph Conrad, Polish exile and merchant seaman, we witness the emergence of a peculiarly *overdetermined* instance of the conflict between Romantic individualism and social organicism which I have traced in the work of George Eliot. Conrad's conservative patriot father became a nationalist rebel against the Russian domination of Poland – an exiled and imprisoned pan-Slavic mystic, from whom Conrad inherited a belief in his subjugated fatherland as a corporate body ('an organic living thing')[2] with a messianic sense of its historical destiny. Yet this Romantic idealist heritage was in conflict with the pragmatic conservative realism which Conrad imbibed from his mother's family, the landowning Bobrowskis, who advocated a cautious constitutionalism and a stern renunciation of the Romantic ego. The Polish nobility to which Conrad belonged were divided: the aristocracy was effectively incorporated into the Russian ruling class, leaving landed gentry like the Bobrowskis and Conrad's own family to devise ways of throwing off the imperial yoke. Aspiring to national independence, but deprived of their social hegemony by Russian imperialism, they were hesitant in embracing the one 'extreme' means – revolution – by which this could be achieved. Poland for Conrad thus came to symbolise an ideal fusion of national corporateness and liberal enlightenment; it was a 'spontaneous unity', yet with its 'almost exaggerated respect for individual rights', allied itself with European liberalism against Slav 'fanaticism'.[3]

Conrad's self-imposed exile from Poland, as seaman and artist, flamboyantly affirms his freedom from an intolerably claustrophobic imperialism. Yet at the same time both art and the merchant service recreate the organic unity which had been brutally splintered in Poland. The ship is an organic community which, with its hierarchical structure of stable functions, curtails subversive individualism and the anarchic imagination. But, like Poland, it also represents a form of collective isolation threatened by alien forces, and so – especially for an officer socially removed from the crew – pitches the individual into lonely, testing confrontation with his own problematic identity. Art similarly, symbolises the supreme autonomy of a personal imagination free from repressive rules; but it is also an organic whole which demands the abnegation of the individual ego. English society itself offered Conrad an ideal resolution of the conflicting ideological imperatives he inherited from his Polish context; it became a welcome enclave for the conservative *émigré* in flight from European political turbulence.[4] Its tolerant, pragmatic individualism united with the organic, Romantic nationalist heritage of the merchant service to provide Conrad with precisely the ideological conjuncture he sought. England, Conrad believes, is 'the only barrier to the pressure of infernal doctrines born in continental backslums';[5] its settled, hierarchic traditionalism is a bastion against that 'fraternity [which] tends to weaken the national sentiment, the preservation of which is my concern'.[6] Conrad's entry into English letters, then, is far from the inruption of an 'alien' ideology into English history, the intrusion into the native social formation of a 'class-subject' produced by foreign forces. His expatriate status is relevant only as one among several possible modes of contradictory unity with the dominant native ideology. 'Expatriatism' is not a 'totalisation' of Conrad's individual position as 'subject' within either Polish or English society; it is, rather, a set of objective ideological relations occupied by the historical subject Joseph Conrad, one determined in the last instance by the internal articulations of the native ideology.

As Avrom Fleishman has argued,[7] Conrad directly inherits the organicist tradition of nineteenth-century Romantic humanism. His positive values, incarnate above all in the virile solidarity of the ship's crew, are the reactionary Carlylean imperatives of work, duty, fidelity and stoical submission – values which bind men spontaneously to the social whole. Yet his fiction, with its recurrent motif of the divided self, is also shot through with a guilty, lawless Romantic individualism which struggles to subject itself to communal discipline. Conrad's social organicism, in other words, is united with an extreme, sometimes solipsistic individualism – a metaphysical scepticism as to the objective nature of social values, a distrust of ideals as the irrational reflexes of egoism and illusion, a view of human societies as essentially 'criminal' organisations of selfish interests, a deep-rooted subjectivism which sees the world as desperately enigmatic, a sense of history as cyclical or absurd.

This ideological conjuncture in Conrad's texts is determined in the last instance by the imperialist character of the English capitalism he served; and it is overdetermined by his Polish experience, with its conflict of organicist idealism and political disillusionment. Nineteenth-century imperialism demanded the production of a corporate, messianic, idealist ideology; but it demanded this at precisely the point where mid-Victorian faith in progress was being eroded into pessimism, subjectivism and irrationalism by (in the last instance) the very economic depression which catalysed the intensified exploitation of the Empire. Imperialism threw into embarrassing exposure the discrepancy between its Romantic ideals and sordid material practice; it also bred an awareness of cultural relativism at precisely the point where the absolute cultural hegemony of the imperialist nations needed to be affirmed. The fatal disjuncture between fact and value, ideal and reality, matter and spirit, Nature and consciousness which pervades Conrad's work is a product of these contradictions.

Conrad's contemptuous rejection of humanitarianism springs in part from a recognition of the imperialist exploitation it rationalises. Yet while denouncing crudely unidealistic forms of imperialism, he is ideologically constrained to discover in the British variant a saving 'idea' – a Romantic commitment to the welding of politically amorphous tribal societies into truly 'organic' units. His onslaught upon nakedly exploitative Belgian or American imperialism is at root that of the traditionalist English conservative radically distrustful of bourgeois 'materialism' and 'commercialism'. It is only when such activity is graced by an organic ideal, as in the merchant service, that the contradiction between his own Romantic nationalism, and the brutal realities of colonialism, can be 'resolved'. Conrad neither believes in the cultural superiority of the colonialist nations, nor rejects imperialism outright. The 'message' of *Heart of Darkness* is that Western civilisation is at base as barbarous as African society – a viewpoint which disturbs imperialist assumptions to the precise degree that it reinforces them.

This conflict between organic solidarity and sceptical individualism is mediated in Conrad's aesthetic. He writes of the artist as snatching 'a passing phase of life' and showing its vibration, colour and form in an effort to evoke 'the latent feeling of fellowship with all creation – and the subtle but invincible conviction of solidarity that knits together the loneliness of innumerable hearts. . .'.[8] The ideological function of art is to affirm human solidarity against disintegrative individualism; yet to characterise its materials as vibrant and ephemeral ironically underscores the individualist impressionism which is to be ideologically overcome. For Conrad, art consists in a scrupulous refinement of recalcitrant language into concrete image and expressive nuance; for him, as for Henry James, the novel constitutes a cunningly fashioned organic unity, which in turn implies a redefinition of the writer as fastidious Flaubertian *worker* of his text. (Writing, he once commented, is a form of *action*.) Yet in redefining the writer as a worker, *fin-de-siècle* aestheticism severs him at the same moment from a social context. The author is a worker, but his product no longer has an assured audience. The confident mid-Victorian pact between producer and consumer has partly collapsed – a collapse reflected in the increasingly problematic status of the writer's productive means, language itself. The author must intensively 'work' his text precisely because he can no longer rely on 'ordinary language' as a nexus with his consumers, trapped as he is within an ideology which views human communication itself as no more than transiently consoling illusion. Indeed, Dickens is perhaps the last historical point at which sheer verbal exuberance has not come to signify writing-as-object – *écriture*, in Roland Barthes's sense of the term.[9] Conrad's calculated linguistic colourfulness offers a significant contrast. The text must be subtly structured into complex unity, but it is what it fails to articulate which matters most – the restlessly allusive suggestions which leave its meanings multiple, ambiguous and unachieved, the merely 'adjectival' hints of meaning which F. R. Leavis correctly identifies in *Heart of Darkness*.[10] The work, that is to say, is at once organically closed and verbally open-ended; images must be clearly etched, but

'Every image floats uncertainly in a sea of doubt . . . in an unexplored universe of incertitudes.'[11] Conrad proceeds in this letter to Edward Garnett, to question the very reality of the *reader*, coupling the formal question of how to write with the problem of his own precarious status as literary producer. What Conrad does, in effect, is to combine a Romantic aesthetic with a 'productive' one. The end of art is to penetrate the phenomenal world to reveal its elusive essence; yet this task, which as it stands is a mere commonplace of idealist aesthetics, requires a crippling amount of sweated labour. Fiction struggles constantly to deny its own artifice, to present itself as 'natural' and translucent; yet this effort must always be self-defeating. The artist, like Marlow, constantly betrays the truth in his attempt to convey it more precisely.

It is, indeed, with the discovery of Marlow as a narrative device that Conrad is able to 'solve' the question of how to write. For the ploy of the narrator allows the epistemological problem of how to communicate the real to be incorporated into the formal structures of the text itself. Writing a story, discovering a form, becomes for Conrad paradigmatic of the epistemological difficulties which beset him; to construct a narrative is to construct a moral order. But that order is condemned to be as precarious and provisional as the act of writing itself – a fragile and perilous enterprise, ceaselessly constructed and deconstructed as that adventure into the unknown which is narrative unfolds its course. In working his fiction, then, the writer is shaping a vacuum, sculpting a void. Work for Conrad is a self-sacrificial sharing in the social totality, but like Kurtz's labours in *Heart of Darkness* merely exposes one's estrangement from the eternally elusive Nature which is to be reduced to order. Aesthetic form must vanquish the inchoate, as imperialism strives to subdue the 'disorganisation' of tribal society to 'rational' structure; yet such ordering always contains its own negation.

Each of Conrad's novels, indeed, is alive with such a subversive negation of its organic unity. Ideological dissonances emerge in his fiction not, as with Dickens, in an exploitation of open-ended, internally discrepant forms, but in the calculative organisation of interlacing patterns around a central absence. At the centre of each of Conrad's works is a resonant silence: the unfathomable enigma of Kurtz, Jim and Nostromo, the dark, brooding passivity of James Wait in *The Nigger of the Narcissus*, the stolid opacity of McWhirr in *Typhoon*, the eternal crypticness of the 'Russian soul' in *Under Western Eyes*, the unseen bomb-explosion and mystical silence of the idiot Stevie in *The Secret Agent*, Heyst's nonexistent treasure in *Victory*.[12] These absences are determinate – they demarcate the gaps and limits of the Conradian ideology, represent the 'hollow's' scooped out by a collision or exclusion of meanings.

The elusiveness of Lord Jim, for example – one produced by the novel's densely-layered narrative technique – is essentially that of the cypher to which Jim is reduced by the mutual cancellation of two contradictory perspectives on him. He can be seen at once as Romantic colonialist, strenuously shaping his own destiny, and as the inexorably determined plaything of a mechanistic cosmos. A similar mutual cancellation inheres in the formal structure of *Under Western Eyes*, where the heroic but 'fanatical' Russian soul, and the humane but humdrum empiricism of the English narrator, put each other continually into question in a spiral of overlapping ironies. The sturdy silence of McWhirr embodies the ineffable values of the organicist tradition, values of dogged fidelity and unreflective heroism which can be shown but not said. The brooding passivity of James Wait, conversely, signifies an anarchic dissolution of social order too metaphysically deep-seated to be articulable. The heart of darkness in the story of that title is imperialism itself, which, since it can be figured only as farcical fantasy and metaphysical evil, must necessarily remain obscure; but it is also the African societies which imperialism plunders, societies which appear, in imperialist fashion, as baffling enigmas. The bomb-explosion in *The Secret Agent*, like Jim's jump from his ship, cannot be directly presented: it suggests a kind of cataclysmic transformation, an unpredictable 'leap' in an organically evolving Nature, which the novel's conservative ideology can accommodate only as impenetrable mystery. The absent centre of *Nostromo* is in part Nostromo himself, but also the silver of which he is the agent – the inert, opaque matter around which the human action frenetically swirls. As the determining structure of which the novel's characters are the bearers (the true protagonist of the book, as Conrad commented), the silver is the unifying principle of the entire action; but since that action has for Conrad no coherent historical intelligibility, it is a principle which must of necessity be dramatically absent. It is precisely in these absent centres, which 'hollow' rather than scatter and fragment the organic forms of Conrad's fiction, that the relations of that fiction to its ideological context is laid bare.

'It is evident', Conrad wrote to Garnett,' that my fate is to be descriptive, and descriptive only. There are things I *must* leave alone.'[13] This, precisely, is Conrad's major problem of form, determined by – and determining – the ideological matrix in which his writing is set. For it is not a matter of Conrad's forms 'expressing' an ideology; it is rather a question of the ideological contradictions which his literary forms inevitably produce. The characteristic Conradian work is a exotic tale of *action*, richly and concretely rendered, on whose margins play a set of sceptical questions about the very reality of action itself. The tale or yarn 'foregrounds' action as solid and unproblematic; it assumes the unimpeachable realities of history, character, the objective world. Yet these assumptions are simultaneously thrown into radical doubt by the penumbra of spectral meanings which surround the narrative, crossing and blurring its contours. If the narrative is reduced to a yarn, those crucial meanings dissolve; if the meanings are directly probed, it is the narrative which evaporates. What unifies dramatic action and 'metaphysical' intimation is mood: the exoticism of the one matches the esotericism of the other. In working the *genre* of the adventure story, then, Conrad 'produces' his own ideology in a determinate form. The adventure story gives rise to a simple, solid specificity of action, which is in turn confronted with its corrosive negation – haunted like the ship *Narcissus* or *The Secret Sharer* with the ghost it must exorcise if the narrative is to survive. Such survival is for Conrad ideologically as well as artistically essential: faith, work and duty must not be allowed to yield to scepticism if the supreme fiction of social order is to be sustained. It is for this reason that Conrad the pessimist insists that the artist's task is not to convey moral nihilism, but to cherish undying hope.[14] Yet that hope can never be anything other than ambiguous. The naturalistic form of *The Secret Agent* thickens and reifies the material world to a point where its revolutionary destruction seems naturally unthinkable; yet this very thickening lends men and objects an air of grotesque mystery which merges with the book's fear of the anarchic unknown.

If such 'metaphysical materialism' is needed to confirm the naturalness of the given, it also banishes that realm of subjectivity which is an equally necessary protest against bourgeois positivism. Within a dispassionately deadlocked world, then, violent change (Winnie), motion (Verloc), spiritual vision (Stevie) must insist on thrusting themselves into the text, if only in mysterious ways. Stevie's silence is that of the 'mystical' which can be shown but not stated; the text *speaks* its contradictions, rather than speaks of them. Its discourse is circled by the abyss on whose brink the nihilist Professor is continually poised – the Professor, who, wired up for instant self-consignment to eternity, is thus a graphic image of the text itself. For *The Secret Agent* is able to reveal the truth of itself only by that ceaseless process of 'self-detonation' which is irony. Only by the revolutionary act of negating its every proposition and reconstructing itself *ex nihilo* could it articulate the real; yet this, it knows, is impossible, for it is doomed to work with discourses riddled with ideological contradiction – or, as the novel itself would say, condemned to the eternal inauthenticity of language. But the work cannot allow itself to disappear down the abyss of the unspeakable, allowing its propositions to be retrospectively cancelled, leaving itself with absolutely nothing to say. If it resembles the Wittgenstein of the *Tractatus Logico-Philosophicus* in its commitment to the transcendent, it must also mime the Wittgenstein of *Philosophical Investigations* in its consecration of that vast, stalemated 'game' which is society. Value, identified with a despised humanitarianism of which anarchist dreams are an even more degenerate extension, is thus forced beyond the frontiers of the world, exiled beyond articulation. Yet precisely because of this, everything seems to be left exactly as it was; and this provides the text with a kind of resolution, or, better, with the illusion of one. The world, as with the *Tractatus*, just is 'everything that is the case'; and in this sense there is no need for a resolution *because there is nothing, it seems, to resolve.* Stalemated games are in one way unachieved, in another way complete; the world goes on, and this is at once the question, and the answer, of the text. The need for value, and the recognition of its utter vacuity: it is here that the deepest contradiction of Conrad's enterprise, one integral to the imperialist ideology he shared, stands revealed.

Notes

1. Florence Hardy, *The Life of Thomas Hardy* (London, 1962), p. 177.
2. Joseph Conrad, *Notes on Life and Letters* (London, 1921), p. 157.
3. Joseph Conrad, *A Personal Record* (London, 1921), p. xii.
4. See Perry Anderson, 'Components of the National Culture', *New Left Review* 50, July/August 1968, for an analysis of the conservative 'white emigration' into England crucially relevant to Conrad, Henry James and T. S. Eliot. See also my own *Exiles and Emigrés* (London, 1970).
5. *Life and Letters*, ed. G. J. Aubry (New York, 1927), p. 84.
6. Ibid., p. 269.
7. *Conrad's Politics* (Baltimore, 1967), Chapter III.
8. Preface to *The Nigger of the Narcissus* (London, 1921), p. viii.
9. See *Writing Degree Zero* (London, 1967). This contradiction comes to a head in 'modernism', where (as with Joyce) a scrupulously precise refinement of meaning paradoxically transforms the work into a self-regarding linguistic object radically closed to its audience, defying them in the act of apparently communicating more exactly.

10. *The Great Tradition* (Harmondworth, 1962), p. 198.

11. *Letters from Conrad*, ed. Edward Garnett (London, 1927), p. 153.

12. It is perhaps worth interpolating that the most striking Victorian example of the absent-centred work is *In Memoriam*. The absent centre around which the poem broods and hovers is the blank left by the death of Arthur Hallam, which fragments the poem formally into a series of brief meditations. But that absence is an ideologically determinate one, since the poem is not primarily about Hallam's death, but about the whole spectrum of ideological anxieties and insecurities (science, rationalism, loss of faith, fear of revolution) which that blankness brings into blurred focus. Hallam is the empty space congregated with these almost inarticulable anxieties. The melancholy of the poem (c.f. Freud: melancholy is grief without an object) reflects the fact that it is ideologically prohibited from knowing precisely why it is sad; it is a classic document of bourgeois ideological insecurity which can only obliquely know itself as such, displacing its anxieties to the personal figure of Hallam.

13. *Letters to Garnett*, p. 94.

14. *Notes on Life and Letters.*

Stephen Greenblatt: The Cultivation of Anxiety: King Lear and His Heirs

I want to begin this essay far from the Renaissance, with a narrative of social practice first published in the *American Baptist Magazine* of 1831. Its author is the Reverend Francis Wayland, an early president of Brown University and a Baptist minister. The passage concerns his infant son, Heman Lincoln Wayland, who was himself to become a college president and Baptist minister:

My youngest child is an infant about 15 months old, with about the intelligence common to children of that age. It has for some months been evident, that he was more than usually self willed, but the several attempts to subdue him, had been thus far relinquished, from the fear that he did not fully understand what was said to him. It so happened, however, that I had never been brought into collision with him myself, until the incident occurred which I am about to relate. Still I had seen enough to convince me of the necessity of subduing his temper, and resolved to seize upon the first favorable opportunity which presented, for settling the question of authority between us.

On Friday last before breakfast, on my taking him from his nurse, he began to cry violently. I determined to hold him in my arms until he ceased. As he had a piece of bread in his hand, I took it away, intending

Reprinted from *Raritan*, 2 (1982), pp. 92–114.

to give it to him again after he became quiet. In a few minutes he ceased, but when I offered him the bread he threw it away, although he was very hungry. He had, in fact, taken no nourishment except a cup of milk since 5 o'clock on the preceding afternoon. I considered this a fit opportunity for attempting to subdue his temper, and resolved to embrace it. I thought it necessary to change his disposition, so that he would receive the bread *from me* and also be so reconciled to me that he would *voluntarily* come to me. The task I found more difficult than I had expected.

I put him into a room by himself, and desired that no one should speak to him, or give him any food or drink whatever. This was about 8 o'clock in the morning. I visited him every hour or two during the day, and spoke to him in the kindest tones, offering him the bread and putting out my arms to take him. But throughout the whole day he remained inflexibly obstinate. He did not yield a hair's breadth. I put a cup of water to his mouth, and he drank it greedily, but would not touch it with his hands. If a crumb was dropped on the floor he would eat it, but if *I* offered him the piece of bread, he would push it away from him. When I told him to come to me, he would turn away and cry bitterly. He went to bed supperless. It was now twenty-four hours since he had eaten anything.

He woke the next morning in the same state. He would take nothing that I offered him, and shunned all my offers of kindness. He was now truly an object of pity. He had fasted thirty-six hours. His eyes were wan and sunken. His breath hot and feverish, and his voice feeble and wailing. Yet he remained obstinate. He continued thus, till 10 o'clock, A.M. when hunger overcame him, and he took from me a piece of bread, to which I added a cup of milk, and hoped that the labor was at last accomplished.

In this however I had not rightly judged. He ate his bread greedily, but when I offered to take him, he still refused as pertinaciously as ever. I therefore ceased feeding him, and recommenced my course of discipline.

He was again left alone in his crib, and I visited him as before, at intervals. About one o'clock, Saturday, I found that he began to view his condition in its true light. The tones of his voice in weeping were graver and less passionate, and had more the appearance of one bemoaning himself. Yet when I went to him he still remained obstinate. You could clearly see in him the abortive efforts of the will. Frequently he would raise his hands an inch or two, and then suddenly put them down again. He would look at me, and then hiding his face in the bedclothes weep most sorrowfully. During all this time I was addressing him, whenever I came into the room, with invariable kindness. But my kindness met with no suitable return. All I required of him was, that he should come to me. This he would not do, and he began now to see that it had become a serious business. Hence his distress increased. He would not submit, and he found that there was no help without it. It was truly surprising to behold how much agony so young a being could inflict upon himself.

About three o'clock I visited him again. He continued in the state I have described. I was going away, and had opened the door, when I thought that he looked somewhat softened, and returning, put out my hands, again requesting him to come to me. To my joy, and I hope gratitude, he rose up and put forth his hands immediately. The agony was over. He was completely subdued. He repeatedly kissed me, and would do so whenever I commanded. He would kiss any one when I directed him, so full of love was he to all the family. Indeed, so entirely and instantaneously were his feelings towards me changed, that he preferred me now to any of the family. As he had never done before, he moaned after me when he saw that I was going away.

Since this event several slight revivals of his former temper have occurred, but they have all been easily subdued. His disposition is, as it never has been before, mild and obedient. He is kind and affectionate, and evidently much happier than he was, when he was determined to have his own way. I hope and pray that it may prove that an effect has been produced upon him for life.*

The indignation and disgust that this account immediately excited in the popular press of Jacksonian America, as it does in ourselves, seem to me appropriate but incomplete responses, for if we say that tyranny here masquerades as paternal kindness, we must also remember that, as Kafka once remarked of his father, 'love often wears the face of violence'. Wayland's behaviour reflects the relentless effort of generations of evangelical fathers to break the child's will, but it would be a mistake to conceive of this effort as a rejection of affective familial bonds or as a primitive disciplinary pathology from which our own unfailing decency toward the young has freed itself. On the contrary, Wayland's struggle is a strategy of intense familial love, and it is the sophisticated product of a long historical process whose roots lie at least partly in early modern England, the England of Shakespeare's *King Lear*.

Wayland's twin demands – that his son take food directly from him and come to him voluntarily, as an act of love and not forced compliance – may in fact be seen, from the perspective of what French historians call the *longue durée*, as a domesticated, 'realistic', and, as it were, bourgeoisified version of the love test with which Shakespeare's play opens. Lear too wishes to be the object – the preferred and even the sole recipient – of his child's love. He can endure a portion of that love being turned elsewhere, but only when he directs that it be so divided, just as Reverend Wayland was in

* Wayland's letter is reprinted in full in William G. McLoughlin, 'Evangelical Childrearing in the Age of Jackson: Francis Wayland's Views on When and How to Subdue the Willfullness of Children,' *Journal of Social History* 9 (1975), pp. 20–43; it was first brought to my attention by Philip Greven, *The Protestant Temperament: Patterns of Child-Rearing, Religious Experience, and the Self in Early America* (New York, 1977).

the end pleased that the child 'would kiss any one when I directed him'. Such a kiss is not a turning elsewhere but an indirect expression of love for the father.

Goneril, to be sure, understands that the test she so successfully passes is focused on compliance: 'you have obedience scanted', she tells Cordelia, 'And well are worth the want that you have wanted' (I, i). But Lear's response to his youngest daughter's declaration that she does not love him all suggests that more than outward deference is at stake: 'But goes thy heart with this?' From Cordelia at least he wants something more than formal obedience, something akin to the odd blend of submission to authority and almost erotic longing depicted at the close of Wayland's account: 'He repeatedly kissed me, and would do so whenever I commanded. . . . As he had never done before, he moaned after me when he saw that I was going away.'

To obtain such love, Wayland withholds his child's food, and it is tempting to say that Lear, in disinheriting Cordelia, does the same. But what is a technique for Wayland is for Lear a dire and irreversible punishment: the disinheriting and banishment of Cordelia is not a lesson, even for the elder sisters, let alone for Cordelia herself, but a permanent estrangement, sealed with the most solemn oaths. Wayland's familial strategy uses parental discipline to bring about a desired relationship rather than to punish when the relationship has failed. In his account, the taking away of the child's food *initiates* the love test, whereas in *King Lear* the father's angry cancellation of his daughter's dowry signals the abandonment of the love test and the formal disclaimer of all paternal care. In the contrast between this bitter finality and a more calculating discipline that punishes in order to fashion its object into a desired shape, we glimpse the first of the differences that help to account for the resounding success of Wayland's test and the grotesque and terrifying failure of Lear's.

A second crucial difference is that by the early nineteenth century the age of the child who is tested has been pushed back drastically; Wayland had noticed signs of self-will in his infant son for some months, but had not sought to subdue it until he was certain that the child could 'fully understand what was said to him'. That he expected to find such understanding in a fifteen-month-old reflects a transformation in cultural attitudes toward children, a transformation whose early signs may be glimpsed in Puritan child-rearing manuals and early seventeenth-century religious lyrics and that culminates in the educational philosophy of Rousseau and the poetry of Wordsworth.

King Lear, by contrast, locates the moment for testing, for Cordelia at least, precisely in what was for Shakespeare's England the age that demanded the greatest attention, instruction, and discipline, the years between sexual maturity at about fifteen and social maturity at about twenty-six. This was, in the words of a seventeenth-century clergyman quoted by Keith Thomas, 'a slippery age, full of passion, rashness, wilfulness', upon which adults must impose restraints and exercise shaping power. The Elizabethan and Jacobean theatre returned almost obsessively to the representation of this age group, which, not coincidentally, constituted a significant portion of the play-going population. Civic officials, lawyers, preachers, and moralists joined dramatists in worrying chiefly about what Lawrence Stone in *The Family, Sex and Marriage in England 1500–1800* calls 'potentially the most unruly element in any society, the floating mass of young unmarried males', and it was to curb their spirits, fashion their wills, and delay their full entry into the adult world that the educational system and the laws governing apprenticeship addressed themselves. But girls were also the objects of a sustained cultural scrutiny that focused on the critical passage from the authority of the father or guardian to the authority of the husband. This transition was of the highest structural significance, entailing complex transactions of love, power, and material substance, all of which, we may note, are simultaneously at issue when Lear demands of his youngest daughter a declaration she is unwilling or unable to give.

Love, power, and material substance are likewise at issue in the struggle between Reverend Wayland and his toddler, but all reduced to the proportions of the nursery: a kiss, an infantile gesture of refusal, a piece of bread. In the nineteenth-century confrontation, punishment is justified as exemplary technique, and the temporal frame has shifted from adolescence to infancy. Equally significant, the spatial frame has shifted as well, from the public to the private. Lear is of course a king, for whom there would, in any case, be no privacy, but generally Renaissance writers do not assume that the family is set off from public life. On the contrary, public life is itself most frequently conceived in familial terms, as an interlocking, hierarchical system of patriarchal authorities, while conversely the family is conceived as a little commonwealth. Indeed the family is widely understood in the sixteenth and early seventeenth centuries as both the historical source and the ideological justification of society: 'for I admit,' writes Bacon, 'the law to be that if the son kill his father or mother it is petty treason, and that there remaineth in our laws so much of the ancient footsteps of *potestas patria* and natural obedience, which by the law of God is the very instance itself, and all other government and obedience is taken but by equity.' In other words, the Fifth Commandment – 'Honour they father and mother' – is the original letter of the law which equity 'enlarges', as the Elizabethan jurist Edmund Plowden puts it, to include all political authority.

This general understanding of the enlargement by which the state is derived from the family is given virtually emblematic form in representations of the ruling family; hence the supremely public nature of Lear's interrogations of his daughters' feelings toward him does not mark him off, as other elements in the play do, from the world of Shakespeare's audience, but rather registers a central ideological principle of middle- and upper-class families in the early modern period. Affairs of family shade into affairs of state, as Gloucester's anxious broodings on the late eclipses of the sun and moon make clear: 'Love cools, friendship falls off, brothers divide: in cities mutinies; in countries, discord; in palaces, treason; and the bond crack'd twixt son and father' (I, ii). The very order of the phrases here, in their failure to move decisively from private to public, their reversion at the close to the familial bond, signals the interinvolvement of household and society. By the time of Jacksonian America, the family has moved indoors, separated from civil society, which in turn has been separated from the state. Reverend Wayland's account of his domestic crisis is also, of course, intended for public consumption, but it was published anonymously, as if to respect the protective boundaries of the family, and more important still, it makes public a private event in order to assist the private lives of others, that is, to strengthen the resolve of loving parents to subdue the temper of their own infants.

We will return later to the temporal and spatial problems touched upon here – the cultural evaluation of differing age groups and the status of privacy – but we should first note several of the significant continuities between Renaissance child-rearing techniques and those of nineteenth-century American evangelicals. The first, and ground of all the others, is the not-so-simple fact of observation: these parents pay attention to their children, testing the young to gauge the precise cast of their emotion and will. This is more obviously the case with Reverend Wayland, who when his child was scarcely a year old was already scrutinising him for signs of self-will. The fathers in Shakespeare's play seem purblind by comparison: Lear apparently cannot perceive the difference between his eldest daughters' blatant hypocrisy and his youngest daughter's truth, while Gloucester evidently does not know what his eldest (and sole legitimate) son's handwriting – his 'character' – looks like and is easily persuaded that this son (with whom he had talked for two hours the night before) wishes to kill him. This seeming obliviousness, however, signifies not indifference but error: Lear and Gloucester are hopelessly inept at reading their children's 'characters', but the effort to do so is of the utmost importance in the play, which, after all, represents the fatal consequences of an incorrect 'reading'. We may say, with the Fool, that Lear was 'a pretty fellow' when he had 'no need to care' for his daughter's frowns (I, iv), but this indifference only exists outside the play itself, or perhaps in its initial moments; thereafter (and irreversibly) parents must scrutinise their children with what Lear, in a moment of uncharacteristic self-criticism, calls a 'jealous curiosity' (I, iv). In initiating the plot against Edgar, Edmund gauges perfectly his father's blend of credulity and inquisitorial curiosity: 'Edmund, how now! what news?. . . . Why so earnestly seek you to put up that letter?. . . . What paper were you reading?. . . . What needed then that terrible dispatch of it into your pocket?. . . . Let's see: come; if it be nothing, I shall not need spectacles' (I, ii). Children in the play, we might add, similarly scrutinise their fathers: 'You see how full of changes his age is,' Goneril remarks to Regan in their first moment alone together; 'the observation we have made of it hath not been little' (I, i). The whole family comes to exist *sub specie semioticae*; everyone is intent on reading the signs in everyone else.

This mode of observation is common to Shakespeare's play and Wayland's account, but not because it is intrinsic to all family life: intense paternal observation of the young is by no means a universal practice. It is, rather, learned by certain social groups in particular cultures and ages. Thus there is virtually no evidence of the practice in late medieval England, while for the seventeenth century there is (given the general paucity of materials for intimate family history) quite impressive evidence, especially for the substantial segment of the population touched by Puritanism. For example, the Essex vicar Ralph Josselin (1617–83) has left in his diary a remarkably full record of his troubled relationship with his son, particularly during the latter's adolescence. 'My soule yearned over John,' notes one characteristic entry, 'oh lord overcome his heart.' The conflict between them reached a crisis in 1674, when, in a family discussion held in the presence of his wife and four daughters, Josselin put the following proposition before his twenty-three-year-old heir:

John set your selfe to fear God, & bee industrious in my business, refrain your evill courses, and I will passe by all past offences, setle all my estate on you after your mothers death, and leave you some stocke on the ground and within doores to the value of an £100 and desire of you, out of your marriage portion but £400 to provide for my daughters or otherwise to charge my land with so much for their porcions; but if you continue your ill courses I shall dispose my land otherwise, and make only a provision for your life to put bread in your hand.

The father's strategy was at least temporarily successful, as John prudently accepted the offer and 'owned his debauchery'.

Josselin's insistence upon the economic consequences of dis-obedience provides an immediate link to *King Lear*, where the father's power to alter portions and to disinherit is of crucial import-ance. We should note that primogeniture was never so inflexibly established in England, even among the aristocracy, as to preclude the exercise of paternal discretion, the power to bribe, threaten, reward, and punish. Lear's division of the kingdom, his attempt both to set his daughters in competition with each other and to dispose of the normative practice than a daring attempt to use the paternal power always inherent in it. This power is exhibited in more conventional form in the subplot: 'And of my land, / Loyal and natural boy,' the deceived Gloucester tells his conniving bastard son, 'I'll work the means / To make thee capable' (II, i). This economic pressure is not, of course, immediately apparent in Rever-end Wayland's dealings with his infant, but Josselin's threat to 'make only a provision . . . to put bread in your hand' curiously anticipates the symbolic object of contention in the Wayland nur-sery and suggests that there too the paternal power to withhold or manipulate the means of sustenance is at issue.

This power should not be regarded as exclusively disciplinary. It is instead an aspect of a general familial concern with planning for the future, a concern that extends from attempts to shape the careers of individual children to an overarching interest in the prosperity of the 'house'. Francis Wayland's struggle with his son is not a flaring-up of paternal anger but a calculated effort to fashion his child's future: 'I hope and pray that it may prove that an effect has been produced upon him for life.' Similarly, Lear's disastrous di-vision of the kingdom is undertaken, he claims, so that 'future strife / May be prevented now' (I, i), and the love test marks the formal entry into his planned retirement.

These efforts to shape the future of the family seem to reflect a conviction that there are certain critical moments upon which a whole train of subsequent events depends, moments whose enabling conditions may be irrecoverable and whose consequences may be irreversible. Such a conviction is formally expressed most often in relation to great public events, but its influence is more widespread, extending, for example, to rhetorical training, religious belief, and, I would suggest, child rearing. Parents must be careful to watch for what we may call, to adapt the rhetorical term, kairotic moments and to grasp the occasion for action. Hence Francis Wayland, wishing to alter his son's nature for life, 'resolved to seize upon the first favorable opportunity which presented, for settling the question of authority between us'. Had the father not done so, he would not only have diminished his own position but risked the destruction of his child's spiritual and physical being. Moreover, Wayland adds, had he received his stubborn child on any other terms than 'the unconditional surrender of his will', he would have permitted the formation of a topsy-turvy world in which his entire family would have submitted to the caprices of an infant: 'He must have been made the center of a whole system. A whole family under the control of a child 15 months old!' This carnivalesque reversal of roles would then have invited further insurrections, for 'my other children and every member of my family would have been entitled to the same privilege'. 'Hence,' Wayland concludes, 'there would have been as many supreme authorities as there were individuals, and contention to the uttermost must have ensued.'

King Lear depicts something very much like such a world turned upside down: Lear, as the Fool says, has made his daughters his mothers, and they employ on him, as in a nightmare, those disciplinary techniques deemed appropriate for 'a slippery age, full of passion, rashness, willfulness'. 'Old fools are babes again,' says Goneril, 'and must be us'd / With checks as flatteries, when they are seen abus'd' (I, iii). In the carnival tradition, tolerated – if uneasily – by the medieval church and state, such reversals of role, provided they were temporary, could be seen as restorative, renewing the proper order of society by releasing pent-up frustrations and potentially disruptive energies. As we know from a family account, even Francis Wayland could allow his children occasional bursts of festive inversion, always returning in the end to the supreme paternal authority that his early discipline had secured. But in *Lear* the role reversal is permanent, and its effect is the disintegration of the entire kingdom. Wayland similarly links permanent disorder in the family to chaos in the political, moral, and theological realms; indeed his loving struggle with his son offers, he suggests, a precise and resonant analogy to God's struggle with the sinner: it is infinitely kind in God to resist the sinner's will, 'for if he were not resisted, he would destroy the happiness of the universe and himself together'.

Here again, in Wayland's conviction that the fate of the universe may be linked to the power struggle in his nursery, we may hear an echo of *Lear*:

> O Heavens,
> If you do love old men, if your sweet sway
> Allow obedience, if you yourselves are old,
> Make it your cause; send down and take my part.
>
> (II, iv)

Of course, as these very lines suggest, what is assumed in Wayland is deeply problematical in *Lear*: the fictive nature of the play, reinforced by its specifically pagan setting, seems to have licensed Shakespeare to anatomise the status and the underlying motives of virtually all of the elements that we have noted as common to the two texts. This difference is crucial, and it comes as no surprise that *King Lear* is more profound than Francis Wayland's account of his paternal authority: celebration of Shakespeare's profundity is an institutionalised rite of civility in our culture. We tend to assume, however, that Shakespearean self-consciousness and irony lead to a radical transcendence of the network of social conditions, paradigms, and practices in the plays. I would argue, by contrast, that Renaissance theatrical representation itself is fully implicated in this network and that Shakespeare's self-consciousness is in significant ways bound up with the institutions and the symbology of power it anatomises.

But if its local ideological situation, its historical embeddedness, is so crucial to Shakespeare's play, what accounts for the similarities I have sketched between *King Lear* and Wayland's family narrative? The explanation lies first in the fact that nineteenth-century evangelical child-rearing techniques are the heirs of more widely diffused child-rearing techniques in the late sixteenth and early seventeenth centuries – Wayland's practices may be seen almost fully articulated in a work like John Robinson's *Of Children and Their Education*, published in 1628 though written some years earlier – and second in the fact that the Renaissance English drama was one of the cultural institutions that expressed and fashioned just those qualities that we have identified as enabling the familial love test in the first place. That is, the mode of the drama, quite apart from any specific content, depended upon and fostered in its audience *observation*, the close reading of gesture and speech as manifestations of character and intention; *planning*, a sensitivity to the consequences of action (i.e., plot) and to kairotic moments (i.e., rhetoric); and sense of *resonance*, the conviction, rooted in the drama's medieval inheritance, that cosmic meanings were bound up with local and particular circumstances.

I am not, of course, suggesting that the nineteenth-century American minister was fashioned by the Renaissance theatre (a theatre his seventeenth-century religious forebears detested and sought to close) nor that without the theatre Renaissance child-rearing techniques would have been far different. But the theatre was not merely the passive reflector of social forces that lay entirely outside of it; rather, like all forms of art, indeed like all utterances, the theatre was itself a *social event*. Artistic expression is never perfectly self-contained and abstract, nor can it be derived satisfactorily from the subjective consciousness of an isolated creator. Collective actions, ritual gestures, paradigms of relationship, and shared images of authority penetrate the work of art and shape it from within, while conversely the socially overdetermined work of art, along with a multitude of other institutions and utterances, contributes to the formation, realignment, and transmission of social practices.

Works of art are, to be sure, marked off in our culture from ordinary utterances, but this demarcation is itself a communal event and signals not the effacement of the social but rather its successful absorption into the work by implication or articulation. This absorption – the presence within the work of its social being – makes it possible, as Bakhtin has argued, for art to survive the disappearance of its enabling social conditions, where ordinary utterance, more dependent upon the extraverbal pragmatic situation, drifts rapidly toward insignificance or incomprehensibility. Hence art's genius for survival, its delighted reception by audiences for whom it was never intended, does not signal its freedom from all other domains of life, nor does its inward articulation of the social confer upon it a formal coherence independent of the world outside its boundaries. On the contrary, artistic form itself both expresses and fashions social evaluations and practices.

Thus the Renaissance theatre does not by virtue of the content of a particular play reach across a void to touch the Renaissance family; rather the theatre is itself already saturated with social significance and hence with the family as the period's central social institution. Conversely, the theatre contributes, in a small but by no means entirely negligible way, to the formal condensation and expression of patterns of observation, planning, and a sense of resonance. Hence it is fitting that when Cordelia resists Lear's paternal demand, she does so in an antitheatrical gesture, a refusal to perform: the theatre and the family are simultaneously at stake.

To these shared patterns that link the quasi-mythical family of

King Lear to the prosaic and amply documented family of Francis
Wayland, we may now add four further interlocking features of
Wayland's account that are more closely tied not to the mode of
the theatre as a whole but to the specific form and content of
Shakespeare's tragedy: these are the absence or displacement of the
mother, an affirmation of absolute paternal authority, an overriding
interest in the will and hence in differentiating voluntary from
merely forced compliance, and a belief in salutary anxiety.

Francis Wayland's wife was alive in 1831, but she is entirely,
even eerily, missing from his account. Where was she during the
long ordeal? In part her absence must depend upon her husband's
understanding of the theological significance of the incident: in
Francis Wayland's Christianity, there is no female intercessor, no
Mother of Mankind to appeal to the stern Father for mercy upon
a wayward child. Even if Mrs Wayland did in fact try to temper
(or reinforce) her husband's actions, he might well have regarded
such intervention as irrelevant. Moreover, we may speculate that
the timing of the incident – what we have called the perception of
the kairotic moment – is designed precisely to avoid such irrelevant
interventions. We do not know when any of the Wayland children
were weaned, but fifteen months would seem about the earliest age
at which the disciplinary withdrawal of food – the piece of bread
and the cup of milk – could be undertaken without involving the
mother or the nurse.

Thus the father is able entirely to displace the nurturing female
body and with this displacement make manifest his 'supreme
authority' in the family, a micropolitics that, as we have seen, has
its analogue both in the human world outside the home and in the
divine realm. Between the law of the father and the law of God
there is a perfect fit; between the father's authority and worldly
authorities there is a more complicated relation, since Wayland,
though an absolutist within his family, could not invoke in Jacksonian America a specific model of absolute power. The most he can
do is to invoke, in effect, a generalised image of the social world
and of the child as misfit: had his son been left unchecked, he
'would soon have entered a *world where other and more powerful beings
than he* would have opposed his will, and his disposition which I
had cherished must have made him miserable as long as he lived'.

This social vision does not mean that Wayland's primary interest
is in outward compliance; on the contrary, a 'forced yielding,' as
he terms it, is worthless. 'Our voluntary service he requires,' says
Milton's Raphael of the Divine Father in *Paradise Lost*,

> Not our necessitated, such with him
> Finds no acceptance, nor *can* find, for how
> Can hearts, not free, be tri'd whether they serve
> Willing or no . . .
> . . . freely we serve.
> Because we freely love.

The proper goal is conversion, and to achieve this the father cannot rely on physical compulsion. He employs instead a technique of disciplinary kindness designed to show the child that his misery is entirely self-inflicted and can only be relieved by a similarly voluntary and inward surrender. In short, Wayland attempts to generate in his son a salutary anxiety that will lead to a tranformation of the will.

With salutary anxiety we return powerfully to the mode and the content of *King Lear*. The very practice of tragedy depends upon a communal conviction that anxiety may be profitably and even pleasurably cultivated. That is, tragedy goes beyond the usual philosophical and religious *consolations* for affliction, and both exemplifies and perfects techniques for the creation or intensification of affliction. To justify such techniques, Renaissance artists could appeal to the theoretical account of tragedy that originated with Aristotle and was substantially elaborated in the sixteenth century, especially in Italy. But like most such theories, this one was inert until it intersected with a set of powerful social practices in the period.

From the perspective of Wayland's account, we may say that the most enduring of these practices is the Protestant cultivation of a sense of sin, the deliberate heightening of an anxiety that can only be relieved by a divine grace whose effect can only be felt by one who has experienced the anxiety. (I should emphasise that I am speaking here not simply of a set of theological propositions but of a programme, prescribed in great detail and carried out by English Protestants from Tyndale onward.) To this religious practice, we may add the child-rearing techniques that also appear in Wayland's account, techniques that once again made a self-conscious and programmatic attempt to arouse anxiety for the child's ultimate good. But what is lost by early nineteenth-century America is the practice of salutary anxiety at the symbolic centre of society, that is, in the characteristic operations of royal power. That power, concentrated and personalised, aroused anxiety not only as the negative limit but as the positive condition of its functioning. The monarchy, let us remind ourselves, did not conceive its purpose as the furthering of the subject's pursuit of happiness, nor was the political centre of society a point at which all tensions and contradictions disappeared. On the contrary, Elizabethan and Jacobean charismatic absolutism battened on as well as suffered from the anxiety that arose from the instability of favour, the unresolved tensions in the religious settlement, the constantly proclaimed threats of subversion, invasion, and civil war, the spectacular public maimings and executions, and even the conspicuous gap between the monarch's ideological claim to perfect wisdom, beauty, and power and the all-too-visible limitations of the actual Elizabeth and James. The obedience required of the subject consisted not so much in preserving a genuine ignorance of this gap but in behaving as if the gap, though fully recognised, did not exist. The pressure of such a performance, demanded by the monarch's paradoxical yoking of the language of love and the language of coercion and registered in the subject's endless effusions of strained but not entirely hypocritical admiration, was itself an enhancement of royal power.

Throughout his career Shakespeare displays the deepest sensitivity to this production of salutary anxiety, a production he simultaneously questions and assimilates to his own authorial power. The fullest metatheatrical explorations of the phenomenon are in *Measure for Measure* and *The Tempest*, where both Dukes systematically awaken anxiety in others and become, for this reason, images of the dramatist himself. But Shakespeare's fullest embodiment of the practice is *King Lear*, and the vast critical literature that has grown up around the play, since the restoration of the text in the early nineteenth century, bears eloquent witness to the power of this anxiety to generate tireless expressions of love. *King Lear* characteristically incorporates several powerful and complex representations of salutary anxiety, the most notable of which, for our purposes, is the love test itself, a ritual whose intended function seems to have been to allay the retiring monarch's anxiety by arousing it in others. As the opening words of the play make clear, the division of the kingdom has in effect already taken place, with the shares carefully weighed. Lear's pretence that this prearranged legal agreement is a contest – 'which of you shall we say doth love us most?' – infuses symbolic uncertainty into a situation where apparently no real uncertainty exists. This is confirmed by his persistence in the test even when its declared occasion has been rendered wholly absurd by the disposition of the first two-thirds of the kingdom, complete with declarations that possession is 'perpetual', 'hereditary ever'. Lear wants his children to experience the anxiety of a competition for his bounty without having to endure any of the actual consequences of such a competition; he wants, that is, to produce in them something like the effect of a work of art, where emotions run high and practical effects seem negligible.

Why should Lear want his children, even his 'joy' Cordelia, to experience such anxiety? Shakespeare's sources, going back to the distant folk tale with its salt motif, suggest that Lear wishes his full value to be recognised and that he stages the love test to enforce this recognition, which is crucially important to him because he is about to abdicate and hence lose the power to compel the defence of his children. Marks of deference such as kneeling for blessings, removing the hat, and sitting only when granted leave to do so, were of great significance in medieval and early modern families, though John Aubrey testifies that by the mid-seventeenth century they seemed strained and arbitrary. They figured as part of a complex, interlocking system of public signs of respect for wealth, caste, and, at virtually every level of society, age. The period had a deep gerontological bias. It told itself constantly that by the will of God and the natural order of things authority belonged to the old, and it contrived, through such practices as deferral of marriage, prolonged apprenticeships, and systematic exclusion of the young from office, to ensure that this proper arrangement of society be observed. At stake, it was thought, was not only a societal arrangement – the protection, in an economy of scarcity, of the material interests of gerontological hierarchy against the counterclaims of the young – but the structure and meaning of a world where the old in each generation formed a link with the old of the preceding generation and so, by contiguity, reached back to the ideal, sanctified order at the origin of time.

But paradoxically the late Middle Ages and the early modern period also kept telling itself that without the control of property and the means of production, age's claim to authority was pathetically vulnerable to the ruthless ambitions of the young. Sermons and, more generally, the writings of moralists over several centuries provide numerous monitory tales of parents who turn their wealth over to their children and are, in consequence, treated brutally. 'Your father were a fool,' Gremio, echoing the moral of these tales, tells Tranio in *The Taming of the Shrew*, 'To give thee all, and in his waning age / Set foot under thy table' (II, i).

The story of King Lear in its numerous retellings from at least the twelfth century on seems to have served precisely as one of these admonitions, and Shakespeare's Edmund, in the forged letter he passes off as Edgar's, gives full voice to the fears of the old, that is, to their fantasy of what the young, beneath the superficial marks of deference, are really thinking:

This policy and reverence of age makes the world bitter to the best of our times; keeps our fortunes from us till our oldness cannot relish them. I begin to find an idle and fond bondage in the oppression of aged tyranny, who sways, not as it hath power, but as it is suffer'd. (I, ii)

This recurrent nightmare of the old seems to challenge not only the material well-being of fathers but the conception of the natural order of things to which the old appeal in justification of their prerogatives. 'Fathers fear,' writes Pascal, 'that the natural love of their children can be erased. What kind of nature is this, that can thus be erased? Custom is a second nature that destroys the first. But what is nature? Why isn't custom natural? I am very much afraid that this nature is only a first custom, as custom is a second nature.' Shakespeare's *King Lear* is haunted by this fear, voiced not in the relative privacy of the *Pensées* but in the public agony of family and state relations: '. . . let them anatomise Regan, see what breeds about her heart. Is there any cause in nature that makes these hard hearts?' (III, vi).

But it would be misleading simply to associate Shakespeare's play with this uneasiness without specifying the practical measures that medieval and early modern fathers undertook to protect themselves when retirement, always frowned upon, could not be avoided. Such situations arose most frequently in Shakespeare's own class of origin, that is, among artisans and small landowners whose income depended upon continual personal productivity. Faced with a precipitous decline in such productivity, the old frequently did have to transfer a farm or workshop to the young, but for all the talk of the natural privileges and supernatural protection of the aged, there was, as we have seen, remarkably little confidence in either the inherent or customary rights of parents. On the contrary, as Alan Macfarlane has noted in *The Origins of English Individualism*, 'contemporaries seem to have been well aware that without legal guarantees, parents had no rights whatsoever'. There could even be ritual acknowledgement of this fact, as testimony in a thirteenth-century lawsuit suggests: having agreed to give his daughter in marriage to Hugh, with half of his land, the widower Anseline and the married couple were to live together in one house. 'And the same Anseline went out of the house and handed over to them the door by the hasp, and at once begged lodging out of charity'.

Once a father had given up his land, he became, even in the house that had once been his own, what was called a 'sojourner'. The connotations of the word are suggested by its use in the Author-ised Version of the Old Testament: 'We are strangers before Thee, and sojourners, as were all our fathers. Our days on the earth are as a shadow, and there is none abiding' (1 *Chron*, 29).

Threatened with such a drastic loss of their status and authority, parents facing retirement turned, not surprisingly, to the law, obtaining contracts or maintenance agreements by which, in return for the transfer of family property, children undertook to provide food, clothing, and shelter. The extent of parental anxiety may be gauged by the great specificity of many of these requirements – so many yards of woollen cloth, pounds of coal, or bushels of grain – and by the pervasive fear of being turned out of the house in the wake of a quarrel. The father, who has been, in Sir Edward Coke's phrase, 'the guardian by nature' of his children, now has these children for his legal guardians. The maintenance agreement is essentially a medieval device, linked to feudal contractualism, to temper the power of this new guardianship by stipulating that the children are only 'depositaries' of the paternal property, so that, in the words of William West's early seventeenth-century legal manual *Simboleography*, 'the self same thing [may] be restored whensoeuer it shall please him that so leaueth it'. Thus the maintenance agreement can 'reserve' to the father some right or interest in the property that he has conveyed to his children.

We are, of course, very far from the social world of *King Lear*, which does not represent the milieu of yeomen and artisans, but I would argue that Shakespeare's play is powerfully situated in the midst of precisely the concerns of the makers of these maintenance agreements: the terror of being turned out of doors or of becoming a stranger even in one's own house; the fear of losing the food, clothing, and shelter necessary for survival, let alone dignity; the humiliating loss of parental authority; the dread, particularly powerful in a society that adhered to the principle of gerontological hierarchy, of being supplanted by the young. Lear's royal status does not cancel but rather intensifies these concerns: he will 'invest' in Goneril and Regan, along with their husbands, his 'power, / Pre-eminence, and all the large effects / That troop with majesty', but he wants to retain the hundred knights and 'The name and all th'addition to a king' (I, i). He wishes, that is, to avoid at all costs the drastic loss of status that inevitably attended retirement in the early modern period, and his maddened rage, later in the play, is a response not only to his daughter's vicious ingratitude but to the horror of being reduced to the position of an Anseline:

> Ask her forgiveness?
> Do you but mark how this becomes the house:

'Dear daughter, I confess that I am old;
Age is unnecessary: on my knees I beg
That you'll vouchsafe me raiment, bed, and food.'

(II, iv)

His daughter, in response, unbendingly proposes that he 'return and sojourn' – a word whose special force in this context we have now recovered – 'with my sister'.

Near the climax of this terrible scene in which Goneril and Regan, by relentlessly diminishing his retinue, in effect strip away his social identity, Lear speaks as if he had actually drawn up a maintenance agreement with his daughters:

Lear: I gave you all –
Regan: And in good time you gave it.
Lear: Made you my guardians, my depositaries,
          But kept a reservation to be follow'd
          With such a number. (II. iv)

But there is no maintenance agreement between Lear and his daughters; there could be none, since as Lear makes clear in the first scene, he will not as absolute monarch allow anything 'To come betwixt our sentence and our power' (I, i), and an autonomous system of laws would have constituted just such an intervention. For a contract in English law implied bargain consideration, that is, the reciprocity inherent in a set of shared obligations and limits, and this understanding that a gift could only be given with the expectation of receiving something in return is incompatible with Lear's sense of his royal prerogative, just as it is incompatible with the period's absolutist conception of paternal power and divine power.

Lear's power draws upon the network of rights and obligations that is sketched by the play's pervasive language of service, but as Kent's experience in the first scene makes clear, royal absolutism is at the same time at war with this feudal legacy. Shakespeare's play emphasises Lear's claim to unbounded power, even at the moment of his abdication, since his 'darker purpose' sets itself above all constraints upon the royal will and pleasure. What enables him to lay aside his claim to rule, the scene suggests, is the transformation of power into a demand for unbounded love, a love that then takes the place of the older contractual bond between parents and children. Goneril and Regan understand Lear's demand as an aspect of absolutist theatre; hence in their flattering speeches they discursively *perform* the impossibility of ever adequately expressing their love: 'Sir, I love you more than word can wield the matter /

. . . . A love that makes breath poor and speech unable; / Beyond all manner of so much I love you' (I, i). This cunning representation of the impossibility of representation contaminates Cordelia's inability to speak by speaking it; that is, Goneril's words occupy the discursive space that Cordelia would have to claim for herself if she were truly to satisfy her father's demand. Consequently, any attempt to represent her silent love is already tainted: representation is theatricalisation is hypocrisy and hence is misrepresentation. Even Cordelia's initial aside seems to long for the avoidance of language altogether and thus for an escape from the theatre. Her words have an odd internal distance, as if they were spoken by another, and more precisely as if the author outside the play were asking himself what he should have his character say and deciding that she should say nothing: 'What shall Cordelia speak? Love, and be silent' (I, i). But this attempt to remain silent – to surpass her sisters and satisfy her father by refusing to represent her love – is rejected, as is her subsequent attempt to say nothing, that is, literally to speak the word 'nothing'. Driven into discourse by her father's anger, Cordelia then appeals not like her sisters to an utter dependence upon paternal love but to a 'bond' that is both reciprocal and limited. Against paternal and monarchical absolutism, Cordelia opposes in effect the ethos of the maintenance agreement, and this opposition has for Lear the quality of treason.

Lear, who has, as he thinks, given all to his children, demands all from them. In place of a contract, he has substituted the love test. He wants, that is, not only the formal marks of deference that publicly acknowledge his value, but also the inward and absolute tribute of the heart. It is in the spirit of this demand that he absorbs into himself the figure of the mother; there can be no division for Lear between authority and love. But as the play's tragic logic reveals, Lear cannot have both the public deference and the inward love of his children. The public deference is only as good as the legal constraints that Lear's absolute power paradoxically deprives him of, and the inward love cannot be adequately represented in social discourse, licensed by authority and performed in the public sphere, enacted as in a court or theatre. Lear had thought to set his rest – the phrase means both to stake everything and to find repose – on Cordelia's 'kind nursery', but only in his fantasy of perpetual imprisonment with his daughter does he glimpse, desperately and pathetically, what he sought. That is, only when he has been decisively separated from his public authority and locked away from the world, only when the direct link between family and state power has been broken, can Lear hope, in the dream of the prison as nursery, for his daughter's sustaining and boundless love.

With this image of the prison as nursery we return for the last time to Francis Wayland, who, to gain the love of his child, used the nursery as a prison. We return, then, to the crucial differences, as we sketched them, between the early seventeenth- and early nineteenth-century versions of salutary anxiety, differences between a culture in which the theatre was a centrally significant and emblematic artistic practice, profoundly linked with family and power, and a culture in which the theatre had shrivelled to marginal entertainment. The love test for Wayland takes place in the privacy of the nursery where he shuts up his fifteen-month-old infant. In consequence, what is sought by the father is not the representation of love in public discourse, but things prior to and separate from language: the embrace, the kiss, the taking of food, the inarticulate moaning after the father when he leaves the room. It is only here, *before* verbal representation, that the love test could be wholly successful, here that the conditional, reciprocal, social world of the maintenance agreement could be decisively replaced by the child's absolute and lifelong love. And, we might add, the father did not in this case have to renounce the public tribute entirely; he had only to wait until he ceased to exist. For upon the death of Francis Wayland, Heman Lincoln Wayland collaborated in writing a reverential two-volume biography of his father, a son's final monument to familial love. Lear, by contrast, dies still looking on his daughter's lips for the words that she never speaks.

Alan Sinfield: *Macbeth*: History, Ideology and Intellectuals

It is often said that Macbeth is about 'evil', but we might draw a more careful distinction: between the violence which the State considers legitimate and that which it does not. Macbeth, we may agree, is a dreadful murderer when he kills Duncan. But when he kills Macdonwald – 'a rebel' (I. ii. 10) – he has Duncan's approval:

> For brave Macbeth (well he deserves that name),
> Disdaining Fortune, with his brandish'd steel,
> Which smok'd with bloody execution,

Reprinted from *Critical Quarterly*, 28 (1986), pp. 63–77.

> Like Valour's minion, carv'd out his passage,
> Till he fac'd the slave;
> Which ne'er shook hands, nor bade farewell to him,
> Till he unseam'd him from the nave to th' chops,
> And fix'd his head upon our battlements.
> *Duncan.* O valiant cousin! worthy gentleman!
>
> (I. ii. 16–24)[1]

Violence is good, in this view, when it is in the service of the prevailing dispositions of power; when it disrupts them it is evil. A claim to a monopoly of legitimate violence is fundamental in the development of the modern State; when that claim is successful, most citizens learn to regard State violence as qualitatively different from other violence and perhaps they don't think of State violence as violence at all (consider the actions of police, army and judiciary as opposed to those of pickets, protesters, criminals and terrorists). *Macbeth* focusses major strategies by which the State asserted its claim at one conjuncture.

Generally in Europe in the sixteenth century the development was from Feudalism to the Absolutist State.[2] Under Feudalism, the king held authority among his peers, his equals, and his power was often little more than nominal; authority was distributed also among overlapping non-national institutions such as the church, estates, assemblies, regions and towns. In the Absolutist State, power became centralised in the figure of the monarch, the exclusive source of legitimacy. The movement from one to the other was of course contested, not only by the aristocracy and the peasantry, whose traditional rights were threatened, but also by the gentry and urban bourgeoisie, who found new space for power and influence within more elaborate economic and governmental structures. Because of these latter factors especially, the Absolutist State was never fully established in England. Probably the peak of the monarch's personal power was reached by Henry VIII; the attempt of Charles I to reassert that power led to the English Revolution. In between, Elizabeth and James I, and those who believed their interests to lie in the same direction, sought to sustain royal power and to suppress dissidents. The latter category was broad; it comprised aristocrats like the Earls of Northumberland and Westmoreland who led the Northern Rising of 1569 and the Duke of Norfolk who plotted to replace Elizabeth with Mary Queen of Scots in 1571, clergy who refused the State religion, gentry who supported them and who tried to raise awkward matters in Parliament, writers and printers who published criticism of State policy, the populace when it complained about food prices, enclosures, or anything.

The exercise of State violence against such dissidents depended upon the achievement of a degree of legitimation – upon the acceptance by many people that State power was, at least, the lesser of two evils. A principal means by which this was effected was the propagation of an ideology of Absolutism, which represented the English State as a pyramid, any disturbance of which would produce general disaster, and which insisted increasingly on the 'divine right' of the monarch. This system was said to be 'natural' and ordained by 'God'; it was 'good' and disruptions of it 'evil'. This is what some Shakespeareans have celebrated as a just and harmonious 'world picture'. Compare Perry Anderson's summary: 'Absolutism was essentially just this: *a redeployed and recharged apparatus of feudal domination*, designed to clamp the peasant masses back into their traditional social position.'[3]

The reason why the State needed violence and propaganda was that the system was subject to persistent structural difficulties. *Macbeth*, like very many plays of the period, handles anxieties about the violence exercised under the aegis of Absolutist ideology. Two main issues come into focus. The first is the threat of a split between legitimacy and actual power – when the monarch is not the strongest person in the State. Such a split was altogether likely during the transition from Feudalism to the Absolutist State; hence the infighting within the dominant group in most European countries. In England the matter was topical because of the Essex rebellion in 1599: it was easy for the charismatic earl, who had shown at Cadiz that Englishmen could defeat Spaniards, to suppose that he would make a better ruler than the aging and indecisive Elizabeth, for all her legitimacy. So Shakespeare's Richard II warns Northumberland, the kingmaker, that he is bound, structurally, to disturb the rule of Bolingbroke:

> thou shalt think,
> Though he [Bolingbroke] divide the realm and give thee half,
> It is too little, helping him to all.[4]

Jonathan Dollimore and I have argued elsewhere that the potency of the myth of Henry V in Shakespeare's play, written at the time of Essex's ascendancy derives from the striking combination in that monarch of legitimacy and actual power.[5] At the start of *Macbeth* the manifest dependency of Duncan's State upon its best fighter sets up a dangerous instability (this is explicit in the sources). In the opening soliloquy of Act I scene vii Macbeth freely accords to Duncan entire legitimacy: he is Duncan's kinsman, subject and host, the king has been 'clear in his great office', and the idea of his deposition evokes religious imagery of angels, damnation and cherubins. But that is all the power the king has that does not depend upon Macbeth; against it is ranged 'Vaulting ambition', Macbeth's impetus to convert his actual power into full regal authority.

The split between legitimacy and actual power was always a potential malfunction in the developing Absolutist State. A second problem was less dramatic but more persistent. It was this: what is the difference between Absolutism and tyranny? – having in mind contemporary occurrences like the Massacre of St Bartholomew's in France in 1572, the arrest of more than a hundred witches and the torturing and killing of many of them in Scotland in 1590–1, and the suppression of the Irish by English armies. The immediate reference for questions of legitimate violence in relation to *Macbeth* is the Gunpowder Plot of 1605. This attempted violence against the State followed upon many years of State violence against Roman Catholics: the Absolutist State sought to draw religious institutions entirely within its control, and Catholics who actively refused were subjected to fines, imprisonment, torture and execution. Consider the sentence passed upon Jane Wiseman in 1598:

The sentence is that the said Jane Wiseman shall be led to the prison of the Marshalsea of the Queen's Bench, and there naked, except for a linen cloth about the lower part of her body, be laid upon the ground, lying directly on her back: and a hollow shall be made under her head and her head placed in the same; and upon her body in every part let there be placed as much of stones and iron as she can bear and more; and as long as she shall live, she shall have of the worst bread and water of the prison next her; and on the day she eats, she shall not drink, and on the day she drinks she shall not eat, so living until she die.[6]

This was for 'receiving, comforting, helping and maintaining priests', and refusing to reveal, under torture, who else was doing the same thing, and for refusing to plead. There is nothing abstract or theoretical about the State violence to which the present essay refers. Putting the issue succinctly in relation to Shakespeare's play, what is the difference between Macbeth's rule and that of contemporary European monarchs?

In *Basilikon Doron* (1599) King James tried to protect the Absolutist State from such pertinent questions by asserting an utter distinction between 'a lawfull good King' and 'an usurping Tyran':

The one acknowledgeth himselfe ordained for his people, having received from God a burthen of government, whereof he must be countable: the other thinketh his people ordeined for him, a prey to his passions and inordinate appetites, as the fruites of his magnanimitie: And therefore, as their ends are directly contrarie, so are their whole actions, as meanes, whereby they preasse to attaine to their endes.[7]

Evidently James means to deny that the Absolutist monarch has anything significant in common with someone like Macbeth. Three aspects of James's strategy in this passage are particularly revealing. First, he depends upon an utter polarisation between two kinds of ruler. Such antitheses are characteristic of the ideology of Absolutism: they were called upon to tidy the uneven apparatus of Feudal power into a far neater structure of the monarch versus the rest, and Protestantism tended to see 'spiritual' identities in similarly polarised terms. James himself explained the function of demons like this: 'since the Devill is the verie contrarie opposite to God, there can be no better way to know God, then by the contrarie'.[8] So it is with the two kinds of rulers: the badness of one seems to guarantee the goodness of the other. Second, by defining the lawful good king against the usurping tyrant, James refuses to admit the possibility that a ruler who has *not* usurped will be tyrannical. Thus he seems to cope with potential splits between legitimacy and actual power by insisting on the unique status of the lawful good king, and to head off questions about the violence committed by such a ruler by suggesting that all his actions will be uniquely legitimate. Third, we may notice that the whole distinction, as James develops it, is in terms not of the *behaviour* of the lawful good king and the usurping tyrant, respectively, but in terms of their *motives*. This seems to render vain any assessment of the actual manner of rule of the Absolute monarch. On these arguments, any disturbance of the current structure of power relations is against God and the people, and consequently any violence in the interest of the status quo is acceptable. Hence the legitimate killing of Jane Wiseman. (In fact, the distinction between lawful and tyrannical rule eventually breaks down even in James's analysis, as his commitment to the State leads him to justify even tyrannical behaviour in established monarchs.)[9]

It is often assumed that *Macbeth* is engaged in the same project as King James: attempting to render coherent and persuasive the ideology of the Absolutist State. The grounds for a Jamesian reading are plain enough – to the point where it is often claimed that the play was designed specially for the king. At every opportunity Macbeth is disqualified ideologically and his opponents ratified. An entire antithetical apparatus of nature and supernature – the concepts through which a dominant ideology most commonly seeks to establish itself – is called upon to witness against him as usurping tyrant. 'Nature' protests against Macbeth (II. iv), Lady Macbeth welcomes 'Nature's mischief' (I. v. 50) and Macbeth will have 'Nature's germens tumble all together, / Even till destruction sicken' (IV. i. 59–60). Good and evil are personified absolutely by Edward the Confessor and the Witches, and the language of heaven and hell runs through the play; Lady Macbeth conjures up 'murth'ring ministers' (I. v. 48) and Macbeth acknowledges 'The deep damnation of his [Duncan's] taking-off' (I. vii. 20). It all seems organised to validate James's contention, that there is all the difference in this world and the next between a usurping tyrant and a lawful good king. The whole strategy is epitomised in the account of Edward's alleged curing of 'the Evil' – actually scrofula – 'A most miraculous work in this good King' (IV. iii. 146–7): James himself knew that this was a superstitious practice, and he refused to undertake it until his advisers persuaded him that it would strengthen his claim to the throne in the public eye.[10] As Francis Bacon observed, notions of the supernatural help to keep people acquiescent (e.g. the man in pursuit of power will do well to attribute his success 'rather to divine Providence and felicity, than to his own virtue or policy').[11] *Macbeth* draws upon such notions more than any other play by Shakespeare. It all suggests that Macbeth is an extraordinary eruption in a good State – obscuring the thought that there might be any pronity to structural malfunctioning in the system. It suggests that Macbeth's violence is wholly bad, whereas State violence committed by legitimate monarchs is quite different.

Such manoeuvres are even more necessary to a Jamesian reading of the play in respect of the deposition and killing of Macbeth. Absolutist ideology declared that even tyrannical monarchs must not be resisted, yet Macbeth could hardly be allowed to triumph. Here the play offers two moves. First, the fall of Macbeth seems to result more from (super)natural than human agency: it seems like an effect of the opposition of good and evil ('Macbeth / Is ripe for shaking, and the Powers above / Put on their instruments' – IV. iii. 237–9). Most cunningly, although there are material explanations for the moving of Birnam Wood and the unusual birth of Macduff, the audience is allowed to believe, at the same time, that these are (super)natural effects (thus the play works upon us almost as the Witches work upon Macbeth). Second, in so far as Macbeth's fall is accomplished by human agency, the play is careful to suggest that he is hardly in office before he is overthrown. The years of successful rule specified in the chronicles are erased and, as Paul points out, neither Macduff nor Malcolm has tendered any allegiance to Macbeth.[12] The action rushes along, he is swept away as if he had never truly been king. *Even so*, the contradiction can hardly vanish altogether. For the Jamesian reading it is necessary for Macbeth to be a complete usurping tyrant in order that he shall set off the lawful good king, and also, at the same time, for him not to be a ruler at all in order that he may properly be deposed and killed. Macbeth kills two people at the start of the play: a rebel and the king, and these are apparently utterly different acts of violence. That is the ideology of Absolutism. Macduff also, killing Macbeth, is killing both a rebel and a king, but now the two are apparently the same person. The ultimate intractability of this kind of contradiction disturbs the Jamesian reading of the play.

Criticism has often supposed, all too easily, that the Jamesian reading of *Macbeth* is necessary on historical grounds – that other views of State ideology were impossible for Shakespeare and his contemporaries. But this was far from being so: there was a well-developed theory allowing for resistance by the nobility,[13] and the Gunpowder Plotters were manifestly unconvinced by the king's arguments. Even more pertinent is the theory of the Scotsman George Buchanan, as we may deduce from the fact that James tried to suppress Buchanan's writings in 1584 after his assumption of personal rule; in *Basilikon Doron* he advises his son to 'use the Law upon the keepers' of 'such infamous invectives' (p. 40). With any case so strenuously overstated and manipulative as James's, we should ask what alternative position it is trying to put down. Arguments in favour of Absolutism constitute one part of *Macbeth*'s ideological field – the range of ideas and attitudes brought into play by the text; another main part may be represented by Buchanan's *De jure regni* (1579) and *History of Scotland* (1582). In Buchanan's view sovereignty derives from and remains with the people; the king who exercises power against their will is a tyrant and should be deposed.[14] The problem in Scotland is not unruly subjects, but unruly monarchs: 'Rebellions there spring less from the people than from the rulers, when they try to reduce a kingdom which from earliest times had always been ruled by law to an absolute and lawless despotism.'[15] Buchanan's theory is the virtual antithesis of James's; it was used eventually to justify the deposition of James's son.

Buchanan's *History of Scotland* is usually reckoned to be one of the sources of *Macbeth*. It was written to illustrate his theory of sovereignty and to justify the overthrow of Mary Queen of Scots in

1567. In it the dichotomy of true lawful king and usurping tyrant collapses, for Mary is the lawful ruler *and* the tyrant, and her deposers are usurpers *and yet* lawful also. To her are attributed many of the traits of Macbeth: she is said to hate integrity in others, to appeal to the predictions of witches, to use foreign mercenaries, to place spies in the households of opponents and to threaten the lives of the nobility; after her surrender she is humiliated in the streets of Edinburgh as Macbeth fears to be. It is alleged that she would not have shrunk from the murder of her son if she could have reached him.[16] This account of Mary as arch-tyrant embarrassed James, and that is perhaps why just eight kings are shown to Macbeth by the Witches (IV. i. 119). Nevertheless, it was well established in protestant propaganda and in Spenser's *Faerie Queene*, and the Gunpowder Plot would tend to revivify it. Any recollection of the alleged tyranny of Mary, the lawful ruler, prompts awareness of the contradictions in Absolutist ideology, disturbing the customary interpretation of *Macbeth*. Once we are alert to this disturbance, the Jamesian reading of the play begins to leak at every joint.

One set of difficulties is associated with the theology of good, evil and divine ordination which purports to discriminate Macbeth's violence from that legitimately deployed by the State. I have written elsewhere of the distinctive attempt of Reformation Christianity to cope with the paradoxical conjunction in one deity of total power and goodness, and will here only indicate the scope of the problem. *Macbeth*, in the manner of Absolutist ideology and Reformation Christianity, strongly polarises 'good' and 'evil', but, at the same time, also like the prevailing doctrine, it insists on complete divine control of all human events. This twin determination produces a deity that sponsors the 'evil' it condemns and punishes. Orthodox doctrine, which was Calvinist in general orientation, hardly flinched from this conclusion (for example, James said in his *Dæmonologie* that fallen angels are 'Gods hang-men, to execute such turnes as he employes them in').[17] Nevertheless, fictional reworkings of it often seem to point up its awkwardness, suggesting an unresolvable anxiety. Traditional criticism registers this factor in *Macbeth* in its inconclusive debates about how far the Witches make Macbeth more or less excusable or in charge of his own destiny. The projection of political issues onto supposedly (super)natural dimensions seems to ratify the Absolutist State but threatens also to open up another range of difficulties in contemporary ideology.

Macbeth also reveals a range of directly political problems to the reader rendered wary by Buchanan's analysis. They tend to break down the antithesis, upon which James relied, between the usurping tyrant and the legitimately violent ruler. Many of them have been noted by critics, though most commonly with the idea of getting them to fit into a single, coherent reading of the play. For a start, Duncan's status is in doubt: it is unclear how far his authority runs, he is imperceptive, and his State is in chaos well before Macbeth's violence against it (G. K. Hunter in the introduction to his Penguin edition (1967) registers unease at the 'violence and bloodthirstiness' of Macbeth's killing of Macdonwald (pp. 9–10)). Nor is Malcolm's title altogether clear, since Duncan's declaration of him as 'Prince of Cumberland' (I. iv. 35–42) suggests what the chronicles indicate, namely that the succession was not necessarily hereditary; Macbeth seems to be elected by the thanes (II. iv. 29–32).

I have suggested that *Macbeth* may be read as working to justify the overthrow of the usurping tyrant. Nevertheless, the *awkwardness* of the issue is brought to the surface by the uncertain behaviour of Banquo. In the sources he collaborates with Macbeth, but to allow that in the play would taint King James's line and blur the idea of the one monstrous eruption. Shakespeare compromises and makes Banquo do nothing at all. He fears Macbeth played 'most foully for't' (III. i. 3) but does not even communicate his knowledge of the Witches' prophecies. Instead he wonders if they may 'set me up in hope' (III. i. 10). If it is right for Malcolm and Macduff, eventually, to overthrow Macbeth, then it would surely be right for Banquo to take a clearer line.

Furthermore, the final position of Macduff appears quite disconcerting, once we read it with Buchanan's more realistic, political analysis in mind: Macduff at the end stands in the same relation to Malcolm as Macbeth did to Duncan in the beginning. He is now the king-maker on whom the legitimate monarch depends, and the recurrence of the whole sequence may be anticipated (in production this might be suggested by a final meeting of Macduff and the Witches).[18] For the Jamesian reading it is necessary to feel that Macbeth is a distinctively 'evil' eruption in a 'good' system; awareness of the role of Macduff in Malcolm's State alerts us to the fundamental instability of power relations during the transition to Absolutism, and consequently to the uncertain validity of the claim of the State to the legitimate use of violence. Certainly Macbeth is a murderer and an oppressive ruler, but he is one version of the Absolutist ruler, not the polar opposite.

Malcolm himself raises very relevant issues in the conversation in which he tests Macduff: specifically tyrannical qualities are invoked. At one point, according to Buchanan, the Scottish lords 'give the benefit of the doubt' to Mary and her husband, following

the thought that 'more secret faults' may be tolerated 'so long as
these do not involve a threat to the welfare of the state' (*Tyrannous
Reign*, p. 88). Macduff is prepared to accept considerable threats to
the welfare of Scotland:

> Boundless intemperance
> In nature is a tyranny; it hath been
> Th' untimely emptying of the happy throne,
> And fall of many kings. But fear not yet
> To take upon you what is yours: you may
> Convey your pleasures in a spacious plenty,
> And yet seem cold – the time you may so hoodwink:
> We have willing dames enough; there cannot be
> That vulture in you, to devour so many
> As will to greatness dedicate themselves,
> Finding it so inclin'd.

(IV, iii. 66–76)

Tyranny in nature means disturbance in the metaphorical kingdom
of a person's nature but, in the present context, one is likely to
think of the effects of the monarch's intemperance on the literal
kingdom. Macduff suggests that such behaviour has caused the fall
not just of usurpers but of kings, occupants of 'the happy throne'.
Despite this danger, he encourages Malcolm 'To take upon you
what is yours' – a sinister way of putting it, implying either Malcolm's title to the State in general or his rights over the women he
wants to seduce or assault. Fortunately the latter will not be necessary, there are 'willing dames enough': Macduff is ready to mort-
gage both the bodies and (within the ideology invoked in the play)
the souls of women to the monster envisaged as lawful good king.
It will be all right, apparently, because people can be hoodwinked:
Macduff allows us to see that the virtues James tries to identify
with the Absolutist monarch are an ideological strategy, and that
the illusion of them will probably be sufficient to keep the system
going.

Nor is this the worst: Malcolm claims more faults, and according
to Macduff 'avarice / Sticks deeper' (lines 84–5): Malcolm may
corrupt not merely people but property relations. Yet this too is to
be condoned. Of course, Malcolm is not actually like this, but the
point is that he well could be, as Macduff says many kings have
been, and that would all be acceptable. And even Malcolm's eventual protestation of innocence cannot get round the fact that he has
been lying. He says 'my first false speaking / Was this upon myself'
(lines 130–1) and that may indeed be true, but it nevertheless
indicates the circumspection that will prove useful to the lawful

good king, as much as to the tyrant. In Holinshed the culminating vice claimed by Malcolm is lying, but Shakespeare replaces it with a general and rather desperate evocation of utter tyranny (lines 91–100); was the original self-accusation perhaps too pointed? The whole conversation takes off from the specific and incomparable tyranny of Macbeth, but in the process succeeds in suggesting that there may be considerable overlap between the qualities of the tyrant and the true king.

Macbeth allows space for two quite different interpretive organisations: against a Jamesian illustration of the virtues of Absolutism we may produce a disturbance of that reading, illuminated by Buchanan. This latter makes visible the way religion is used to underpin State ideology and undermines notions that established monarchs must not be challenged or removed and that State violence is utterly distinctive and legitimate. It is commonly assumed that the function of criticism is to resolve such questions of interpretation – to go through the text with an eye to sources, other plays, theatrical convention, historical context and so on, deciding on which side the play comes down and explaining away contrary evidence. However, this is neither an adequate programme nor an adequate account of what generally happens.

Let us suppose, to keep the argument moving along, that the Jamesian reading fits better with *Macbeth* and its Jacobean context, as we understand them at present. Two questions then present themselves: what is the status of the disturbance of that reading, which I have produced by bringing Buchanan into view? And what are the consequences of customary critical insistence upon the Jamesian reading?

On the first question, I would make three points. First, the Buchanan disturbance *is in the play*, and inevitably so. Even if we believe that Shakespeare was trying to smooth over difficulties in Absolutist ideology, to do this significantly he must deal with the issues which resist convenient inclusion. Those issues must be brought into visibility in order that they can be handled, and once exposed they are available for the reader or audience to seize and focus upon, as an alternative to the more complacent reading. A position tends to suppose an *op*position. Even James's writings are vulnerable to such analysis, for instance when he brings up the awkward fact that the prophet Samuel urgently warns the people of Israel against choosing a king because he will tyrannise over them. This prominent biblical instance could hardly be ignored, so James quotes it and says that Samuel was preparing the Israelites to be obedient and patient.[19] Yet once James has brought Samuel's pronouncement into visibility, the reader is at liberty to doubt the king's tendentious interpretation of it. It is hardly possible to deny the reader this scope: even the most strenuous closure can be repudiated as inadequate. We are led to think of the text not as propounding a unitary and coherent meaning which is to be discovered, but as handling a range of issues (probably intractable issues, for they make the best stories), and as unable to control the development of radically divergent interpretations.

Second, the Buchanan disturbance has been activated, in the present essay, as a consequence of the writer's scepticism about Jamesian ideological strategies and his concern with current political issues. It is conceivable that many readers of *Macbeth* will come to share this outlook. Whether this happens or not, the theoretical implication may be taken: if such a situation should come about, the terms in which *Macbeth* is customarily discussed would shift, and eventually the Buchanan disturbance would come to seem an obvious, natural way to consider the play. That is how notions of appropriate approaches to a text get established. We may observe the process, briefly, in the career of the Witches. For many members of Jacobean audiences, Witches were a social and spiritual reality: they were as real as Edward the Confessor, perhaps more so. As belief in the physical manifestation of supernatural powers, and especially demonic powers, weakened, the Witches were turned into an operatic display, with new scenes, singing and dancing, fine costumes and flying machines. In an adaptation by Sir William Davenant, this was the only stage form of the play from 1674 to 1744, and even after Davenant's version was abandoned the Witches' divertissements were staged, until 1888.[20] Latterly we have adopted other ways with the Witches – being still unable, of course, to contemplate them, as most of Shakespeare's audience probably did, as phenomena one might encounter on a heath. Kenneth Muir comments: 'with the fading of belief in the objective existence of devils, they and their operations can yet symbolize the workings of evil in the hearts of men' (New Arden *Macbeth*, p. lxx). Recent critical accounts and theatrical productions have developed all kinds of strategies to make the Witches 'work' for our time. These successive accommodations of one aspect of the play to prevailing attitudes are blatant, but they illustrate the extent to which critical orthodoxy is not the mere response to the text which it claims to be: it is *remaking* it within currently acceptable parameters.[21] The Buchanan disturbance may not always remain a marginal gloss to the Jamesian reading.

Third, we may assume that the Buchanan disturbance was part of the response of some among the play's initial audiences. It is in the nature of the matter that it is impossible to assess how many people inclined towards Buchanan's analysis of royal power. That there were such may be supposed from the multifarious challenges to State authority – culminating, of course, in the Civil War. *Macbeth* was almost certainly read against James by some Jacobeans. This destroys the claim to privilege of the Jamesian reading on the ground that it is historically valid: we must envisage diverse original audiences, activating diverse implications in the text. And we may demand comparable interpretive license for ourselves. Initially the play occupied a complex position in its ideological field, and we should expect no less today.

With these considerations about the status of the Buchanan disturbance in mind, the question about the customary insistence on the Jamesian reading appears as a question about the politics of criticism. Like other kinds of cultural production, literary criticism helps to influence the way people think about the world; that is why the present essay seeks to make space for an oppositional understanding of the text and the State. It is plain that most criticism has not only reproduced but endorsed Jamesian ideology, so discouraging scrutiny, which *Macbeth* can promote, of the legitimacy of State violence. That we are dealing with live issues is shown by the almost uncanny resemblances between the Gunpowder Plot and the 1984 Brighton Bombing, and in the comparable questions about State and other violence which they raise. My concluding thoughts are about the politics of the prevailing readings of *Macbeth*. I distinguish conservative and liberal positions; both tend to dignify their accounts with the honorific term 'tragedy'.

The conservative position insists that the play is about 'evil'. Kenneth Muir offers a string of quotations to this effect: it is 'Shakespeare's "most profound and mature vision of evil"; "the whole play may be writ down as a wrestling of destruction with creation"; it is "a statement of evil"; "it is a picture of a special battle in a universal war . . ."; and it "contains the decisive orientation of Shakespearean good and evil" '.[22] This is little more than Jamesian ideology writ large: killing Macdonwald is 'good' and killing Duncan is 'evil', and the hierarchical society envisaged in Absolutist ideology is identified with the requirements of nature, supernature and the 'human condition'. Often this view is elaborated as a sociopolitical programme, allegedly expounded by Shakespeare and implicitly endorsed by the critic. So Muir writes of 'an orderly and closely-knit society, in contrast to the disorder consequent upon Macbeth's initial crime [i.e. killing Duncan, not Macdonwald]. The naturalness of that order, and the unnaturalness of its violation by Macbeth, is emphasized . . .' (New Arden *Macbeth*, p. li). Irving Ribner says Fleance is 'symbolic of a future rooted in the acceptance of natural law, which inevitably must return to reassert God's harmonious order when evil has worked itself out'.[23]

This conservative endorsement of Jamesian ideology is not intended to ratify the Modern State. Rather, like much twentieth-century literary criticism, it is backward-looking, appealing to an earlier and preferable supposed condition of society. Roger Scruton comments: 'If a conservative is also a restorationist, this is because he lives close to society, and feels in himself the sickness which infects the common order. How, then, can he fail to direct his eyes towards that state of health from which things have declined?'[24] This quotation is close to the terms in which many critics write of *Macbeth*, and their evocation of the Jamesian order which is allegedly restored at the end of the play constitutes a wistful gesture towards what they would regard as a happy ending for our troubled society. However, because this conservative approach is based on an inadequate analysis of political and social process, it gains no purchase on the main determinants of State power.

A liberal position hesitates to endorse any State power so directly, finding some saving virtue in Macbeth: 'To the end he never totally loses our sympathy'; 'we must still not lose our sympathy for the criminal.'[25] In this view there is a flaw in the State, it fails to accommodate the particular consciousness of the refined individual. Macbeth's imagination is set against the blandness of normative convention and for all his transgressions, perhaps because of them, Macbeth transcends the laws he breaks. In John Bayley's version: 'His superiority consists in a passionate sense for ordinary life, its seasons and priorities, a sense which his fellows in the play ignore in themselves or take for granted. Through the deed which tragedy requires of him he comes to know not only himself, but what life is all about.'[26] I call this 'liberal' because it is anxious about a State, Absolutist or Modern, which can hardly take cognisance of the individual sensibility, and it is prepared to validate to some degree the recalcitrant individual. But it will not undertake the political analysis which would press the case. Hence there is always in such criticism a reservation about Macbeth's revolt and a sense of relief that it ends in defeat: nothing could have been done anyway, it was all inevitable, written in the human condition. This retreat from the possibility of political analysis and action leaves the State virtually unquestioned, almost as fully as the conservative interpretation.

Shakespeare, notoriously, has a way of anticipating all possibilities. The idea of literary intellectuals identifying their own deepest intuitions of the universe in the experience of the 'great' tragic hero who defies the limits of the human condition is surely a little absurd; we may sense delusions of grandeur. *Macbeth* includes much more likely models for its conservative and liberal critics in the characters of the two doctors. The English Doctor has just four and a half lines (IV. iii. 141–5) in which he says King Edward is coming and that sick people whose malady conquers the greatest efforts of medical skill await him, expecting a heavenly cure for 'evil'. Malcolm, the king to be, says 'I thank you, Doctor'. This doctor is the equivalent of conservative intellectuals who encourage respect for mystificatory images of ideal hierarchy which have served the State in the past, and who invoke 'evil', 'tragedy' and 'the human condition' to produce, in effect, acquiescence in State power.

The Scottish Doctor, in V. i and V. iii, is actually invited to cure the sickness of the rulers and by implication the State: 'If thou couldst, Doctor, cast / The water of my land, find her disease . . .' (V. iii. 50–1). But this doctor, like the liberal intellectual, hesitates to press an analysis. He says: 'This disease is beyond my practice' (V. i. 56), 'I think, but dare not speak' (V. i. 76), 'Therein the patient / Must minister to himself' (V. iii. 45–6), 'Were I from Dunsinane away and clear, / Profit again should hardly draw me here' (V. iii. 61–2). He wrings his hands at the evidence of State violence and protects his conscience with asides. This is like the liberal intellectual who knows there is something wrong at the heart of the system but will not envisage a radical alternative and, to ratify this attitude, discovers in Shakespeare's plays 'tragedy' and 'the human condition' as explanations of the supposedly inevitable defeat of the person who steps out of line.

By conventional standards, the present essay is perverse. But an oppositional criticism is bound to appear thus: its task is to work across the grain of customary assumptions and, if necessary, across the grain of the text, as it is customarily perceived. Of course, literary intellectuals don't have much influence over State violence, their therapeutic power is very limited. Nevertheless, writing, teaching, and other modes of communicating all contribute to the steady, long-term formation of opinion, to the establishment of legitimacy. This contribution King James himself did not neglect. An oppositional analysis of texts like *Macbeth* will read them to expose, rather than promote, State ideologies.

Notes

1. *Macbeth* is quoted from the New Arden Shakespeare, 9th edn., ed. Kenneth Muir (London: Methuen, 1962).

2. See Nicos Poulantzas, *Political Power and Social Classes*, translation editor Timothy O'Hagan (London: New Left Books, 1973), pp. 157–68; Perry Anderson, *Lineages of the Absolute State* (London: New Left Books, 1974).

3. Anderson, *Lineages of the Absolute State*, p. 18. For further studies of the scope of Absolutist ideology in England see V. G. Kiernan, 'State and nation in Western Europe', *Past and Present*, 31 (1965), 20–38; W. T. MacCaffrey, 'England: the Crown and the new aristocracy, 1540–1600', *Past and Present*, 30 (1965), 52–64; Alan Sinfield, 'Power and ideology: an outline theory and Sidney's *Arcadia*', *English Literary History*, 52 (1985), 259–77. On attitudes to government and *Macbeth* see Michael Hawkins, 'History, politics and *Macbeth*' in *Focus on 'Macbeth'*, ed. John Russel Brown (London: Routledge,1982).

4. *King Richard II*, ed. Peter Ure, New Arden edn. (London: Methuen, 1956), V. i. 59–61.

5. Jonathan Dollimore and Alan Sinfield, 'History and ideology: the instance of *Henry V*', in *Alternative Shakespeares*, ed. John Drakakis (London: Methuen, 1985).

6. John Gerard, *The Autobiography of an Elizabethan*, trans. Philip Caraman (London: Longman, 1951), pp. 52–3.

7. *The Political Works of James I*, ed. Charles Howard McIlwain (New York: Russell and Russell, 1965), p. 18.

8. King James the First, *Dæmonologie (1597), Newes from Scotland (1591)* (London: Bodley Head, 1924), p. 55.

9. See James, *The Trew Law of Free Monarchies*, in *Political Works*, ed. McIlwain, pp. 56–61, 66.

10. Henry Paul, *The Royal Play of 'Macbeth'* (New York: Octagon Books, 1978), p. 373.

11. Francis Bacon, *Essays*, introduction by Michael J. Hawkins (London: Dent, 1972). See further Jonathan Dollimore, *Radical Tragedy* (Brighton: Harvester, 1984), specially ch. 5; Alan Sinfield, *Literature in Protestant England 1560–1660* (London: Croom Helm, 1983), ch. 7.

12. Paul, *The Royal Play of 'Macbeth'*, p. 196.

13. See W. D. Briggs, 'Political ideas in Sidney's *Arcadia*', *Studies in Philology*, 28 (1931) 137–61, and 'Philip Sidney's political ideas', *ibid.*, 29 (1932), 534–42.

14. See *The Tyrannous Reign of Mary Stewart, George Buchanan's Account*, trans. and ed. W. A. Gatherer (Edinburgh University Press, 1958), pp. 12–3; James E. Philips, 'George Buchanan and the Sidney circle', *Huntington Library Quarterly*, 12 (1948/9), 23–55; I. D. McFarlane, *Buchanan* (London: Duckworth, 1981), pp. 392–440.

15. *The Tyrannous Reign of Mary Stewart*, p. 49; see also p. 99.

16. *The Tyrannous Reign of Mary Stewart*, pp. 72, 86, 91, 111, 119, 145, 153; cf. *Macbeth*, III. i. 48–56; V. vii. 17–8; III. v. 130–1; V. viii. 27–9.

17. King James, *Dæmonologie*, p. 20. See further Sinfield, *Literature in Protestant England*, specially chapters 2, 6.

18. However, as Jim McLaverty points out to me, the play has arranged that Macduff will not experience temptation from his wife. In the chronicles Malcolm's son is overthrown by Donalbain; in Polanski's film of *Macbeth* Donalbain is made to meet the Witches.

19. *The Trew Law of Free Monarchies*, in *Political Works*, ed. McIlwain, pp. 56–61; referring to I Sam. 8:9–20.

20. See Hunter, *Macbeth*, Penguin edition, pp. 33–4; Dennis Bartholomeusz, '*Macbeth*' and the Players (Cambridge University Press, 1969). On the Witches and the ideological roles of women in the play see Peter Stallybrass, '*Macbeth* and witchcraft', in Brown, ed., *Focus on 'Macbeth'*.

21. See further Jonathan Dollimore and Alan Sinfield, eds, *Political Shakespeare* (Manchester University Press, 1985), chs. 7, 9, 10.

22. Muir in the New Arden *Macbeth*, p. xlix, quoting G. Wilson Knight, L. C. Knights, F. C. Kolbe, Derek Traversi. See also Irving Ribner, *Patterns in Shakespearean Tragedy* (London: Methuen, 1960), p. 153; Robert Ornstein, *The Moral Vision of Jacobean Tragedy* (University of Wisconsin,1965), p. 230; Hunter, Penguin edition, p. 7.

23. Ribner, *Patterns in Shakespearean Tragedy*, p. 159.

24. Roger Scruton, *The Meaning of Conservatism* (Harmondsworth: Penguin, 1980), p. 21.

25. A. C. Bradley, *Shakespearean Tragedy*, 2nd edn. (London: Macmillan, 1965), p. 305; Wayne Booth, 'Macbeth as tragic hero', *Journal of General Education*, 6 (1951), revised for *Shakespeare's Tragedies*, ed. Laurence Lerner (Harmondsworth: Penguin, 1963), p. 186. See also Hunter, Penguin edition, pp. 26–9; Wilbur Sanders, *The Dramatist and the Received Idea* (Cambridge University Press, 1968), pp. 282–307.

26. John Bayley, *Shakespeare and Tragedy* (London: Routledge, 1981), p. 199; see also p. 193. I am grateful for the stimulating comments of Russell Jackson, Tony Inglis, Peter Holland and Jonathan Dollimore.

Edward W. Said: Jane Austen and Empire

We are on solid ground with V. G. Kiernan when he says that 'empires must have a mould of ideas or conditioned reflexes to flow into, and youthful nations dream of a great place in the world as young men dream of fame and fortunes'.[1] It is, I believe, too simple and reductive a proposition to argue that everything in European

Reprinted from *Raymond Williams: Critical Perspectives*, ed. Terry Eagleton (Oxford, 1989), pp. 150–64.

and American culture is therefore a preparation for, or a consolidation of, the grand idea of empire that took over those societies during 'the age of empire' after 1870 but, conversely, it will not do to ignore those tendencies found in narrative, or in political theory, or in pictorial technique that enable, encourage, and otherwise assure the readiness of the West during the earlier parts of the nineteenth century to assume and enjoy the experiences of empire. Similarly, we must note that if there was cultural resistance to the notion of an imperial mission there was not much support for such resistance in the main departments of cultural thought. Liberal though he was, John Stuart Mill – as a particularly telling case in point – could still say that 'the sacred duties which civilized nations owe to the independence and nationality of each other, are not binding towards those to whom nationality and independence are certain evil, or at best a questionable good'.[2]

Why that should be so, why sacred obligation on one front should not be binding on another, are questions best understood in the terms of a culture well grounded in a set of moral, economic and even metaphysical norms designed to approve a satisfying local, that is European, order in connection with the denial of the right to a similar order abroad. Perhaps such a statement appears preposterous, or extreme. In fact, I think, it formulates the connection between a certain kind of European well-being and cultural identity on the one hand, and, on the other, the subjugation of imperial realms overseas in too fastidious and circumspect a fashion. Part of the difficulty today in accepting any sort of connection at all is that we tend to collapse the whole complicated matter into an unacceptably simple causal relationship, which in turn produces a rhetoric of blame and consequent defensiveness. But I am *not* saying that the major thing about early nineteenth century European culture was that it *caused* late nineteenth century imperialism, and I am not therefore implying that all the problems of the contemporary non-European, formerly colonial, world should be blamed on Europe. I am saying, however, that European culture often, if not always, characterised itself in such a way as simultaneously to validate its own preferences while also advocating those preferences in conjunction with distant imperial rule. Mill certainly did: he always recommended that India not be given independence. When for a variety of reasons imperial rule occupied Europe with much greater intensity after 1880, this schizophrenic practice became a useful habit.

The first thing to be done now is more or less to jettison the simple causal mode of thinking through the relationship between

Europe and the non-European world. This also requires some lessening of the hold on our thought of the equally simple sequence of temporal consecutiveness. We must not admit any notion, for instance, of the sort that proposes to show that Wordsworth, Jane Austen and Hazlitt because they wrote before 1857 actually caused the establishment of formal British governmental rule over India. What we should try to discern instead is a counterpoint between overt patterns in British writing about Britain and representations of what exists in the world beyond the British Isles. The inherent mode for this counterpoint therefore is not temporal, but spatial. How do writers in the period before the great age of explicit and programmatic colonial expansion in the late nineteenth century – the scramble for Africa say – situate and see themselves and their work in the larger world? We will find some striking but careful strategies employed, most of them deriving from expected sources – the positive ideas of home, of a nation and its language, of proper order, good behaviour, moral values.

But positive ideas of this sort do more than validate 'our' world. They also tend to devalue other worlds and, perhaps more significantly from a retrospective point of view, they do not prevent or inhibit or provide a resistance to horrendously unattractive imperialist practices. No, we are right to say that cultural forms like the novel or the opera do not cause people to go out and imperialise; perhaps Carlyle did not drive Rhodes directly, and he certainly cannot be 'blamed' for the problems of today's South Africa. But the genuinely troubling issue is how little the great humanistic ideas, institutions, and monuments, which we still celebrate as having the power historically to command our approving attention, how little they stand in the way of an accelerating imperial process during the nineteenth century. Are we not entitled to ask therefore how this body of humanistic ideas coexisted so comfortably with imperialism, and why until the resistance to imperialism *in the imperial domain*, among Africans, Asians, Latin Americans, developed, there was little significant opposition or deterrance to empire at home? May we suspect that what had been the customary way of distinguishing 'our' home and order from 'theirs' grew into a harsh political rule for accumulating more of 'them' to rule, study and subordinate? Do we not have in the great humane ideas and values promulgated by mainstream European culture precisely that 'mould of ideas and conditioned reflexes' of which V. G. Kiernan speaks, into which the whole business of empire would later flow?

The extent to which these ideas are actually invested in distinctions between real places has been the subject of Raymond Williams's richest book, *The Country and the City*. His argument concerning the interplay between the rural and the urban in England admits of the most extraordinary transformations, from the pastoral populism of Langland, through Ben Jonson's country-house poems, the picture of Dickens's London, right up to visions of the metropolis in twentieth-century literature. And while he does tackle the export of England into the colonies Williams does so, in my opinion, less centrally, less expansively than the practice actually warrants. Near the end of *The Country and the City*, Williams suggests that 'from at least the mid-nineteenth century, and with important instances earlier, there was this large context [the relationship between England and the colonies, and its effects on the English imagination which, Williams correctly says, 'have gone deeper than can easily be traced'] within which every idea and every image was consciously and unconsciously affected.' He goes on quickly to list 'the idea of emigration to the colonies' as one such image prevailing in various novels by Dickens, the Brontës, Gaskell, and he quite rightly shows that 'new rural societies', all of them colonial, enter the imaginative metropolitan economy of English literature via Kipling, early Orwell, Somerset Maugham. After 1880 there comes a 'dramatic extension of landscape and social relations': this corresponds more or less exactly with the great age of empire.[3]

It is dangerous to disagree with Williams. Yet I would venture to say that if one began to look for something like an imperial map of the world in English literature it would turn up with amazing centrality and frequency well before the middle of the nineteenth century. And not only turn up with an inert regularity that might suggest something taken for granted, but – much more interestingly – threaded through, forming a vital part of the texture of linguistic and cultural practice. For there were established English interests in America, the Caribbean and Asia from the seventeenth century on, and even a quick inventory will reveal poets, philosophers, historians, dramatists, novelists, travel writers, chroniclers, and fabulists for whom these interests were to be traced, cared for, prized, and regarded with a continuing concern. A similar argument could be made for France, Spain and Portugal, not only as overseas powers in their own right, but as competitors with the British. How then can we examine these interests at work in England *before* the age of empire that officially occurred during the last third of the nineteenth century?

We would do well to follow Williams's lead, and look at that period of crisis following upon widescale land enclosure at the end of the eighteenth century. Not only are old organic communities dissolved, and new ones forged under the impulse of parliamentary activity, industrialisation, and demographic dislocation, but, I would suggest, there occurs a new process of relocating England (and in France, France) within a much larger circle of the world map. During the first half of the eighteenth century, Anglo-French competition in India was intense; in the second half there were numerous violent encounters between them in the Levant, the Caribbean and of course in Europe itself. Much of what we read today as major pre-Romantic literature in France and England contains a constant stream of references to the overseas dominions: one thinks not only of various encyclopaedists, the Abbé Reynal, de Brosses, and Volney, but also of Edmund Burke, Beckford, Gibbon, and William Jones.

In 1902 J. A. Hobson described imperialism as the expansion of nationality, implying that the process was understandable mainly by considering *expansion* to be the more important of the two terms, since 'nationality' was a fixed quantity.[4] For Hobson's purposes nationality was in fact fully formed, whereas a century before it was in the process of *being formed*, not only at home, but abroad as well. Between France and Britain in the late eighteenth century there were two contests: the battle for strategic gains in such places as India, the Nile delta and the Caribbean islands, and the battle for a triumphant nationality. Both battles place 'Englishness' in contrast with 'the French', and no matter how intimate and closeted such factors as the supposed English or French 'essence' appear to be, they were almost always thought of as being (as opposed to already) made, and being fought out with the other great competitor. Thackeray's Becky Sharp, for example, is as much an upstart as she is because of her half-French heritage. Earlier, the upright abolitionist posture of Wilberforce and his allies developed partly out of desire to make life harder for French hegemony in the Antilles.[5]

These considerations, I think, suddenly provide a fascinatingly expanded dimension to *Mansfield Park*, by common acknowledgement the most explicit in its ideological and moral affirmations of all Austen's novels. Williams once again is in general dead right: Austen's novels all express an 'attainable quality of life', in money and property acquired, moral discriminations made, the right choices put in place, the correct 'improvements' implemented, the finely nuanced language affirmed and classified. Yet, Williams continues,

What [Cobbett] names, riding past on the road are classes. Jane Austen, from inside the houses, can never see that, for all the intricacy of her social description. All her discrimination is, understandably, internal and exclusive. She is concerned with the conduct of people who, in the complications of improvement, are repeatedly trying to make themselves into a class. But where only one class is seen, no classes are seen.[6]

As a general description of how by the effect of her novels Austen manages to elevate certain 'moral discriminations' into 'an independent value', this is excellent. Where *Mansfield Park* is concerned, however, a good deal more needs to be said and in what follows I should like to be understood as providing greater explicitness and width to Williams's fundamentally correct survey. Perhaps then Austen, and indeed, pre-imperialist novels generally, will appear to be more implicated in the rationale for imperialist expansion than at first sight they have been.

After Lukács and Proust, we have become so accustomed to regarding the novel's plot and structure as constituted mainly by temporality that we have overlooked the fundamental role of space, geography and location. For it is not only Joyce's very young Stephen Dedalus who sees himself in a widening spiral at home, in Ireland, in the world, but every other young protagonist before him as well. Indeed we can say without exaggeration that *Mansfield Park* is very precisely about a whole series of both small and large dislocations in space that must occur before, at the end of the novel, Fanny Price, the niece, becomes the mistress of Mansfield Park. And that place itself is precisely located by Austen at the centre of an arc of interests and concerns, spanning the hemisphere, two major seas, and four continents.

As in all of Austen's novels, the central group that finally emerges with marriage and property 'ordained' is not based principally upon blood. What her novel enacts is the disaffiliation (in the literal sense) of some members of a family, and the affiliation between others and one or two chosen and tested outsiders: in other words, blood relationships are not enough for the responsibilities of continuity, heirarchy, authority. Thus Fanny Price – the poor niece, the orphaned child from the outlying port city of Portsmouth, the neglected, demure and upright wallflower – gradually acquires a status commensurate with, and even superior to, her more fortunate relatives. In this pattern of affiliation and of assumption of authority, Fanny Price is relatively passive. She resists the misdemeanours and the importunings of others, and very occasionally she ventures actions on her own: all in all, though, one has the impression that Austen has designs for her that Fanny herself can scarcely comprehend, just as throughout the novel Fanny is thought of by everyone as 'comfort' and 'acquisition' despite herself. Thus, like Kim O'Hara, Fanny is both device and instrument in a larger pattern, as well as novelistic character.

Fanny, like Kim, requires direction, requires the patronage and outside authority that her own impoverished experience cannot provide. Her conscious connections are to some people and to some places, but as the novel reveals there are *other* connections of which she has faint glimmerings that nevertheless demand her presence and service. What she comes into is a novel that has opened with an intricate set of moves all of which taken together demand sorting-out, adjustment and re-arrangement. Sir Thomas Bertram has been captivated by one Ward sister, the others have not done well, and so 'an absolute breach' opens up; their 'circles were so distinct', the distances between them were so great that they have been out of touch for eleven years (*MP*, p. 42);[7] fallen on hard times, the Prices seek out the Bertrams. Gradually, and even though she is not the eldest, Fanny becomes the new focus of attention as she is sent to Mansfield Park, there to begin her new life. Similarly, the Bertrams have given up London (the result of Lady Bertram's 'little ill health and a great deal of indolence') and come to reside entirely in the country.

What sustains this life materially is the Bertram estate in Antigua, which is not doing well. Austen takes considerable pains to show us two apparently disparate but actually convergent processes; the growth of Fanny's importance to the Bertrams' economy, including Antigua, and Fanny's own steadfastness in the face of numerous challenges, threats and surprises. In both processes, however, Austen's imagination works with a steel-like rigour through a mode that we might call geographical and spatial clarification. Fanny's ignorance, when as a frightened ten-year-old she arrives at Mansfield, is signified by her inability to 'put the map of Europe together' (*MP*, p. 54), and for much of the first half of the novel the action is concerned with a whole range of things whose common denominator, misused or misunderstood, is space. Not only is Sir Thomas in Antigua to make things better there and at home, but at Mansfield Park Fanny, Edmund, and her Aunt Norris negotiate where she is to live, read and work, where fires are to be lit, the friends and cousins concern themselves with the improvement of the estates, and the importance of chapels (of religious authority) to domesticity is debated and envisioned. When, as a device for stirring things up, the Crawfords (the tinge of France that hangs over their background is significant) suggest a play, Fanny's discomfiture is polarisingly acute. She cannot participate, although with all its confusion of roles and purposes, the play, Kotzebue's *Lovers' Vows*, is prepared for anyway.

We are to surmise, I think, that while Sir Thomas is away tending his colonial garden, a number of inevitable mis-measurements (associated explicitly with feminine 'lawlessness') will occur. Not only are these apparent in innocent strolls through a park, in which people lose and catch sight of each other unexpectedly, but most clearly in the various flirtations and engagements between the young men and women left without true parental authority, Lady Bertram being too indifferent, Mrs Norris unsuitable. There is sparring, there is innuendo, there is a perilous taking on of roles: all of this of course is crystallised in preparations for the play, in which something dangerously close to libertinage is about to be (but never is) enacted. Fanny, whose earlier sense of alienation, distance and fear all derive from her first uprooting, has now assumed a sort of surrogate consciousness of what is right and how far is too much. Yet she has no power to implement her uneasy awareness, and until Sir Thomas suddenly returns from 'abroad' the rudderless drift continues.

When he does appear, preparations for the play are immediately stopped, and in a passage remarkable for its executive dispatch, Austen narrates the re-establishment of Sir Thomas's local rule:

It was a busy morning with him. Conversation with any of them occupied but a small part of it. He had to reinstate himself in all the wonted concerns of his Mansfield life, to see his steward and his bailiff – to examine and compute – and, in the intervals of business, to walk into his stables and his gardens, and nearest plantations; but active and methodical, he had not only done all this before he resumed his seat as master of the house at dinner, he had also set the carpenter to work in pulling down what had been so lately put up in the billiard room, and given the scene painter his dismissal, long enough to justify the pleasing belief of his being then at least as far off as Northampton. The scene painter was gone, having spoilt only the floor of one room, ruined all the coachman's sponges, and made five of the under-servants idle and dissatisfied; and Sir Thomas was in hopes that another day or two would suffice to wipe away every outward memento of what had been, even to the destruction of every unbound copy of 'Lovers' Vows' in the house, for he was burning all that met his eye.

(*MP*, p. 206)

The force of this paragraph is unmistakable. This is not only a Crusoe setting things in order: it is also an early Protestant eliminating all traces of frivolous behaviour. There is nothing, however, in *Mansfield Park* that would contradict us were we to assume that

Sir Thomas does exactly the same things – on a larger scale – in Antigua. Whatever was wrong there, and the internal evidence garnered by Warren Roberts suggests that economic depression, slavery, and competition with France were at issue[8] – Sir Thomas was able to fix, thereby maintaining his control over his colonial domain. Thus more clearly than anywhere else in her fiction Austen synchronises domestic with international authority, making it plain that the values associated with such higher things as ordination, law and propriety must be grounded firmly in actual rule over and possession of territory. What she sees more clearly than most of her readers is that to hold and rule Mansfield Park is to hold and rule an imperial estate in association with it. What assures the one, in its domestic tranquillity and attractive harmony, is the prosperity and discipline of the other.

Before both can be fully secured, however, Fanny must become more actively involved. For this, I believe, Austen designed the second part of the book, which contains not only the failure of the Edmund-Mary Crawford romance as well as the disgraceful profligacy of Maria and Henry Crawford, but Fanny Price's redis-covery and rejection of her Portsmouth home, the injury and inca-pacitation of Tom (the eldest) Bertram, the launching of William Price's naval career. This entire ensemble of relationships and events is finally capped with Edmund's marriage to Fanny, whose place in Lady Bertram's household is taken by Susan Price, her sister. I do not think it is an exaggeration to interpret the concluding sections of *Mansfield Park* as the coronation of an arguably *unnatural* (or at the very least, illogical) principle at the heart of a desired English order. The audacity of Austen's vision is disguised a little by her voice, which despite its occasional archness is understated and notably modest. But we should not misconstrue the limited references to the outside world, her lightly stressed allusions to work, process and class, her apparent ability to abstract (in Ray-mond Williams's phrase) 'an everyday uncompromising morality which is in the end separable from its social basis'. For in fact Austen is far less diffident, far more severe than that.

The clues are to be found in Fanny, or rather in how rigorously we wish to consider Fanny. True, her visit home upsets the aesthetic and emotional balance she has become accustomed to at Mansfield Park, and true, she has begun to take for granted the wonderful luxuries there as something she cannot live without. These things, in other words, are fairly routine and natural consequences of get-ting used to a new place. But Austen is talking about two other matters we must not mistake. One is Fanny's newly enlarged sense of what it means to be at home; this is not merely a matter of expanded space.

> Fanny was almost stunned. The smallness of the house, and thinness of the walls, brought every thing so close to her, that, added to the fatigue of her journey, and all her recent agitation, she hardly knew how to bear it. *Within* the room all was tranquil enough, for Susan having disappeared with the others, there were soon only her father and herself remaining; and he taking out a newspaper – the customary loan of a neighbour, applied himself to studying it, without seeming to recollect her existence. The solitary candle was held between himself and the paper, without any reference to her possible convenience; but she had nothing to do, and was glad to have the light screened from her aching head, as she sat in bewildered, broken, sorrowful contemplation.
>
> She was at home. But alas! it was not such a home, she had not such a welcome, as – she checked herself; she was unreasonable . . . A day or two might shew the difference. *She* only was to blame. Yet she thought it would not have been so at Mansfield. No, in her uncle's house there would have been a consideration of times and seasons, a regulation of subject, a propriety, an attention towards every body which there was not here.
>
> (*MP*, pp. 375–6)

In too small a space you cannot see clearly, you cannot think clearly, you cannot have regulation or attention of the proper sort. The fineness of Austen's detail ('the solitary candle was held between himself and the paper, without any reference to her possible convenience') renders very precisely the dangers of unsociability, of lonely insularity, of diminished awareness that are rectified in larger and better administered spaces.

That such spaces are not available by direct descent, by legal title, by propinquity, contiguity or adjacence (Mansfield Park and Portsmouth are after all separated by many hours' journey) is precisely Austen's point. To earn the right to Mansfield Park you must first leave home as a kind of indentured servant, or to put the case in extreme terms, as a kind of transported commodity; this clearly is the fate of Fanny and William, but it also contains the promise for them of future wealth. I think Austen saw what Fanny does as a domestic or small-scale movement in space that corresponds to the longer, more openly colonial movements of Sir Thomas, her mentor, the man whose estate she inherits. The two movements depend on each other.

The second matter about which Austen speaks, albeit indirectly, is a little more complex, and raises an interesting theoretical issue. To speak about Austen's awareness of empire is obviously to speak about something very different, very much more alluded to almost casually, than Conrad's or Kipling's awareness of empire. Nevertheless, we must concede that Antigua and Sir Thomas's trip there play a definitive role in *Mansfield Park*, a role which, I have been saying, is both incidental, because referred to only in passing, and absolutely important, because although taken for granted it is crucial to the action in many ways. How then are we to assess the few references to Antigua, and as exactly as possible what are we to make of them interpretively?

My contention is that Austen genuinely presages Kipling and Conrad, and that far from being a novelist only dedicated to the portrayal and elucidation of domestic manners, Austen by that very odd combination of casualness and stress reveals herself to be *assuming* (just as Fanny assumes, in both senses of the word) the importance of empire to the situation at home. Let me go further. Since Austen refers to and uses Antigua as she does in *Mansfield Park*, there needs to be a commensurate effort on the part of her readers to understand concretely the historical valences in the reference. To put it differently, we should try to understand *what* she referred to, why she gave it the role she did, and why, in certain sense, she did not avoid the choice, keeping in mind that she might *not* have made use of Antigua. Let us now proceed to calibrate the signifying power of the references to Antigua in *Mansfield Park*; how do *they* occupy the place they do, what are they doing there?

According to Austen, no matter how isolated and insulated the English *place* is (e.g. Mansfield Park), it requires overseas sustenance. Sir Thomas's property in the Caribbean would have had to be a sugar plantation maintained by slave labour (not abolished until the 1830s): these are not dead historical facts but, as Austen certainly knew, the results of evident historical processes. Before the Anglo-French competition to which I referred earlier, there is for Britain the major distinguishing characteristic between its empire and all earlier ones (the Spanish and Portuguese principally, but also the Roman). That was that earlier empires were bent, as Conrad puts it, on loot, the transport of treasure from the colonies to Europe, with very little attention to development, organisation, system; Britain and, to a lesser degree, France were deeply concerned with how to make the empire a long-term profitable and, above all, an on-going concern. In this enterprise the two countries competed, nowhere with more observable results than in the slave colonies of the Caribbean, where the transport of slaves, the functioning of large sugar plantations dedicated exclusively to sugar production, the whole question of sugar markets which raised problems of protectionism, monopolies, and price: all these were more or less constantly, competitively at issue.

Far from being something 'out there', British colonial possessions in the Antilles and Leeward Islands were during the last years of the eighteenth century and the first third of the nineteenth a crucial setting for Anglo-French colonial competition. Not only was the export of revolutionary ideas from France there to be registered, but there was a steady decline in British Caribbean profits: the French sugar plantations were producing more sugar at less cost. By the end of the century, however, the slave rebellions generated in and out of Haiti were incapacitating France and spurring British interests to more intervention, and greater power locally. Yet compared with their prominence for the home market during the eighteenth century, the British Caribbean sugar plantations of the nineteenth century were more vulnerable to such countervailing forces as the discovery of alternative sugar supplies in Brazil and Mauritius, the emergence of a European beet-sugar industry, and the gradual dominance of free trade (as opposed to monopolistic) ideology and practice.

In *Mansfield Park* – and I speak here both of its formal characteristics as well as its contents – a number of all these currents converge. The most important of course is the complete subordination of colony to metropolis. Sir Thomas is absent from Mansfield Park, and is never seen as *present* in Antigua, which requires at most a half dozen references in the novel, all of them granting the island the merest token importance to what takes place in England. There is a passage from John Stuart Mill's *Principles of Political Economy* which catches the spirit of Austen's use of Antigua:

These are hardly to be looked upon as countries, carrying on an exchange of commodities with other countries, but more properly as outlying agricultural or manufacturing estates belonging to a larger community. Our West Indian colonies, for example, cannot be regarded as countries with a productive capital of their own . . . [but are, rather,] the place where England finds it convenient to carry on the production of sugar, coffee and a few other tropical commodities. All the capital employed is English capital; almost all the industry is carried on for English uses; there is little production of anything except for staple commodities, and these are sent to England, not to be exchanged for things exported to the colony and consumed by its inhabitants, but to be sold in England for the benefit of the proprietors there. The trade with the West Indies is hardly to be considered an external trade, but more resembles the traffic between town and country.[9]

To some extent Antigua is like London or Portsmouth, a less

desirable urban setting than the country estate at Mansfield Park. Unlike them, however, it is a place producing goods, sugar, to be consumed by all people (by the early nineteenth century every Britisher used sugar), although owned and maintained by a small group of aristocrats and gentry. The Bertrams and the other characters in *Mansfield Park* constitute one sub-group within the minority, and for them the island is wealth, which Austen regards as being converted to propriety, order, and at the end of the novel, comfort, an added good. But why 'added'? Because, Austen tells us pointedly in the final chapters, she wants to 'restore every body, not greatly in fault themselves, to tolerable comfort, and to have done with all the rest' (*MP*, p. 446).

This can be interpreted to mean, first, that the novel has done enough in the way of destabilising the lives of 'everybody', and must now set them at rest: actually Austen does say this explicitly as a bit of meta-fictional impatience. Second, it can mean what Austen implicitly suggests, that everybody may now be finally permitted to realise what it means to be properly at home, and at rest, without the need to wander about or to come and go. Certainly this does not include young William, who, we are right to assume, will continue to roam the seas in the British navy on whatever missions, commercial and political, may still be required. Such matters draw from Austen only a last brief gesture (a passing remark about William's 'continuing good conduct and rising fame'). As for those finally resident in Mansfield Park itself, more in the way of domesticated advantages is given to these now fully acclimatised souls, and to none more than to Sir Thomas. He understands for the first time what has been missing in his education of his children, and he understands it in the terms paradoxically provided for him by unnamed outside forces so to speak, the wealth of Antigua and the imported example of Fanny Price. Note here how the curious alternation of outside and inside follows the pattern identified by Mill of the outside *becoming* the inside by use and, to use Austen's word, 'disposition':

Here [in his deficiency of training, of allowing Mrs Norris too great a role, of letting his children dissemble and repress feeling] had been grievous mismanagement; but, bad as it was, he gradually grew to feel that it had not been the most direful mistake in his plan of education. Some thing must have been wanting *within*, or time would have worn away much of its ill effect. He feared that principle, active principle, had been wanting, that they had never been properly taught to govern their inclinations and tempers, by that sense of duty which can alone suffice. They had been instructed theoretically in their religion, but never required to bring it into daily practice; to be distinguished for elegance and accomplishments – the authorized object of their youth – could have had no useful influence that way, not moral effect on the mind. He had meant them to be good, but his cares had been directed to the understanding and manners, not the disposition; and of the necessity of self-denial and humility, he feared they had never heard from any lips that could profit them.

(*MP*, p. 448)

What was wanting *within* was in fact supplied by the wealth derived from a West Indian plantation and a poor provincial relative, both brought in to Mansfield Park and set to work. Yet on their own, neither the one nor the other could have sufficed; they require each other and then, more important, they need executive disposition, which in turn helps to reform the rest of the Bertram circle. All of this Austen leaves to her reader to supply in the way of literal explicitation.

And that is what reading her necessarily entails. But all these things having to do with the outside brought in, seem to me unmistakably *there* in the suggestiveness of her allusive and abstract language. A 'principle wanting within' is, I believe, intended to evoke for us memories of Sir Thomas's absences in Antigua, or the sentimental and near-whimsical vagary on the part of the three variously deficient Ward sisters by which a niece is displaced from one household to another. But that the Bertrams did become better if not altogether good, that some sense of duty was imparted to them, that they learned to govern their inclinations and tempers, and brought religion into daily practice, directed disposition: all of this did occur because outside (or rather outlying) factors were lodged properly inward, became native to Mansfield Park, Fanny, the niece, its final spiritual mistress, Edmund, the second son, its master.

An additional benefit is that Mrs Norris is dislodged from the place: this is described as 'the great supplementary comfort of Sir Thomas's life' (*MP*, p. 450). For once the principles have been interiorised, the comforts follow: Fanny is settled for the time being at Thornton Lacey 'with every attention to her comfort'; her home later becomes 'the home of affection and comfort'; Susan is brought in 'first as a comfort to Fanny, then as an auxiliary, and at last as her substitute' (*MP*, p. 456), when the new import takes Fanny's place by Lady Bertram's side. Clearly the pattern established at the outset of the novel continues, only now it has what the novel has intended to give it all along, an internalised and retrospectively guaranteed rationale. This is the rationale that Raymond Williams describes as 'an everyday, uncompromising morality which is in the end separable from its social basis and which, in other hands, can be turned against it'.

I have tried to show that the morality in fact is not separable from it social basis, because right up to the last sentence of the novel Austen is always affirming and repeating a geographical process involving trade, production, and consumption that pre-dates, underlies, and guarantees the morality. Most critics have tended to forget or overlook that process, which has seemed less important to the morality than in devising her novel Austen herself seemed to think it was. But interpreting Jane Austen depends on *who* does the interpreting, *when* it is done, and no less important, from *where* it is done. If with feminists, with great Marxist critics sensitive to history and class like Williams, with historical and stylistic critics, we have been sensitised to the issues their interests raise, we should now proceed to regard geography – which is after all of significance to *Mansfied Park* – as not a neutral fact (any more than class and gender are neutral facts) but as a politically charged one too, a fact beseeching the considerable attention and elucidation its massive proportions require. The question is thus not only how to understand and with what to connect Austen's morality and its social basis, but *what* to read of it.

Take the casual references to Antigua, the case with which Sir Thomas's needs in England are met by a Caribbean sojourn, the uninflected, unreflective citations of Antigua (or the Mediterranean, or India, which is where Lady Bertram in a fit of distracted impatience requires that William should go 'that I may have a shawl. I think I will have two shawls' (*MP*, p. 308). They stand for something significant 'out there' that frames the genuinely important action *here*, but not for something too significant. Yet these signs of 'abroad' include, even as they repress, a complex and rich history, which has since achieved a status that the Bertrams, the Prices and Austen herself would not, could not recognise. To call this status 'the Third World' begins to deal with its realities, but it by no means exhausts its history with regard to politics or cultural activities.

There are first some prefigurations of a later English history as registered in fiction to be taken stock of. The Bertram's usable colony in *Mansfield Park* can be read proleptically as resulting in Charles Gould's San Tome mine in *Nostromo*, or as the Wilcoxes' Anglo-Imperial Rubber Company in Forster's *Howards End*, or indeed as any of these distant but convenient treasure spots in *Great Expectations*, or in Jean Rhys's *Wide Sargasso Sea*, or *Heart of Darkness*, resources to be visited, talked about, described or appreciated – for domestic reasons, for local metropolitan benefits. Thus Sir Thomas's Antigua already acquires a slightly greater density than the discrete, almost reticent appearances it makes in the pages of *Mansfield Park*. And already our reading of the novel begins to distend and open up at those points where ironically Austen was most economical and her critics most (dare one say it?) negligent. Her 'Antigua' is therefore not just a slight but definite way of marking the outer limits of what Williams calls domestic improvements, or as a quick allusion to the mercantile venturesomeness of acquiring overseas dominions as a source for local fortunes, or one reference among many attesting to a historical sensibility suffused not just with manners and curtsies but with contests of ideas, struggles with Napoleonic France, awareness of seismic economic and social change. Not just those things, but also strikingly early anticipation of the official age of Empire, which Kipling, Conrad and all the others, will realise a full three-quarters of a century later.

Second, we must see 'Antigua' as a reference for Austen held in its precise place in her moral geography, and in her prose, by a series of historical changes that her novel rides like a vessel sitting on a mighty sea. The Bertrams could not have been possible without the slave trade, sugar, and the colonial planter class; as a social type Sir Thomas would have been familiar to eighteenth- and early nineteenth-century readers who knew the powerful influence of the class in domestic British politics, in plays (like Cumberland's *The West Indian*) and in numerous other public ways. As the old system of protected monopoly gradually disappeared, and as a new class of settler-planter displaced the old absentee system, the West Indian interest lost its dominance: cotton manufacture, open trade, abolition reduced the power and prestige of people like the Bertrams whose frequency of sojourn in the Caribbean decreased appreciably.

Thus in *Mansfield Park* Sir Thomas's infrequent trips to Antigua as an absentee plantation-owner *precisely* reflect the diminishment of his class's power, a reduction immediately, directly conveyed in the title of Lowell Ragatz's classic *The Fall of the Planter Class in the British Caribbean, 1763–1833* (published in 1928). But we must go further and ask whether what is hidden or allusive in Austen – the reasons for Sir Thomas's rare voyages – are made sufficiently explicit in Ragatz? Does the aesthetic silence or discretion of a great novel in 1814 receive adequate explication in a major work of historical research written a full century later? If so, can we assume that the process of interpretation is thereby fulfilled, or must we go on to reason that it will continue as newer material comes to light?

Consider that for all his learning Ragatz still finds it in himself to speak of 'the Negro race' as having the following characteristics: 'he stole, he lied, he was simple, suspicious, inefficient, irresponsible, lazy, superstitious, and loose in his sexual relations.'[10] Such 'history' as this therefore gave way (as Austen gave way to Ragatz) to the revisionary work of Caribbean historians like Eric Williams and C. L. R James, works in which slavery and empire are seen directly to have fostered the rise and consolidation of *capitalism* well beyond the old plantation monopolies, as well as a powerful ideological system whose original connection to actual economic interests may have passed, but whose effects continued for decades.

> The political and moral ideas of the age are to be examined in the very closest relation to the economic development . . .
> An outworn interest, whose bankruptcy smells to heaven in historical perspective, can exercise an obstructionist and disruptive effect which can only be explained by the powerful services it had preciously rendered and the entrenchment previously gained . . .
> The ideas built on these interests continue long after the interests have been destroyed and work their old mischief, which is all the more mischievous because the interests to which they correspond no longer exist.[11]

Thus Eric Williams in *Capitalism and Slavery* (1961). The question of interpretation, and indeed of writing itself, is tied to the question of interests, which we have seen are at work in aesthetic as well as historical work, then and now. We cannot easily say that since *Mansfield Park* is a novel, its affiliations with a particularly sordid history are irrelevant or transcended, not only because it is irresponsible to say that, but because we know too much to say so without bad faith. Having read *Mansfield Park* as part of the structure of an expanding imperialist venture, it would be difficult simply to restore it to the canon of 'great literary masterpieces' – to which it most certainly belongs – and leave it at that. Rather, I think, the novel points the way to Conrad, and to theorists of empire like Froude and Seeley, and in the process opens up a broad expanse of domestic imperialist culture without which the subsequent acquisition of territory would not have been possible.

Notes

1. V. G. Kiernan, *Marxism and Imperialism* (New York, 1974), p. 100.
2. J. S. Mill, *Disquisitions and Discussions*, vol. III (London, 1875), pp. 167–8.

3. Raymond Williams, *The Country and the City* (London, 1973), p. 281.

4. J. A. Hobson, *Imperialism* (1902; repr. Ann Arbor, 1972), p. 6.

5. This is most memorably discussed in C. L. R. James, *The Black Jacobins: Toussaint L'Ouverture and the San Domingo Revolution* (1938; repr. New York, 1963), especially ch. II, 'The Owners'.

6. Williams, *The Country and the City*, p. 117.

7. Jane Austen, *Mansfield Park*, ed. Tony Tanner (1814; repr. Harmondsworth, 1966). All references to this edition of the novel are indicated parenthetically after the citation as *MP*. The best account of the novel is in Tony Tanner's *Jane Austen* (Cambridge, Mass. 1986).

8. Warren Roberts, *Jane Austen and the French Revolution* (London, 1979), pp. 97–8. See also Avrom Fleishman, *A Reading of Mansfield Park: An Essay in Critical Synthesis* (Minneapolis, 1967), pp. 36–9, and *passim*.

9. J. S. Mill, *Principles of Political Economy* vol. III, ed. J. M. Robson (Toronto, 1965), p. 693. The passage is quoted in Sidney W. Mintz, *Sweetness and Power: The Place of Sugar in Modern History* (New York, 1985), p. 42.

10. Lowell Joseph Ragatz, *The Fall of the Planter Class in the British Caribbean, 1763–1833: A Study in Social and Economic History* (1928: repr. New York, 1963), p. 27.

11. Eric Williams, *Capitalism and Slavery* (New York, 1961), p. 211.

INDEX